Shakespeare's Mad Men

SQUARE ONE
First-Order Questions in the Humanities

Series Editor: **PAUL A. KOTTMAN**

SHAKESPEARE'S
MAD MEN

A Crisis of Authority

Richard van Oort

STANFORD UNIVERSITY PRESS
Stanford, California

Stanford University Press
Stanford, California

©2023 by Richard van Oort. All rights reserved.

No part of this book may be reproduced or transmitted in any form or by any means, electronic or mechanical, including photocopying and recording, or in any information storage or retrieval system without the prior written permission of Stanford University Press.

Printed in the United States of America on acid-free, archival-quality paper
Library of Congress Cataloging-in-Publication Data

Names: Van Oort, Richard, author.
Title: Shakespeare's mad men : a crisis of authority / Richard van Oort.
Other titles: Square one (Series)
Description: Stanford, California : Stanford University Press, 2022. | Series: Square one : first order questions in the humanities | Includes bibliographical references and index.
Identifiers: LCCN 2022003628 (print) | LCCN 2022003629 (ebook) | ISBN 9781503632905 (cloth) | ISBN 9781503633575 (paperback) | ISBN 9781503633582 (ebook)
Subjects: LCSH: Shakespeare, William, 1564-1616. King Lear. | Shakespeare, William, 1564-1616. Measure for measure. | Shakespeare, William, 1564-1616—Characters. | English drama—17th century—History and criticism. | Characters and characteristics in literature. | Mentally ill in literature. | Ethics in literature.
Classification: LCC PR2819 .V36 2022 (print) | LCC PR2819 (ebook) | DDC 822.3/3—dc23/eng/20220428
LC record available at https://lccn.loc.gov/2022003628
LC ebook record available at https://lccn.loc.gov/2022003629

Cover art: Sheila Jones
Cover design: Rob Ehle
Typeset by Elliott Beard in Minion Pro 10/14

Contents

Foreword by PAUL A. KOTTMAN	vii
Introduction	1
1 The King's Last Potlatch	13
2 The Judge, the Duke, His Wife, and Her Lover	117
Conclusion	225
Afterword	233
Notes	237
Bibliography	273
Index	279

Foreword by PAUL A. KOTTMAN

Richard van Oort is engaged in an ambitious study of the ethical and anthropological significance of Shakespeare's plays. Van Oort calls it "ethical" *and* "anthropological" because, to borrow words from the anthropologist Eric Gans, van Oort sees "humanity [as] the species for which the central problem of survival is posed by the relations within the species itself rather than with those of the external world."

The title *Shakespeare's Mad Men* does not so much allude to a psychological state of certain characters as to an ethical situation or predicament. The first-order question van Oort asks might be put like this: How is the survival of human beings qua human beings explicable in light of "humanity's violence toward itself," and what can Shakespeare's plays teach us about this?

In *Shakespeare's Mad Men*, van Oort treats *King Lear* and *Measure for Measure* as works that develop in dialogue with Shakespeare's attempts elsewhere (in *Julius Caesar, Hamlet, Othello, Macbeth*, and *Coriolanus*) to consider how violent competition with rivals is endemic. Van Oort builds upon theories expounded by René Girard and Harry Berger Jr. in their work on "mimetic desire" and Shakespeare's "theater of envy." So long as the power center of a culture was occupied by gods, not human beings, resentment was handled through ritual sacrifice—actual killing. But as cultures become more secular and variegated, resentment gets directed toward the "center's real human occupant"—away from "an inaccessible sacred center." The violence this unleashes threatens to spin out of control.

"Mad men," van Oort proposes, attempt to mitigate such violence by trying to renounce the center—both King Lear and Duke Vincentio in

Measure for Measure ostensibly abdicate their political authority. By doing so, they test the strengths and weakness, possibilities and limitations, of ethical life unmoored from the violent rivalries churning at its center. These plays by Shakespeare can therefore be read as explorations of how and whether human life and culture can plausibly be shown to survive its own internal, violent threats.

Insofar as van Oort's book is, as I believe it is, excellent at doing what I have just described it to be doing, then, I also believe, readers interested in these issues will learn a lot from it.

But van Oort's book can also be read in another way, as exemplifying an important response to another first-order question in the humanities: How does one put theoretical reflections by cultural anthropologists or linguists or philosophers and poetic works, like Shakespeare's plays, in profitable conversation with one another around a common first-order question, such as humanity's relation to its own violence?

After all, van Oort's suggestion is that Shakespeare has something crucial to say *to* an anthropologist like Eric Gans, not just something to say *about* debates in which cultural anthropologists can and do engage without ever mentioning Shakespeare's work and which might be thought to get along just fine without whatever Shakespeare's plays are capable of teaching. At the same time, what Shakespeare has to teach us, van Oort thinks, can only be properly appreciated if we also bear in mind ways in which linguists or cultural anthropologists independently articulate their questions, shape discourses, and generate concepts.

One obvious but underappreciated fact to bear in mind is that Shakespeare cannot, so to speak, put himself into those contemporary conversations in which his words might be most useful. For one thing, Shakespeare is dead—and so whatever insights his work might bequeath are wholly dependent upon engagement with it by living readers, audiences, theater practitioners, students, and teachers. For another thing, and just as pointedly, contemporary conversations—in the written work of anthropologists or philosophers but also in the mouths of thoughtful people who talk with one another about human life and its violence—occur every day without unfolding as the production of a work of dramatic poetry.

As Plato's Socrates took pains to note, rational conversations about the sorts of problems van Oort invokes with terms like "ethics" or "anthropology"—the ability to talk rationally amongst ourselves about any of this—requires that we stop, and perhaps even put away, dramatic productions that keep us wallowing in the pain and suffering of human tragedies. This implies not just that rational conversations about human life and violence can get along just fine without the help of dramatic poetry but—rather more forcefully—that rational conversation must demonstrate, in order to take place at all, that it need not cultivate attention to, or unfold as, works of dramatic poetry.

For all these reasons and more, a direct and unmediated dialogue between theoretical reflection and the poetry of Shakespeare is not in the cards. And here is where a thoughtful critic like van Oort can be of enormous help. The thoughtful literary critic can tend to the needs of both poetry and theoretical conversation for each other—and for our overall self-understanding—in ways that neither can adequately do for itself.

Shakespeare's Mad Men

Introduction

Shakespeare's Mad Men is a sequel to *Shakespeare's Big Men*.[1] The mad men of my title are, specifically, King Lear and *Measure for Measure*'s Duke Vincentio. There are, of course, other mad men in Shakespeare. One thinks especially of Hamlet, whose madness begins as a self-conscious role but ends in real madness, or Macbeth, whose nightly hallucinations and feverish fits are a consequence of his enormous guilt. In the most general sense, Shakespeare's mad men constitute a subcategory of Shakespeare's big men. Not all big men are mad, but, in Shakespeare at any rate, all mad men are also big men. Commenting on the "cycle of change" the tragic hero undergoes, Maynard Mack notes, with some surprise, "how many of Shakespeare's heroes are associated with this disease" of "madness."[2] No doubt madness, which may be described as a total collapse of the protagonist's customary sense of his standing in the world, is something that disproportionately affects Shakespeare's tragic heroes, all of whom share a "monstrous" desire to possess the public (tragic) center. Hence the depth of their resentment when the center eludes them. When Othello calls Desdemona a "cunning whore of Venice," he seems to have gone quite mad, as does Coriolanus when he deliberately goads the plebeians into banishing him. But quite apart from having already discussed Hamlet, Macbeth, Othello, and Coriolanus in *Shakespeare's Big Men*, I intend something a bit more specific by the term *mad men*. Lear's madness is a consequence of his *refusal* to renounce the center despite his very public abdication of the throne in the play's first scene. This refusal produces an extended inner conflict between his public and private selves that eventually leads to madness. While the Duke in *Measure for Measure* doesn't suffer a similarly dramatic psychological breakdown, he is (like Lear) insincere in his abdication of state authority to the point that first Lucio (like Lear's Fool) accuses him of playing "a mad fantastical trick" (3.2.91),* and then Angelo worries that the Duke's "wisdom" might be "tainted" to the point of "madness" (4.4.4–5).[3] In each case, madness appears to be the moral and psychological cost of a failed attempt to renounce the center upon which the protagonist's political authority rests. This is also the sense intended by Ariel when he accuses Alonso, Sebastian, and Antonio of usurping their proper selves and drowning in madness. "I have made you mad," he says, "And even with suchlike valor men hang and drown / Their proper selves" (*Tempest* 3.3.58–60). We don't normally think of Alonso, Sebastian, and Antonio as mad in the same sense that Lear is mad because we tend to view madness as a purely psychological problem. As I will try to show, Shakespeare's view of madness is ethical rather than psychological. Madness afflicts those whose renunciation of the center is fake or insincere.

Stanley Cavell and Harry Berger, whose arguments I will consider more closely in the pages to follow, have usefully suggested that Lear's madness is a method for dealing with shameful feelings and a guilty conscience. Cavell stresses Lear's shame; Berger, Lear's guilt. Both argue that Lear uses madness to avoid confronting the truth of his (evil) treatment of Cordelia. I agree that Lear's madness can be seen as, in Cavell's terms, a shameful moral avoidance of the other. But I also think we can sharpen the discussion by tracing categories such as shame and guilt to the anthropological hypothesis I introduced in *Shakespeare's Big Men*. While the current book can (I hope) be profitably read without knowledge of its precursor, a brief look back, just to get our bearings, may help to make the road ahead a little smoother.

---

*Unless otherwise indicated, all references to Shakespeare's plays are to *The Complete Works of Shakespeare*, 6th ed., edited by David Bevington (New York: Pearson Longman, 2009).

As Marshall Sahlins's classic anthropological study shows, the big man only looks big next to his fellow mortals, who contribute to the big man's feasts not because they are especially public-minded or altruistic but because they enjoy consuming the stupendous amounts of food he makes available through his talent for entrepreneurship and people management.[4] The big man is good at throwing parties, but the prospect of a good party is the only means he has to cajole his clients into helping him amass enough foodstuffs to prove he is better than his rivals, all of whom would dearly love to unseat him by humiliating him with a bigger and better party than the one he has just thrown. As Eric Gans points out, the big man is a usurper of the ritual center, a position formerly reserved for the gods under whose auspices the community's foodstuffs are distributed.[5] By taking over the role of central economic redistributor, the big man turns a sacred and moral difference (all are equal compared to the god or gods) into an ethical and economic one (not all are equal compared to the big man).

It follows that a king may be defined as a big man in possession of a sacred title, which he inherits from his forbears and passes on to his heirs. The sacred title allows for continuity and enables the king to accumulate a surplus that he redistributes not merely at the next potlatch or public feast but to his heirs, a task Shakespeare depicts Lear undertaking in the first scene in which he appears.[6] Continuity is, of course, much desired by people generally. It is not just a preoccupation of the king and his immediate heirs but of his subjects too. But once the center is opened to ethical and economic differentiation, continuity will tend to accentuate initially small differences between the big man and his clients into much larger differences that eventually get reflected in a permanently stratified social order. This is the fate of all agrarian societies. In his great book on the structure of human history, Ernest Gellner cites the Islamic proverb "Subjection enters the house with the plough" and argues that the differential economic surplus is turned into a differential moral surplus, which is ultimately projected onto a hierarchical world picture representing the different levels of human society.[7] The king and his retainers own the surplus, and this gives them a higher ethical standing as well as a lock on political authority. The king is a big man with a sacred crown and, more to the point, an army of thugs ready to obey him because everyone's status, from the lowest slave to the highest prince, depends upon reinforcing these economic and ethical differences.

Whereas the big man has to demonstrate his credentials by throwing ever more lavish parties, the king merely has to point to the royal bloodline. As far as the king is concerned, lavish parties are a perk of the job and must be paid for by somebody else. Once a noble, always a noble, which also implies (sadly, since it describes the vast majority of those living in preindustrial agrarian conditions) once a peasant, always a peasant.

And yet the king is still only a glorified big man. His humble anthropological ancestry serves as a reminder that even the greatest kings are usurpers of the ritual center toward which all human authority aspires. From the point of view of the undying sacred center, the king is bound to appear, for all his magnificent pomp and ceremony, faintly ridiculous, a point the young and beautiful Christian novitiate Isabella eloquently makes in her great speech about the brevity and pettiness of human authority. Dressed in a little brief authority, the big man thunders like an angry ape, making the angels either weep or, if angels were not immortal, laugh themselves to death.

King Lear and *Measure for Measure* suggest two possible outcomes to this situation, neither of them enviable. Either the king is killed by his rivals, or he will go mad playing all kinds of "mad fantastical tricks" to keep both his subjects and himself distracted from the guilt he experiences as an impersonator of the gods, whose omnipotence he shamefully apes in his attempt to possess the inaccessible sacred center. *Shakespeare's Big Men* examines the former problem: the desire to accede to the center from the periphery, a movement that is inherently tragic because it entails violent competition with one's rivals (that's the weeping or tragic part). *Shakespeare's Mad Men* examines the latter problem: the paradoxical attempt to renounce the center and all the envy, jealousy, and resentment that attends one's ruthless pursuit of it by returning to the shelter of the anonymous periphery in the hope of discharging both shame, by being unknown or unrecognized, and guilt, by unburdening one's heavy conscience. Renunciation of desire is thus essentially an ironic or comic gesture, which may explain Shakespeare's increasing interest in tragicomedy and romance toward the end of his career when he had exhausted his ethical experiments in tragedy. Our very humanity depends upon the "comic" capacity to renounce desire and, more precisely, the resentment that accompanies it.

What is the point of reading Shakespeare in this rather peculiar and unorthodox fashion? Am I saying that Shakespeare is a protoanthropologist? Are his dramas to be understood as aesthetic attempts to address basic ethical questions that philosophers like Stanley Cavell, cultural anthropologists like Marshall Sahlins, social theorists like Eric Gans, or literary critics like Harry Berger are also interested in exploring?[8] That is indeed what I am saying, and the point deserves emphasizing. My readings of the plays are not intended as purely literary or aesthetic exercises. The thesis that Shakespeare explores the ambivalent position of the big man who absorbs and purges the desire and resentment directed at him is not offered as a purely literary or aesthetic claim. As Gans in particular has shown, the ambivalent aesthetic experience of desire and resentment toward *any* central figure can be traced genetically—which is to say, historically—to a hypothesis concerning symbolic representation in general.[9] Since humans are the only creatures who represent the world symbolically, this hypothesis must be not merely historical but anthropological. Furthermore, since symbolic representation—in a word, language—is irreducible to more basic perceptual modes of representation (whose origins *can* be explained in straightforward Darwinian terms), it follows that the hypothesis must be irreducible to more basic nonsymbolic biological evolutionary processes. In other words, it must be originary.

This is just another way of saying that the experience of desire and resentment, or indeed of any other fundamental anthropological category (e.g., love, guilt, shame, morality, ethics, linguistic and economic exchange, and so on), is irreducible to an MRI scan of neurons firing in the brain. It is no doubt thrilling to discover that Albany's line uttered to Goneril—"A father, and a gracious agèd man, / Whose reverence even the head-lugged bear would lick, / Most barbarous, most degenerate, have you madded" (4.2.42–44)—produces "prompt activation in the visual association cortex."[10] But this observation tells us nothing about why Albany says what he says, or why Goneril replies the way she does. In short, it misses the point of the sentence, which is not to reduce Shakespeare's words to iconic and indexical representations within the listener's or reader's brain, but to understand their various meanings in the context of a dramatic and dialogic scene. The latter (the dramatic scene), not the former (the individual brain), is what we mean by language, the function of which is not in the first place to excite one's neurons but to communicate meaning to someone else. Needless to say, without a brain you cannot speak (or understand when spoken to). But without a brain you can't do anything because you're dead. In other words, the reduction of language to brain processes misses the salient feature of language: namely, its irreducibly social and dialogic—in a word, its scenic—structure or essence. Attempts to reduce language to yet more elementary components within this scene are condemned to failure. From the point of view of biological evolution, the paradox of language origin is that the first word must have been situated on this anthropological scene before it could be represented internally within the brain, which is to say, selected for biologically. The language areas of the brain are a response to, not the cause of, the origin of this dialogic and interactive anthropological scene.

The same point is made by the neuroscientist and evolutionary anthropologist Terrence Deacon, who observes that from a Darwinian perspective, language can only be seen as an "evolutionary anomaly."[11] One cannot generalize from basic internal iconic and indexical representational processes to the intersubjective originary scene of human language. Language is not simply a generalization of more basic perceptual processes. If it were, we would expect many other social mammals, in particular our nonhuman primate cousins, to use language. But they don't.[12] This is not simply anthropocentric prejudice. On the contrary, to hold that chimpanzees can talk does a far greater disservice to chimpanzees because it assumes, on the basis of our own peculiar facility for representing the world abstractly, collectively, and aesthetically, that language—symbolic representation—represents the norm when it comes to explaining how other animals communicate. In short, we take the evolutionarily eccentric case (language, symbolic representation) and project it onto other animal communication systems. This has the highly prejudicial consequence of regarding these other species—chimpanzees being the exemplary instance—as somehow less evolved. "No analytic method," Deacon writes, "could be more perverse."[13] Or, I might add, more anthropocentric. Treating chimpanzees as characters just like us may make for an entertaining aesthetic experience (as in *Planet of the Apes*), but it makes for poor science and even poorer anthropology.

The fact is I do not learn the meaning of the word *tree* by generalizing from my perception of specific trees. Rather, I learn the word only after I have been initiated into the joint attentional scene upon which specifically human (symbolic) cognition depends.[14] The notion that language can be traced to more basic iconic and indexical perceptual and representational processes epitomizes the dead end of empiricist theories of language. Nietzsche had already pointed out the incoherence of the empiricist picture of language, and by the early twentieth century it was being systematically dismantled by anthropologists (Durkheim), linguists (Saussure), and philosophers (Wittgenstein).

What makes language so interesting from an evolutionary point of view is precisely the fact that it relies upon a highly unusual and highly counterintuitive representational strategy.[15] We can agree with Derrida that language is the fundamental cultural institution.[16] We know of no human society, past or present, without language, just as we know of no human society without religion. It therefore appears that human society does not exist without either language or some concept of the sacred. But why is that the case? How do we explain this curious fact? The wager of the current book is that Shakespeare can help us to understand such fundamental anthropological categories as language, morality, and the sacred. Theoretical and methodological polemics aside, the present book is offered very much in the spirit of an ongoing dialogue concerning Shakespeare's contribution to human self-understanding. If we are to build constructively on Derrida's celebrated claim that human culture is grounded on the trace or deferral among the signs of the language system, then we must turn this purely metaphysical observation into a hypothesis concerning the origin of humanity as the language-using animal.

How, then, does Gans explain the origin of language? Instead of attempting to trace language back to more basic, already existing animal communication systems, Gans proposes that the human scene of representation emerges in the breakdown of preexisting iconic and indexical representational strategies. More precisely, language emerges when a centrally perceivable appetitive object (e.g., the carcass of a large prey animal) becomes too dangerous as an object of widespread ethical conflict to remain unguarded by specifically symbolic prohibition. Other social animals (e.g., chimpanzees, wolves) have well-developed pecking orders that allow conflict over disputed objects to be defused or constrained. The alpha goes before the beta, which goes before the next animal in the pecking order, and so on. Of course, conflict is never wholly absent; the beta may fight the alpha. But these challenges for dominance are never represented as moral challenges to the existing social order, which is to say, they are never represented as ethically motivated usurpations of scenic centrality. Animal representation remains unmediated by the collective and dramatic aesthetic scene, with its structure of a sacred center around which the peripheral human group assembles to represent itself collectively (as in sacrificial ritual). What makes the originary (human) sign different from an indexical (animal) signal is that the scene on which the linguistic-symbolic sign is produced deliberately undermines the indexical correlation between the sign and its referent. Smoke is an index of fire because combustion naturally produces airborne particles. Indexical reference inheres in this empirical contiguity between the sign (smoke) and its referent (fire). Pointing with one's index finger, on the other hand, is precisely *not* an example of an indexical sign. When one points to an object for the benefit of someone else, one has introduced a third party into the sign-referent relation. The "presence" of the centrally designated object is now mediated by the social and moral relationship between the interlocutors. I can only understand that you are pointing out something for my benefit if I can imagine that the object is significant to both of us. In short, the object is not merely perceptually present to me but symbolically present to each of us as participants in the same scene of representation. The object's significance is given by its presence on this scene, which is produced by our shared collective and aesthetic attention. But if you are sharing attention toward the object with me, then neither you nor I can appropriate it without also undermining the scene in which this form of shared symbolic and aesthetic attention is produced. Hence Gans's claim that language originates as an "aborted gesture of appropriation." In the normal (animal) case, the alpha would proceed to take his piece of the appetitive object. But in the originary (human) case, the pecking order no longer provides a viable method for dealing with the problem of intraspecific conflict. Only when the gesture of appropriation is converted into a symbol of each individual's renunciation of the object can the specifically ethical task of economic redistribution take place. But central redistribution is precisely *not* a continuation of the animal pecking order. On the contrary, redistribution now takes place as a communal and sacred act, which is to say that each portion received by the members of the group is sanctioned by the preceding symbolic moment of linguistic renunciation. In this moment of deferral of appetitive appropriation, the specifically human capacity for symbolic representation is born. The originary scene includes within itself all the categories necessary for human thought: desire, resentment, shame, guilt, linguistic and economic exchange, the moral, the ethical, the sacred, and the aesthetic. These basic anthropological categories will be returned to repeatedly in my attempt to develop a picture of Shakespeare's plays as "ethical discovery procedures."[17]

The notion that Shakespeare has something urgent to teach us about our fundamental humanity appears contentious only from a point of view that considers the problem of human origin to be a purely scientific problem, one that will eventually be resolved by researchers working in such empirical fields as evolutionary biology, neuroscience, and paleoanthropology. But this is already to concede too much to the scientists, who cannot grasp the specific nature of the problem without erasing the category of the human altogether. No doubt the massive imbalance in intellectual authority and prestige between the sciences and the humanities is a sign of the increasing irrelevance of the latter when it comes to addressing the practical problems of the modern world. Humanists are not going to invent more fuel-efficient cars or greener technologies. Nor are they going to cure cancer or design more powerful computer processors. But before we concede all the important questions to the scientists, we must remember that science exists only because humans have survived long enough to invent what is, historically speaking, a very recent and very peculiar worldview, one in which serious cognition is associated with a universal method (science) rather than with a particular ethical and cultural stance (religion). More precisely, the scientific and technological revolutions upon which our modern world depends would not be possible without the decentralizing of sacred monarchal authority that begins in the West with the rise of early Christianity, passes through the Reformation, and reemerges in the political experiments of liberalism, fascism, and communism, all of which are a response to the rise of a decentralized economic exchange system. Why a society with a free market and a secular system of political governance emerged when it did is not a question science is equipped to answer. And it cannot answer it because it is in the first place an ethical question, not an empirical one.[18]

It should be no surprise to those working in the humanities that the problem of human origin is also a specifically ethical or anthropological problem. To claim that Shakespeare has something important to teach us about ourselves is, likewise, to adopt an ethical viewpoint on the significance of his works. This does not mean that Shakespeare invented *ex nihilo* the anthropological perspective adopted in this book. What it means is that Shakespeare's plays may be understood as aesthetic reflections on the historical conditions of modern anthropological thought.[19] The ethical changes in social organization spread by Christianity brought a new cultural and aesthetic self-consciousness. This new self-consciousness reflects the awareness that the aesthetic scene is structured not just by an unapproachable divine center but by a human periphery existing on the margins of the old center. This focus on the human periphery leads to a greater focus on the ethical problem of resentment, a problem that lies at the core of modern anthropological thought, as Nietzsche realized. The most persuasive answer to the question of why we need yet another book on Shakespeare is to point to this ethical motivation.

When Albany accuses Goneril of ingratitude toward her father, he worries that her offense will breed further evil until society "must perforce prey on itself." Shakespeare's characters repeatedly return to this dismal vision of the total collapse of humanity's civilizing institutions. But this collapse is never represented by Shakespeare as a consequence of malign natural or supernatural influences (though, of course, his characters may represent violence in ways that shift blame away from themselves, as Gloucester does when he blames Edgar's disloyalty on the "late eclipses in the sun and moon"). Shakespeare's plays are concerned not with the violent spectacle of humans being destroyed by vengeful gods or natural disasters but with the violent spectacle of humans destroying *themselves*. In short, Shakespeare's plays are above all concerned with the ethical question of the survival of humanity in the face of humanity's violence toward itself. That this is also the basic premise of a generative anthropology suggests the relevance of the latter when it comes to reading Shakespeare. As Gans succinctly puts it in his definition of generative anthropology, "*Humanity is the species for which the central problem of survival is posed by the relations within the species itself rather than those with the external world.*"[20] If the readings I provide in the following chapters have anything lastingly meaningful to say, it will be because they succeed in connecting Shakespeare not just to his particular historical context in early modern England but also to our global and ethically fragile human community.

It has become unfashionable to refer to Shakespeare's universality. We live in an age opposed to universalism, essentialism, or anything that smacks of the (white male) privilege of traditional cultural authority.

Unless, of course, we are scientists. Scientists are obliged to apply a privileged and universal method if they are to be taken seriously by their peers, who are naturally suspicious of the results of experiments that cannot be replicated in their own laboratories. For those skeptical of the notion that Shakespeare might offer insight into our universal humanity, I offer not a universal method but the term "Shakespearean anthropology" or, better yet, Shakespeare's "ethical discovery procedure." The latter does not imply that I am applying a method akin to the empirical methods of science (an "-ology"). But nor am I applying an "-ism" or political doctrine (e.g., Marxism, Freudianism, feminism, postcolonialism, etc.). I am trying to think in terms of Shakespeare's ethical and dramatic aesthetic experiments. The point is not that my version of Shakespeare should be identical to yours. That would defeat the purpose of dialogue. The point is that whereas the finer historical details of Shakespearean drama may be of interest only to specialists, the ethical origins of humanity are relevant to us all.[21]

The heuristic exercise of tracing Shakespeare's dramatic experiments to a hypothetical originary anthropological scene is, despite appearances, an opening to, not a closing down of, further critical work. No one, not even Shakespeare, has a monopoly on human self-understanding. If readers find my analyses of *King Lear* and *Measure for Measure* the least bit compelling, that is sufficient evidence that my attempt to initiate a dialogue concerning Shakespeare's "ethical discovery procedure" has been worthwhile.

ONE

The King's Last Potlatch

In classical tragedy, the hero suffers for his usurpation of the center, which is another way of saying that the center is off-limits to all but the gods. In Shakespeare's "neoclassical" drama, this paradoxical relationship between divine center and human periphery is unpacked and reflected upon.[1] Shakespeare's tragic protagonists do not so much offend the gods, whose unquestioned position at the center they unknowingly usurp; they offend their fellow humans, whose worldly desires are in conflict with their own. Rivalry for the center is thus the sine qua non of Shakespearean tragedy. As Harry Berger's analyses show so well, Shakespeare's characters collude in violent suffering, whether their own or that of others.[2] All are complicit in the convergence of desire upon the center. Insofar as we are spectators of this scene, we too conspire in the protagonist's downfall. His suffering is a condition of our resentful identification with the "monstrous" desire of all those who aspire to centrality.

Hamlet at his uncle's table foreshadows Cordelia at her father's. But unlike Hamlet, who is condemned to remain attached to the scene he despises, Cordelia is banished from Lear's court. Hamlet is a prince and, as Claudius very publicly insists, the King's chosen successor. In contrast, Cor-

13

delia has no real chance of occupying her father's throne. Her best chance of approaching it would be to participate in her father's "darker purpose" (1.1.36), which would have yielded her a "third more opulent" (1.1.86) than the portions of his kingdom already divided among her older sisters. When she defies her father's wishes, she severs herself from the center and, therefore, from the scene of rivalry that defines it. But her absence from this scene is only temporary. When in the fourth act she returns to rescue her father, she does so with an army at her back. Like all the major characters, she suffers for her transgression of the sacred center toward which the desires of the human periphery are directed.

Do Cordelia's actions make her a tragic "big man" like Hamlet or Coriolanus? In the opening scene, she is certainly encouraged to play that role by her father. As René Girard observes, Lear's love contest is an attempt to incite maximum conflict and rivalry among those who stand to gain from the King's abdication.[3] In this sense, Cordelia is perhaps more aware than Hamlet of the dangers of the center. In refusing to participate in the King's test of filial love and loyalty, she attempts to avoid the rivalry it provokes among the contestants.

We can see this more clearly if we compare Cordelia's predicament to Hamlet's. Hamlet's loyalty is very pointedly insisted upon in his first stage appearance. Dressed in black on the occasion of his uncle's marriage and coronation, Hamlet conspicuously signals his loyalty not to the new King but to the old. As Wilson Knight observes, Hamlet's allegiances are to death rather than life.[4] While the rest of the court accepts Claudius's leadership, Hamlet remains stubbornly attached to the memory of his father, an image associated, as Horatio's account of the ghost in the opening scene makes clear, with rivalry, conflict, and death. Hamlet's sardonic first line ("A little more than kin, and less than kind") expresses what was already apparent in his wordless conduct, namely, his resentment. In contrast, Cordelia's first line, also delivered as an aside, makes clear her love: "What shall Cordelia speak? Love and be silent" (1.1.62). In her case, what is silenced is love, not resentment. To be sure, once she is forced to speak by the King, she cannot avoid inciting *his* resentment. A. C. Bradley already detected in Cordelia "a touch of personal antagonism and pride" and "a nature so strong" that she could not but help feel "resentment" and "hatred" in the face of her father's and sisters' hypocrisy.[5] Could she not have swallowed her pride and humored her father? After all, his announcement is to be a grand public gesture, his last as the reigning monarch. Hamlet is at least begrudgingly conciliatory when he consents to the King's request to remain in Denmark as, in Claudius's words, "Our chiefest courtier, cousin, and our son" (1.2.117). No doubt Lear's love test is more unseemly than Claudius's avuncular blandishments, but Bradley imagines that another heroine—Desdemona or Imogen, for instance—could "have made the unreasonable old King feel that he was fondly loved" without seeming "to compete for a reward."[6] That Cordelia cannot do this makes her, in Bradley's opinion, a truly tragic figure. She is not, after all, blameless, a fact that makes her suffering tragic as opposed to merely pathetic. She arouses pity *and* fear, alienation *and* identification.

Critics writing after Bradley have tended to agree with him.[7] Cordelia's response to Lear is not free of the resentment that hangs so ominously over the scene. She has, Berger says, good reasons to avoid "Lear's setting his rest on her kind nursery" and "would like to break free of the parental bondage, get out from under, though she is not likely to admit that to herself."[8] When Lear presents her with the love test, he unwittingly provides his daughter with a way out. She will accept his terms of the relationship by saying nothing. Moreover, when she asserts that she must give half her love to her husband, she reinforces Lear's dismal view. "She acknowledges," Berger writes, "the father's right to compete with the husband but feels it oppressive and strains from it."[9] For Berger, Cordelia's relationship to her father is shot through with the same ambivalence that structures the tragedy as a whole. She wants to break free from the center, but she also refuses to break free. She accepts her independence (her exile), but only to return as Lear's one true daughter. Berger underscores her parting words to her sisters:

Time shall unfold what plighted cunning hides;
Who covers faults, at last shame them derides. (1.1.284–85)

She unwillingly consigns her father to her sisters' care, but only to predict that *their* evil treatment of him will vindicate *her* status as Lear's one true daughter: "*They* will do the bad things that will bring Lear to realize how he has mistreated and misprized the daughter who loved him most."[10]

Berger's larger argument is that there exists a persistent undercurrent working against the more highly visible flow of evil away from the good characters and onto the bad. The moral contrast between good and bad characters, which the casual reader or playgoer accepts as self-evident by the time the play concludes, turns out to be much less clear upon closer inspection. Taking his cue from Lear's self-exculpatory line that he is "[m]ore sinned against than sinning" (3.2.60), Berger argues that Lear's focus on his own victimhood is typical of the good characters, who tend to downplay their involvement with evil by projecting their sins onto others. Their refusal to acknowledge their complicity is, moreover, abetted by the bad characters who function as "ethical vacuums" or scapegoats for the better characters.[11] In protesting her own innocence and her sisters' duplicity, Cordelia participates, quite unconsciously, in this larger sacrificial dynamic.

As I suggested, Berger picks up on Bradley's acknowledgment that Cordelia is not blameless when it comes to her role in the events that will ultimately lead to her downfall and her father's. She must, Bradley says, be accorded a "share in her father's sufferings" in the "part she plays in the opening scene."[12] Certainly, Bradley's view of Cordelia is not as bleak as Berger's, but it opens the way to Berger's ethical analysis of how the play redistributes the burden of guilt more widely among the characters. Berger seeks to reverse the flow of resentment draining so precipitously onto the scapegoat, conveniently marked as "Villain" or "Bastard" or "Evil Older Sister," by taking a closer look at those pointing their fingers. Like the detective who uncovers all manner of sins among the witnesses he interviews, Berger's hawkish attention to language and motive turns up of lot of unexpected dirt. Everybody has something to hide, not only from others but above all from themselves.

According to Bradley, our ethical judgment of the central characters is a necessity of Shakespearean tragedy, which presents us with individuals who suffer, not because they unknowingly offend the gods, but because they fail to live up to their better selves. Bradley believes that this applies no less to Cordelia than to Lear. Shakespeare sought to heighten the tragic effect by presenting Cordelia with "the one demand which she is unable to meet."[13] Rather than following her sisters and humoring her father by playing his dismal game, she chooses this moment to call him (and them) to account. Moreover, this is done in front of the entire court at what is supposed to be the King's farewell ceremony, his last public duty before he can "crawl toward death" (1.1.41). Lear was looking forward to his final grand gesture, especially the part in which he would bestow the "more opulent" third on his favorite daughter. Unfortunately, things don't work out as he intended. The youngest daughter calls his bluff. But why does she choose to antagonize her father at precisely this point? Couldn't she have played along with the others? If she objects to this unseemly mixing of private love with public show, then surely the time to protest is not now, in front of the crowd, but later, when her father won't be embarrassed by what might easily be perceived as a rival show aimed at exposing his hypocrisy and upstaging him at his grand farewell.

But Cordelia's refusal to delay her protest to a more fitting occasion is precisely the point. She cannot delay. Shakespeare is writing a tragedy, not a romantic novel. There is no private space to which Cordelia can retreat to express her love. She is condemned to choose between, on the one hand, the hypocrisy of the public scene occupied by her father and, on the other, total rejection of it. There is no middle ground. In the contest for centrality, a contest assumed by tragedy, resentment inevitably triumphs over love. Love obliges you to renounce the public center, but tragedy—and more precisely, the conflict among rival desires upon which tragedy is based—demands that you pursue it. That is why love is always crushed in Shakespeare's tragedies. They depict what happens when desire is given free rein unconstrained by love (Cordelia) or faith (Kent). Shakespeare's plays are not just excellent dramatic entertainment; they are also ethical analyses of the very highest order.

Am I saying that Cordelia represents love? That is partly what I am saying. Cordelia is rejected by Lear because his renunciation of the center remains incomplete. As long as Lear is blind to love, he is incapable of the spiritual regeneration he hopes his retirement will bring. "How should I your true love know / From another one?" Ophelia sings. "By his cockle hat and staff, / And his sandal shoon" comes the reply in the song (4.5.23–26). The cockle hat and staff represent the pilgrim on his way to the shrine of Saint James of Compostela in northern Spain. Ophelia's song, as John Vyvyan notes, employs the metaphor of love as a pilgrimage of the soul. The image is much favored by Shakespeare.[14] Ophelia, of course, is rejected by her lover, who is blinded by resentment and the desire for revenge. Love is incompatible with resentment, and when Hamlet rejects Ophelia and kills her father, it is clear that he is on a pilgrimage of hate, not love. Whence the symbolic significance of the fifth act, the first scene of which begins in a graveyard and ends with Hamlet and Laertes in a death struggle over Ophelia's grave. When love dies, hate triumphs and leaves the stage littered with corpses. The symbolism of this struggle between love and hate occurs throughout Shakespeare, and we should not be surprised to find it in *King Lear*.

Unlike Romeo or Hamlet, Lear is an old man. But the pilgrimage of love applies to him too. Indeed, his advanced age makes the quest to find it all the more urgent:

> Know that we have divided
> In three our kingdom; and 'tis our fast intent
> To shake all cares and business from our age,
> Conferring them on younger strengths while we
> Unburdened crawl toward death. (1.1.37–41)

Why does Lear renounce the throne? It must be because the regeneration he craves remains elusive. He suspects that his duties as a king—which is to say, as a being defined by the center—may have something to do with the spiritual vacuum in his life. With death approaching, he seeks to put things right. But he doesn't grasp the full nature of the problem. Much more will be required than a ceremonial farewell in which he bestows the duties of the state on younger strengths. Part of the difficulty is that he has become so habituated to his public role that he sets about his new task by simply reproducing the old habits of authority and rulership. He thinks he is doing the right thing by dividing his kingdom so that "future strife / May be prevented" (1.1.44–45). But the absurd terms of the exchange—"Which of you shall we say doth love us most" (1.1.51)—show that he is still trapped in the language of public self-centralization.

Lear's first test occurs, and he fails. He divides his kingdom between Goneril and Regan, the representatives of false love, and rejects Cordelia, whose love is true. The point is not just that Cordelia refuses to exchange love for a material reward. It is that Lear is blind to love and, so, to Cordelia. Kent's admonishment, "See better, Lear" (1.1.159), underscores the point. And so does Regan's line uttered to Goneril at the end of the scene: "Yet he hath ever but slenderly known himself" (1.1.296–97). Lear fails to see love. From this blindness the whole tragedy springs.

Most readers are shocked at Lear's response to Cordelia. How can he disown the child he loves most? Certainly, from a strictly realistic point of view Lear's actions are difficult to accept. Bradley explains it as the reaction of a man, otherwise accustomed to getting what he wants, who finds his best laid plan thwarted. When Cordelia denies him the pleasure of gifting her the more opulent third, he explodes in anger and denies his child precisely what he had hoped to give.[15] Stanley Cavell takes Bradley's analysis a step further. What terrifies Lear is that Cordelia threatens to expose the hollowness and shamefulness of his bargain: "Cordelia is alarming precisely because he *knows* she is offering the real thing, offering something a more opulent third of his kingdom cannot, must not, repay; putting a claim upon him he cannot face. She threatens to expose both his plan for returning false love with no love, and expose the necessity for that plan—his terror of being loved, of needing love."[16] I think Cavell gets it right. Cordelia unsettles Lear because she calls his bluff. She offers true love, which cannot be exchanged for something it is not (land, money). As the king of France puts it, "She is herself a dowry" (1.1.245). To look beyond her, as Burgundy does, is to miss the entire point:

> Love's not love
> When it is mingled with regards that stands
> Aloof from th'entire point. (1.1.242–44)

The Rejection of Love

Critics such as Cavell and Berger are keenly aware of the text's ethical complexities. They show how the characters are constantly testing each other as they jostle for position in larger social structures that variously constrain and liberate them. What these critics do not address, at least not to the extent I think the subject deserves, is how *King Lear* reproduces a broader ethical—ultimately, anthropological—pattern to be found more widely in Shakespeare. I have already commented on some of the similarities between *Hamlet* and *King Lear*. Hamlet at his uncle's table anticipates Cordelia at her father's. But whereas Hamlet rejects love, Cordelia *is* love. In this sense, it is Lear who more closely approximates Hamlet. Just as Hamlet rejects Ophelia, so Lear rejects Cordelia. Hamlet's rejection of Ophelia occurs in the third act, the act in which revenge plays its trump card in the guise of the Mousetrap play and hoists the hero by his own petard. Hamlet had intended to trap the King, but instead he succeeds only in baiting himself. In transparent emulation of the murderer Lucianus ("nephew to the King"),

Hamlet renews his bloodthirsty desire for revenge: "Now could I drink hot blood" (3.2.389). And where is the King? He is kneeling in repentance, overwhelmed by guilt and fearing for his soul:

> O bosom black as death,
> O limèd soul that, struggling to be free,
> Art more engaged! Help, angels! (3.3.67–69)

In this image of the kneeling King, we find a third analogy to Lear. For does not the one king remind us of the other? Does not Claudius on his knees remind us of Lear kneeling before his daughter in the play's fourth act? The difference, of course, is that Lear suffers a good deal more than Claudius to get to this point.

In this respect, the worlds of *Hamlet* and *King Lear* are quite different. *Hamlet* is a revenge tragedy. From the beginning, the play is dominated by its big men competing with one another. This rivalry includes not just the younger generation (Hamlet, Laertes, and Fortinbras, all of whom are presented as rivals for the throne at some point in the play) but their fathers and uncles too.[17] Is it any wonder that the women should be so marginal in this environment? And is it any wonder that Hamlet's father's ghost haunts Elsinore? If revenge is to prosper, its evil spirit must be kept alive. Hamlet represents his devotion to the memory of his father as filial piety, but Shakespeare shows that it is something much more sinister. Even Laertes warns his sister about the dangers of all this hypermimetic male chest-thumping when he advises her to keep well back from the fray:

> Fear it, Ophelia, fear it, my dear sister,
> And keep you in the rear of your affection,
> Out of the shot and danger of desire. (1.3.33–35)

It's too bad Laertes doesn't follow his own advice. As usual, the men are too busy lecturing the women to notice that the faults they see so vividly in their female counterparts apply much more accurately to themselves. The same blindness is evident in Hamlet when he unleashes a torrent of invective on Ophelia: "God hath given you one face, and you make yourselves another" (3.1.145–46). But it is Hamlet, not Ophelia, who hides himself behind a mask. More precisely, love is masked—ultimately, overwhelmed—by resentment, the indispensable fuel of revenge.

By looking back to *Hamlet*, we can begin to get a sense of what Shakespeare is up to in *King Lear*. *Hamlet* is largely told from the point of view of the prince, who is a rival for the center occupied by Claudius. Admittedly, he is a reluctant rival. That is why the seed of resentment, so conspicuous in the prince's first stage appearance, must be carefully nursed into action. Resentment, as Nietzsche realized, is *impotent* rage.[18] Even the thought of a dear father murdered fails to motivate the prince to kill Claudius. Instead, he decides to wear an antic disposition and play the fool. When we turn from Hamlet to Claudius, the ethical salience of the comparison gets clearer still. Claudius on his knees is the closest the King will get to spiritual regeneration in a world otherwise obsessed with blood revenge. He considers forgiveness but only to dismiss it:

> But oh, what form of prayer
> Can serve my turn? "Forgive me my foul murder"?
> That cannot be, since I am still possessed
> Of those effects for which I did the murder:
> My crown, mine own ambition, and my queen. (3.3.51–55)

Claudius cannot face forgiveness because it doesn't fit with his ethical picture of the world. It conflicts with the rules by which he and his rivals conduct themselves. I think this is what attracted Shakespeare to Saxo's *Amleth* in the first place. It transparently depicts the brutal ethic of blood revenge. Claudius's ruthless cunning has won him the throne, which is no more than he deserves. It is worth recalling that in the original legend, Feng (Claudius's prototype) kills his brother publicly in an open contest for the leadership. There is no clandestine shilly-shallying behind closed doors. What would be the point of now throwing it away after all the hard work has been done? In contrast, Lear decides to give up the throne before he dies. Rather than being ousted by others, he will oust himself.

We tend to think of Cornwell, Goneril, and Regan as monsters, but in fact they have shown remarkable restraint in tolerating the old man on the throne for so long. Macbeth wasn't so hesitant. Nor was Claudius. But Lear preempts everyone by abdicating before he dies. Politically, this might seem an unwise strategy.[19] But the political reasons for the King's abdication are left purposely vague by Shakespeare. We are not in the world of *Julius Caesar* where political rivals compete endlessly for supremacy. If *Julius Caesar* and *Hamlet* are focused on the approach to the center, *King Lear* is much more about the (failed) attempt to retreat from it. We should understand Lear's abdication not as a political move but a moral one. In this sense, he is closer to Duke Vincentio in *Measure for Measure* or Prospero in *The Tempest*. Like these mysterious and shadowy figures, he wants to liberate himself from the public scene to explore a world he has thus far neglected: the world within himself.

Lear renounces the throne to explore his inner moral life. This is a step in the right direction. Certainly, it is a step very few of Shakespeare's other kings have the courage to take. As long as he occupies the seat of power, he will be beset by flatterers and false loves who may, furthermore, turn out to be murderers and regicides. But the renunciation is incomplete.[20] The abdication does not lead to the expected spiritual transformation. Initially, nothing changes. He continues to treat his children as subjects who must satisfy the royal will.

Lear's specific test—a test that is quite different from the tests encountered by Shakespeare's other tragic protagonists—is to see his children not as subjects who must conform to his will but as human beings to love. Unfortunately, he fails the test miserably. He knows what to do: he must give up the throne. But he doesn't know what to do next, how to feel once he has stripped away the royal identity. He has to learn everything all over again, except this time there are no guidelines to follow, no models for him to emulate, no servants to carry out his commands. There is only Cordelia, whom he has to acknowledge. Only then can he really love.[21]

Masters and Slaves

Lear is trying to make the dialectical leap from Hegel's feudal master, whose will dominates everyone, to the much less stable, and therefore much more uncertain, relationship of strict moral reciprocity. The latter configuration is unstable because you constantly have to renew your attention to the other, whose being cannot be fixed into a preexisting social role or category. Lear's particular vulnerability—where he is to be tested and where he fails—is in his capacity for genuine reciprocity, which is also the basis of love and friendship. What we need from the other, as Hegel understood, is reciprocal recognition.[22] But neither master nor slave can recognize the other as an equal. Instead, they are locked in a destructive cycle based on dominance and false love. Lear is imprisoned in this cycle. His tantrums are a manifestation of the old world of hierarchy and authority that has defined him throughout his long life. His identity as a king, an identity he wants to shed but keeps reverting to, stands in the way of his capacity to see others as equals rather than inferiors. Moral reciprocity can only be discovered when the layers of bad-faith hierarchy, and the contempt that goes with bad-faith hierarchy, fall away and the individual shines through. Cordelia represents that possibility for Lear. We see it, but Lear does not. A terrifying leap of faith, a complete moral transformation, is required for him to see what lies right before his eyes. Like Paul blinded on the road to Damascus, the scales must fall from his eyes. (Hence the Gloucester subplot.)

Cordelia is Lear's favorite child. He wants her to care for him in his old age, so he makes a great show of gifting her the more opulent third of the kingdom. This is a mistake. In return for their share of the inheritance, Goneril and Regan give him a flattering show of false love. But when Lear turns to his youngest, he is confronted not by flattery but truth. She can give him nothing in exchange, not because she is poor and he is rich, but because she *is* love. In the face of love, Lear is powerless, a feeling he finds intolerable. Whence the violence of his reaction. Stung by what he does not understand, he reacts by hurling her violently from his presence: "Hence, and avoid my sight!" (1.1.124). But the "grave of love" is also the "womb of hate."[23] Once Lear disowns Cordelia, he leaves himself vulnerable to the false loves of Goneril and Regan. That way disaster lies:

> The barbarous Scythian,
> Or he that makes his generation messes
> To gorge his appetite, shall to my bosom
> Be as well neighbored, pitied, and relieved
> As thou my sometime daughter. (1.1.116–20)

We might wonder why Lear is so quick to accept the false loves of Goneril and Regan. The answer is given by Lear himself. He furiously clutches them to his bosom because they speak the same insincere and servile language, the language of lordship and bondage. Nor should we be surprised that they treat him as he has treated them. They are willing conspirators in the suffering he brings on himself. The point is not that had Cordelia humored her father all would have been well. On the contrary, conspiring with the false loves of Goneril and Regan would merely hasten Lear's suffering. Humoring Lear means competing for the center. Cordelia and Kent will not collude in this show of false love. Both are exiled for their honesty. Love and faith have no place in this world. Kent says, "Freedom lives hence and banishment is here" (1.1.184). In banishing love, Lear has banished precisely what he needs to survive. What follows is a terrible personal pilgrimage to discover the truth of his error.

Why does Kent disobey the King's order? Why does he not only refuse to leave the country but insist on staying close to the very man who has banished him? Kent reminds me a bit of Coriolanus. Both speak out against the hypocrisy of flattery and are banished for doing so. Both then disguise themselves to facilitate their return to the scene of their original banishment. The difference, of course, is that whereas Kent remains in disguise, Coriolanus sheds his disguise to renew his old identity and his vengeful assault on the center from which he has been expelled. Unlike Kent, who is shielded by his (secret) devotion to the more central other (Lear), Coriolanus cannot refuse the center's violence. His whole life has been devoted to its service. As far as he is concerned, the man who speaks rather than fights is by definition a false flatterer and a coward. Clearly, from Coriolanus's point of view, an old man like Lear cannot be considered a serious rival. In Coriolanus's nascent Roman Republic, men too old to fight are automatically retired from the center to the periphery, where they participate vicariously, as Menenius does, in the warlike feats of the younger generation. Coriolanus is more resentful than Kent because his claim to the center is both greater and more urgent. Unlike the younger generation in *King Lear*, Kent has no desire to engage in the contest for centrality.[24] On the contrary, his faith never swerves from believing in Lear's authority. This faith is tested by Lear's actions. Kent sees that Lear is making a mistake in rejecting Cordelia, which is why he protests so vociferously and also why he risks his life by returning (in disguise) to serve the King. As Bradley observes, Kent is the only character who never wavers from seeing Lear as something "terrible" and "grand," "the Lear of Lear's prime."[25]

But is this a mistake? If Lear has to learn to cast off his old identity in order to see better, then doesn't Kent contribute to Lear's blindness? In continuing to serve Lear as though nothing has changed, doesn't Kent exacerbate, rather than resolve, the fundamental problem? Bradley appears to acknowledge this difficulty when he observes that Kent does not always serve Lear's best interests. Bradley is thinking of the moment when Kent is placed in the stocks. Why does Kent lose his temper so easily with Oswald?

Isn't he merely playing into the hands of Lear's enemies, whose chief aim is to further the King's discomfiture? Bradley concedes that Kent "illustrates the truth that to run one's head unselfishly against a wall is not the best way to help one's friends."[26] Indeed it is not. But Bradley misses something that is crucial to understanding Kent's function. Like many of Shakespeare's characters, Kent has a double role. He is a character in his own right, but he is also a representation of an aspect within Lear. Bradley seems to intuit this possibility when he observes that one of the reasons Kent is so well loved by readers is because he reminds us of Cordelia when "she is out of sight."[27] But I think this reminder goes much deeper than Bradley realizes. If Cordelia represents love, Kent represents the faith Lear lacks. When Lear disowns Cordelia, Kent tries to dissuade the King from making a grave mistake. But Lear refuses to listen. He will not put his unconditional trust in Cordelia. Consequently, love and faith are banished, and in their absence, the imposters—false love and bad faith—prosper. It is not a coincidence that the second scene of the play begins with a soliloquy from Edmund, the personification of false love and bad faith.

Shakespeare gives us a clue to the development of this allegorical picture when Kent draws his sword on the servile Oswald:

> Draw, you rascal! You come with letters against the King, and take Vanity the puppet's part against the royalty of her father. Draw, you rogue, or I'll so carbonado your shanks—draw, you rascal! (2.2.35–38)

Kent accuses Oswald of playing the role of Vanity in a morality play. Oswald is Goneril's trusted servant, and Kent includes her in his reference to Vanity (i.e., Oswald is the servant or "puppet" of Vanity). But what Kent cannot be aware of is his own role in Shakespeare's allegory. Oswald has been entrusted with relaying secret messages between Goneril and Regan. His services are necessary if the sisters are to secure Lear's defeat. At this point, their main concern is to reduce Lear's train of one hundred knights. The knights had been a condition of the King's abdication, but the sisters are understandably reluctant to tolerate a private army loyal to the old King. Kent, of course, is loyal to Lear and we may take his presence here as a metonymy of Lear's one hundred knights. We are, therefore, witnessing a contest between the forces loyal to the old King, represented by Kent, and those loyal to the new pretenders, represented by Oswald. When Kent draws his sword on Oswald, he is assaulting not just Oswald, but anybody whose faith in the old King has diminished since the abdication.

Thus the duel is between Vanity and Faith. If these terms are felt to be too old-fashioned, we can say that the contest is between narcissism or self-love, on the one hand, and trust or selflessness, on the other. Without faith or trust, there is only self-love or vanity. That this contest involves an inward conflict is apparent in Kent's explanation of his actions. When Cornwell asks Kent why he is so angered by Oswald (who, let's face it, hasn't behaved particularly poorly), Kent says:

> That such a slave as this should wear a sword,
> Who wears no honesty. Such smiling rogues as these,
> Like rats, oft bite the holy cords atwain
> Which are too intrinse t'unloose; smooth every passion
> That in the natures of their lords rebel,
> Bring oil to fire, snow to their colder moods,
> Renege, affirm, and turn their halcyon beaks
> With every gale and vary of their masters,
> Knowing naught, like dogs, but following. (2.2.73–81)

This account is unlikely to win much favor from a judge or magistrate tasked with keeping the peace. Kent is basically accusing Oswald of being a sycophant or yes-man. No doubt this is true. But it is hardly a crime, and it is not deserving of physical assault. To read the scene so literally, however, is to look for an explanation in the wrong place. Most critics recognize that the scene is implausible.[28] Kent's reaction is too extreme, even for someone of Kent's blunt and choleric temperament. But the implausibility disappears when we understand the scene allegorically (i.e., as a representation of a conflict within Lear). Kent's reaction is exaggerated precisely because the forces of vanity or self-love are in the ascendance. The King's abdication, which was itself motivated by vanity, has broken "the holy cords atwain," and now every fool is rushing in to grab a piece of the royal authority. Power has been denuded of sacred constraint. Kent sees only chaos and disorder among the new contenders:

> I have seen better faces in my time
> Than stands on any shoulder that I see
> Before me at this instant. (2.2.94–96)

What Kent fails to see is that he is himself a sign of the disorder in the realm. He can proclaim his loyalty to the old King all he wants, but the King has abdicated and nobody can believe in a ruler without power. The fact that Kent is forced to adopt a disguise tells us that it has become more or less impossible to distinguish true from false faith. In other words, Kent is fighting a losing battle. Only madmen and fools behave the way he does, which is why Lear's company in the middle of the play is reduced to Edgar and the Fool.[29] Bradley is right that Kent is hardly helping the King's cause, but what Bradley does not see is that Kent is also Lear's alter ego. In Maynard Mack's useful formulation, Kent functions "as a screen on which Shakespeare flashes, as it were, readings from the psychic life of the protagonist, possibly even of his subconscious life, which could not otherwise be conveyed in drama at all."[30] Kent's beating of Oswald is a hysterical attempt to reassert the King's vanquished authority. Such antics are plainly ridiculous. Kent and Lear succeed only in making themselves laughing stocks. When Lear arrives at Gloucester's home to find Kent asleep in the stocks, he cannot believe his eyes. The humiliation is too much to bear. Cornwall and Regan have made a mockery of him. The whole business of Lear's unruly hundred knights is of a piece with this image of Kent in the stocks. Kent is a metonymy of the knights, who are themselves a metonymy of the King. By putting Kent in the stocks, Cornwall, Regan, and Goneril signal their intent toward Lear. He must put a lid on his ridiculously self-centered behavior, or they will pack him off to the nearest retirement home.

In this contest between Vanity and Faith, Vanity wins. Moreover, this victory is not merely an external victory of the younger strengths represented by Edmund, Goneril, Regan, and Cornwall. It is, much more, a moral defeat of Lear's better self. By catering to the forces of vanity, Lear has orchestrated his own moral defeat. It was, after all, his vanity that led him to reject Cordelia. And it is his vanity that requires him to be accompanied by a hundred knights. We should not be surprised, therefore, when Goneril and Regan take aim at precisely this aspect of Lear's self. They have been schooled by their father and know where to hurt him. The knights are a crutch for Lear's fragile ego, which now needs more reassurance than ever. Like a woman's wardrobe or a man's golf equipment, they function as a security blanket in menacing and uncertain times. As Lear crawls toward death, he clings to these appurtenances in the vain hope that they will continue to shield him from discovering the awful truth about himself and the society of which he is a part. But events conspire to thrust him face-to-face with the violence that lies at the secret heart of the human social order.

First, however, Lear must pierce through the layers of vanity that shield the self from observing this violence in the cold light of day. When Lear removes himself to Goneril's home, he does not think further than when his next meal or hunting expedition will occur. But if the old man is to feast and hunt, others will have to cook the food, keep his hunting boots clean, and the horses fed and watered. This obviously requires a lot of work, and it is understandable that Goneril might object to having to cater for so many. A hundred knights are a hundred mouths to feed. Her main objection, however, appears to be that her father's retainers are unruly and ill mannered:

> Here do you keep a hundred knights and squires,
> Men so disordered, so debauched and bold
> That this our court, infected with their manners,
> Shows like a riotous inn. Epicurism and lust
> Makes it more like a tavern or a brothel
> Than a graced palace. (1.4.238–43)

It is tempting to dismiss Goneril's objection as self-serving and exaggerated. Perhaps it is. We are all given to presenting the facts in a light most favorable to ourselves. But can there be any disagreement about the facts? She finds the new household arrangements difficult and feels compelled to speak out. Perhaps she exaggerates, but the fact of the matter is that Lear is behaving as though nothing has changed and he is still very much in charge. This wouldn't be so bad if she just had to care for him. But when he can order around a hundred knights, the burden becomes quite oppressive. What upsets her most are his insults and abuse of her staff: "Every hour / He flashes into one gross crime or other / That sets us all at odds" (1.3.4–6). Lear is behaving like a spoiled child. But unlike a child, he has a hundred knights to amplify his imperious behavior. Who can blame her for wanting to put an end to it? Such behavior is unattractive in an adult, let alone in a man of his age: "Old fools are babes again, and must be used / With checks as flatteries, when they are seen abused" (1.3.20–21).

When Goneril suggests, quite reasonably, that he "disquantity" his train a "little" (1.4.246), Lear reacts as though she has put him in the stocks and the entire country is laughing at him. Outraged that she should have the "power to shake" his "manhood" (1.4.296), Lear unleashes a blistering curse that reflects his peculiar sense of love and obligation:

> Hear, Nature, hear! Dear goddess, hear!
> Suspend thy purpose if thou didst intend
> To make this creature fruitful!
> Into her womb convey sterility;
> Dry up in her the organs of increase,
> And from her derogate body never spring
> A babe to honor her! If she must teem,
> Create her child of spleen, that it may live
> And be a thwart disnatured torment to her!
> Let it stamp wrinkles in her brow of youth,
> With cadent tears fret channels in her cheeks,
> Turn all her mother's pains and benefits
> To laughter and contempt, that she may feel
> How sharper than a serpent's tooth it is
> To have a thankless child! (1.4.274–88)

The speech is hopelessly self-pitying and resentful. Curses are the last resort of the impotent, and Lear *is* powerless. He has resigned his authority and, shockingly, he is now being given a taste of his own medicine. The tyrant is being tyrannized. Unable to tolerate this new and highly uncomfortable feeling, he orders his men to saddle up and storms out. He reminds Goneril that he has another daughter, who will "flay" her "wolvish visage" (1.4.307). His parting shot is a threat. She will see his former power restored. There will be a reckoning:

> Thou shalt find
> That I'll resume the shape which thou dost think
> I have cast off forever. (1.4.307–9)

What follows, however, merely underscores the ridiculousness and incongruity of Lear's beliefs about himself. He arrives at Gloucester's home expecting a sympathetic reception. Instead, he finds his messenger in the stocks (shameful sight!) and his second daughter inside too busy to greet him. He tries desperately to excuse her rudeness. Perhaps Cornwall is unwell and she cannot leave his bedside. It is left to Gloucester to pass messages between the ungracious hosts and their unwanted guest, who is forced to stand outside in the cold. When Regan and Cornwall finally do emerge, the reception is far from warm. Regan scolds him for his childishness and selfishness. Wasn't the agreement to remain a month with Goneril? Why has he come to see her? Is her sister really so unreasonable? Are not his knights unruly and riotous? Regan advises that he apologize to Goneril and finish the month as planned. The whole scene has the flavor of an unpleasant custody battle between the sisters, with the obvious difference that the object of contention is a tiresome and irritable old father rather than a jealously guarded child.

Goneril arrives and all the principal characters (except Cordelia and Albany) are again on stage. It is the second Big Family Meeting, a repeat, or a parody, of the opening scene. But this time Lear has no bargaining power. He has given his wealth away, as the Fool never ceases to remind him. Nonetheless, he remains as stubborn as ever. He refuses to apologize and absolutely refuses to reduce his train of beloved knights to fifty. His egocentrism and vanity will not allow it. Goneril, too, will not budge (my house, my rules). Regan, forewarned by Goneril's letter, sees her cue and announces that if he is going to stay with her, she can accept no more than twenty-five knights. Lear does the math. Goneril now appears (rather awkwardly, given how he has treated her) the more agreeable of the two daughters. "Those wicked creatures," he says, "yet do look well-favored / When others are more wicked" (2.4.258–59). He makes a last desperate but futile attempt to play the daughters against each other. Goneril's fifty outbids Regan's twenty-five: "I'll go with thee. / Thy fifty yet doth double five-and-twenty, / And thou art twice her love" (2.4.260–62). We are back to the dismal terms of the love auction. The family dynamic is well rehearsed (it always is), and the players slip comfortably into their familiar roles. Lear steps obediently into his own trap and is hoisted by his own petard. Goneril and Regan press home the unhappy point, a point their father has taught them only too well: "What can you offer in return? Nothing? But nothing will come of nothing." As he himself surely must see, the terms of exchange require that they reduce his train of knights to zero. Lear is, as the Fool says, "an O without a figure" (1.4.189–90). Or, as his daughters would no doubt put it if they were alive today, his net worth is exactly zero. They are the ones paying the bills. Downsizing is necessary. Lear bellows helplessly and stumbles out into the storm.

Tempests of the Mind

At this point, it is easy to let our emotions get the better of us. But we must show forbearance lest we, too, are hoisted by our own petard. The line between good and evil appears to be getting quite stark, and it is tempting to exaggerate the difference to satisfy our need for catharsis and poetic justice. In Berger's view, the text, if read with sufficient patience, is rather more ambivalent about where precisely guilt lies. Dramatic performance inevitably pushes us away from textual ambivalence and toward a decisive emotional catharsis. It is, after all, shameful to see, in vivid three-dimensional reality, an old man locked out in such dreadful weather. Our sympathy naturally goes toward the vulnerable and the weak, and Lear unmistakably is shown to be a victim when he is so cruelly locked out in the storm. In this sense, the dramatic picture is heartrendingly obvious. Lear shivering on the heath is the victim of his two evil daughters, who are cozily tucked up inside Gloucester's warm home. They have reduced the former king to an unloved, unhoused old fool.

Berger calls this the "conventional reading" of the play, and it is certainly compatible with the view Lear adopts of himself.[31] Here we must remind ourselves of a fundamental distinction, namely, the distinction between Lear's perspective and Shakespeare's.[32] This may seem like an obvious difference. But when Lear is turned out on the heath, we are liable to forget it because these scenes are so overwhelmingly dominated by one character. To adopt a term we normally apply to novels rather than drama, Lear comes close to performing the role of a first-person narrator. He begins to tell his story. Once he has been exiled from family and court, he usurps the center of *our* attention utterly. Of course, Lear has a tendency to dominate the scenes in which he appears: he is given to violent outbursts whenever his vanity is threatened. But up to this point his presence on stage has been public rather than private. Thus, he appears as part of the preexisting structure of court or family (usually both). His role is determined by the part he plays in the social order, with all the rules that go with it. Once Lear is on the heath, however, all of this preexisting cultural and institutional machinery falls away. Like Edgar, who functions as a mirror in which Lear sees himself, Lear becomes "unaccommodated man," "the thing itself" (3.4.105–6). The heath scenes are Shakespeare's attempt to reduce the tragic scene to its most minimal, most originary elements.

The same point can be made by observing that Lear, unusually for a tragic protagonist, doesn't have any soliloquies. This peculiar fact is explained when we realize that the heath scenes function as one long, extended soliloquy. Unlike Hamlet or Iago, both of whom are hyperconscious of the distinction between public and private (which is to say, the distinction between their private, highly resentful view of the world and the public view consented to by others), Lear has no similar sense of irony or self-awareness. That is why he is so humorless. As Wilson Knight remarks, he lacks the comic spirit, which otherwise might have saved him.[33] In this sense, the speeches of the Fool and Edgar, which intersperse Lear's furious monologues, are closer to asides or meta-commentaries. Lear barely notices them. When he does, his hearing is highly selective. He reinterprets everything they say as confirmations of his own point of view. The effect is quite bizarre. It is comic to us but not to Lear. Lear is off in his own world, trying desperately to create some order from the disorder around him.

The first indication of the storm occurs just after Lear, in his failed negotiation with Regan and Goneril, delivers his desperate speech on the difference between animal need and human desire. All animals, including humans, need food and shelter to survive and reproduce. But only humans project onto these fundamental biological realities an additional symbolic aesthetic or sacred significance. A house, for example, is not merely a place to shelter from the elements. It must also appear attractive to other humans, who can imagine it as a place of hospitality, warmth, and civilized order—in short, as a place they, too, would like to inhabit.[34] This capacity to project onto objects a purely imaginary or symbolic function is a peculiar feature of human thinking. We do not merely perceive the external world in terms of our biological needs; we represent it collectively as part of a larger symbolic order. My house is desirable because it possesses a recognizable form or style. Yes, it protects me from the sun and rain, but so will a hole in the ground. I like *this* house because it reflects my identity and style, which is to say, my place in a universe of other tastes and styles that collectively make up the human concept of a house.

Lear makes a version of this argument when Goneril and Regan deny him so much as one knight to serve him ("What need one?"):

Oh, reason not the need! Our basest beggars
Are in the poorest thing superfluous.

> Allow not nature more than nature needs,
> Man's life is cheap as beast's. (2.4.266–69)

Even beggars have possessions that transcend their physical needs. Strip them of these useless but symbolically significant objects and you strip them of their humanity. Lear continues by pointing out that his daughters wear things which serve no necessary purpose. They are valued for purely aesthetic reasons:

> Thou art a lady;
> If only to go warm were gorgeous,
> Why, nature needs not what thou gorgeous wear'st,
> Which scarcely keeps thee warm. (2.4.269–72)

Should they be stripped of these useless objects (jewelry, ribbons)? Lear's argument is that these objects serve a purely symbolic function. They define who they are and therefore cannot be removed without also removing their sense of identity. We might disagree that having an army of knights counts as a fundamental human right, but we can certainly understand Lear's point that life can't be reduced to bare survival without missing precisely what makes a human life meaningful and therefore worth living.[35]

But what exactly *does* make life meaningful? We can grant Lear his general point while still remaining skeptical that the sheer accumulation of useless objects will in itself contribute to human happiness. It may be, for example, that Lear has projected his desire for meaning onto things that are only making his life *more* miserable. Certainly, that seems to be the case with his beloved knights. They have become a kind of fetish, which only seems to exacerbate the underlying problem. The fact that he engages in an absurd bidding war with Regan and Goneril suggests that they function as objects to be acquired and jealously protected rather than as independent actors whom he might learn to love and whose company he might learn to enjoy. Lear never mentions the name of a single knight. Instead, he treats them as nameless servants to carry out his commands. His jealous protection of them appears to be motivated by the air of superiority they allow him to maintain. He may not be king, but with one hundred knights at his service he can still boss a lot of people around.

Am I suggesting that Goneril and Regan are actually doing Lear a favor by stripping him of his knights? There is an undeniable upside to Lear's (brief) experience of life without servants or armed retainers. Insofar as they represent his former life, the knights are an obstacle to Lear's moral transformation. He cannot understand the world differently until he experiences it differently. To do that he must live life not from the center but the periphery. Like Cordelia and Kent, he must become an exile. The first two acts are the lead-up to Lear's exile. Lear must be unkinged before he can be kinged by love with a crown of flowers. The unkinging is the hard part. Lear has a deep-seated fear of appearing weak and impotent, which is why he surrounds himself with the accoutrements of kingship. The knights represent power.[36] Strip him of these symbols and you strip him of his manhood. After pointing out the hypocrisy of his daughters, who have reduced him to impotence (bare life) while flaunting their own potency, Lear calls on the gods for patience. He fears he will break out into impotent (womanish) tears:

> You heavens, give me that patience, patience I need!
> You see me here, you gods, a poor old man,
> As full of grief as age, wretched in both.
> If it be you that stirs these daughters' hearts
> Against their father, fool me not so much
> To bear it tamely; touch me with noble anger,
> And let not women's weapons, water drops,
> Stain my man's cheeks. (2.4.273–80)

He worries that in his wretchedness he will be overwhelmed by self-pity and tears, a woman's response he is determined to avoid. He tells himself it may be the gods who are behind his daughters' poor treatment of him, a thought which suggests that he is fortune's fool. He begs the gods not to prompt him to further foolishness (woman's tears). Rather, they must prompt him to noble anger, which is, of course, how the gods in their superhuman potency respond to indignities inflicted on them:

>   No, you unnatural hags,
> I will have such revenges on you both
> That all the world shall—I will do such things—
> What they are yet I know not, but they shall be
> The terrors of the earth. You think I'll weep;
> No, I'll not weep.   *Storm and tempest.* (2.4.280–85)

Lear's hesitancy and vagueness rather blunts the menace of the threat. He is battling to maintain his composure as tears of self-pity well up inside him. It is all he can do to smother them. This rather inept reference to revenge is the best he can muster.

As the stage direction indicates, here we get the first evidence of the storm. The flash of lightning and the sound of thunder coincide with Lear's threat. But what does this intrusion of the natural world into the human world mean? How is it to be interpreted? For Lear the storm reflects and amplifies his suffering. Berger calls the storm a "metonymic amplifier" of Lear's "torn state," presumably because the lightning strikes and claps of thunder are metonymically contiguous with Lear's inner turmoil.[37] The storm provides a fitting backdrop, a welcome echo, to the fury within Lear.

Lear's interpretation of the storm is an egocentric one. The storm reflects *his* preoccupations. And, indeed, the image of Lear on the heath does seem slightly melodramatic, even sentimental.[38] There he stands, exposed and vulnerable, inviting the elements to vent their rage on him:

> Blow, winds, and crack your cheeks! Rage, blow!
> You cataracts and hurricanoes, spout
> Till you have drenched our steeples, drowned the cocks!
> You sulfurous and thought-executing fires,
> Vaunt-couriers of oak-cleaving thunderbolts,
> Singe my white head! (3.2.1–6)

The very fact that Lear recognizes the difference between the internal and external tempests suggests that there is a certain amount of bad faith in his performance. When Kent attempts to usher him into the hovel, Lear refuses. The physical assault of the storm provides a welcome distraction from the prospect of more troubling thoughts within: "This tempest will not give me leave to ponder / On things would hurt me more" (3.4.24–25). Lear is like the man who refuses to sleep because his nightmares are worse than his waking experiences. Better the storm outside than the one that visits him internally.

Some critics have noted that Lear's rage on the heath is a bit too stagey, as if he were deliberately cultivating an image of himself as a victim in order to avoid the more terrible and difficult acknowledgment of his own evil. H. A. Mason, for example, remarks that Lear is "play-acting humility," and he sees in Lear's antics on the heath too much "posturing" and "spouting," as though "he is enjoying the spectacle he imagines he is offering."[39] But what motivates this posturing? Mason believes it is Lear's self-protective ego, which repeatedly kicks in when threatened. The more events conspire to expose Lear as a foolish and impotent old man, the more loudly he proclaims the earth-shattering significance of his daughters' ingratitude. To diminish the significance of his hurt would be disastrous for his ego, which is in danger of collapsing altogether in the face of the cascading indignities his vanity suffers. Even those small gestures Lear begins to make toward others, such as when he asks the Fool if he is cold, or when he notes Edgar's nakedness, are merely reflections of his own self-centered preoccupations. He is cold, so the Fool must be cold. He has been reduced to penury by his daughters, so poor naked Tom must have evil daughters who have done the same to him. Nonetheless, these small gestures represent a step in the right direction, even if they remain sheltered behind Lear's extreme egoism. At least he recognizes that he is not alone in his suffering. In these moments, he turns his attention toward those on the margins rather than venting his fury on the center he cannot bear to renounce.

Berger agrees with Mason but goes further in his analysis of Lear's self-deception. Lear's exposure on the heath is the outcome of his actions at the beginning when he rejected Cordelia and put himself in the care of Goneril and Regan. There is a perverse moral safety in doing so, Berger says, because by making "Regan and Goneril his chastisers," he "can more easily goad them into treating him shabbily." The tactic is necessary if he is to avoid recognizing his own hand in their violence: "He can evade arousing his guilty awareness of the extent to which he has already victimized them, and he can do this by making himself their victim and making them his scapegoats."[40] Lear's main challenge, then, is to maintain the integrity of this moral picture, which is repeatedly threatened by the damaging thought that his daughters' evil is but the mirror image of his own. This dangerous and self-destructive thought is what Berger calls Lear's "darkest purpose," which Berger sees pressing for release in the scenes on the heath. Thus, Lear's apostrophe to the storm, in which he begs the "great gods" to "find out their enemies now" (3.2.49–51), ambivalently refers both to his imagined persecutors (Regan, Goneril, Cornwall) and, more horribly and shamefully, to himself:

> Tremble, thou wretch,
> That hast within thee undivulgèd crimes
> Unwhipped of justice! Hide thee, thou bloody hand,
> Thou perjured, and thou simular of virtue
> That art incestuous! Caitiff, to pieces shake,
> That under covert and convenient seeming
> Has practiced on man's life. Close pent-up guilts,
> Rive your concealing continents and cry
> These dreadful summoners grace! I am a man
> More sinned against than sinning. (3.2.51–60)

The image of villainy conjured by Lear, Berger says, is "melodramatic, hyperbolic, and simplistic," but the exaggerated picture is necessary if Lear is to displace "its reference from himself to the world at large."[41] By hewing so closely to the melodramatic formula, Lear successfully avoids fitting himself to the image. That way madness lies.

I have no real disagreement with those critics who discern a certain amount of bad faith lurking in the old King's diatribes on the heath. Lear's moral picture of the world is bound to falter once he has been exiled from his exalted position at the center. The paradoxical oscillation between center and periphery is something all of Shakespeare's tragic protagonists undergo. Lear's experience of dispossession is certainly more dramatic. Unlike Hamlet, who remains pretty much permanently on the periphery relative to Claudius (which is why he can delay carrying out his vengeful fantasy for so long), Lear's position on the periphery occurs only after having first occupied the center for a very long time. In a move quite unprecedented in Shakespearean tragedy, he renounces the throne. This extraordinary move creates unique problems for the hero, who has to unlearn what he had once taken for granted. *King Lear* is Shakespeare's version of Hegel's historical parable of master and slave. Lear is a man who gets to experience both sides of the master-slave dialectic. This double experience, which is full of bad faith and false love, leads to a crisis that is only resolved by Lear's acceptance of Cordelia, who represents the love and moral reciprocity that Lear failed to recognize as long as he was king.

Lear's experience of injustice occurs only after he has been expelled from the center. In this sense, his suffering is a precondition of his moral transformation. The discovery that he is not in the first place a king (i.e., someone who is ontologically superior to his subjects) but a morally equal human being is a genuine revelation for him. Nowadays, we tend to take this view very much for granted, but for most of human history people didn't believe in it so fervently. In general, the universal moral law of the equality of souls takes a backseat to the laws of actual human societies, which are, of course, full of morally scandalous but ethically necessary hierarchies. This is not to say that earlier peoples didn't experience resentment. On the contrary, resentment is an infallible indicator of infractions against our intuition of moral reciprocity. This intuition makes us extremely sensitive to imbalances of status, power, and authority. Consequently, we tell ourselves all kinds of stories to explain why these imbalances exist. As a king, Lear was not in the habit of justifying his centrality. What kind of king explains or justifies his superiority? Once exiled to the periphery, however, he begins to question the center's unquestioned superiority, which now seems more problematic than he had assumed. His initial response is to stage an imaginary coup by invoking the destructive forces of nature. The storm will expose the sham behind all those false occupiers of the center. But if the current occupiers are false, then so was he. After all, he put them there. They have learned all their sneaky tricks from him. But what are the consequences of this revelation that the center is filled with imposters? Morally, where does it put the former King? Is he as evil as its current occupants?

Conscience of a King

If Mason and Berger are right about the extent of Lear's complicity in evil, then we would expect Shakespeare to represent the hero's temptation toward it. Typically, these temptation scenes are not hard to spot. Brutus is tempted by Cassius into the conspiracy against Caesar. Hamlet is tempted by the ghost to kill Claudius. Othello is tempted by Iago to kill Desdemona. And Macbeth is tempted by the witches to kill Duncan. Whether human or supernatural, these figures of temptation perform a double function. They are, on the one hand, independent agents and, on the other, aspects of the protagonist's soul. When Cassius tempts Brutus, he says, "Tell me, good Brutus, can you see your face?" Brutus replies, "No, for the eye sees not itself / But by reflection, by some other things" (1.2.51–53). Cassius then promptly declares that he will perform the role of mirror for Brutus:

> I, your glass,
> Will modestly discover to yourself
> That of yourself which you yet know not of. (1.2.68–70)

What hidden part of himself does Brutus discover when he looks at Cassius? Shakespeare leaves us in no doubt about the answer. The centerpiece of Cassius's seduction of Brutus is an extremely salacious and gossipy story of the scandal of Caesar's centrality. I will not cite all thirty-five lines of Cassius's marvelous story, but the essential points are as follows: Caesar is (a) a pathetic swimmer, (b) weak and given to fever, and (c) prone to girlish cries for water. And this man is become a god! And Cassius must bend his body if Caesar carelessly but nod on him! Oh Brutus, the scandal of it![42]

So, what hidden part of Brutus does Cassius reflect back to his noble interlocutor? Like a figure in an old morality tale, Cassius personifies Envy. Shakespeare shows us that Brutus is being tempted by Envy. Why, we might ask, would Shakespeare represent Brutus's inner world in this roundabout allegorical fashion? Because Brutus must keep Envy hidden from himself. We see Envy creeping up on Brutus, but he does not. In fact, he disguises it by insisting on calling this rather sneaky emotion something else, namely, honor. As far as he is concerned, the assassination is motivated by much nobler thoughts than the vulgar and commonplace experience of envy. That is why he is so concerned that the conspirators avoid, at all costs, appearing envious.[43]

Shakespeare's other temptation scenes follow a similar pattern. Hamlet is depicted as melancholy and resentful in the opening court scene. He claims he is grieving for his dead father. Then Horatio brings him news of the ghost, which sets up the first temptation scene. The ghost delivers an accusation that sounds suspiciously like Hamlet's first soliloquy. Hamlet's uncle is an incestuous villain, his mother faithless, and his father a veritable Hyperion. Only one additional detail is added. His uncle is a murderer! The serpent that did sting his father's life now wears his crown. The temptation scene has the same function vis-à-vis Hamlet as it did vis-à-vis Brutus—a preexisting but impotent feeling surfaces and is put into murderous action. In Brutus's case the passion (or subjective inner state) is envy, and the action is the murder of Caesar. In Hamlet's case the passion is resentment, and the action is the murder of Claudius. In both cases, a lot more blood ends up being spilled. Shakespeare traces the violent conflict of tragedy to these extremely common passions.[44]

Othello and Macbeth also have their temptation scenes. Othello's is doubtless the most extended in all of Shakespeare. Iago tempts his general with jealousy, the green-eyed monster which doth mock the meat it feeds on. By the end of the scene, Othello kneels before Iago and, in an obvious parody of his vow of love to Desdemona, pledges his soul to revenge:

> Arise, black vengeance, from the hollow hell!
> Yield up, O love, thy crown and hearted throne
> To tyrannous hate! (3.3.462–64)

Jealousy, personified in Iago, is transformed into vengeance and the murder of love (Desdemona). Macbeth undergoes a similar transformation. Confronted by the witches on the heath, he hears that he will be "king hereafter." Murderous ambition takes hold of his soul, and he kills the sleeping Duncan. Scotland becomes another Golgotha, and the seas turn blood red.

A proper analysis of Shakespeare's temptation scenes would require a much lengthier exposition. We do not have time for that here—and, in any case, I have attempted it elsewhere[45]—but I hope this brief summary at least gives the reader an idea of the basic elements employed by Shakespeare in his representation of the protagonist's temptation. When we turn to *King Lear*, however, we are confronted by an important difference. Unlike Brutus, Hamlet, Othello, or Macbeth, Lear is not tempted to commit an evil action he has hitherto avoided. Rather, he is offered the opportunity to renounce an evil he has unconsciously and habitually conspired to reproduce. Lear's division of the kingdom can hardly be seen *in itself* as a temptation. Morally speaking, the abdication is commendable. It shows the King is concerned for his soul, a fact that stands in marked contrast to Shakespeare's other tragic heroes. Connected to this fact is Lear's age. Lear feels death approaching, and that is why he bestows "all cares and business" onto "younger strengths" (1.1.39–40). What these facts suggest is that Lear arrives at a privileged stage in his life, one that eludes Shakespeare's other tragic heroes. Unlike them, he stands at the threshold of peaceful death. Can he put the violence behind him? Can he renounce the center?

> The oldest hath borne most; we that are young
> Shall never see so much nor live so long. (5.3.331–32)

Lear's advanced age means that he has already experienced and survived many temptations. This does not make him a saint. Far from it. But it does mean that what appears as a temptation to a younger person is unlikely to appear so to him. Lear's temptation is less about the self's approach to the desirable center and much more about the difficulty of retreating from it. To see the difference, consider this soliloquy delivered by Brutus. It occurs in his second temptation scene, just before he is visited by Cassius and the conspirators:

> It must be by his death. And for my part
> I know no personal cause to spurn at him,
> But for the general. He would be crowned.
> How that might change his nature, there's the question.
> It is the bright day that brings forth the adder,
> And that craves wary walking. Crown him—that—
> And then I grant we put a sting in him
> That at his will he may do danger with.
> Th'abuse of greatness is when it disjoins
> Remorse from power. And to speak truth of Caesar,
> I have not known when his affections swayed
> More than his reason. But 'tis a common proof
> That lowliness is young ambition's ladder,
> Whereto the climber-upward turns his face;
> But when he once attains the upmost round
> He then unto the ladder turns his back,
> Looks in the clouds, scorning the base degrees
> By which he did ascend. So Caesar may.
> Then, lest he may, prevent. And since the quarrel
> Will bear no color for the thing he is,
> Fashion it thus: that what he is, augmented,
> Would run to these and these extremities;
> And therefore think him as a serpent's egg
> Which, hatched, would, as his kind, grow mischievous;
> And kill him in the shell. (2.1.10–34)

The image of young ambition's ladder is highly instructive. Brutus worries that Caesar will get to the top first. Once there, he will turn his back on those below and become insufferably arrogant, scornful, and contemptuous. Therefore, lest he may, prevent. Crush the snake in the shell! Brutus is an advocate of preventative pest management. Don't wait for the snake to strike—find the nest and exterminate the eggs! Of course, the argument is obviously self-serving. Brutus doesn't see the irony that his pest management program applies not just to Caesar but to all (himself included) who are enviously clasping the rungs of young ambition's ladder.

The point I wish to make is that Lear is at the top of ambition's ladder. He has won the race, turned his back on the other competitors, and is comfortably able to scorn the base degrees by which he did ascend. Even more than Caesar, Lear has experienced the ruthlessness and cruelty of the brutal contest for centrality. Now an old man, he wants to put this violent chapter of his life behind him. Unlike Caesar, who did not have the luxury of announcing his retirement, Lear renounces the crown. But after Lear divides the kingdom, he more or less carries on as if nothing has changed. His temptation involves less an envious and ambitious desire to occupy the center than a refusal to renounce its corrupting influence. A lifetime at the top has immunized him against the regenerative powers of humility, charity, gratitude, and love. Instead, his soul has been dominated by envy, pride, scorn, anger, and contempt. In Cordelia, he is given the opportunity to recognize love, but accepting her would require a genuine abdication not merely of the seat of power but of those negative passions that have come to dominate his soul. I think Berger is right to suggest that Lear opts for the familiar rather than the unfamiliar path. He throws himself at Goneril and Regan because he recognizes them as kindred and like-minded spirits. Their hypocrisy, contempt, and cruelty are cozily familiar. They possess the tools of the center's trade and are aching to get their hands on Lear's pile. Next to them, Cordelia's offer of love is a totally alien experience. It is not a path Lear is willing to risk, even though, deep down, he knows it is the right one. He will only surrender himself into her care if she will become a willing partner in his diabolical game of power. When she refuses, he does too.

But is this evil? Lear is not being tempted to murder anyone. Othello kills Desdemona, but Lear does not kill Cordelia. Nor does Hamlet kill Ophelia. Nonetheless, both Ophelia and Cordelia die unpleasant and tragic deaths. This should give us a clue to Lear's temptation. Lear does not murder Cordelia, but like Hamlet he conspires in spreading evil that leads directly to the heroine's death. Shakespeare underscores the point when he has Kent utter the following prophetic words:

> Revoke thy gift,
> Or whilst I can vent clamor from my throat
> I'll tell thee thou dost evil. (1.1.167–69)

The "gift" Kent advises the King to revoke is the more opulent third he had intended to bestow upon Cordelia but that he has now rashly divided between the husbands of his eldest daughters. Kent objects not to Lear's initial division of the kingdom, which he already knew about, but to Cordelia's banishment, which has led to this further unplanned division of the remaining third. Obviously, Kent cannot know that the King, in pledging himself to Goneril and Regan, has doomed Cordelia.[46] But by calling the King's action evil, he makes clear to us that Lear, like his tragic precursors, has been tempted and has chosen the wrong path.

What makes Lear's evil seem less wicked than Othello's or Macbeth's or even Hamlet's is that it is cleverly disguised by Lear himself as a noble renunciation of power. How can evil exist without power? But powerlessness is what Lear fears most of all. He dismisses Cordelia because real love requires an absolute surrender of power. Claudius on his knees and overwhelmed by remorse knew what he had to do. But he could not do it because he could not countenance giving up "those effects for which I did the murder: / My crown, mine own ambition, and my queen" (*Hamlet*, 3.3.54–55). Lear remains as attached to power as Claudius. His public renunciation is, therefore, an act of bad faith. The internal passions do not follow the external command. One can see this in the intemperate responses he gives whenever the topic of reducing his train of knights arises. Goneril is the first to point out that the knights follow Lear's own poor example:

> You strike my people, and your disordered rabble
> Make servants of their betters. (1.4.253–54)

Goneril is not lying. We have seen Lear strike Oswald. Kent is merely following his master's example when he humiliates Oswald, first by tripping him, then by striking him in Gloucester's courtyard. Of course, Oswald is afflicted with the same vanity as Lear, but that is no excuse. It merely shows that pride and contempt have spread outwards from the King to his subordinates.

We should understand Lear's conduct in Goneril's house in the same way we understand Kent's placement in the stocks. Both incidents represent an inversion within Lear himself. He does not possess rulership of his baser passions. On the contrary, they rule him:

> Detested kite, thou liest!
> My train are men of choice and rarest parts,
> That all particulars of duty know
> And in the most exact regard support
> The worships of their name. Oh, most small fault,
> How ugly didst thou in Cordelia show!
> Which, like an engine, wrenched my frame of nature
> From the fixed place, drew from my heart all love,
> And added to the gall. Oh, Lear, Lear, Lear!
> Beat at this gate that let thy folly in
> And thy dear judgment out! (1.4.261–71)

We should not be misled by the reference to Cordelia. Lear is not admitting to his fault in rejecting her. Rather, he is comparing Goneril's current attempt to restrain his unruliness with Cordelia's earlier snub of his pride. Next to this latest outrage, Cordelia's appears small. When Lear says that Cordelia's fault unsettled him so much that love vanished from his heart, he is lying to himself. She offered love and, in return, he gave her hate. It is the huge shame of this action that Lear cannot bear to countenance, which is why he reacts with such venom toward Goneril. She functions as a scapegoat onto whom he can vent the accusations that should really be directed at himself: "Detested kite, thou liest!" But it is Lear who lies, not Goneril.

In 1.4 and 2.4, we witness the consequences of the hero's fatal decision to expel Cordelia. Lear has been tempted, he has failed the test, and now his soul is being steadily overwhelmed. Lear is dimly aware that he is experiencing an abdication of his proper self:

> LEAR
> > Does any here know me? This is not Lear.
> > Does Lear walk thus, speak thus? Where are his eyes?
> > Either his notion weakens, or his discernings
> > Are lethargied—Ha! Waking? 'Tis not so.
> > Who is it that can tell me who I am?
>
> FOOL
> > Lear's shadow. (1.4.223–28)

Lear's shadow is the dark side of his soul, and it is in danger of possessing him completely. All the evils he notices so assiduously in his daughters, beginning with the "most small fault" he attributes to Cordelia, can be applied with far greater precision to himself. He accuses Goneril of having "scornful eyes" (2.4.166) and striking him "with her tongue / Most serpentlike upon the very heart" (2.4.160–61). But her scorn and venomous tongue are no match for his. We should see Lear's growing hysteria not as a response to the evil within Goneril and Regan but rather as a furious attempt to hide from himself the shameful evil of his shadow self. The daughters, Cordelia included, function as scapegoats to divert Lear from attending to his own shame. Or, to put the same point differently, they are mirrors in which Lear sees a distorted version of himself. Hence the hysteria of his reaction to them. Goneril, the most formidable of the sisters, brings this response out most clearly. In 2.4, Lear admits that despite her fierce and scornful eyes, she is his flesh and blood:

> But yet thou art my flesh, my blood, my daughter—
> Or rather a disease that's in my flesh,
> Which I must needs call mine. Thou art a boil,
> A plague-sore, or embossèd carbuncle
> In my corrupted blood. (2.4.222–26)

Lear comes close to acknowledging the evil within himself but only to reject it. The image of his daughter as a disease poisoning his flesh implies that he can be healed by expelling her. Claudius had the same thought about Hamlet, whom he sent to England to be murdered: "Do it, England, / For like the hectic in my blood he rages, / And thou must cure me" (4.3.69–71). Violent expulsion of the other is always easier than facing up to one's own shame and guilt.

Hamlet becomes an antic fool after he is tempted by the ghost. Lear, too, increasingly plays the fool in a grotesque attempt to hide his shame by becoming a caricature of the penitent pilgrim. When Regan suggests he reduce his knights by half and return to Goneril, he kneels in mockery and play-acts the humble penitent. When she objects to these "unsightly tricks" (2.4.157), he refuses to stop. He compares himself to the houseless poor and the dowerless Cordelia:

> Return to her? And fifty men dismissed?
> No! Rather I abjure all roofs, and choose

> To wage against the enmity o'th'air,
> To be a comrade with the wolf and owl—
> Necessity's sharp pinch. Return with her?
> Why, the hot-blooded France, that dowerless took
> Our youngest born—I could as well be brought
> To knee his throne and, squirelike, pension beg
> To keep base life afoot. (2.4.208–16)

How exactly is returning to Goneril with fifty knights comparable to being homeless and dowerless? The hyperbole makes a mockery of those who really are forced to "abjure all roofs," to "knee" and "pension beg" to "keep base life afoot." One can see what Mason means when he says that Lear, when he is locked out, is "play-acting humility."[47] For here he is *before* he has been locked out already rehearsing for his grand solo performance. It is hard not to agree with those critics who regard Lear's exile as self-inflicted. He is practically begging Regan and Goneril to throw him out so he can wage his fury against the "enmity o'th'air." His daughters must be thinking that the old man's desire for some fresh Gloucestershire air is really quite a good idea.

When does Lear stop play-acting and genuinely begin to feel humility? Bradley believes it occurs when Kent attempts to persuade Lear to take shelter in the hovel. Lear is momentarily distracted from his furious self-aggrandizing performance and notices the Fool shivering beside him:

> My wits begin to turn.
> Come on, my boy. How dost, my boy? Art cold?
> I am cold myself.—Where is this straw, my fellow?
> The art of our necessities is strange,
> And can make vile things precious. Come, your hovel.—
> Poor fool and knave, I have one part in my heart
> That's sorry yet for thee. (3.2.67–73)

For Bradley, this represents a turning point toward "the inmost shrine of love," as Lear "comes in his affliction to think of others first, and to seek, in tender solicitude for his poor boy, the shelter he scorns for his own bare head." For the first time, we see Lear begin to triumph over his vanity, egoism, hatred, and impatience. The struggle is protracted, and his inner passions continue to threaten to overwhelm him, but this first selfless gesture toward the Fool, followed by his prayer to "houseless poverty" and the encounter with poor Tom indicate, for Bradley at any rate, that Lear has turned a corner and is now on an upward trajectory. These scenes, Bradley says, are "stages" in Lear's "purification," leading ultimately to the hero's "redemption."[48]

We can sharpen Bradley's remarks by putting them in more resolutely anthropological terms. Lear's self-pity, anger, and desire for vengeance begin to abate once he turns his attention away from the violent center and toward the human periphery. When Lear implores the gods to wreak havoc on himself and his enemies, he is invoking the sacred power of the center, which stands opposed to all human desire—as, for example, the Tree of Knowledge stands opposed to Adam and Eve's desire to eat its fruit. But this sacred power is itself a product of human desire, which is created not by the forbidden object at the center but by the desiring humans on the periphery. Because human desire is learned or, as Girard says, "imitated," it thrives on the scarcity created by prohibition.[49] That which is widely available ("common," "cheap") can scarcely be desirable. If it is not surrounded by prohibition and mystery, why on earth would you want to pursue it? The same goes for the institution of sacred kingship. A king can only exist if he has subjects to worship and obey him. A society of one hundred individuals, all of whom are kings, is by definition not monarchal. Politically, it would have no center and therefore no sacred hierarchy by which to govern. Or, to put the same point differently, it would have multiple centers all equal in authority and, therefore, all equally impotent. Each would be free to command while ignoring the commands of others. Lear on the heath waging war "against the enmity o'th'air" is in this situation. Stripped of real power, he play-acts his authority in his rage against the storm. Lear is a bit like Hamlet after the players arrive in Elsinore and he has recited and then listened to the lurid speech about Pyrrhus's hellish revenge. Unable to carry out real revenge, Hamlet furiously unpacks his heart with words and play-acts revenge. But there is an important difference. Hamlet eventually satisfies his desire for violent and bloody revenge. Lear never does. Or perhaps it would be more accurate to say he gets his revenge accidentally. All his enemies die *before* he can kill them. Only the Captain dies by his hand. But that is not really revenge. Murder, yes, but murder in the second rather than first degree.

Bradley is right that Lear's desire for vengeance begins to ebb when he turns to the Fool. By the time he is reunited with Cordelia, it has slackened significantly. Hamlet, of course, is never reunited with Ophelia. Revenge is incompatible with love, which is why Ophelia dies in the fourth act. When Hamlet and Laertes seek to outface each other over Ophelia's grave, their exaggerated and theatrical exclamations of love are no more sincere than Regan's and Goneril's during the love contest. Love motivates neither Hamlet nor Laertes. On the contrary, both are buoyed by the evil spirit of revenge that has haunted the play from the beginning. Why does Hamlet scream his love to the world only after Ophelia dies? His hysterical and exaggerated proclamation of love shows how easy it is to use the name of love as a pretext for the destructive passions (e.g., resentment, pride, vanity, jealousy, hatred). The similarity to Lear when he abdicates is not a coincidence. On the contrary, Shakespeare is remarkably consistent when it comes to representing the conflict between love and its enemies.

But just as Hamlet's soul will not go down without a long and protracted struggle (whence Hamlet's famous delay), so too Lear's will not rise without an epic inner battle. Lear's fight with his inner demons is so great it almost overwhelms him. Concerned for his master's sanity, Kent attempts to usher Lear into the shelter of the hovel multiple times, but each time Lear balks.[50] Why? What great significance does the hovel possess that makes Lear so reluctant to enter? The answer is Edgar, or, more accurately, Edgar's transformation into poor Tom the Bedlam beggar. The hovel represents a threshold Lear is hesitant to cross but which Edgar, a hunted fugitive, embraces wholeheartedly:

> I will preserve myself, and am bethought
> To take the basest and most poorest shape
> That ever penury, in contempt of man,
> Brought near to beast. My face I'll grime with filth,
> Blanket my loins, elf all my hairs in knots,
> And with presented nakedness outface
> The winds and persecutions of the sky.
> The country gives me proof and precedent
> Of Bedlam beggars who with roaring voices
> Strike in their numbed and mortified arms
> Pins, wooden pricks, nails, sprigs of rosemary;
> And with this horrible object, from low farms,
> Poor pelting villages, sheepcotes, and mills,

> Sometimes with lunatic bans, sometimes with prayers,
> Enforce their charity. Poor Turlygod! Poor Tom!
> That's something yet. Edgar I nothing am. (2.3.6–21)

Edgar decides to do exactly what Lear threatens to do. He will present his "nakedness" to "outface" the "winds and persecutions of the sky." The difference is that he will do it unconditionally and without reserve. There are no halfway measures for Edgar. He will even castigate his bare flesh with pins, thorns, and nails. He will feel what wretches feel. Compare Edgar's speech with the speech Lear utters when he stands before the hovel, having ushered the Fool inside:

> Poor naked wretches, whereso'er you are,
> That bide the pelting of this pitiless storm,
> How shall your houseless heads and unfed sides,
> Your looped and windowed raggedness, defend you
> From seasons such as these? Oh, I have ta'en
> Too little care of this! Take physic, pomp;
> Expose thyself to feel what wretches feel,
> That thou mayst shake the superflux to them
> And show the heavens more just. (3.4.28–36)

Compared with Edgar's transformation, Lear's is tepid and lukewarm. The words fly up, his thoughts remain below. He expresses some high-minded ideas, but they come off as a little too self-serving. He says he's never noticed poverty in the realm before. Really? This sounds highly implausible. Poverty and famine strike agrarian societies frequently and without mercy. Of course, the king—assuming he remains in power—always gets to eat, even in the harshest famine. His storehouse is never entirely bare. In lean years, the king's storehouse will get low, and this will be a sign that outside the castle the peasants are starving, perhaps in very great numbers. But if the storehouse runs out completely, this just means that the king has either foolishly given his food away to others, which never happens, or has failed to protect it. Agrarian societies are distinguished from hunter-gatherer societies by the fact that there is a centrally maintained and centrally protected storehouse. This last point is key. The king cannot merely be a symbolic king. He must command a militia, an army of thugs, who can protect the storehouse from other thugs. The whole point of having a king is to protect the central depot, which will naturally be an object of contention, especially in lean years. That is why sacred kingship is unknown to hunter-gatherers. Why swear fealty to a lord if there is nothing he can give you in return when times are tough and there's not enough food to go around? In other words, the king is more aware than his subjects of the dangers of famine, as it is precisely then that he is most likely to be overthrown.

What about Lear's statement that he wants "to feel what wretches feel"? Is it sincere? To my ears, Lear sounds a bit like a government official talking about his plan to end homelessness. He is full of compassion for those less fortunate than himself. But does he know what it's like to sleep in a doorway in the freezing cold? His authenticity seems questionable. The "houseless heads and unfed sides" function more as props for his own self-aggrandizement. Evidence that this is indeed the case comes when the Fool, frightened by Edgar, starts from the hovel. When Edgar emerges, Lear sees one of those "poor naked wretches" he had just been pitying, but his reaction to Edgar shows that his compassion for the poor is simply a pretext to talk about himself and his own (self-inflicted) hardships: "Didst thou give all to thy daughters? And art thou come to this?" (3.4.48–49). Lear can explain Edgar's wretchedness only by fitting it, quite absurdly, to a highly sentimental and melodramatic picture of himself.

Nonetheless, Edgar serves as a touchstone against which Lear can begin to measure himself. When Lear asks, "What hast thou been?" (3.4.83), Edgar replies:

> A servingman, proud in heart and mind, that curled my hair, wore gloves in my cap, served the lust of my mistress' heart, and did the act of darkness with her; swore as many oaths as I spake words, and broke them in the sweet face of heaven. One that slept in the contriving of lust and waked to do it. Wine loved I deeply, dice dearly, and in woman out-paramoured the Turk. (3.4.84–91).

Edgar does not let up with this excoriating picture of his past selves, eventually fragmenting himself into a kaleidoscope of metonyms and metaphors: "False of heart, light of ear, bloody of hand, hog in sloth, fox in stealth, wolf in greediness, dog in madness, lion in prey" (3.4.91–93). When Lear looks at Edgar, he sees not just a poor naked wretch but a caricature of the fallen self. In particular, he sees pride, envy, and wrath—the three deadliest of the seven deadly sins—parading before him, reflecting aspects of his own sinful nature. His false heart (pride), light ear (envy), and bloody hand (wrath) have led to the banishment of Cordelia and Kent.

Lear marvels at how Edgar can survive the storm in his nakedness, which suggests to him the possibility of liberation. Edgar has shed the layers of sin obscuring his proper self. His nakedness is a purification of the soul. Lear wants to follow his example:

> Thou ow'st the worm no silk, the beast no hide, the sheep no wool, the cat no perfume. Ha! Here's three on 's are sophisticated; thou art the thing itself. Unaccommodated man is no more but such a poor, bare, forked animal as thou art. Off, off, you lendings! Come, unbutton here. (3.4.102–8).

At this point, Gloucester enters with a torch. The two storylines—the Lear plot and the Gloucester plot—collide and intertwine. Henceforth Lear is onstage with either Edgar or Gloucester (usually both) until his reunion with Cordelia. What is Shakespeare trying to tell us by weaving these two plots together?

Fantasies of Parricide

As most readers notice, the subplot is a mirror image of the main plot. Lear embraces the false love of Goneril and Regan; Gloucester embraces the false love of Edmund. Lear rejects the true Cordelia; Gloucester rejects the true Edgar. Lear is punished by being locked out; Gloucester is punished by being blinded. Lear is reunited with the true Cordelia; Gloucester is reunited with the true Edgar. But what, in the end, is the point of this curious mirroring of the plots? It cannot simply be a means to amplify Lear's tragedy. For why would it need amplifying? Shakespeare does not use subplots in this way. Typically, they are used to provide a comment, often ironic or critical, on elements of the main plot, in particular, the protagonist.

We have already seen how Edgar's transformation into poor Tom functions as a criticism of Lear's much less convincing transformation of himself into a humble occupant of the periphery.[51] Lear's representation of himself as a victim is a strategy of self-centralization. He wants all the world to know that he is the most persecuted man in human history. Never has a father experienced such ingratitude! Lear's melodrama deserves all the thunder and lightning the gods can muster. It must be a storm to end all storms because the injustice done to Lear outdoes all previous injustices. But how does Gloucester fit into this bombastic scheme? What is his function vis-à-vis Lear?

Let's go over the basic facts. When Cornwall urges his host to shut the door after Lear has stormed out, Gloucester has to make a decision. Does he obey Cornwall and shut the door on Lear, or does he disobey Cornwall and shelter the King? Initially, he tries to do both. He shuttles between house and heath fretting about the King's health and the unjust "injunction" "to bar [his] doors" (3.4.148). But this (negative) injunction from his superiors ("Don't help the old man! Shut your doors! Leave him outside!") is then transformed into a statement—a belief—about Regan and Goneril's evil intent: "His daughters seek his death" (3.4.161). Whether Gloucester means that the daughters hope Lear will die of exposure or plan to murder him remains unclear at this stage. But there is a third possibility. Gloucester may be telling himself a story to justify his actions. The story goes something like this: "If I don't succor Lear, he will die because of their cruelty. This is more than I can bear, so I will rescue him." In his third and final visit, which occurs just as Lear falls into a sleep that, as Kent puts it, "might yet have balmed thy broken sinews" (3.6.98), Gloucester is no longer on a relief mission. Urgent and breathless, he bursts in and exclaims, "I have o'erheard a plot of death upon him" (3.6.89). If the King doesn't leave immediately, he will be dead in "half an hour" (3.6.93). Gloucester says he has a litter ready to hurry the King to Dover where "welcome and protection" await him (3.6.92).

These are the facts of the story. But they are the facts as told from Gloucester's point of view. I am particularly interested in the progression from the injunction to shut the door on the King to, first, the statement in 3.4 that his daughters seek his death and, second, the statement in 3.6 that he has overheard a plot to kill the King. Let's put our detective hats on for a moment and treat all statements by the witness with skepticism. What does the witness have to gain? Why does he tell the story the way he does? Can his statements be corroborated by other witnesses? The last question is the most easily answered. Nobody else has heard of a plot to kill the King. Nor do any of the accused plotters mention it themselves. This suggests that, at the very least, Gloucester has privileged or clandestine knowledge. At worst, it suggests that Gloucester has made up the story.

Let's keep this last possibility in mind and review the facts, this time from the point of view of the accused parties. First, remember that up until

Gloucester's blinding there have been no alarming acts of violence depicted onstage. The only violence has been pretended or hypothetical, as in Edmund's toy fight (with Edgar) followed by his self-inflicted wound. Lear has talked a great deal about the horrible cruelty of his daughters, but so far there has been no evidence of it either from the daughters or their husbands. If anything, what we see is the reverse. The only hint of genuine violence has come from the old man himself. For example, he strikes Goneril's servant, Oswald. It's true that Cornwall places Kent in the stocks, but this is a response to Kent's violence. Besides, placing someone in the stocks is not painful. The objective is to humiliate the occupant, not inflict physical pain. My point is that despite Lear's outrage at the way he has been treated, no one so much as lays a finger on him. Moreover, Lear's exposure on the heath is self-inflicted. He slams the door on his children, preferring the hostility of the storm to the humiliation of having to stay inside without the ego-boosting presence of his precious knights. Never once does he consider going back inside. He never even checks to see if the doors are locked. Cornwall, Regan, and Goneril are no doubt steely in their refusal to get sucked into Lear's self-pity, but they are not willfully cruel. Here is what they say after Lear has stormed out:

CORNWALL
    Let us withdraw. 'Twill be a storm.

REGAN
    This house is little. The old man and 's people
    Cannot be well bestowed.

GONERIL
    'Tis his own blame hath put himself from rest,
    And must needs taste his folly.

REGAN
    For his particular, I'll receive him gladly,
    But not one follower.

GONERIL
    So am I purposed. Where is my lord of Gloucester?

CORNWALL
    Followed the old man forth. (2.4.289–97)

Regan and Goneril aren't particularly concerned that Lear has abandoned the house. The consensus seems to be that Lear's decision is for the best. Once he gets cold and wet, he'll return, but without those tiresome knights. At this point, Gloucester reenters. He had followed Lear but returns almost immediately. The following exchange takes place:

GLOUCESTER
    The King is in high rage.

CORNWALL
                    Whither is he going?

GLOUCESTER
    He calls to horse, but will I know not whither.

CORNWALL
    'Tis best to give him way. He leads himself.

GONERIL *[to Gloucester]*
    My lord, entreat him by no means to stay.

GLOUCESTER
    Alack, the night comes on, and the bleak winds
    Do sorely ruffle. For many miles about
    There's scarce a bush.

REGAN
                    Oh, sir, to willful men
    The injuries that they themselves procure
    Must be their schoolmasters. Shut up your doors.
    He is attended with a desperate train,
    And what they may incense him to, being apt
    To have his ear abused, wisdom bids fear.

CORNWALL
    Shut up your doors, my lord; 'tis a wild night.
    My Regan counsels well. Come out o'th' storm. (2.4.298–311)

The second act closes with the suggestion that there is worse weather to come. But the storm that threatens the occupants of the house is internal rather than external. Evil is about to overwhelm them. The King is in "high rage" and attended by a "desperate train," who may (Regan says) "incense him" to that which "wisdom bids us fear." "We should," she says, "shut the door to the night's evil." But the evil on the heath turns out to be nothing compared to the evil inside the house. Outside the old King raves. His train consists of no more than the Fool and a lunatic beggar. What do Cornwall, Regan, and Goneril have to fear? The answer, of course, is themselves. Albany puts the point succinctly:

> It will come,
> Humanity must perforce prey on itself,
> Like monsters of the deep. (4.2.49–51)

It takes only a whisper to raise these monsters of the deep. Regan says that Lear is "apt" to have his "ear abused." Earlier, Curran had "whispered ... ear-kissing arguments" to Edmund about "likely wars ... twixt the Dukes of Cornwall and Albany" (2.1.7–11). And, of course, Edmund has whispered in his father's ear the horrible story of Edgar's treachery. Regan is unsurprised to hear the latter news. She suspects that Edgar must have been a "companion with the riotous knights / That tended upon my father" (2.1.94–95). Edmund confirms her suspicions, "Yes, madam, he was of that consort" (2.1.97). "No marvel, then," she replies, "though he were ill affected. / 'Tis they have put him on the old man's death, / To have th'expense and spoil of his revenues" (2.1.98–100).

Is any of this true? Unfortunately, nobody bothers to find out, least of all Gloucester. Edmund and Regan are quite unscrupulous in their pursuit of power. They will happily tell lies about others if it means they can get one step closer to the seat of power. If you want to climb young ambition's ladder, you can't be too squeamish about what you do to get to the top. You must not let cold and heartless facts push you from your goal, which is to hoodwink your interlocutor and get a leg up on your rivals. It is essential, therefore, to let the facts take a backseat to the intended effect you want your story to have on your audience. And you do that by putting yourself in the best possible light and your rivals in the darkest shade. Don't be shy about foregrounding your heavenly purity while emphasizing the unspeakable evil of your enemies.

Queen Margaret in *Richard III* knows a thing or two about this narrative strategy. She is everybody's scapegoat at the beginning of the play, so when the once-powerful Queen Elizabeth and Duchess of York also find themselves victimized by Richard, they turn to her for moral consolation and some self-help therapy. "O thou well skilled in curses, stay awhile," Elizabeth says to Margaret, "And teach me how to curse my enemies!" (4.4.116–17). Despite being former rivals, the women become allies in their hatred of Richard, who by the end of the play becomes the biggest scapegoat of all. Margaret's reply to Elizabeth is thus also Shakespeare's ironic comment on the audience's complicity in the scapegoating of Richard. Here is what the delightful Margaret says:

> Forbear to sleep the nights, and fast the days;
> Compare dead happiness with living woe;
> Think that thy babes were sweeter than they were
> And he that slew them fouler than he is.
> Bett'ring thy loss makes the bad causer worse;
> Revolving this will teach thee how to curse. (4.4.118–23)

This is excellent advice for the impotent and resentful. Note that we in the audience are also impotent and resentful because we can do nothing about the reprehensible actions represented on the stage before us. If you find yourself in the unjust position of a Margaret or an Elizabeth and cannot take revenge on your persecutor (because he is too powerful and you are too weak), then your best bet is to go public with the outrage. But now you have another problem. Who will listen? How do you get your audience to share your resentment? Simple. You exaggerate. Don't hold back! Emphasizing the innocence of the victim and the wickedness of the persecutor is the only way to get the audience's attention.

Richard III is an early play and Shakespeare's use of irony is not at all subtle. Dramatically, the play is a triumph. Theater audiences immediately fall in love with Richard because the irony is so obviously stageworthy. He hoodwinks his onstage interlocutors while slyly winking at us.[52] By the time Shakespeare wrote *King Lear*, he had put aside this rather stagey use of dramatic irony. The irony of his mature work is infinitely more subtle. Edmund, for example, is no Richard of Gloucester, despite the superficial similarities between the two. He is much closer to Iago, who of course nobody, least of all Othello, suspects of being a villain. We don't boo, hiss, or laugh at Iago or Edmund. The whole point of their villainy is that it appears honest, reasonable, and impeccably logical.

Why is Gloucester so quick to believe Edmund's story about Edgar? Why doesn't he bother to check the facts by talking directly to Edgar? Berger points out that Gloucester's credulity is not as preposterous as it appears. In a society based on primogeniture, the firstborn is—by definition, we might say—impatient to replace the father. "The heir," Berger says, "is a potential enemy and competitor, the eventual replacement whose appearance prophesies his father's death."[53] Just as Lear fears a revolt from his heirs and perversely appears to provoke it by dividing his kingdom, so too Gloucester secretly fears a challenge from his heir. That is why he is so quick to believe Edgar is a traitor: "Abhorred villain! Unnatural, detested, brutish villain!" (1.2.78–79). The reaction seems exaggerated. How can Edgar be transformed so quickly in Gloucester's mind from loving and dutiful son to hated and disloyal villain? But this shocking exaggeration is very much the point. In the eyes of the father, the son can only be an unnatural villain once the taboo of patricide has been transgressed even if the transgression remains purely imaginary. The father thinks that the son thinks that the son wants to murder the father. As Freud famously pointed out, it is every father's worst nightmare and every son's favorite dream. I think this is why Gloucester later assumes that Regan and Goneril seek Lear's death. Lear calls his daughters all kinds of horrible names, but he never accuses them of conspiring to kill him. Nor do Goneril and Regan ever give any indication that they want to kill their father. Of course, lack of evidence does not mean that the desire does not exist. The whole point of an unconscious or latent desire is that it can't ever be ruled out.[54] It could surface at any time. But it is surely significant that Lear has daughters rather than sons, a fact which makes the fear of patricide less prominent to Lear than to Gloucester. In any case, Gloucester clearly projects his own anxieties about his treacherous son onto Lear. We can see this association unfolding in Gloucester's mind when he first broaches the idea of Lear's daughters' patricidal intentions:

> His daughters seek his death. Ah, that good Kent!
> He said it would be thus, poor banished man.
> Thou sayest the King grows mad; I'll tell thee, friend,
> I am almost mad myself. I had a son,
> Now outlawed from my blood; he sought my life
> But lately, very late. I loved him, friend,

No father his son dearer. True to tell thee,
The grief hath crazed my wits. (3.4.161–68)

Kent has just told Gloucester that the King's "wits begin t'unsettle" (3.4.160). The thought of the King's madness prompts these reflections on the cause of Gloucester's own grief and crazed wits. He too has been betrayed by a tenderly loved child who now seeks his death. The two plots (Lear's and Gloucester's) and their attendant unruly passions (grief, rage, hatred, desire for vengeance) merge seamlessly into one another. The speech is Gloucester's, but we are not really sure whose perspective we are getting. Gloucester's perspective is mapped onto Lear, which maps back onto Gloucester again. His daughters are cruel, my son is cruel; Edgar wants to kill me, Regan and Goneril want to kill him. The narrative irony of this layering of perspectives is accentuated by the fact that Gloucester is talking to Kent, whom he doesn't recognize. Gloucester is looking directly at "poor banished" Kent but doesn't see him. In short, Gloucester suffers from the same blindness as Lear. In his preoccupation with his own (purely fictional) miseries, he projects those same miseries onto others. Just as Edgar seeks to end Gloucester's life, so Goneril and Regan seek to end Lear's.

It's time to consider the moment in the play when light seems to be utterly extinguished and all is, in Gloucester's bleak words, "dark and comfortless" (3.7.88). But rather than take the victim's perspective, which is admittedly very difficult not to do given the graphic cruelty of the action performed before our eyes, let's consider the scene from the perspective of the evil persecutor. Why is the Duke of Cornwall so enraged? What terrible crime has Gloucester committed? Cornwall is enraged because he believes Gloucester is conspiring with an invading force. He repeatedly refers to Gloucester as a *traitor*—an accurate description given the evidence in his possession, which includes Gloucester's clandestine letter from the French invaders. The interrogation proceeds logically from this evidence. Thus, his first question is about the letter: "Come, sir, what letters had you late from France?" (3.7.43). His second concerns the extent of Gloucester's "confederacy" with the French (3.7.45). Gloucester's answer attempts, unconvincingly, to obscure his guilt:

I have a letter guessingly set down,
Which came from one that's of a neutral heart,
And not from one opposed. (3.7.48–50)

If the letter were neutral, why would Gloucester have hidden it? And why would he have dispatched the King to meet a "neutral" party? Cornwall is not fooled by Gloucester's clumsy evasions. His next question gets straight to the point: "Where hast thou sent the King?" (3.7.53). "To Dover," Gloucester replies (3.7.54). Oswald had already reported that Lear with "some five- or six-and-thirty of his knights" had gone to Dover, "where they boast / To have well-armèd friends" (3.7.16–20). Now this third crucial fact is confirmed.

Let us give credit where credit is due. At least Cornwall seeks to confirm the facts, something Gloucester, when hearing an equally shocking story of betrayal and treachery, does not bother to do. At least Cornwall insists on questioning the accused before he puts out the accused's eyes. Of course, Cornwall is unspeakably cruel. That is indisputable. But we should not let the graphic cruelty of Cornwall's actions blind us to Gloucester's faults. When Gloucester proclaims Edgar an outlaw and condemns him to death ("Let him fly far. / Not in this land shall he remain uncaught; / And found—dispatch" [2.1.55–57]), he does so on the basis of an unconfirmed and ultimately false story. Like Cornwall, he is blinded by fear, resentment, rage, and an insatiable desire for vengeance. Gloucester loses his eyes because he fails to see this elementary truth. He is blind to his own evil.

At this point, Gloucester realizes the game is up. He can no longer pretend to be the Duke's faithful ally. Not only has he admitted to conspiring with foreign invaders, he has also admitted to sending the retired King to these same invaders. What possible motive does Gloucester have for actions which must look, to Cornwall at any rate, like treason? This is the point of Cornwall's final question: "Wherefore to Dover?" (3.7.56). Gloucester's reply is addressed not so much to Cornwall but to himself: "I am tied to th' stake, and I must stand the course" (3.7.57). This seems like an odd thing to say during a cross-examination, but one can understand why Gloucester chooses to see things in this light. Rather than admit to conspiring in violent rebellion, it is morally preferable to see oneself as the target of somebody else's violence. Regan, no doubt impatient at Gloucester's self-pitying reply, reiterates the question: "Wherefore to Dover?" Gloucester's reply is directed at her:

Because I would not see thy cruel nails
Pluck out his poor old eyes, nor thy fierce sister
In his anointed flesh rash boarish fangs.

> The sea, with such a storm as his bare head
> In hell-black night endured, would have buoyed up
> And quenched the stellèd fires;
> Yet, poor old heart, he holp the heavens to rain.
> If wolves had at thy gate howled that dern time,
> Thou shouldst have said, "Good porter, turn the key."
> All cruels else subscribe. But I shall see
> The wingèd Vengeance overtake such children. (3.7.59–69)

I think it's safe to assume that Cornwall did not enter the room intending to gouge out Gloucester's eyes. To be sure, Cornwall had no intention of handling Gloucester gently. He had instructed Edmund to leave with Goneril because the "revenges" he had in mind for the "traitorous" Gloucester were "not fit for your beholding" (3.7.7–9). Nonetheless, I think it makes sense to see the particular method of torture, if not the torture itself, as an unplanned response to Gloucester's extraordinary depiction of Lear's suffering. In a cruel and ironic twist, Cornwall inflicts the very punishment on Gloucester that Gloucester imagines Regan and Goneril inflicting on Lear.[55]

Here we must pause and ask ourselves a basic question. Do the sisters intend to kill their father? Are they, like the cunning but ultimately fantastical Edgar, also wicked parricides? Unfortunately for Gloucester, there is no evidence that they want to kill their father. Nor is there any evidence that they want to gouge out his eyes. The whole plot against the father seems to be a product of Gloucester's vivid and fearful imagination. He has modeled their fantastic crime on Edgar's equally fantastic crime. What is more, he has incited the rage of his lord and benefactor (Cornwall) by acting on these false assumptions. Gloucester believes he is saving Lear from Regan's "cruel nails" and Goneril's "boarish fangs," but all he achieves by sharing these lurid images with his interrogators is to unleash Cornwall's cruel imagination. When Gloucester swears that he will see wingèd Vengeance exact retribution on Lear's daughters, Cornwall replies, "See't shalt thou never," and gouges out his victim's first eye. Gloucester's lurid image of Regan plunging her cruel nails into Lear's eyes inspires Cornwall to do exactly what Gloucester feared. He graphically literalizes the metaphor.

We should not forget that Cornwall's charge of treason is true. To see this, we need to go back to 3.3, when Gloucester tells Edmund about a mysterious letter he has just received:

> There is division between the dukes, and a worse matter than that. I have received a letter this night; 'tis dangerous to be spoken; I have locked the letter in my closet. These injuries the King now bears will be revenged home; there is part of a power already footed. We must incline to the King. I will look him and privily relieve him. Go you and maintain talk with the Duke, that my charity be not of him perceived. If he ask for me, I am ill and gone to bed. If I die for't, as no less is threatened me, the King my old master must be relieved. There is strange things toward, Edmund. Pray you, be careful. (3.3.8–20).

Recall that the King has recently stormed out of the house and onto the heath. Gloucester is unsure where to place his loyalties. Does he back the old King, or does he stick with his benefactor, the Duke of Cornwall? The letter tips the balance in favor of Gloucester's former master, the old King. Let's assume the letter comes from Cordelia. Kent has already received clandestine messages from her, and he also refers to a looming conflict between the "cunning" dukes (3.1.21). They are the most powerful figures in the land, and, following the King's abdication, there is a power vacuum. Now that Lear has been shunted to one side, everyone is expecting a showdown between the dukes. But suddenly a third party is thrown into the mix. France has crossed the channel and landed at Dover. Gloucester seems to think that France has come to avenge Lear's injuries: "These injuries the King now bears will be revenged home." But how can Cordelia know about the King's injuries? There has not been sufficient time to exchange messages about the King's nighttime escapade. Furthermore, why does Gloucester refer to injuries that must be "revenged home"? Even if we assume that Gloucester is referring vaguely to Lear's exposure during the storm (hypothermia? exhaustion? mental breakdown?), do these "injuries" deserve retaliation by a foreign power? Are we to suppose that France has landed to rescue the King from hostile parties? But who exactly is holding the King hostage? Lear's exile has been self-inflicted. He walked out of the house and into the storm of his own free will. We should not be surprised if he catches a chill. So, whom exactly is Cordelia supposed to be saving? Has she come to save Lear from himself?

These factual and moral inconsistencies don't really bother us because what these whispered rumors describe is our offstage reaction not to all the messy and conflicting details but to the central emotive fact of Lear's thunderous rage on the heath. But who tells *that* story? Lear, of course! And how does Lear represent himself? As a victim! When we listen to Lear scream about his daughters' ingratitude, we witness a truly pitiable and heart-rending performance. But does anybody ever bother to check the facts? When it comes to narratives of persecution, it is remarkable how determined we are to ignore any facts that contradict the narrator's perspective, especially if the narrator presents himself as a victim of an outrageous injustice. But this should not surprise us at all. Recall the basic principles of cursing, as advised by the champion curser, Queen Margaret. The victim must be allowed to speak freely and without inhibition. To imply that the victim might also be guilty or complicit in evil is to show poor judgment and, what is worse, to enable the victim's persecutor. Do you really want to smear yourself with the unpleasant odor of the evildoer? How exactly does that help the victim's cause? Suggesting that the victim might be complicit in the violence inflicted upon him is unlikely to motivate the audience's warm desire for vengeance. On the contrary, it is all too likely to cool it until, eventually, it is extinguished altogether. Theatrically speaking, this is not a good strategy. The audience demands a violent spectacle, not a dreary lecture on the ironies of the victim's moral indignation.

After receiving word from a mysterious third party, ambivalently both hostile and benevolent, Gloucester decides that he must "incline to the King" (3.3.13–14). But the way he presents the matter to himself is significant. He is not conspiring with a hostile foreign power. He is saving the King. Furthermore, the presence of a foreign power in England means revenge is both possible and likely. That is why he imagines that Cordelia and her French army have come to avenge the indignities inflicted on the King, even though there is no possible way she can know about Lear's exposure, which furthermore was self-inflicted. No matter. The battle lines between good and evil must be drawn, and they must be drawn starkly. There will be a violent reckoning. The audience rubs its hands in eager anticipation. We are as happy to conspire in these dark whispers as the hapless Gloucester. The difference, of course, is that Gloucester loses his eyes, whereas we can modestly avert ours from the graphic violence depicted so shamelessly before us. To put the point slightly differently, Shakespeare anticipates our shameless desire for a cruel and violent spectacle. We are complicit in Gloucester's fantasies of parricide.[56]

Cornwall modestly invites Edmund to avert his eyes by insisting that he accompany Goneril on her return home. The act will be too shameful for him to see. But such modesty seems unnecessary. Edmund is the one who has quite explicitly encouraged the violent spectacle in the first place. He has set up his father, first by inventing the story of Edgar's parricidal plot, then by revealing his father's involvement in the conspiracy with France. And he has done it gleefully and joyfully, without the slightest remorse or hesitation.

Drowning the Stage with Tears

To understand the full significance of Gloucester's blinding we need to make a brief detour to examine the association between weeping and violence. The image of the weeping eye is referred to repeatedly in the play. Weeping often signals an injustice: we weep for the unjustly persecuted victim. But it also signals impotence. If you are weeping, you are not correcting or avenging the injustice about which you are weeping. Avengers do not weep when they kill their victims. Nonetheless, weeping is an important step toward rage and the fulfillment of revenge.

Consider Shakespeare's most famous avenger. After watching the player perform Hecuba's grief by shedding real tears, Hamlet chides himself for being unable to summon any tears in support of his cause. How is he supposed to avenge his father if he can't even shed a tear for him? What, he wonders, would the player do if he were in his shoes?

> He would drown the stage with tears
> And cleave the general ear with horrid speech,
> Make mad the guilty and appall the free,
> Confound the ignorant, and amaze indeed
> The very faculties of eyes and ears. (2.2.562–66)

Hamlet is a terrible avenger because he lacks the necessary moral conviction. He tries very hard to create in his mind a sentimental image of his father as loving, kind, and pure and his uncle as devious, incestuous, and lecherous, but he knows full well that the picture is a caricature and not to be trusted. Hence his fascination for and suspicion of the ghost, which produces a most lurid and melodramatic speech about the heroism and purity of the father next to the lechery and villainy of the uncle.

Unlike Hamlet, Lear has no difficulty producing either tears or horrid speech. In fact, horrid speech and tears are his specialties. After cursing Goneril in the most lurid and sensational terms (Queen Margaret would approve!), he is so impressed by his own speech that he can't hold back the tears that immediately well up inside him:

> Life and death! I am ashamed
> That thou hast power to shake my manhood thus,
> That these hot tears, which break from me perforce,
> Should make thee worth them. Blasts and fogs upon thee!
> Th'untented woundings of a father's curse
> Pierce every sense about thee! Old fond eyes,
> Beweep this cause again, I'll pluck ye out
> And cast you, with the waters that you loose,
> To temper clay. (1.4.295–303)

Even when he's crying, Lear has time to provide a running commentary full of exaggeration and sensational language. It is not Goneril who has made Lear cry, but Lear himself. Most of us have witnessed, either in ourselves or someone else, the emotional release of tears. Once started, they are hard to stop. Small children, of course, frequently vent their hurt and frustration with tears. The violent image of Lear plucking out his weeping eyes to mix with the dust at his feet anticipates Cornwell gouging out Gloucester's eyes and grinding them underfoot. Lear says he's ashamed of his tears. Both his horrid speech (curses) and his tears are signs of his impotence. Men don't cry about their injuries, they get even. But tears are also shed in sympathy for the powerless victim and are, in this sense, a prelude to getting even.

Lear has a keen disciple in Laertes, who doesn't seem to have Hamlet's motivational problems. When Gertrude describes Ophelia's drowning, Laertes is overwhelmed by grief, then rage:

> Too much of water hast thou, poor Ophelia,
> And therefore I forbid my tears. But yet
> It is our trick; nature her custom holds,
> Let shame say what it will. [*He weeps.*] When these are gone,
> The woman will be out. Adieu, my lord.
> I have a speech of fire that fain would blaze,
> But that this folly douts it. (4.7.186–92)

Laertes hasn't yet mastered Lear's trick of weeping and uttering a speech of fire at the same time, but he is a fast learner. At Ophelia's burial, he manages a much better performance. Indeed, it is so effective that Hamlet, who had been spying on the proceedings, can't resist joining in. He steps out from his place of hiding and the two young avengers compete with one another in a grotesque parody of grief over Ophelia's death.

> 'Swounds, show me what thou'lt do.
> Woo't weep? Woo't fight? Woo't fast? Woo't tear thyself?
> Woo't drink up eisel? Eat a crocodile?
> I'll do't. Dost come here to whine?
> To outface me with leaping in her grave?
> Be buried quick with her, and so will I. (5.1.277–82)

Hamlet doesn't quite threaten to pluck out his own eyes, but he will not allow Laertes to hog the limelight. If Laertes will bury himself—eyes, tears, and all—in Ophelia's grave, so will he. Hamlet's dull revenge has been ignited by the exaggerated tears of a rival. Hamlet has figured out how to drown the stage with tears and horrid speech. The audience is about to receive its pound of flesh.

Let us look at a final example. When Lear encounters the blinded Gloucester at Dover, he offers him his eyes:

> If thou wilt weep my fortunes, take my eyes.
> I know thee well enough; thy name is Gloucester.
> Thou must be patient. We came crying hither.
> Thou know'st the first time that we smell the air
> We wawl and cry. (4.6.176–80)

Before he was blinded, Gloucester wept at Lear's misfortunes. But his tears were mistaken. He was weeping over his own misfortunes, which he projected onto Lear. And yet not only was he mistaken about Lear's misfortunes, he was also mistaken about his own. He sought vengeance on Edgar, who was guiltless. His susceptibility to rumor and gossip led him to accept the many whispers circulating in the air, beginning with the rumors about Edgar. Gloucester failed to see what was in front of his eyes. Rather than talk to Edgar directly, he relied on Edmund as an intermediary. He allowed Edmund's narrative to substitute for a face-to-face encounter with Edgar. He then layered onto Edmund's narrative of patricidal persecution elements from Lear's self-pitying narrative of filial ingratitude. Lear's daughters became doubles of Edgar, who was himself a figment of Gloucester's imagination. Even if we put the blame squarely on Edmund, which strikes me as very un-Shakespearean, this would still be the case. The difference is that we add an additional narrative perspective. Edmund invents a story about Edgar and tells it to Gloucester, who accepts it without question as an accurate description of his eldest son. The point is that the story is never confirmed by any fact-checking. Gloucester never hesitates to accept the story's truth. Why he never hesitates is an interesting question. Presumably, he suspected Edgar of disloyalty all along. Edmund, just like Iago whispering in Othello's ear, does not so much sow the seed of parricidal suspicion; he waters it. He confirms a narrative that had long existed in Gloucester's mind and was waiting for release. What triggers its release, moreover, is not just Edmund's story, but the events in the play's first scene. In 1.2, Gloucester enters the stage muttering the following thoughts to himself:

> Kent banished thus? And France in choler parted?
> And the King gone tonight? Prescribed his power,
> Confined to exhibition? All this done
> Upon the gad? (1.2.23–26)

If Kent, who possesses the same noble rank as Gloucester, can be banished and stripped of his estate, then so can he. This eventuality seems all the more likely now that the King has abdicated. The lions are circling, and it is no time for weak old men like himself. When Gloucester sees Edmund guiltily hide the incriminating letter, his suspicions are confirmed. He sees conspiracies sprouting in every corner. Edmund, Edgar—someone, everyone—is up to no good. The young are rising up to unseat their elders. He is the next target. These late eclipses in the sun and moon predicted it.

Incidentally, these remarks explain a peculiar line uttered by Edgar at the end of the play. Edmund is dying from a wound inflicted by Edgar, who reveals his identity. The brothers exchange forgiveness, and Edgar says something rather tasteless about their father: "The dark and vicious place where thee he got / Cost him his eyes" (5.3.175–76). Most readers assume that Edgar is moralizing rather crassly.[57] Gloucester's whoring cost him his eyes. But I think this is rather unfair to Edmund's mother. Why should she, or her room or bed, be a "dark and vicious" place?[58] It seems much more likely that Shakespeare intended us to understand "dark and vicious place" as referring to a place within Gloucester himself. Edmund is a bastard and a villain, but if there is one thing this play tells us, it is that we should be cautious about accepting the most obvious moralizing labels. It was Gloucester's desire for a scapegoat, not Edmund's, that led him to believe the things he did. He feared patricide, so he scapegoated Edgar. He feared Regan and Goneril, so he turned them into monsters who wanted to gouge out Lear's eyes with their cruel nails and rash their boarish fangs into his anointed flesh. In this sense, it was indeed the dark and vicious place in Gloucester that cost him his eyes. Fear and resentment so obscured his vision that his eyes became quite useless. Of course, I am interpreting Gloucester's blindness metaphorically. His moral blindness is represented by the removal of his eyes. Gloucester loses his eyes when resentment triumphs over love. Allegorically, this conflict between love and resentment is represented by the rise of the faithless Edmund and the descent of the faithful Edgar. Gloucester has two sons, but we never see him on stage with both. It is either one or the other. Up until he is blinded, it is Edmund; afterward, it is Edgar. Edmund's triumph culminates with his father's blindness. Once Gloucester discovers that he has been betrayed by Edmund, he never seeks vengeance again. Instead, he directs violence inwards, toward himself.

Shakespeare underscores this change within Gloucester in the moments immediately before and after the blinding. When Gloucester says, "But I shall see / The wingèd Vengeance overtake such children," Cornwall replies, "See't shalt thou never," and gouges out an eye. Wingèd Vengeance immediately swoops down on Gloucester, Cornwall, and the brave servant who takes "the chance of anger" and comes to Gloucester's aid (3.7.82). Gloucester loses his second eye; Cornwall and the servant, their lives. But Gloucester still believes in anger's privilege and wingèd Vengeance and now calls on his bastard son to avenge his suffering: "Edmund, enkindle all the sparks of nature / To quit this horrid act" (3.7.89–90). Regan spitefully reveals the truth to Gloucester:

> Thou call'st on him that hates thee. It was he
> That made the overture of thy treasons to us,
> Who is too good to pity thee. (3.7.91–93)

Instantly, Gloucester's desire for vengeance vanishes. Now, instead of asking for vengeance, he repents:

> Oh, my follies! Then Edgar was abused.
> Kind gods, forgive me that, and prosper him! (3.7.94–95)

The reason that Edmund is not on stage is now clear. It's not that he is squeamish about violence but that Shakespeare does not want to undermine the allegorical picture of Gloucester's divided soul. The blinding scene occurs when Gloucester's inner conflict reaches its nadir. Thereafter, he begins a slow and arduous upward climb. Allegorically, we would expect to see this conflict represented with Edmund onstage for the blinding but departing at the point Gloucester realizes his error and asks the gods for forgiveness, at which point Edgar would arrive to indicate the inner change. But this would be dramatically clumsy, so Shakespeare excludes Edmund from the scene and waits until the next scene to reunite Gloucester with Edgar. Gloucester's resentment and desire for vengeance have vanished. Now he feels remorse, shame, and guilt. This is also why Edgar remains disguised. Gloucester's moral transformation is far from complete. He is no longer fearful and resentful, but he is far from ready to embrace Edgar. Shame and guilt stand in the way.

Act 3 closes in total darkness. The outer darkness mirrors the inner darkness. The blinded Gloucester is thrust out of the house and told by Regan to "smell / His way to Dover" (3.7.96–97). But Gloucester's exile is, paradoxically, also a new opening. Shakespeare indicates this change by the entrance of Edgar, who delivers a soliloquy of hope:

> Yet better thus, and known to be contemned,
> Than still contemned and flattered. To be worst,
> The lowest and most dejected thing of fortune,
> Stands still in esperance, lives not in fear.
> The lamentable change is from the best;
> The worst returns to laughter. (4.1.1–6).

Edgar is talking about his own fortunes, not his father's. But if his father is to recover his proper self, he must look up, not down. He must also look inward rather than outward, study himself, not his rivals. The first step is to recognize his mistake: "I stumbled when I saw" (4.1.19). But Gloucester's admission of guilt is incomplete. He still sees himself as a victim, not of his son, but of the cruel gods: "As flies to wanton boys are we to th' gods; / They kill us for their sport" (4.1.36–37). The logical consequence of this nihilistic fatalism is to embrace death. At Dover, he may walk to his death: "There is a cliff, whose high and bending head / Looks fearfully in the confinèd deep" (4.1.72–73). But violence, whether directed at others or self-inflicted, is not a solution. Self-harm is no doubt an improvement over harm to others, but it is hardly a solution to the fundamental ethical problem of human violence.

Bradley sees in Gloucester's journey to the cliff face at Dover a pilgrimage analogous to Lear's. "His sufferings," Bradley says, "purify and enlighten him," and "he dies a better and wiser man."[59] More recently, critics have tended to dispute Bradley's optimistic interpretation. Most have focused their attention on Edgar, whose actions appear at best insensitive and at worst gratuitously cruel, even sadistic. Why does Edgar lead his father to Dover? Why doesn't he reveal his true identity? He has heard his father say he longs to see his son "in his touch" (4.1.23). Why does he deny his father this easily granted pleasure? Why does he instead continue to play this silly pretense of being a lunatic beggar?

Cavell answers this question by suggesting that Edgar is not exempt from the evil that envelops the world of *King Lear*. Certainly, he is not as bad as Edmund, Cornwall, Regan, or Goneril, but he is quite bad enough. In this sense, he is like Lear and Gloucester. Their goodness is sadly and tragically compromised.[60] The particular crime Edgar commits is of a piece with his father's crime (and Lear's too). He studiously, laboriously, and cruelly avoids recognition. Rather than reveal himself to his father, he pretends he is someone else. Why? Because he is ashamed of himself. After all, he committed the same crime as his father. Instead of talking to the old man about this crazy story invented by his envious brother, he acted as though he were guilty and rushed off to hide like an animal in the thickets and gullies of the heath. In short, he acted like an outlaw. No wonder his father believes him to be guilty. Edgar behaves like a criminal!

The Parable of the Cliff

Cavell believes that the great secret to *King Lear* is the human propensity for shame, which always gets in the way of love or reciprocal acknowledgment of the other. Shameful thoughts are the prelude to shameful acts. We are, deep down, unpleasant creatures, harboring dark and filthy desires. For example, we insist on clothing ourselves to avoid the shame of others seeing us naked. This sense of shame is so strong that we invent all kinds of narratives to disguise ourselves from one another. In *King Lear*, Cavell sees the "avoidance of love" arising from this deep sense of shame. Rather than mutual love, we engage in mutual shame and mutual envy. We are so ashamed of ourselves that we find it difficult, sometimes impossible, to love each other, to recognize each other as individuals unattached to obfuscating but soothingly familiar and comforting narrative stereotypes. We are like the movie actress who can only be seen in a certain light from a certain angle. This is great when the right light and the right angle exist, but what happens when they don't? The actress is suddenly thrown into an existential crisis.[61] Her world crumbles, and she has to hide and wait for the right light and the right angle before she can emerge again.

According to Cavell, Edgar finds himself in this situation when he sees his blinded father stumbling out of the gate of his estate. He is shocked at the brutality of his father's injuries. But he is also ashamed of himself. His actions have contributed to his father's suffering. To reveal himself would mean exposing his shame and guilt, which he is unwilling to do. Cavell also suggests that Edgar is unprepared for the shock of seeing his father in this horribly mutilated state. Gloucester is in pain, helpless, and vulnerable. This is not the father Edgar remembers, and he is caught utterly off-balance. What can the child do when he sees the father so vulnerable and powerless? The normal paternal relationship, with its reassuring strength and familiarity, is undermined.[62] It is not easy for the child to throw off the shackles and behave as though he is the one in charge and the father is the one who needs to be cared for. It would be difficult enough to do this for a stranger. How much more difficult to do it for a parent, whose role has always been defined as the caregiver and protector of the child. So Edgar hides behind his mask, which saves him from having to acknowledge his father. Faced with this new intolerable reality, Edgar shrinks back into his disguise as the poor mad beggar. It is an act of self-preservation. But it is also an act of cowardice. Fear prompts him to delay, perhaps forever, the moment when the two can honestly acknowledge one another and talk about all those things they are too ashamed to talk about. Life is difficult enough without having to open up about one's secret and shameful feelings. Better to keep moving toward Dover and the cliff.[63]

Holding to this hypothesis, Cavell reads the cliff scene as a further instance of the avoidance of love. Edgar invents this spectacular narrative about the dizzying precipice precisely so he can avoid referring to the facts.

Anything is better than having to talk about the shameful reality of his relationship to his father, so he diverts both his own and his father's (and the audience's) attention to this alternative, purely fictional reality. Cavell doesn't buy the traditional reading of this scene, which is that Edgar is seeking to cure his father of nihilistic despair. Readers more inclined to Bradley's salvational interpretation of Gloucester's pilgrimage up the imaginary slope have marveled at the power of Edgar's imagination. How impressive it is! How easily we, like Gloucester, accept it as a substitute for the real thing! Harold Goddard, for instance, says that Edgar's description of the cliff face is a triumph of the play and makes "this place that exists only in the imagination more real than the actual chalk cliffs of Albion." When Gloucester falls to his imagined death, he is reborn and purified: "Imagination has exorcised the suicidal temptation. Gloucester is done with the idea of voluntary death. The father is converted by the child."[64]

Let us call Goddard's reading, which probably represents the consensus among most readers, the optimistic reading.[65] These readers accept Edgar's view that the father is suicidal and depressed. Something must be done to heal him. The near-death experience, expertly created by the loving and attentive son, cures the father, at least for the time being. Of course, it is always possible that he may suffer a relapse. But psychological ailments are not cured overnight. The son is doing his best for the despairing father. Goddard stresses the healing effects of Edgar's imagination, which he reads as a sly reference by Shakespeare to the healing effects of poetry more generally. In this sense, Shakespeare is a forerunner of the romantic poets and, indeed, Goddard quotes William Blake approvingly: "He who does not imagine in stronger and better lineaments and in stronger and better light than his perishing and mortal eye can see does not imagine at all."[66] Goddard's reading of the play, like Bradley's, is based on the assumption that literature has the power to redeem and ennoble humanity. To see what is before one's eyes is to see nothing much. Humans are so much more than flesh and bones. Shakespeare and Blake, Goddard suggests, want to show us not just the flesh and bones, but the human soul in all its truth, beauty, and transcendence.

This optimistic picture of humanity is no longer especially fashionable, particularly among humanities professors. We tend to be a good deal more skeptical of the redeeming power of literature because we are a lot more skeptical about human beings, who seem to be capable of goodness knows what crimes.[67] In this sense, Cavell's reading is a sign of the times. He regards Edgar's explanation of his father's fall as a justification of further cruelty rather than a purifying exorcism of Gloucester's inner demons. Fiction does not purify. On the contrary! It obscures or disguises dark and nasty impulses. For Cavell, there is nothing liberating or purifying about Edgar's narrative. To see it as full of spiritual or transcendent meaning (purifying the soul, exorcising despair, etc.) is to miss the point, which is that there is nothing there but two men awkwardly going to great lengths to avoid each other. "To fill this scene with nourishing, profound meaning," Cavell says, "is to see it from Edgar's point of view; that is, to avoid what is there."[68] Edgar says he is saving his father from suicidal despair—"Why I do trifle thus with his despair / Is done to cure him" (4.6.33–34)—but what he is really doing, according to Cavell, is avoiding the painful and shameful reality of sitting down with his father and having that heart-to-heart, face-to-face conversation in which each man recognizes the other without the obfuscating mask of the victimary narrative. Like passengers crammed together on the subway, we stare at our phones so we don't have to acknowledge the other's existence. Presumably, the narratives on those screens are full of nourishing, profound meaning that distracts us from the more demanding task of acknowledging the singular reality of those annoying bodies pressing uncomfortably upon us.

Perhaps Cavell sets the bar too high. Perfect moral reciprocity is, after all, difficult to maintain all the time. Indeed, is it impossible to avoid lapsing into narratives that put the other, even if only momentarily, at a disadvantage. This imbalance occurs even in the most equal and harmonious of circumstances. Consider, for example, a conversation with a friend. Your only aim is to hear what your friend has to say before responding with your own thoughts that build on what your friend has said. In a genuine conversation, each takes turns listening and speaking. The shared goal is to allow the conversation to continue unobstructed by any need beyond the needs of the conversation itself. Even in this ideal example, however, small asymmetries and hierarchies emerge because when you are speaking, I must listen. This asymmetry is, of course, only temporary. I grant you the right to speak because you in turn will grant me the right to speak so that the conversation can advance, which is, after all, the point of having the conversation in the first place. We are enjoying one another's presence not because we have some other end in view, but because your presence is what is desirable to me and vice versa. In other words, we "acknowledge" one another in the full human sense of the word Cavell finds lacking in Edgar's interactions with his father.

Unfortunately, human interaction does not consist only of conversations between equal partners. Much of life involves getting others to do things that you would rather not do yourself. Hierarchies inevitably emerge, and when they do, we invariably fail to attend to the other with the same uncompromising sense of reciprocity we intuitively know we all deserve. Yes, we are all equal, which is to say, equally deserving of the other's attention, but the attention space is limited, and we can't attend to everybody all the time with the same equal attention. Inevitably, we devote much of our attention to ourselves rather than others. "To thine own self be true," Polonius says to his son, no doubt hoping that if Laertes is true to himself, he will be true to others too. Unfortunately, the self is divided into multiple conscious and unconscious parts, and the imperative to be true to oneself is therefore shot through with ambiguity. Which self should I be true to? Hamlet and Laertes are true to a part of themselves, but tragically it is the vengeful part, and the upshot is much suffering and death, not just for themselves but a lot of other people too. Is Edgar being true to himself when he adopts the disguise of poor Tom? Obviously not. He says, "Edgar I nothing am." Edgar is a much more complex person than poor Tom, which is why Edgar repeatedly breaks character when he is playing the role of poor Tom. Nonetheless, poor Tom is a part of Edgar; otherwise he would not be able to play the role at all. Cavell is right to suggest that in maintaining his disguise Edgar shamefully retreats from his father. But I'm not sure he is right to assume that by revealing himself Edgar could have cured his father of his despair and therefore avoided the charade of the imaginary suicidal plunge.[69] What if Edgar did reveal himself and his father had died on the spot? Wouldn't he have regretted not going through with the charade?

Edgar's tactic of putting his father through what seems like unnecessary psychological hardship and cruelty is not unusual in Shakespeare's plays. There are many instances of falsely advertised deaths that Shakespeare's heroes and heroines have to endure. In *Much Ado about Nothing*, Claudio believes he has killed his sweetheart, Hero. (Admittedly, the news of her death does not appear to upset him unduly, at least not until he discovers that his vilification of her was based on a falsehood.) In *Measure for Measure*, Angelo believes he has killed Claudio, and Isabella believes that her brother is dead. In *The Winter's Tale*, Leontes believes he has killed Hermione and Perdita. In *The Tempest*, Alonso believes his son is drowned, and, of course, the courts of Naples and Milan believe that Prospero and Miranda have perished when they are cast adrift in a leaky boat on the open ocean. In each of these cases, the motive for the pretense is to get the guilty characters to repent so that forgiveness can be granted. When Isabella, in *Measure for Measure*, kneels beside Mariana and begs for Angelo's life, she believes her brother to be dead by Angelo's command. Her mercy is therefore genuine, not a pretense. The same applies to Angelo's remorse. He believes he's killed Claudio, and his repentance is therefore sincere. He accepts the penalty for his sin, which is death. When he discovers that Claudio is alive, the discovery does not absolve him of his sin. He had intended Claudio's death, commanded it, and believed it to be successfully executed. Now he must repent. Only once he has repented can he be forgiven. Of course, many readers regard the Duke in *Measure for Measure* to be even crueler and more sadistic than Edgar, who at least does not pretend that murder has occurred.[70] No doubt telling Gloucester that he had killed his son—a far more devastating fiction than the tale of the cliff—would push Gloucester over the edge completely.

Incidentally, Shakespeare elsewhere gives us an example of a son who encounters his blind father, pretends he is someone else, and reports that the blind father's son is dead. I am thinking of Lancelot and his blind father, Gobbo, in *The Merchant of Venice*. Of course, in this case we laugh at the pretense, which seems to be just more of Lancelot's foolery. Nonetheless, there is a more serious side to it. Lancelot has just uttered a long soliloquy in which he debates whether he should flee the stingy Jew and take up service with the more enticing and open-handed Venetians. Should he abandon Shylock and serve Bassanio, who is now flush with a good chunk of Shylock's borrowed cash? Lancelot may be given to foolery, but he is no fool when it comes to judging which way the wind is blowing. Long before anybody else, he senses that Shylock's days as a secure and wealthy employer are numbered. The Venetians will not tolerate the upstart Jew much longer, and, sooner or later, his wealth will be snatched from him by those wily Venetians. Even though Lancelot's conscience counsels him to stay with the Jew, the fiend at his elbow prompts him to run into the arms of the newly rich Bassanio, whose wealth Lancelot rightly senses will soon be spectacularly multiplied. Giddy at the prospect of a new and much wealthier master,

Lancelot is on his way to Bassanio's home when he encounters his father, Gobbo. Being blind, Gobbo does not recognize his son and assumes he has bumped into a stranger, whom he addresses as "[m]aster young gentleman" (2.2.36) before politely inquiring for directions to Shylock's home. Doing nothing to dispel his father's false assumption, the son announces that Lancelot, after whom Gobbo inquires, is not, as far as he knows, a "poor man's son" (2.2.48) but a prosperous gentleman and, moreover, that Master Lancelot is "deceased" (2.2.61). When Gobbo hears that his son is dead he is distraught: "Marry, god forbid! The boy was the very staff of my age, my very prop" (2.2.63–64). Gobbo, who is old, poor, and blind, needs his son if he is to survive. How can Lancelot be so cruel to pretend the son is dead? No doubt, there is some deep shame in Lancelot, which tempts him to engage in this little power trip over his father. More precisely, Lancelot believes that by serving Bassanio he will rise in the social hierarchy. The lowly serving boy his father remembers has died, and the new wealthier Lancelot, whose loyalties have shifted to the young, attractive, and soon-to-be-extravagantly-rich Bassanio, will rise from the ashes of the old. Does Lancelot really want his father to get in the way of his new venture? Won't the old blind man be a burden on his ambitions? Happily, Lancelot has second thoughts about casting off his poor blind father. He eventually reveals himself to his father and the two end up joining Bassanio's rapidly growing and very spiffily dressed staff.

Lancelot appears in a romantic comedy, so his strategy of avoidance, to use Cavell's term, is easily passed off as harmless tomfoolery. But behind the tomfoolery is the sobering thought that Lancelot is reproducing, in somewhat ham-fisted and exaggerated fashion, the behavior of his new Venetian masters. The irresistible movement away from Shylock is a deliberate strategy of avoidance. The Venetians are infinitely more subtle than Shylock in the games of avoidance they play. But beneath those games lies the hard fact of scapegoating. In this sense, Shylock fulminating about his pound of flesh is merely reflecting back to the Venetians the cruelty that they obscure behind all their glitter and gold: "The villainy you teach me I will execute, and it shall go hard but I will better the instruction" (3.1.67–69). Unfortunately for Shylock, he does not better the instruction. On the contrary, when it comes to scapegoating and the avoidance of the other, he is a clumsy amateur among immensely skilled professionals. In his tomfoolery, Lancelot is, paradoxically, closer to Shylock than the Venetians. Presumably, this is also why he is the only one to express any guilt for abandoning Shylock.

How, then, should we interpret the cliff scene? Is it, as the traditionalists maintain, a morally commendable spiritual healing of the father by his faithful son? Or is it, as the antitraditionalists argue, a cruel exploitation of the father by a sadistic son playing the role of a lunatic beggar? In favor of the traditionalists is the text, which shows that Edgar has, at this point, shed his role as the mad beggar. He no longer talks in riddles and nonsense. On the contrary, his description of the cliff is vivid and clear—so clear, in fact, that we can easily picture it in our minds. The crispness and clarity of the picture is something Goddard admires deeply and is the main reason he regards the scene as the cornerstone of the play. We *see* the cliff clearly in our mind's eye even though there is nothing to see in reality.

Goddard's point is well taken, but I am inclined to think that Shakespeare is playing a double trick on us. All readers, whether traditionalists or antitraditionalists, believe that Gloucester is duped. But what if he isn't? What if Gloucester suspects—is perhaps certain—that the lunatic beggar is his son Edgar? We know that he already associates poor Tom with Edgar. When the blinded Gloucester is led out of the gates of his estate by his old and faithful tenant, they encounter poor Tom on the road. Gloucester recalls seeing him the night before:

> I'th' last night's storm I such a fellow saw,
> Which made me think a man a worm. My son
> Came then into my mind, and yet my mind
> Was then scarce friends with him. I have heard more since. (4.1.32–35)

Obviously, when Gloucester saw poor Tom the night before, he wasn't blind. He recognized, if only subconsciously, the physical similarity between poor naked Tom and his son Edgar. But the association was painful, Edgar being for him a would-be parricide. Saying that they were "scarce friends" is, of course, a massive understatement, which underscores the fact that Gloucester is now looking back on his former self with deep shame. He finds it difficult to admit to himself the extent of his former hatred of Edgar. The terse sentence—"I have heard more since"—is another understatement, ridiculously inadequate in its attempt to sum up Gloucester's interrogation, his blinding, and Regan's cruel taunt that he had been betrayed by Edmund. Does the penny now drop? Does Gloucester realize that the lunatic beggar he saw last night was in fact his son Edgar?

Much of what follows makes better sense if we *do* make this assumption. Everyone assumes that Gloucester wants to commit suicide, but that doesn't sit with what Gloucester says in the lead-up to his encounter with Edgar. His first thought is not for himself but for his guide, an old man and long-time tenant, whose service goes back to when Gloucester's father ran the estate. The old tenant's loyal service of "fourscore years" (4.1.14) is meant, I think, to remind us that despite Gloucester's woeful situation, there is still much good in the world. Gloucester is concerned for his tenant's safety:

> Good friend, begone.
> Thy comforts can do me no good at all;
> Thee they may hurt. (4.1.15–17)

When the old man objects that Gloucester cannot see his way without a guide, Gloucester utters a confession that presumably is lost on the old man: "I have no way and therefore want no eyes; / I stumbled when I saw" (4.1.18–19). This despairing admission is then generalized into a gnomic statement that seeks to recuperate an element of good from his misfortune: "Full oft 'tis seen / Our means secure us, and our mere defects / Prove our commodities" (4.1.19–21). The thought that he might learn from his terrible experience leads to a heartfelt affirmation of his desire to live:

> O dear son Edgar,
> The food of thy abusèd father's wrath!
> Might I but live to see thee in my touch,
> I'd say I had eyes again! (4.1.21–24)

At this point they encounter poor Tom. Why, after having just expressed a warm desire to live, would Gloucester suddenly decide to kill himself? Furthermore, his selfless desire to put the old man out of harm's way does not strike me as the despairing actions of a suicide. Nor do his subsequent actions fit with this image of a despairing suicide. Why ask the old man to fetch clothes for poor Tom? Why give Tom his purse? Are these to be understood as his last noble gestures before he bids goodbye to the world? If so, they seem grotesquely out of place, oddly self-aggrandizing rather than despairing or nihilistic. Suicide is born of despair or unbearable pain or both, not out of generosity or altruism. Certainly, Gloucester is in pain, but the physical pain is nothing compared to his psychological pain—the shame, guilt, and remorse for what he has done.

I think it makes much more sense to assume that Gloucester, despite his physical blindness, suspects or intuits—imagines secretly to himself—that Tom may indeed be Edgar. This is ironic, of course, but it fits with the radical shift in Gloucester's perspective after the blinding. He sees that he had wrongly persecuted Edgar and consequently feels shame, remorse, and guilt. The scales fall from his eyes, and he is, so to speak, reborn. His greatest wish is to be forgiven by his son. That is all that matters. And that is why he has to live. Gloucester has shed the negative passions that had once so dominated him: fear, self-pity, resentment, anger, and the desire for vengeance. He now sees clearly what he has to do. He needs to find Edgar and he needs to kneel before him and ask forgiveness. But what if Edgar wants revenge? That is understandable and to be expected. And that is why Gloucester devises the plan to have Edgar lead him to the cliff. He more than anyone understands the temptation of revenge. To prove his remorse to Edgar, he will offer him the opportunity to inflict on him what he had intended to inflict on Edgar—his death.

If Gloucester knows that poor Tom is Edgar, why doesn't he come straight out and say it? Why does he humor Edgar's silly lunatic-beggar act? This is where the antitraditionalists are closer to the mark than the traditionalists. They suspect that Edgar's noble desire to cure his father hides something much more sinister. Cavell believes it hides Edgar's shame. He is ashamed for two reasons: first, he conspired in the events leading to his father's injuries (he didn't have the courage to confront his father face-to-face and dispel the lies); and second, his father is weak, impotent, and vulnerable, and he can't stand the shame of seeing the once powerful paterfamilias appear so pathetically decrepit. Obviously, these are shameful feelings and must at all costs be kept hidden to maintain one's self-respect. The charade provides a welcome distraction from the shame of having to recognize his father, which would also entail recognizing the darker side of himself. Following in Cavell's footsteps, Berger is even harder on Edgar. He believes that Edgar wants revenge and that the cliff scene is a trial run for, as Berger puts it, the "execution" of the father,[71] which occurs in the sharp tale Edgar relates at the end, a tale which literally breaks his father's "flawed heart" (5.3.200).[72]

I think Cavell and Berger are on to something, but I disagree that Gloucester is the victim of Edgar's machinations when he is led up the imaginary slope. On the contrary, Gloucester anticipates and even welcomes Edgar's desire for revenge, which is just retribution for what he has done to his son. In a sharp comment, Cavell notes that Gloucester never intended to go to Dover. When Regan shoves him out of the house and tells him to "smell / His way to Dover" (3.7.96–97), she must (Cavell says) be thinking of her father.[73] Cavell believes that Regan's cruel taunt is what gives Gloucester the idea, first, to go to Dover and, second, to commit suicide: "What the text suggests is that, rather than taking a plan for suicide as our explanation for his insistence on using Dover cliff, we ought to see his thought of the cliff, and consequently of suicide, as *his* explanation of his otherwise mysterious mission to Dover."[74] In other words, Gloucester hears the word *Dover*, associates it with steep white cliffs, and in a final imaginative leap associates the cliffs with a desperate leap into the abyss below. The suicidal leap provides him with a pretext—an excuse—for a journey he otherwise had no intention of taking. Gloucester is like the man who accidentally steps onto the wrong train, discovers that it is going to Paris, and then, embarrassed by his error, explains to the lady next to him that he is fulfilling a lifelong dream of visiting the Eiffel Tower.

I have no problem with Cavell's suggestion, but I think that rather than suicide, Gloucester associates the cliff with that famous ancient punishment in which the pharmakon is collectively nudged off the steep Tarpeian Rock. If Edgar wants revenge, then Gloucester will offer it to him. In other words, Shakespeare's ethical interest in the cliff scene is focused not primarily on the despairing victim (Gloucester) but on the agent of temptation and prosecutor of revenge (Edgar). As far as Shakespeare is concerned, Gloucester is not the main problem. Vengeance is not on Gloucester's mind. On the contrary, he feels shame, guilt, and remorse. His repentance is genuine. The problem is rather Edgar. Will he demand vengeance? The cliff scene is his test, not Gloucester's.

Gloucester keenly senses that poor Tom is not who he claims to be. When Gloucester's tenant describes Tom as "[m]adman and beggar too" (4.1.30), Gloucester is immediately skeptical: "He has some reason, else he could not beg" (4.1.31). Gloucester is not fooled by Tom's mad act—madmen don't beg. Indeed, he strongly suspects that poor mad Tom is none other than poor mad—resentful, angry, vengeful—Edgar. But he will not reveal he knows his son's secret until his son is ready to reveal himself, which will occur only when the son's desire for vengeance has subsided. It may be that the son kills the father before the hoped-for reunion, but that is a risk the father is willing to take. He cannot hope for his son's forgiveness without also expecting a fair bit of resentment and wrath. Who can expect a child, after being abandoned and persecuted by a parent, to turn around and magnanimously say, "Never mind, I forgive you, forget about it"?

The antitraditionalists are therefore right to focus on Edgar rather than Gloucester. But both the traditionalists and the antitraditionalists are wrong to believe that Gloucester is duped by Edgar's tale of the imaginary cliff. Shakespeare gives us plenty of signs that Gloucester is not fooled by his son's deception:

GLOUCESTER
When shall I come to th' top of that same hill?

EDGAR
You do climb up it now. Look how we labor.

GLOUCESTER
Methinks the ground is even.

EDGAR
         Horrible steep.
Hark, do you hear the sea?

GLOUCESTER
        No, truly.

EDGAR
Why, then your other senses grow imperfect
By your eyes' anguish.

GLOUCESTER
       So may it be, indeed.
Methinks thy voice is altered, and thou speak'st
In better phrase and matter than thou didst.

EDGAR
You're much deceived. In nothing am I changed
But in my garments.

GLOUCESTER
      Methinks you're better spoken. (4.6.1–10)

Gloucester does not know whether Edgar will punish him or not. But the two have walked all the way from Dover, and, presumably, Gloucester has continually had Edgar in his "touch" (4.1.23). He has gotten to know his son better than ever before. He has experienced his gait, his smell, and his touch, all in the most intimate physical proximity. One wonders what they talked about. It's clear that Edgar has been unable to maintain his disguise very effectively. By the time they reach the cliff, Edgar is talking normally, like the Edgar we heard before he became poor Tom. Gloucester notices the change and comments on it. Edgar denies it, but Gloucester is unconvinced. I think this is why he stubbornly repeats his observation, which acknowledges the plain fact of the change. We cannot fail to notice it too. Edgar is no longer spouting mumbo jumbo. Gloucester also expresses skepticism that they are climbing to the verge of a high cliff or that they are near the sea. When Edgar replies, unconvincingly, that the injuries to Gloucester's eyes have dulled his other senses, Gloucester politely concedes the point, but one gets the feeling that he is humoring his son (as parents often do). I am not suggesting that Gloucester is being condescending. On the contrary, the whole point of having his son lead him to the cliff is to undergo penance. The traditionalists are not wrong to see in Gloucester's journey a kind of pilgrimage. It is done with the utmost clarity of purpose and sincerity.

In the scene directly after his blinding, Gloucester had expressed a burning desire to see his son. I don't deny that Gloucester comes close to despair at this point, but the despair is overtaken by a stronger desire to live so he can see his son in his touch again. Only then can he die in peace. His repentance is thus a sped-up version of Lear's much more drawn-out struggle. Lear begins the play thinking about dying peacefully—"crawl[ing] towards death," as he puts it. Gloucester only thinks about it once he casts out the fear of dying violently at the hands of a parricidal son. He no longer has a fear of dying. If Edgar leads him to the edge of a cliff in order to get his revenge, then so be it.

If Gloucester is not duped by Edgar, if he knows there is no real cliff, why does he jump? Why doesn't he insist that Edgar lead him to a real cliff? Because that would defeat the purpose of the test, which is not to kill but to heal. The fact that it is Edgar who needs to heal, not Gloucester, is, I suppose, Shakespeare's little joke on his audience.

Gloucester's blindness makes him utterly dependent upon Edgar, the son he had once distrusted. Gloucester's past misdeeds weigh heavily upon him. Rather than looking Edgar in the eye and asking if the malicious stories about him were true, he chose to believe Edmund, and he deliberately put as much distance as possible between Edgar and himself.[75] For Gloucester's former self, an abstract narrative label—"Edgar, the envious parricide"— was preferable to having a face-to-face dialogue. From our perspective, Gloucester's actions at the beginning of the play may appear stupid, but before we dismiss him as an idiot, we would do well to understand his motivations. It is always easier to vent one's fear, resentment, and anger on an abstraction than an actual living and breathing person standing directly before one's face. Genuine dialogue is difficult because it requires that we put aside our resentments and open ourselves to the other's point of view. But this openness requires that we have faith in the fundamental reciprocity at the core of the human scene of interaction, which is most simply defined by our capacity to talk to one another unburdened by the hierarchies that structure the social group, whether family, tribe, or modern state.[76] This faith in dialogue is precisely what Gloucester lacked. Instead, he was blinded by fear, resentment, and a violent desire for revenge, all three of which were cruelly visited upon him in the scene of his blinding. The point is not that Gloucester got what he deserved. Rather, it is that resentment can never be resolved in one final violent solution; it can only be deferred by increasing the degrees of freedom among the individuals on the periphery. The lesson of tragedy is that the more we feed resentment, the more violent the central conflict becomes, until humanity, as Albany puts it, "must perforce prey on itself, / Like monsters of the deep" (4.2.50–51).

What is the answer to this dismal prospect? How can humanity avoid devouring itself? Shakespeare's answer is simple. Instead of feeding the monster, we must starve it. Instead of nourishing the fear or grudge or petty sense of injured merit, we must stamp it out immediately. If we don't, it will quickly metastasize into seething resentment, rage, and an unstoppable hunger for vengeance. Both Gloucester and Lear allow their pride and sense of injured merit to spread like cancer. Their fear and resentment grow into a full-blooded desire for revenge. Gloucester suffers much more cruelly than Lear, but he is also the first to recover from the nightmare. After he is blinded, he cries out for vengeance: "Edmund, enkindle all the sparks of nature / To quit this horrid act" (3.7.89–90). Seconds later, the desire for vengeance has vanished. Now he seeks forgiveness:

> Oh, my follies! Then Edgar was abused.
> Kind gods, forgive me that, and prosper him! (3.7.94–95)

The sin was his alone. He cannot project it onto somebody else. This is the first step in his recovery, which is also the first step in the recovery of humanity. Gloucester has to take responsibility. He acknowledges his fault ("Oh, my follies!"). The next step is to repent. This step is more difficult because it requires not just the acknowledgment of a fault but the demonstration that the fault has been corrected. Gloucester realizes that Edgar was the victim of his evil, and he asks the gods to forgive him and let Edgar prosper. But asking the gods for forgiveness is not enough. He must also demonstrate that his repentance is genuine. This realization is the main reason why Gloucester doesn't collapse into total abject despair. On the contrary, he expresses a burning desire to live to see his son Edgar in his touch again:

> Might I but live to see thee in my touch,
> I'd say I had eyes again! (4.1.23–24)

He could say he has eyes again because the encounter would allow him to see Edgar as if for the first time—that is, as someone who deserves his compassion and humility, not his wrath. If he can demonstrate to Edgar that his repentance is genuine, then perhaps his son will forgive him. When Edgar says, "Give me thy arm / Poor Tom shall lead thee" (4.1.77–78), Gloucester's wish comes true. Gloucester has eyes again, both literally and metaphorically. He has Edgar's eyes to guide him, but he also has Edgar in his touch again. What remains for him to do—no easy task—is to convince his son of the sincerity of his repentance.

Now consider the matter from Edgar's point of view. When Edgar leaves Gloucester at the edge of the imaginary cliff, he is not ready to forgive his father. If he were, he would have stopped pretending and would never have led his father on this fictional suicide mission. The antitraditionalists are correct when they detect a fair bit of discontent and ill-will in Edgar. He says he is trying to cure his father of despair, but this is just a convenient story to avoid acknowledging the more difficult truth that he is still angry at his father, who, let us not forget, put a price on his head. Gloucester must sense this, which is why he chooses to accept Edgar's version of reality. But remember, he has made the mistake of trusting a lie before. He knows Edgar is lying about the cliff. He cannot feel the incline and he cannot hear the sea. He also knows that Edgar's disguise is wearing thin. He no longer talks like a lunatic. On the contrary, his language is crystal clear. These are encouraging signs. It means that though his son is not prepared to reveal himself, at least he does not want revenge. Healing is slowly taking place. A death wish is being exorcised; the traditionalists are right about that. But it is much more Edgar's death wish than Gloucester's that is exorcised. On that point, we can agree with the antitraditionalists.

Is this a double bluff? The son thinks his father wants to commit suicide. The father thinks the son wants revenge. The son pretends to lead the father to the cliff's edge. The father knows the son is pretending and concludes that the son may not be fully committed to revenge. What does the father do? He tips forward and plays dead. How does the son react? He is terrified:

> And yet I know not how conceit may rob
> The treasury of life, when life itself
> Yields to the theft. Had he been where he thought,
> By this had thought been past. Alive or dead?—
> Ho, you, sir! Friend! Hear you, sir! Speak!—
> Thus might he pass indeed. (4.6.42–47)

Has Edgar killed his father by words alone? The first sentence expresses disbelief that mere "conceit" could rob the "treasury of life." But this confident assumption is swiftly undermined by the thought that life might yield—might willingly open its doors—to death. The alarm system has been disabled, and the thief can enter to take whatever he wants, even the treasury of life itself. Imagination is no longer conceived as harmless; it is represented as a thief who may enter the body (through its glassy essence, the eyes, windows to the soul), steal its treasure (the mind, the soul), and thus end life. The next sentence offers another version of the idea that thought (representation, imagination) is synonymous with life. If thinking is the essence of an individual life, then the thought that thinking has ended is another way to describe death. Edgar is now frantic as he looks at his unconscious father. Is he no longer capable of thought? Is he unconscious? In a coma? Hearing? Speaking? Dead or alive? When Lear looks for signs of life in Cordelia, he's a much better medical student than Edgar. He looks for symptoms, not thoughts or words. He checks her pulse, her breathing. Will her warm breath mist a cold mirror? Edgar, on the other hand, is focused intently on his father's capacity to think or talk—"Hear you, sir! Speak!" When his father doesn't speak, there follows the laconic line, "Thus might he pass indeed." Is it possible that a man might die by thought alone? "Have I," Edgar wonders, "killed him with my story of the cliff?"

The more we emphasize that this is Edgar's test rather than Gloucester's, the more sense we can make of what otherwise makes little sense. If we assume that Gloucester is duped by Edgar, we are not only faced with the ludicrous notion that Gloucester cannot trust his other senses; we are also stuck with the unconvincing idea that the only salient fact about Gloucester after his blinding is his suicidal despair. But this does not stack up with many other facts about Gloucester, including his selfless actions toward his old tenant, his repentance, and his sharp observations about Edgar's transformation. I think it is much more plausible to see that Gloucester oscillates between hope and despair not because he wants to end his life, which would be merely despairing, but because he longs to be recognized by Edgar. He lives in hope of receiving forgiveness, but he despairs that Edgar may not be able to grant it. When Gloucester, after his imaginary fall, says, "Away, and let me die," he may be sincere. But he is sincere not because he believes he's fallen, but because he feels his son may have abandoned him. He feels vulnerable and helpless, even though he hasn't fallen from a great height. It takes him a few moments to realize that Edgar hasn't abandoned him. When Edgar says that it was the fiend that left his side, Gloucester's despair once more gives way to hope. For the first time, Edgar calls him "thou happy father" (4.6.72). It is, no doubt, a manner of speaking, but it is also a slip of the tongue and further confirmation that Edgar is nearer to shedding his disguise. The fiend that departed from Gloucester's side was the fiend in Edgar much more than the fiend in Gloucester. Gloucester, we know, is no longer possessed by resentment and the desire for vengeance. The fiend is therefore far more likely to succeed in tempting Edgar, who is still smarting from the injustice of his exile. Edgar's description of the fiend at Gloucester's elbow is a touching eulogy to the figure of poor mad Tom:

> As I stood here below, methought his eyes
> Were two full moons; he had a thousand noses,

> Horns whelked and waved like the enridgèd sea.
> It was some fiend. (4.6.69–72)

Can Gloucester really believe in this ridiculous parody of evil? Shakespeare deliberately exaggerates to make a fundamental point. Gloucester remembers poor Tom from the night before when he eagerly rushed to rescue Lear from his daughters, whose cruel rapier-like fingernails and huge boarish fangs (oh horror!) Gloucester conjured out of thin air in an obscene attempt to whet his appetite for righteous retribution. But he also remembers how his fearful and resentful habit of preposterous exaggeration only succeeded in fanning the flames of his resentment and the resentment of his enemies. He now knows much better that this farcical image of evil is childish and unhelpful. He won't make the same mistake a second time. His heart is no longer full of vengeance. What fills him with boundless hope is not just the thought that the fiend has left his side but that it has also left Edgar's. After all, here it *is* Edgar's image of evil, not Gloucester's. The fact that it has departed is a hopeful sign that Edgar's desire for vengeance has departed too:

> Henceforth I'll bear
> Affliction till it do cry out itself
> "Enough, enough," and die. (4.6.75–77)

The traditionalists are right to hear in Gloucester's words a triumphant affirmation of life. Hearing that Edgar has abandoned the disguise of poor mad Tom, Gloucester senses that the desire for vengeance is ebbing in his son too. This gives him renewed hope that his pilgrimage of repentance and reconciliation is working. He will endure further affliction until affliction itself, both his own and his son's, expires.

Monstrous Conspiracy

Gloucester's imaginary leap from the steep Tarpeian Rock is followed by his bizarre encounter with Lear, who has somehow managed to evade his attendants and is wandering alone on the high Dover cliffs. At court, Lear wore a crown. On the heath, he was bareheaded. Now, he wears a crown of flowers. It is, of course, a mock crown, but it nonetheless singles him out as the exceptional figure, the one marked for *sacrifice*. John Holloway, noticing a common sacrificial pattern in Shakespeare's tragedies, describes Lear in this scene as "Jack-a-Green, at once hero and victim of a popular ceremony."[77] The tragedy is moving irresistibly to its conclusion, which means the death of the protagonist. Lear begins the play at the center, but events conspire to distance him from his former illustrious position, pushing him to the margins before returning him to the center as a mock king marked for death. On the heath, he was reduced to a court that consisted of the Fool, Edgar, and Kent. Now he has nobody. If he is "every inch a king" (4.6.107), his ludicrous appearance is sufficient to disabuse anyone of the idea that he is a figure to be feared and obeyed. "When I do stare," Lear says, "see how the subject quakes" (4.6.108). But nobody quakes, least of all Gloucester, who cannot even see if Lear is staring at him.

Does this make Lear merely pitiful? Has the admirable and enviable hero finally become the pitiable and unenvied victim? Certainly, all signs are pointing in that direction, but the old Lear, the Lear we saw at the beginning, will not go down without a fight. In his lunatic state of mind, he is still able to mint coin—"No, they cannot touch me for coining. I am the King himself!" (4.6.83-84)—and conscript soldiers—"There's your press money" (4.6.86-87). He will need these troops if he is to get his revenge: "And when I have stol'n upon these son-in-laws, / Then, kill, kill, kill, kill, kill, kill!" (4.6.186-87). Mixed in with this desire for vengeance, however, are other feelings that threaten to undermine it. First, there is the realization that his former authority stood on shaky ground. He was surrounded by false flatterers—"they flattered me like a dog" (4.6.96-97)—an idea that suggests an unflattering picture of his former self: "There thou mightst behold the great image of authority: a dog's obeyed in office" (4.6.157-59). Second, there is the sense that given the general weakness of human beings, who are constantly giving in to their baser desires, it is hypocritical for the king, or indeed anyone, to mete out punishment:

> Thou rascal beadle, hold thy bloody hand!
> Why dost thou lash that whore? Strip thine own back;
> Thou hotly lusts to use her in that kind
> For which thou whipp'st her. (4.6.160-63)

And finally, there is the sense that, given the arbitrariness of power and justice, compassion and forgiveness are preferable to vengeance and punishment:

> Plate sin with gold,
> And the strong lance of justice hurtless breaks;
> Arm it in rags, a pygmy's straw does pierce it.
> None does offend, none, I say, none. I'll able 'em. (4.6.165–68)

How do these sentiments stack up with the desire to kill? They don't, which is precisely why Lear's mind is unbalanced. He no longer has any moral conviction in the justice of his old cause, which was to punish his enemies and restore himself to power. On the heath, despite lacking an army, he still thought and behaved like a tyrant, commanding the wind and rain to punish his adversaries. But all he got for his efforts was a severe chill: "When the rain came to wet me once and the wind to make me chatter, when the thunder would not peace at my bidding, there I found 'em, there I smelt 'em out. Go to, they are not men o' their words. They told me I was everything. 'Tis a lie. I am not ague-proof" (4.6.100–105).

At the fundamental level, power involves getting others to do things for you. If your commands get fulfilled, you have power. If your commands are ignored, you don't. Truly omnipotent beings (gods) usually don't bother with commands. A mere glance has the power to destroy whatever displeases a god. Kings seek to emulate the omnipotence of gods ("When I do stare, see how the subject quakes"), but they are hampered by the fact that their desires cannot always be anticipated. The solution, of course, is to speak instead of stare. The king can let others know what exactly is on his mind by talking about it. If the beef is too rare and the beer a bit stale, he can send both meat and drink back to the kitchen with instructions to grill the steak for another minute and to send wine instead of beer (please!). Whereas gods seem to possess a perfect fit between their (unspoken) desires and reality, humans are always trying to reconcile their inner desires with words that are not their own but communally shared.

The fact that words are shared—publicly owned, so to speak—is the Achilles' heel in the power relation, at least for humans. Whereas God can say, "Let there be light!" and expect light miraculously to appear, humans are limited by the fact that someone else must first understand the command. Only after it has been understood can any attempt be made to fulfill it (or not fulfill it, as the case may be). Of course, this begs the question of why God needed to say "Let there be light!" at all. Why utter the command if there is nobody to interpret it? Given the perfect fit between God's desires and reality, words become an unnecessary and annoying intermediary between the inner thought and the outer reality.

Presumably, God was just being considerate. He knew that humans, being imperfect, would need language to express their desires to others, who would then be able to discuss the merits of fulfilling (or not fulfilling!) any given individual desire. In fact, God was being particularly canny, because by giving Adam language, he assumed the presence of Eve and other language users (such as the serpent). He then named all the things he had created, which had a truly extraordinary effect. Once named, these objects gained, on top of their obvious material or appetitive relevance (as shelter or food), a purely transcendental or symbolic significance. (Plato, notoriously, proposed the existence of an ideal world of concepts divorced from reality, but concepts, as Durkheim realized, depend on more elementary "ostensive" rituals in which names are attached to communally salient objects in the world, such as food.) In the Edenic garden, these named objects were no longer simply objects to be perceived by Adam's sensorimotor system (a system he shared with other animals); they also possessed an extraperceptual significance that was evident (i.e., symbolically meaningful) only to Adam and other language users (Eve, Satan, etc.). The most obvious consequence of this act of naming was to place all these named objects under a hierarchy of significance with respect to human desire, which was now distinct from basic biological or appetitive need. For example, although there was plenty of food available to Adam and Eve, not all food was created equal when it came to their desires. In purely biological or nutritional terms, all the available foodstuffs were equally consumable, but in metaphoric or symbolic terms, there was a strict hierarchy when it came to what Adam and Eve could and could not eat. Certain food items were strictly prohibited, including (notoriously) the fruit of one tree in particular. But here's the curious fact. If you didn't have language, all you saw was another tree. If you did have language, what you saw was not just a tree, but a tree that was surrounded by an invisible but mighty wall that could not be scaled except in the mind. In *Paradise Lost*, Milton emphasizes this fact by having Eve transgress the prohibition first in her dreams. She dreams she is soaring, godlike, among the clouds after tasting the delicious-because-prohibited fruit. The next day she eats the fruit.[78]

In other words, the really salient fact about God's use of language is not the command he used to bring the world into existence ("Let there be light!") but the command he issued to the first humans ("Do not eat the fruit of that tree!"). Naming is a form of prohibition. You name something only if you want to set it apart from other things. By pointing to this particular tree and ring-fencing it with a special name (Tree of Knowledge of Good and Evil), God encouraged a rebellion. Eve, the more precocious of his students, took the hint.[79] She understood that God was bluffing. His authority was no more powerful than her capacity to understand his commands. That's why Milton shows her transgressing the prohibition in her imagination. The secret to power is not that you must have more thugs and weapons than the next guy. That is hardly a secret. Rather, the secret lies in the step *before* brute coercion takes place. You must get people to believe in you. It is true, of course, that people need stability in their lives, and they will often prefer to stick with a tyrannical dictator if it means their livelihoods, however impoverished, will not be reduced to total chaos. States, especially agrarian states, rely on the inertia of deeply embedded social hierarchies, which are aided and abetted by thugs at every level. But in periods of social turbulence, usually precipitated by the death or resignation of the monarch, loyalties shift, and naked power, though necessary, will not be sufficient to decide on a winner.[80]

Lear's problem is that he has grown so accustomed to issuing commands that he no longer grasps Eve's perspective. Lear expects his commands to be obeyed, not ignored or contradicted. If he has a desire, he expects it to be fulfilled. In this sense, subordinates are seen as extensions of his body. Just as the hand lifts food to the mouth, so other people work to produce the food that eventually ends up on the table. Instead of having to till the soil, sow the wheat, thresh it, mill it, bake the bread, etcetera, you have it all done for you. This is very convenient, of course, but it can also lead to a rather impoverished understanding of the world. In particular, it can lead to the bad habit of judging others as instruments of *your* desire rather than as independent actors with desires of their own. Lear has very much looked at the world in this way. But now he is incensed that his daughters have the temerity to behave as though their needs are equal to his. The very idea is preposterous and can only lead to civil war, both in the body and in the kingdom:

> Filial ingratitude!
> Is it not as this mouth should tear this hand
> For lifting food to't? (3.4.14–16)

Lear must be thinking of the old adage not to bite the hand that feeds you. His daughters depend on him, not he on them. But the image is ambiguous and there is the secondary, ironic sense that Lear is biting the hand that feeds him. As we have seen, this secondary sense is far truer to the facts of the play up to Lear's self-imposed exile. Having renounced the throne, Lear has no power. If he has no power, then he is dependent upon others. He bites the hand that feeds him, and now he has to suffer the consequences.

Critics are divided when it comes to understanding the significance of Lear's bizarre encounter with Gloucester. The traditional view is that it continues the theme of purification. Just as Gloucester is liberated of his despair, so too Lear is cleansed of his anger, tyranny, and desire for vengeance, thus setting the stage for his reunion with Cordelia.[81] The antitraditionalists are skeptical of this idea. In the same way they see much cruelty in Edgar, they see much cruelty in Lear, especially in his taunts of the blind Gloucester. Cavell wonders why Gloucester should be the first person Lear recognizes in his madness. It must be because Gloucester is blind, blindness being a necessity if one is to face up to evil. Like all creatures of the night (e.g., vampires), evil cannot tolerate the light and must hide in secret and dark places. Lear flees his lodgings at Dover because he is too ashamed to face Cordelia. Her light is intolerable to him, and he feels naked and exposed. "A sovereign shame so elbows him" (4.3.43), Kent says, that he cannot bear to be seen by her. Lear manages to give Kent and his other watchers the slip and is now roaming the countryside when he crosses paths with Gloucester and Edgar. Cavell believes that Lear recognizes Gloucester immediately but will not reciprocate Gloucester's desire to be recognized until he has confirmed Gloucester's blindness. That is why he bullies Gloucester into reading the challenge and makes all kinds of insensitive and hurtful comments about Gloucester's eyes: "I remember thine eyes well enough. Dost thou squinny at me? No, do thy worst blind Cupid" (4.6.136–37); "No eyes in your head?" (4.6.145–46); "Get thee glass eyes, / And like a scurvy politician seem / To see the things thou dost not" (4.6.170–72). Once Gloucester's blindness is confirmed, Lear feels secure enough to be recognized: "If thou wilt weep my fortunes, take my eyes. / I know thee well enough; thy name is Gloucester" (4.6.175–76). Like the penitent in the confessional booth, Lear can only acknowledge Gloucester from behind a self-protective screen. Lear's great shame drives him to madness, which functions as a screen to conceal him from *being seen*. Gloucester, however, is blind. He is the first person the mad Lear can bring himself, reluctantly and hesitantly, to acknowledge. It is, Cavell says, Lear's first tentative step toward sanity.[82]

Cavell stresses Shakespeare's habit of associating evil with shame and, in particular, the shame of being seen. I agree with Cavell's stress on the need to keep evil hidden. We can compare Lear's shame with Brutus's shame in *Julius Caesar*. When Cassius and the conspirators arrive at Brutus's home (at night, of course), Brutus asks his servant Lucius (the name means *light*) if he recognizes any of them. Lucius replies:

> No, sir. Their hats are plucked about their ears,
> And half their faces buried in their cloaks,
> That by no means I may discover them
> By any mark of favor. (2.1.73–76)

Like internet trolls, the conspirators shield themselves from recognition. Darkness, disguise, and the anonymity of the crowd are, Shakespeare suggests, the ancient instruments of evil. Despite these obvious signs of malcontent, Brutus orders Lucius to show the conspirators in. When the boy departs, he utters a soliloquy in which he identifies, in the clearest terms possible, the monstrous shamefulness of the conspiracy he is about to join:

> They are the faction. O conspiracy,
> Sham'st thou to show thy dangerous brow by night,
> When evils are most free? Oh, then, by day
> Where wilt thou find a cavern dark enough
> To mask thy monstrous visage? Seek none, conspiracy!
> Hide it in smiles and affability;
> For if thou put thy native semblance on,
> Not Erebus itself were dim enough
> To hide thee from prevention. (2.1.77–85)

Brutus is a divided soul. On the one hand, he acknowledges the deep shamefulness of the conspiracy, which is so evil there is no cavern dark enough to hide its monstrous visage. On the other, he welcomes the conspirators into his house with open arms. If Brutus were to listen to his conscience, which is later figured by the entry of Portia, who sees straight through Brutus's shamefaced evasions, he would have ignored Cassius, closed the door on the conspirators, and returned, as Portia emphatically puts it, to the "wholesome" marriage "bed" rather than daring "the vile contagion of the night" (2.1.265–66). But resentment—what Portia calls "some sick offense within your mind" (2.1.269)—is a powerful and irresistible force, and Brutus is overwhelmed by it. Portia belongs to a long list of heroines who suffer because of the protagonist's fatal decision to join the conspiracy against love.

If we ask why Brutus could at once recognize the monstrous shamefulness of the conspiracy and nonetheless still join it, the only answer we can give is that he chose to ignore what one half of himself, the better half, was telling him. Shame overtakes him precisely because he knows what he is doing is evil and therefore has to be concealed from others, especially those, like Portia, whom he loves and who love him. When Brutus exits the family home with the conspirators to fetch Caesar, whom they intend to murder, we never see Brutus on stage with Portia again. She is dead to Brutus. Later, in the fourth act, her death by suicide is confirmed twice, first by Brutus, then by Messala. To use Cavell's language, shame is the consequence of the "avoidance of love." The protagonist shamefully averts his eyes from his beloved because love is incompatible with evil's monstrous visage.

As these remarks suggest, the avoidance of love is by no means unique to *King Lear*. In play after play, Shakespeare shows that when the protagonist rejects love, he is lost. In the tragedies, the consequence is suffering and death. Gloucester's eyeless face, with its grotesque bleeding sockets, is a brutal literalization of what Brutus calls the "monstrous visage" of the conspiracy against love. In Gloucester's bleeding and blinded face, Lear sees a reflection of himself. Cavell puts great stress on this point. They are "psychically identical," and the two plots fuse to produce "the great image, the double or mirror image, of everyman who has gone to every length to avoid himself, caught at the moment of coming upon himself face to face."[83] Gloucester is the first man Lear recognizes in his madness because he is Lear's mirror image. In Gloucester's blindness toward evil, in his deliberate and painstaking avoidance of love, Lear sees himself. It is a devastating and deeply shameful picture, but it is the first step in recognizing his complicity in the evil that has overwhelmed his kingdom.

Yet no sooner has Lear taken these tentative steps toward recognizing his shameful involvement in the conspiracy against love than he is once again terrified at the prospect of having to face Cordelia. Members of her search party enter. One of them, a gentleman and presumably the leader, says, "Oh, here he is. Lay hand upon him" (4.6.188). When the others move toward Lear, he feels cornered. Hoping to calm Lear, the gentleman says, "Sir, / Your most dear daughter—" (4.6.189), but he cannot finish his sentence. At the mention of his daughter, Lear interrupts him wildly:

> No rescue? What, a prisoner? I am even
> The natural fool of fortune. Use me well;
> You shall have ransom. Let me have surgeons;
> I am cut to th' brains. (4.6.190–93)

As far as Lear is concerned, this is an arrest, not a rescue. Shame again wells up in him, and he resorts to his old tactics. He is a prisoner, a victim, fortune's fool carted off to his execution. Or perhaps they will ransom him. After all, he is—was—the King. He is again mad as a hatter, cut to the brains. The gentleman tries to placate him, "You shall have anything" (4.6.193). But Lear insists on seeing himself as a victim sentenced to die:

> No seconds? All myself?
> Why, this would make a man a man of salt
> To use his eyes for garden waterpots,
> Ay, and laying autumn's dust.
> I will die bravely, like a smug bridegroom. What?
> I will be jovial. Come, come, I am a king,
> Masters, know you that? (4.6.194–200)

He is back to his old tricks. Everything must be overdramatized. The prospect of his arrest and execution is enough to make him weep. Lear returns again to the image of his tearful eyes ("man of salt") mixed with clay ("eyes for garden waterpots"). When we remember that Lear is wearing a crown of flowers, the image of him as a victim about to be sent to the "block" takes on additional resonance.[84] His melodramatic self-presentation turns into a reenactment of a harvest ritual. As Holloway observes, Lear becomes Jack-a-Green, the mock king who dies in the autumn to be reborn in the spring. As if in anticipation of his role as the hero and victim of a sacrificial ritual, the gentleman, upon hearing Lear's last words ("I am a king, / Masters, know you that?"), says, "You are a royal one, and we obey you" (4.6.201). They release Lear from their grip, perhaps even kneel before him. Lear makes a mad dash for the "high-grown" "sustaining corn" (4.4.6–7) from which he had emerged like the green man of popular myth: "Then there's life in't. Come, an you get it, you shall get it by running. Sa, sa, sa, sa" (4.6.202–3).[85] Lear runs from the stage pursued by members of the rescue party, which is now figured as a hunting party. As he watches the mad King with his crown of greenery vanish into the corn, the gentleman makes a choric comment: "A sight most pitiful in the meanest wretch, / Past speaking of in a king!" (4.6.204–5). How the mighty have fallen! The great King has turned into a fugitive. But what is he running from?

Lear is terrorized by the prospect of a rescue. Cordelia has sent out her searchers, and his response is to bolt from them. He cannot bear to face her, because doing so means returning to that shameful scene in which he first commanded her out of his sight. As Kent notes, the memory of that scene, with all its troubling consequences, overwhelms him: "these things sting / His mind so venomously that burning shame / Detains him from Cordelia" (4.3.46–48). Anything, even death itself, is better than having to face Cordelia's love. In seeing her, he will have to bear the full shameful weight of his rejection of her. Cordelia has returned to save Lear, but she is ultimately saving him from himself, not from Goneril and Regan. Despite what Lear tells himself on the heath, or what Gloucester tells himself in the lead-up to his blinding, or what Cordelia tells herself in the reconciliation scene, Goneril and Regan are not the evil monsters they are frequently made out to be. As scapegoats, they enable the good characters to shift the burden of guilt away from themselves and onto those marked by their villainy. But as we have seen, Regan and Goneril's contribution to Lear's suffering has been minimal. Even the lockout is a ruse cooked up by Lear as an excuse to vent his impotent rage on the heath. At worst, they can be accused of coldly standing by as he madly and willfully destroys himself. Of course, the same coldhearted voyeurism applies to us. We, too, are keen and willing observers of the scene of Lear's destruction. Do we also share Lear's shame? What terrible truth has Lear seen that keeps him from his reunion with Cordelia? Can we see it too? Will it change us for the better?

Gloucester, newly recovered from his own ordeal, is moved by Lear's suffering, and he utters a quiet prayer: "You ever-gentle gods, take my breath from me; / Let not my worser spirit tempt me again / To die before you please!" (4.6.219–21). It is unclear whether Gloucester is responding to his own or to Lear's misfortune. Does he ask not to be tempted by his worser spirit because he sees Lear as a negative example? "Don't be tempted like Lear. Look what happened to him!" Or does Lear's situation remind him of his own? "I was tempted by my worser spirit, and look what happened to me. I won't let that happen again!" Perhaps it does not matter. As Cavell says, in this scene Gloucester and Lear become mirror images of one another. They fuse into a single mythical figure. Let's call this figure the shameful inner reality of Everyman. At this stage, Gloucester appears much keener than Lear to acknowledge the presence of this shameful inner reality, which is presumably why he prays for strength to confront it. Most readers assume that Gloucester is thinking of his recent escape from the clutches of despair. But given what I have argued, I don't think that despair is the fundamental problem for Gloucester. Rather, the temptation concerns our old friend, young ambition's ladder. From the beginning this problem affects all the characters. More specifically, Lear's problem was that he could not renounce those darker traits that held him securely at the top for a very long time. Pride, resentment, envy, and contempt accompany those who embark on climbing this ladder. When Gloucester ascends the imaginary slope and steps over the edge, he doesn't fall headlong to his death. He floats gossamer-like in the air. Or at least that is what Edgar tells him. The notion that Gloucester is saved by words, by mere puffs of air from the mouth, is, I think, crucial to Shakespeare's moral picture. Romantics like Goddard are right to stress the transformative power of the imagination. But the imagination can be used for good or ill. That is the point stressed by the antitraditionalists, such as Cavell and Berger, who see Edgar's cliff narrative as a form of torture.[86]

My view is that the cliff is primarily Edgar's test. He is tempted by revenge but lets his father live. The idea that his father needed to be saved from despair is his way of justifying what otherwise can only be seen as calculated torture. But Edgar still refuses to reveal himself to his father. Why? It can only be because he has not fully exorcised his inner demons. His worser spirit is still tempting him toward disaster. That is why Shakespeare gives Edgar a second temptation. Oswald enters the stage bearing Goneril's treacherous letter to Edmund. He sees Gloucester and believes his fortunes are about to rise:

A proclaimed prize! Most happy!
That eyeless head of thine was first framed flesh
To raise my fortunes. (4.6.229–31)

Oswald is the quintessential social climber. He is motivated by pride, ambition, and envy. When Lear abdicates, he sees his opportunity and immediately ingratiates himself with his mistress, whom he recognizes as someone whose coattails he can ride all the way to the top. Like the other evil characters, he is a caricature and an easy target for the audience's moral indignation. We should therefore exercise the same skepticism we exercised toward the view that Regan and Goneril are the chief villains of the play. In Shakespeare, villainy goes much deeper than what lies on the surface.

Oswald's dramatic and symbolic purpose in this scene is not to kill Gloucester but to tempt Edgar. Gloucester feared Edgar was a parricide. The fear was exaggerated but, as Berger points out, not absurd. From the point of view of the son, the father is "first framed flesh" to raise the son's fortunes, just as from the point of view of the father, the son is "first framed flesh" to inherit the father's title. In other words, father and son are unavoidable rivals. There can only be one head of the family, just as there can only be one king, not two or three. Edgar is now faced with a more urgent problem than when he led his father up the imaginary slope. Revenge is no longer symbolic but real. If he lets Oswald kill his father, he is giving in to his desire for revenge. He becomes a spectator not of a symbolic but a real death. When Gloucester says to Oswald, "Now let thy friendly hand, / Put strength enough to't" (4.6.233–34), many readers interpret this as a return of Gloucester's suicidal despair. He didn't die at the cliff, but at last the gods have sent a villain to put him out of his misery. (So much for not being tempted by his worser spirit.) I find the idea that Gloucester is randomly seesawing between hope and despair unconvincing and, in any case, inattentive to the facts of the text. Gloucester has been hoping for Edgar to reveal himself, but he is repeatedly disappointed. His son continues to pretend he is someone else. He is no longer poor mad Tom, but he remains stubbornly reticent about his true identity. Moments before Oswald appears, Gloucester asks Edgar, "Now, good sir, what are you?" (4.6.223). Edgar replies,

> A most poor man, made tame to fortune's blows,
> Who, by the art of known and feeling sorrows,
> Am pregnant to good pity. (4.6.224–26)

This is an odd way to introduce oneself. Are we supposed to believe that Gloucester is fooled by this statement? Gloucester must be getting tired of his son's tedious and evasive speeches. When it comes to telling fibs to avoid recognition, Edgar is turning into a compulsive liar. The habit is getting annoying.

Edgar's gnomic statement is designed to suggest wisdom and high seriousness, but really it is superficial claptrap. If he were bursting with compassion ("pregnant to good pity"), would he continue to conceal himself from his father? One feels that fortune's blows have dulled Edgar's capacity for compassion. The experience of repeated blows of misfortune rarely heightens one's sensitivity to the misfortunes of others, at least not until one has had sufficient time to recover from one's own traumatic experiences. Very few individuals can survive unscathed from serious persecution.[87] The arrival of the would-be murderer Oswald forces Edgar's submerged bitterness toward his father to the surface. Oswald is a caricature of ambition, envy, and vanity, but the caricature is necessary if Edgar is to recognize those traits within himself. When Edgar stands in front of his father and cudgels Oswald, he is not just battling Oswald. He is also battling within himself those forces Oswald so grotesquely and vividly represents—envy, ambition, pride. There can be no true recognition of the other without first banishing the worser spirit within the self.

Oddly, when Edgar battles Oswald, he adopts yet another alter ego (his third so far). He pretends he is a country lad from one of the southwest counties—Somerset or Cornwall perhaps. Why he feels this is necessary can only be explained by a perverse and increasingly desperate desire to remain hidden from his father. He has no need to hide himself from Oswald. Why, then, does Edgar adopt this new persona instead of carrying on with the somewhat pompous notion of himself as a "poor man made tame to fortune's blows"? Why a rural Somersetshire lad? It must be an instinctive reaction to what Oswald says to him:

> Wherefore, bold peasant,
> Durst thou support a published traitor? Hence,

Lest that th'infection of his fortune take
Like hold on thee. Let go his arm. (4.6.234-37)

Edgar is dressed in the humble clothes fetched by Gloucester's old tenant. Seeing these external markers of his opponent's villainously low station, Oswald addresses him contemptuously. When Edgar responds—"'Chill not let go, zir, without vurther 'cagion" (4.6.238)—he evidently feels obliged to fit himself as closely as possible to Oswald's superficial preconception of him. Alarmingly, Edgar has become so habituated to adopting clichéd and exaggerated—in a word, false—versions of himself that he now finds it easier to adopt these roles willy-nilly. Edgar has become a textbook example of self-avoidance. Lear's sarcastic representation of himself as a kind of anti-Lear applies yet more forcefully to Edgar:

Does any here know me? This is not Lear.
Does Lear walk thus, speak thus? Where are his eyes?
Either his notion weakens, or his discernings
Are lethargied—Ha! Waking? 'Tis not so.
Who is it can tell me who I am? (1.4.223-27)

Whereas Lear never forgets who he is, Edgar does. When Edgar adopted the disguise of poor mad Tom, he said, "Edgar I nothing am" (2.3.21). Unfortunately, Edgar's penchant for disguise and role-playing is in danger of erasing his identity altogether. The longer he avoids his father, the more difficult it becomes to remember who he is.

Consider the scene from Gloucester's perspective. By now he must be beside himself with anxiety and despair that his son will never reveal himself. I imagine Gloucester asking himself the following questions: "Why does my son insist on continuing to play these games? He has passed up on two opportunities for revenge. If he doesn't want to kill me, what does he want?" By this stage Gloucester must be certain that poor Tom (or the slightly pompous self-pitying victim of fortune's blows, or the country bumpkin from Somerset) is none other than his son Edgar. How else can he explain the fact that his devoted guide, whose clothing, smell, and touch has not changed, keeps slipping into these different roles and personalities? If it isn't his son, then he must truly be going mad. But Gloucester is quite certain he isn't mad. He has just compared his own sanity with Lear's insanity:

> The King is mad. How stiff is my vile sense
> That I stand up and have ingenious feeling
> Of my huge sorrows! Better I were distract;
> So should my thoughts be severed from my griefs,
> And woes by wrong imaginations lose
> The knowledge of themselves. (4.6.283–88)

There is nothing wrong with Gloucester's imagination. It remains firmly attached to reality. He is not fooled by Edgar's story of the cliff, nor is he fooled by any of Edgar's crazy disguises. He instantly recognizes Lear's voice. How could he not recognize his son's? Imagine how painful it must be to see your son and not be recognized. Gloucester must truly feel like a ghost, unrecognized by the one person in the world he longs to be recognized by. Why is his son doing this to him? Anything, even death itself, is better than this cruel punishment. If, as Cavell suggests, Lear is scared to face his shame, Gloucester has the opposite problem. His penance is to endure the shame of not being recognized. How would you feel if your eagerly awaited son or daughter stepped off the plane, ignored your furiously waving arms, and walked right past you as if you did not exist? It would be enough to drive you to despair. Gloucester despairs not because of what he did to his son but because of what his son is doing to him.

As Edgar tortures the eyeless Gloucester with nonrecognition, Lear tortures himself with the thought of being exposed to Cordelia's shaming eyes. Gloucester is penitent, remorseful, humble, ready to die if only his son acknowledges and forgives him. But Edgar won't allow it. He will keep his father alive, safe from Oswald and premature violent death, until "vurther 'cagion" (4.6.238). What further occasion is Edgar waiting for? The optimists would have us believe that Edgar is purifying his father. The road to Dover is Gloucester's penitential journey toward death. Once his soul is shriven and absolved, he can die in peace. This puts Edgar in the role of Death, who exhorts Everyman (Gloucester) to reject ill thoughts and embrace Good Deeds, at which point he can die blissfully. No doubt there is some truth to this picture, but it remains partial. Not only does it ignore the conflicting forces within Edgar, it also gives short shrift to Gloucester's point of view. Gloucester's literal blindness may symbolize his inner moral awakening, but it also necessitates a level of physical proximity between father and son that only heightens the cruelty of Edgar's actions. Why does the son prolong the father's life in this cruel fashion? What is the son waiting for?

The most obvious reason for keeping his father alive is that Edgar is not yet ready to usurp the role of earl and patriarch, the (big) man of the family. After Edgar bludgeons Oswald to death, he rummages through his victim's pockets and extracts Goneril's letter. After uttering a touching apology for snooping into somebody else's private correspondence, he breaks the seal and reads the letter. To his horror and disgust, he discovers a plot between Goneril and Edmund, who have exchanged unlawful "reciprocal vows," to kill the Duke of Albany (4.6.266). Enraged at the "murderous lechers" and expressing heartfelt sympathy for their intended victim, Edgar says that he will "in the mature time" (4.6.279) reveal everything to the "death-practiced Duke" (4.6.281). Edgar is morally scandalized by his brother's treachery, but one can't help wishing that he might reflect a little more critically on the similarity of his father's position to that of the Duke of Albany. Ever since Edmund's story of Edgar's parricidal desire to unseat his father, poor old Gloucester has been the reigning champion when it comes to the title of "death-practiced" punchbag. Edmund, Goneril, Regan, Cornwall, Oswald, and Edgar himself have all made their assaults on his much-abused person. There are many victims in Shakespeare, but few can claim to endure as much suffering as Gloucester. When Lear says he is bound upon "a wheel of fire" (4.7.48), we should think of Gloucester, not Lear.

In his rush to defend the Duke of Albany from the evil clutches of Edmund and Goneril, Edgar downplays or forgets his own violence. Of course, Edmund has already claimed, on Cornwall's authority, the title of Earl of Gloucester, although technically he is an imposter, not simply because he is a bastard and Edgar ("the legitimate") is alive but more precisely because his father lives. Regan had told Oswald that if he should happen to see Gloucester on his way to Dover, he should kill the old earl. But she had also said that Edmund had gone to Dover "to dispatch" his father's "nighted life" (4.5.14–15). Presumably, Edmund was wrapping up loose ends. With the father dead and Edgar vanished (to Germany, according to rumor), Edmund is the last Gloucester standing (at least in Britain), and the earldom falls to him. When Edgar kills Oswald, he makes his first definitive, and definitively violent, move back into the ring. There is no avoiding violence in the contest for centrality, which is precisely what Gloucester feared in the first place and why he proclaimed his firstborn a villain. Those critics (like Berger) who regard Edgar's torture of his father as a form of deferred parricide are not wide of the mark. Edgar may not bludgeon his father to death, but nor does he exactly seek to nurse him back to health after his physical and psychological trauma. Cordelia restores Lear's health and sanity with medicinal herbs, music, sleep, doctor's visits, and, most importantly, love and recognition.

Why the big contrast between these two parent-child relationships? Let's just say that there seem to be more unresolved issues between father and son than between father and daughter. My feeling is that this has a lot to do with the fact that ambition's ladder is also a ladder of violence. For obvious reasons, men, and young men in particular, have an advantage when it comes to inflicting violence. It follows that though no one is immune to the blandishments of ambition's ladder (we all experience the desire for centrality), those most likely to succumb to its temptations are those in whom the desire is strongest because they already possess the necessary talent for violence. It is no accident that all of Shakespeare's tragic heroes are, or have been, men of violence. Romeo, Brutus, Hamlet, Othello, Lear, Macbeth, Antony, and Coriolanus are all either professional warriors or serious amateur fighters. Even the least violent of them, Romeo and Lear (the youngest and the oldest respectively), are guilty of murder. It is their failure to manage peacefully their desire for centrality—and, more specifically, their resentment when this desire is thwarted—that leads to their suffering and downfall. Of course, this is not to say that Shakespeare's women do not experience similar temptations. They undeniably do. Goneril and Regan, not to speak of Tamora, Lady Macbeth, Volumnia, or Cymbeline's wife, are as ambitious and resentful as the men with whom they conspire. But the point is not to restrict resentment to men. That is plainly false. The point is to understand why resentment leads to so much violence. This is an ethical question, and it evidently concerned Shakespeare a great deal. His plays do not merely trade on the obvious entertainment value of representing conflict; they seek to understand the anthropological source of violence itself. They are not only excellent theatrical entertainment but also meticulously contrived ethical thought experiments or discovery procedures.

The Promised End?

That Shakespeare did have a final violent conflagration in mind is evident in the fact that the reconciliation scene between Lear and Cordelia does not lead to wider social harmony. In the figure of Cordelia, love scores a notable victory, but in the larger context of the tragedy, war still ends up winning. Playgoers, readers, and critics are appalled by Cordelia's death. Why does she have to die? She and Lear are reconciled, and he is ready to do what he did not do in the beginning—namely, renounce the center unreservedly and live his remaining years in humble retirement on the periphery in the care of his youngest daughter. Why must he now be punished? Lear's picture of their future is moving, but it remains a distant and unfulfilled dream:

> We two alone will sing like birds i'th' cage.
> When thou dost ask me blessing, I'll kneel down
> And ask of thee forgiveness. So we'll live,
> And pray, and sing, and tell old tales, and laugh
> At gilded butterflies, and hear poor rogues
> Talk of court news; and we'll talk with them too—
> Who loses and who wins; who's in, who's out—
> And take upon 's the mystery of things,
> As if we were God's spies; and we'll wear out,
> In a walled prison, packs and sects of great ones,
> That ebb and flow by th' moon. (5.3.9-19)

To ask why Cordelia has to die is to miss the point of the tragedy. Cordelia is a victim of the rivalry for the center, as indeed are all those who die, including Cornwall, Oswald, Gloucester, Regan, Goneril, Edmund, Lear, and (let us not forget) the anonymous and courageous servant. All die because all have participated, whether consciously or not, in the violent agon for the center. Of course, some are more complicit than others. Conspiracy for the center rewards above all the ambitious, the warlike, and the ruthless. In a social order resistant to change, as all preindustrial agrarian societies are, only the most violent individuals will succeed in making their way to the top. As Edmund says to the Captain, to whom he has given secret instructions to kill Cordelia and Lear: "To be tender minded / Does not become a sword" (5.3.32-33).

It is an unfortunate fact that agrarian societies offer few outlets for the talented and ambitious. There is a preponderance of men at the top and, at the very top, a preponderance of extremely violent and ruthless men. Richard of Gloucester and Prince Hal are very different characters, but one thing they share is their ruthlessness when it comes to annihilating their rivals and enemies. If anything, Hal is the more ruthless of the two. Richard doesn't have any friends, and nobody is surprised when the unloved hunchback murders his way to the throne. Harry is much loved, good-looking, and seems to enjoy the riotous company of Falstaff and his low-life tavern friends. But the young prince does not hesitate to stab them in the back when he has no further use for them.

In this context, Cordelia's death is no more senseless than Portia's, Ophelia's, or Desdemona's—or, for that matter, Falstaff's, Bardolph's, and the boy's. If anything, her death is more understandable because it is more easily traceable to actions that are themselves not wholly innocent of ambition or envious rivalry. As Bradley himself points out, Cordelia is not blameless in the events that conspire to produce the tragedy. She deliberately provokes her father's temper, which leads to her expulsion and the elevation of her sisters and their husbands to the front row in the conspiracy for the center. The sense that nobody is really to blame for Lear's expulsion onto the heath can be traced to these seemingly trivial interactions between Lear and his daughters. Why did Cordelia provoke her father? Why did Lear react so tempestuously? Why did Goneril and Regan press the matter of Lear's knights? Why did Lear again lose his temper and refuse to swallow his pride? From these trivial domestic conflicts the tragedy grows and grows, until there is a brutal scene of torture and a full-scale war between Britain and France.

As Berger points out, Cordelia seems to remain blissfully unaware of her own complicity in the violence that shakes Britain. From the very beginning, she anticipates the exposure of her sisters' (concealed) evil and the vindication of her (inner and silent) goodness. When she returns in the fourth act with an army at her back, she insists that her motives are pure:

> O dear father,
> It is thy business that I go about;
> Therefore great France
> My mourning and importuned tears hath pitied.

No blown ambition doth our arms incite,
But love, dear love, and our aged father's right. (4.4.23–28)

Of these lines Berger writes, "I find it disarmingly ingenuous that she has to protest she was not blown across from France by political ambition." Berger evidently suspects that the lady doth protest too much. He also thinks she is overstating the matter when she blames her father's misfortunes on her sisters: "Had you not been their father, these white flakes / Did challenge pity of them" (4.7.31–32). Berger is not fooled by Cordelia's protestations, which he regards as self-serving attempts to present herself in the role of the "merciful redeemer."[88]

Berger's points are shrewd and well taken, but I don't think they will receive their proper due until we trace them back to their originary anthropological roots. I am deeply impressed with the mileage Berger gets from his otherwise rather spare concept of complicity. However, this concept can be better understood once we recognize that complicity in Shakespeare means complicity in the desire for centrality and in the resentment that attends this desire in the human scene of representation, the origin of which we are obliged to take seriously by offering some sort of hypothesis to explain its existence among humans. In other words, I think Berger's close readings of the Shakespearean text would benefit from some anthropological grounding. Whether or not Cordelia is naive or cynically calculating, the point is that she returns to the scene of the original conflict, which is quite explicitly represented by Shakespeare as a contest for centrality. After announcing his retirement, Lear plans to pass his kingdom to his three daughters. In an unusual twist, no doubt motivated by the fact that he has daughters instead of sons, he makes the succession conditional upon receiving a suitably obsequious show of flattery. When the father gives gifts to his daughters, especially gifts as spectacular as these, he expects to be warmly appreciated for his generosity. Presumably, if Lear had sons instead of daughters, he would put them in the boxing ring and tell them to get on with it. (One function of the subplot is to show this difference between male and female heirs. Edgar and Edmund compete in a fight to the death. The tragedy, of course, is that the women follow the men's example and fight to the death too.) Cordelia can say nothing because she sees the hopelessness of her situation. If she says she loves Lear as much as, or more than, her sisters, she is a hypocrite, because that would entail doing the very thing she despises, namely, participating in a vain and envious show of insincere affection. Consequently, she remains true to herself, says nothing (or nothing Lear can admire), and is thrust penniless from the kingdom. Woe to the proud and stubborn! Cordelia is in the situation of Ferdinand, the strong but gentle bull. If Ferdinand fights, he wins a spot in the bullring. But to win the bullring is to defeat his purpose, which is to enjoy the flowers in the green field. Consequently, he is sent to the butcher instead of the matador.[89]

Cordelia's situation is not much better than Ferdinand's. She wins her freedom, but only at the cost of being publicly humiliated and rejected. This is too high a price to pay for the young princess. (She has her pride and feelings too!) Besides, she has a reputation to protect and, in particular, an old score to settle with those pretentious and insufferable sisters who think they're so superior. Happily, the sisters provide her with a perfect pretext to return for some retribution. They have been unspeakably mean to her father, who must be rescued from all this unpleasantness. This last assertion is, admittedly, highly questionable. The old man is given to unpredictable temper tantrums and seems to be suffering from dementia. No matter, old men must not be left to fend for themselves in foul English weather. So the princess returns, this time with an army (the husband, a man of some importance and not to be trifled with, can spare a battalion or two). There is an emotional reconciliation with the father, who recovers his sanity and begs her forgiveness, which she graciously grants. All is well, except that the older sisters are none too pleased that they are now once more in the shade of the youngest daughter. Moreover, there is the question of her army. The handful of knights retained by the old man (purely symbolic, of course, to sooth his vanity) has swelled alarmingly to several battalions. There is another contest, but this time with real swords. The older two sisters gang up on the younger, defeat her, confine her to a cell with the father, and then jealously turn on each other in a bizarre murder-suicide involving a young man of questionable character. Meanwhile, in her cell the young princess briefly enjoys being the apple of her father's eye before she too, in some treacherous shenanigans, dies. The old man is distraught. He has no legacy and dies of a broken heart. When sorrows come, they come not single spies but in battalions.

Obviously, this summary ignores a great deal. But it has the virtue of pinpointing Cordelia's complicity in the contest for centrality. Sharp-eyed readers notice the conspicuous absence of Cordelia's husband, the king of France. Where is he? Why does Shakespeare banish him from the stage after he so dashingly sweeps Cordelia off her feet in her hour of need? All we hear is that after crossing the English Channel a second time (this time armed with his battalions), he is abruptly called back on some urgent business of state. This is most convenient, because it leaves Lear to have Cordelia all to himself. There is no evidence that the relationship is incestuous. But that is not really the point about the king of France's absence. Rather, the point is that Cordelia's desire is in danger of becoming monstrous, in the precise sense Albany uses when he describes how humanity must perforce prey on itself like monsters of the deep. In returning to Lear's bedside, she returns to the originary contest for centrality and therefore risks provoking and suffering the violence that attends this most monstrous and dangerous of desires. Whether or not she has any ambition to wear the crown herself, by returning to the scene of rivalry with her sisters, she cannot fail to inflame the desire that has led Lear—and everyone else—to this dreadful place to begin with. Why else would she insist that she is returning to restore her "aged father's right" (4.4.28)? Right to what? To return to young ambition's ladder? Isn't that precisely what Lear, finally, has learned to renounce?

Berger suggests that Cordelia conceals both from herself and Lear her complicity in the miasma of evil that envelopes the play and its characters. Like Bradley, Berger traces Cordelia's complicity in all this unpleasantness back to the first scene, in which she stubbornly refuses to gratify her father's vanity. Berger, however, sees a great deal more resentment in Cordelia than Bradley is prepared to concede. He cites Cordelia's sarcastic parting shot toward her sisters—"Ye jewels of our father . . . I know what you are" (1.1.272–73)—as evidence that Cordelia is *already* plotting her revenge. Time will unfold what plighted cunning hides. "Cordelia's final two utterances in the first scene," Berger writes, "reveal that the desire for vindication is not entirely free of vindictiveness, that the desire for justification may contain within it traces of the desire for retribution and even, perhaps, revenge."[90]

I agree that there is some evasion or self-deception in Cordelia. She is not innocent when it comes to the central conflict. Certainly, it is touching and heartwarming that no less a man than the king of France accepts her hand when she seems to be at the nadir of her fortunes. But she is still a princess, and one cannot help feeling that France has grasped an opportunity missed by his rival Burgundy. Lear offers the dowerless Cordelia first to Burgundy, who, clearly dismayed by the new terms, politely declines. France, more hot-blooded and passionate, sees Cordelia quite differently. Whereas Burgundy was expecting a peaceful and gentlemanly commercial exchange that would effortlessly augment his territories, warlike France sees a bigger prize that only an ambitious young man could notice. She comes with nothing? No matter, she is herself a dowry, which is to say, a symbol around whom the English commoners can rally. The next time he comes to Britain, he arrives armed to the teeth. Of course, he must have realized he was taking a risk by putting French soldiers on British soil. I think this is why he slips back to Calais once he has Cordelia and his battalions safely deposited at Dover. As long as Cordelia, not he, stands at the head of these suspiciously foreign troops, he knows he has a chance. And if he can put Cordelia on behalf of the old English King at the head, the odds become better still. The invasion must be sold to the British people (and to playgoers and readers) as a rescue mission. Of course, he knows full well that he stands to gain a considerable empire should his wife win this second, much bloodier contest for supremacy over her sisters. We should not forget that the war with which the play ends is a more violent version of the competition with which the play begins.

High-minded readers and critics are appalled by Lear's love contest. It smacks too much of vulgar showmanship and narcissism. Lear behaves like the host of one of those appalling and extremely popular American reality television shows, which deliberately appeal to the contestant's and the audience's baser emotions. But we should remember that the love contest is framed by Lear as a peaceful attempt to *avoid* future strife. Kings are in the business of expanding their territories, not diminishing them. Burgundy and France are not just rivals for Cordelia but rivals for Lear's Britain. This fact is made clear by the events of the play. At his first opportunity, France invades Britain on the pretext of a rescue mission. This pretext would not have been possible if he had not married Cordelia. She is his passport to Britain's riches displayed so tantalizingly on Lear's oversized map, which is purposely designed to incite the maximum amount of envy in all who behold it.[91]

Albany is mindful of the political delicacy of the matter. The presence of French troops on English soil would normally be seen as a transparent power grab. But the fact that Cordelia leads these troops and, moreover, has the old King by her side makes matters ambiguous. Albany is reluctant to fight. He is torn between his loyalty to Cordelia and Lear, on the one hand, and his loyalty to Edmund, Goneril, and Regan, on the other. In the end, the presence of foreign troops sways him toward the latter group, even though morally his heart seems to be with Lear and Cordelia. Before the battle, he says to Edmund:

> Sir, this I heard: the King is come to his daughter,
> With others whom the rigor of our state
> Forced to cry out. *Where I could not be honest,*
> *I never yet was valiant.* For this business,
> It touches us as France invades our land,
> Not bolds the King, with others whom, I fear,
> Most just and heavy causes make oppose. (5.1.22–28; italics added)

I find it peculiar that Albany, in the italicized sentence, interrupts his summary of the situation by reminding himself and his interlocutors of his honesty and valiance. Does he protest these things because he's worried they are in doubt? The need to declare his honesty suggests an uneasiness about his ethical position. He feels that he is on the wrong side of the moral ledger, and it is only because of France's involvement that he can take the side of the morally dubious sisters and the illegitimate Edmund. Goneril thinks her husband is being mealy-mouthed: "Why is this reasoned?" (5.1.30). She advises that they put aside their "domestic and particular broils" (5.1.32) and fight the common enemy, which is France and his proxies—the English "traitors" Cordelia and Lear. Later, after the British victory, Edmund explains that he thought it best to conceal Lear and Cordelia in prison, lest they continue to "pluck the common bosom" to their cause (5.3.51). All of this indicates that behind the rescue mission is a more suspect motive that Cordelia assiduously conceals from herself. Her final lines are oddly detached, almost passionless. Before she and Lear are carted off to prison, she says:

> We are not the first
> Who with the best meaning have incurred the worst.
> For thee, oppressèd King, I am cast down;
> Myself could else outfrown false Fortune's frown.
> Shall we not see these daughters and these sisters? (5.3.3–7)

She once more emphasizes her good motives and bad luck. She came to help her oppressed father, and for that selfless action she is now cast down. She can take it, of course, but she's worried that her father, who isn't as resilient, won't be able to survive this latest blow. Her last sentence suggests that she had been hoping to see her sisters, whom she could blame once more for the terrible suffering inflicted on his frail white head. It wasn't supposed to end this way, but she will exit the stage with her head held high. She may have been defeated on the battlefield, but the moral victory is hers. It's just a shame she can't rub their faces in it one more time.

Edmund secretly commissions the Captain to hang Cordelia in her cell, making it look like suicide, and then to kill Lear too. The plan doesn't work, and only Cordelia is hanged, but before the audience discovers she's dead, Edmund has a sudden change of heart. He confesses his crime and seeks to reverse the order. Why? Why does the acknowledged villain undergo a radical change of heart? Bradley thinks it is because Edmund, who is dying of a wound inflicted by Edgar, sees that his game is up. He is not driven by an unquenchable desire to do evil. He is, rather, a pragmatist; now that there is nothing for him to gain by their deaths, he consents to do some good. Edmund is amoral rather than vindictive. Bradley is also moved by Edmund's laconic line, "Yet Edmund was beloved" (5.3.244). Has the villain been touched by the thought that even he, "[d]espite of [his] own nature" (5.3.249), has the capacity for love? Bradley wants to believe that this is true.[92] And so does Goddard, who thinks that Shakespeare has produced one of those moments when the villain's capacity for goodness comes, as it were, from out of the blue.[93] And why not? If the play shows that there is no wide margin between the good and bad characters, that good is mixed with evil, then why not some good in the otherwise bad Edmund?[94]

Bradley and Goddard make useful points, but I think there is another reason for Edmund's change of heart. Edmund is the play's most accomplished storyteller. Everyone else is following his lead, including Lear himself. Why is he so successful? Because (like Queen Margaret) he knows how to get people's attention. He gets Gloucester's attention by telling him the story of Edgar's treachery. He deliberately fans the flames of fear, resentment, anger, and vengeance. He is so successful that he comes within an inch of the crown itself. This talent for spotting our hidden fears and desires and bringing them out into the open is something that Shakespeare also excels at. He, too, plays with his audience's darker feelings, its hidden desires and resentments. It seems to me that Edmund's abrupt change of heart mirrors our own change of heart. After all, we have aided and abetted the story by identifying with the protagonist's desires. The more we identify with one character, the more we dislike those characters who oppose his desires. Initially, we sympathize with Edmund. His father treats him poorly in the play's brief opening scene, and when he delivers his first soliloquy, which is also the first soliloquy of the play, he quickly takes us into his confidence. We like this young man who shows such wit and humor. He also has an excellent sense of dramatic irony, which is a huge asset when it comes to currying favor with the audience. Certainly, he is more appealing than the rather staid and colorless older brother, or the timorous and credulous father.

We begin, in other words, by taking Edmund's side, at least when it comes to the Gloucester plot. But this puts us in an uncomfortable position once we see Gloucester's eyes put out. Suddenly, our identification with Edmund, the black sheep of the Gloucester family, has been brutally chastised. We want to avert our eyes from this shameful violence. But we are also implicated in it, for we have silently applauded Edmund, whose plight was genuine. What is a talented and ambitious young man to do when the odds are so unfairly stacked against him? We like an underdog and want to see him succeed. The violence is regrettable, but there it is. We cannot blame the author for putting us in this situation. We asked for it, and he gave it to us. As Cavell writes, "We share the responsibility for tragedy."[95] Or as Kenneth Burke puts it in a discussion of the relationship between tragedy and its reception, "The audience consents to the sacrifice."[96]

When Edmund offers to do some good, Shakespeare is giving his audience a shot at expiation for its earlier identification with Edmund's desire. Yes, let him do some good! This is certainly how Bradley feels.[97] Edmund has committed terrible crimes, but he is not beyond redemption. It is never too late to repent. So let Edmund repent! And let Lear and Cordelia live! But Shakespeare will not allow it. We came to see a tragedy—a violent conflagration—and the playwright is determined we witness the consequences of our desire. When Lear enters with Cordelia in her arms, it is, emotionally, a repetition of the blinding scene. Shakespeare is denying us a shot at cheap expiation. We have desired this from the beginning. By identifying with Lear's monstrous desires, we have willed him into this situation. Lear is a victim of our scenic imaginations just as she is a victim of his. We would like to blame their deaths on somebody else, and Edmund is the obvious candidate. After all, he is a villain and a bastard, and, furthermore, he ordered their deaths. But when Edmund abruptly confesses his crime and seeks to reverse the order, Shakespeare deliberately pulls the rug from under us. He denies us our scapegoat. So, when Lear enters with Cordelia in his arms, we are crushed by the sheer arbitrariness of her death. The heroine has survived so much, even the villain wants to save her. So why does she die? Her death makes no more sense to us than if she were to be fatally struck by a runaway bus with malfunctioning brakes. We are at a loss for someone to blame, unless we blame the author himself, which is precisely what motivated Nahum Tate to rewrite the play. In his enormously popular adaptation, which held the stage from 1681 to 1838, Gloucester, Lear, and Cordelia survive; Lear bequeaths the crown to Cordelia; and she marries her sweetheart Edgar (Tate removed the dashing young king of France from the *dramatis personae*).

Obviously, Tate's solution to the apparent senselessness of Cordelia's death is extreme. He turned the play into a heartwarming romantic comedy. Bradley felt ambiguous about Tate's revision, but he thought it made sense as an adaptation for the stage. As far as Bradley was concerned, Shakespeare's play was too big for the stage because it was not really a dramatic but a poetic work, one best appreciated in the privacy of the reader's imagination. Cordelia's death is an instance of this conflict between stage and page. When Lear points at her and with his dying breath says, "Do you see this? Look on her, look, her lips, / Look there, look there!" (5.3.316–17), he dies, Bradley says, in a state of "unbearable *joy*."[98] Lear dies believing that Cordelia lives and therefore that she "does redeem all sorrows" (5.3.271). Bradley sees in Lear's dying speech "the soul in its bare greatness."[99] The difficulty, of course, is that it is hard to represent on the stage the soul, which is by definition ethereal and invisible. There is a risk that, when Lear points at Cordelia's lifeless body and says that he sees her inner and eternal soul, a theatrical audience will dismiss Lear's point of view as deranged or, if the director takes Lear seriously and tries to represent Cordelia's soul (perhaps by suspending a stuffed dove from a wire), the audience will be sent into fits of laughter, which would be highly inappropriate. For Bradley, the representation of the inner soul is the proper stuff of poetry, not the stage, and that is why *King Lear* is best experienced in the privacy of the reader's imagination rather than in the public space of the theater, where depictions of the eternal soul are likely to be seen as pretentious and corny, if not downright ludicrous or absurd. Only in one's imagination is it possible to understand what Lear sees when he points at the lifeless Cordelia, because only in the imagination can we see "that the outward is nothing and the inward is all," that death is merely the outward end of life but that the inward soul lives on.[100]

Goddard is even more certain that Cordelia's death on the stage is transcended by the enduring significance she possesses in the reader's imagination. For Goddard, the key lines to set beside Lear's dying words are a pair of earlier speeches. First, Albany to Goneril:

> If that the heavens do not their visible spirits
> Send quickly down to tame these vile offenses,
> It will come,
> Humanity must perforce prey on itself,
> Like monsters of the deep. (4.2.47–51)

The second speech is Lear to Cordelia in the reunion scene: "You are a spirit, I know. Where did you die?" (4.7.50). Albany feared that humanity would devour itself if the heavens did not send down their visible spirits to tame our vile offenses. But humanity did not devour itself, and that is because Cordelia—a heavenly spirit—tamed Lear's vile offenses.

Both Bradley's and Goddard's interpretations depend upon internalizing the Lear narrative. The actions performed on the stage are externalizations of an internal transformation within the protagonist. That is why both critics accept Lear's point of view when he points at Cordelia's living soul. Goddard goes so far as to suggest that the best measure of *King Lear* is the effect it has on a child's imagination. If the child also sees the miracle, then Shakespeare has succeeded. Goddard admits that adults, who are as a rule more cynical than children, might be skeptical. If they fail to see what Lear sees, then the play is indeed "the darkest document in the supreme poetry of the world."[101] But Goddard says that all this proves is that the despair of the adult is in dialectical tension with the hope of the child. In this sense, the text reflects back to its readers their own prejudices. If you are a hopeful optimist, you will see Cordelia's soul. If you are a jaded pessimist, you will consider Lear to be hopelessly deluded.

But there is a third possibility. Lear's inner transformation, while possibly tending toward some kind of inner redemption, does not lead to a more general or widespread redemption for humanity as a whole. Certainly, there is no redemption for Cornwall, Edmund, Regan, or Goneril. Humanity may not devour itself (thank God!), but one gets the feeling that it wouldn't take too much to set off the whole cycle of violence again. Nor does the fact that Edgar seems to be the one left in charge fill one with much confidence. It's true that he has managed to defer his desire for vengeance for quite a long time, but it's also true, as Berger points out, that when he finally did reveal himself to his father, he ended up killing him. Edgar's sad tale of his father's death follows directly after the duel with Edmund. Berger takes this as a hint to connect Gloucester's death with Edmund's. Edmund accepts Edgar's challenge because he wants to defend his good name. Although the "rule of knighthood" (5.3.148) does not require him to fight an anonymous challenge, Edmund senses that his rival is not a lowly imposter—"thy outside looks so fair and warlike," "thy tongue some say of breeding breathes" (5.3.145–46)—and therefore feels compelled to refute the aspersions cast upon him in the way that all true gentlemen solve their disputes, namely, at the point of a sword:

> Back do I toss those treasons to thy head,
> With the hell-hated lie o'erwhelm thy heart,
> Which—for they yet glance by and scarcely bruise—
> This sword of mine shall give them instant way,
> Where they shall rest forever. (5.3.149–53)

Comparing Edmund's highly vocal protestation of the injustice of the aspersions cast upon him to Edgar's equally vocal protestation to his father when he finally reveals himself, Berger writes, "Edgar's tale of pilgrimage is a keener instrument of justice than Edmund's sword."[102] And it is a keener instrument of justice because Edgar has the weight of tradition and culture on his side. Just as Shylock vainly tries to better the instruction of his Venetian persecutors but only succeeds in failing all the more spectacularly by returning himself to the scapegoat's position, so too Edmund's attempt to play the honorable knight is bound to fail. Edmund suffers from the same difficulty as Shylock. He is a misfit and an outcast and therefore born to play the role of scapegoat. He is a caricature of those vengeful feelings we all possess but few have the decency to own up to.[103]

In a perfect world, there would be no need for a Shylock or an Edmund, for the accusing labels of "vengeful Jew" or "ambitious and spiteful bastard." But in the imperfect world in which we live, these monsters of the deep lurk beneath the surface, where they remain artfully concealed from self-recognition ("Back do I toss those treasons to thy head"). When they do emerge for air, as they inevitably must, they are whacked on the head and returned to the deep, until the next crisis emerges, at which point they are whacked on the head again. The point to be inferred from Berger's analyses is that as long as the good characters insist on projecting their faults onto the bad characters, then the situation is indeed tragic and hopeless. Lear is not redeemed if he does not recognize this fact about himself, and nor are any of the other characters, who share Lear's habit of self-pity and self-exculpation ("I am more sinned against than sinning").

It turns out that only Edmund is truly redeemable, because only he has the decency and the honesty to own up to his incorrigible villainy. His inner monster is his goddess: "I confess my bastardy!" The first step to recovery is to admit your addiction. So goes the homily. When Edmund seeks to do some good, what stands in his way is not his own nature, which he is refreshingly candid about, but the nature of all those who dismiss him as a hopelessly lost cause. When the messenger enters and tells Albany that Edmund is dead, Albany waves him impatiently aside, "That's but a trifle here" (5.3.301). Albany, Edgar, and Kent, all good and worthy men, have no time for Edmund. Their eyes are on the best of them, namely, Lear, and his eyes are on Cordelia, the very best of the best. But did it ever occur to anyone to cast a sideways glance? To resist the tyranny of the center? That would be a sacrilege. It would destroy the integrity of the tragic scene, which requires that all eyes remain firmly fixed on the desirable center, with Lear on his throne and his beloved Cordelia in his lap. But isn't that where we began? And isn't that what Lear expressly wanted to avoid when he implored Cordelia to spend her remaining days in a humble cell far from the center and its fearful, prying eyes?[104]

Shakespeare will not allow it. And nor will we. The anthropological problem underlying the tragedy is less that the reconciliation between Lear and Cordelia remains brief and unfulfilled than that there is no possibility of reconciliation for anyone else, not even for Edgar and Gloucester. As long as we remain irritated by distracting messages about Edmund's death, we participate in the same evasion as the good characters. We have pushed the monster back into the deep.

Yet it will come again. Humanity must perforce prey on itself. The heavenly spirits demand it. And so do we.

TWO

The Judge, the Duke, His Wife, and Her Lover

Let us briefly recall the core idea of this book. My hypothesis is that Shakespeare's plays may be conceived as discovery procedures or heuristics to help us think about the ethical problem of resentment in human societies. Resentment is a problem because it leads to violence (vandalism, theft, assault, rape, murder, war, etc.). All societies must, if they wish to endure, concern themselves with the ethical business of controlling resentment. For most of human history, this task has fallen to religion, which relies on the ritual authority of sacred edicts backed up by, in large agrarian societies, a coercive state. More recently, with the rise of the free market, various modern political systems (liberalism, communism, fascism) have attempted to take on the burden of managing the conflict between, on the one hand, the individual "pursuit of happiness," the different pathways to which proliferate greatly in the consumer era, and, on the other, the resentment produced by the market system, which subjects individuals to the impersonal supply-and-demand laws distilled in the price system. Not all careers and not all individuals are rewarded equally by the market.

As Duke Vincentio in *Measure for Measure* well knows, any attempt by the human occupant of the state's sacred monarchal center to prohibit or coerce desire produces resentment, which is why he resists punishing his subjects to the full extent of the law. When Angelo attempts to crack down on liberty in Vienna by enforcing those laws, everyone resents him. Meanwhile Angelo resents Isabella, whose virtue surpasses his. But what most people miss is the Duke's resentment. The uneasy feeling most of us have reading (or watching) the play's final scene, in which ducal pardons rain down like laser-guided missiles, can be traced to the groundswell of resentment that has been building since the beginning, until it finally explodes in the Duke's mad and extravagant display of potlatch clemency, which (I submit) is designed to humiliate his clients-turned-subjects. Having invaded their innermost private (sex) lives, he takes great pleasure in publicly throwing muck on them.

But why is the Duke resentful? There are doubtless many reasons, but the play's final scene suggests a decisive one. His intended has taken a lover. Isabella wanted to become a bride of God before she met the Duke's friarly avatar. The Duke's proposal of marriage is a way for him to stick it to God, who is the ultimate rival and hence the object of his deepest resentment. Whether Isabella accepts or rejects the Duke is ultimately beside the point. Unlike Shakespeare's romantic comedies, this play is not about love. It is about love's deadly opposite. If *Measure for Measure* is a "problem play," it is because resentment is itself a problem. But resentment is also notoriously hard to spot. It is a secretive and furtive passion, a disease of the soul much given to disguise and deception. Who willingly admits to being resentful? It should not surprise us if the play's trickiest and craftiest character also turns out to be the most resentful.

The Disappearing Act

As we noted in the last chapter, Lear is unusual among Shakespeare's tragic protagonists. Whereas Brutus, Hamlet, Othello, Macbeth, Antony, and Coriolanus compete with their rivals for the center, Lear's first order of business is to renounce it. Of course, the renunciation (as Orwell pointed out) remains insincere and incomplete. Lear does not escape the suffering that afflicts all tragic competitors for the center. But at least he can be consoled by the fact that he occupied it for a very long time, which is more than can be said for Shakespeare's other tragic heroes, all of whom die violently well before Lear's ripe old age of "fourscore and upward."[1]

The Duke in *Measure for Measure* adopts a course of action that appears even more perverse than Lear's. He too renounces power, but unlike Lear, whose actions tend to betray a stubborn attachment to power, the Duke appears only too eager to vacate the center. After hastily handing Escalus and Angelo their commissions, the Duke abandons the rule of Vienna to his subordinates. Angelo wants to accompany him to the city gates, but the Duke pleads for absolute secrecy:

> I'll privily away. I love the people
> But do not like to stage me to their eyes;
> Though it do well, I do not relish well
> Their loud applause and "aves" vehement,
> Nor do I think the man of safe discretion
> That does affect it. Once more, fare you well. (1.1.68–73)

This seems admirable, but it could equally suggest the devious tactics of a guilty conscience. Why does he steal away so guilty-like? Why does he shroud his abdication in so much mystery? When the ruler abdicates, even if the abdication is only temporary, one expects an honest and plainly stated explanation. No wonder Angelo is so hesitant to take up the reins of power. The Duke waves Angelo's reluctance aside—"No more evasion"—and asserts that he has "with a leavened and preparèd choice / Proceeded to [him]" (1.1.51–53). Yet judging by the reactions of both Escalus and Angelo, the commissions come as a surprise *to them*. It becomes clear, in 1.3, that the Duke has considered at some length, first, the need for his abdication and, second, whom to select as his substitute. But already in the first scene we note that the Duke seems to be one step ahead of everyone, including his most senior councilors. The very fact that he has chosen to write down his instructions in a pair of commissions rather than make a grand Lear-like public show tells us that the Duke's "darker purpose" is more carefully planned than Lear's. When it comes to delivering the punchline to his story, it turns out that the Duke has more patience, better timing, and far greater narrative control than Lear. This ought to make us wonder about the Duke's motives.

At this stage, however, we know nothing of the Duke's motives. We learn only that he trusts the older and more senior figure, Escalus, whose knowledge of governorship is so great the Duke does not feel obliged to waste his breath telling him how to do his job:

> Of government the properties to unfold
> Would seem in me t'affect speech and discourse,
> Since I am put to know that your own science
> Exceeds, in that, the lists of all advice
> My strength can give you. (1.1.3–7)

Why then does he deputize Angelo, the younger and less experienced man? Again, no reasons are given other than the suggestion that the time is ripe for the younger man to prove himself:

> Angelo,
> There is a kind of character in thy life
> That to th'observer doth thy history
> Fully unfold. Thyself and thy belongings
> Are not thine own so proper as to waste
> Thyself upon thy virtues, they on thee.
> Heaven doth with us as we with torches do,
> Not light them for themselves; for if our virtues
> Did not go forth of us, 'twere all alike
> As if we had them not. (1.1.27–36)

The speech is slightly admonitory. The Duke implies that Angelo has been hiding his light under a bushel. It is time for him to take center stage and show the people his hidden virtues and potential. Working against this sense of Angelo's hidden virtues, however, is the first sentence, which suggests that the Duke's powers of observation have already fully unfolded Angelo's true story. Does the Duke know more about Angelo than he is letting on? What else has Angelo been hiding? Most people don't make a habit of hiding their virtues. On the contrary, most are all too happy to publicize them. Indeed, one of the peculiar challenges of the radical (Christian) idea of universal moral equality is that it undermines the view that virtue is external and visible, that it can be read off easily and conveniently by identifying where you sit on the ladder of virtuousness. Historically, one's position on this ladder was always tightly connected to one's predestined and unchangeable social station, which was clearly visible by the clothes one wore and the way one talked. Once you push these external markers of virtue inside ("To thine own self be true"), you lose the ability to make these quick and easy judgments. When Hamlet says he has "that within which passes show" (1.2.85), he voices the social and ethical quandary facing all claims to centrality. How do we know that the king is more virtuous than the beggar? Which is the justice and which the thief? One possible solution is to impress upon others your high moral character, which includes not only your temperance and sobriety but your industriousness and fiscal prudence. A well-known sociological hypothesis is that it is the *hiddenness* of virtue that lies behind the ethic of the market system. Once virtue is driven inside and is no longer clearly visible, the onus is on you to prove yourself to your prospective audiences (your friends, lovers, employers, clients, colleagues, etc.). It turns out that it's hard work demonstrating your virtuousness and industriousness. When everyone wears blue jeans, it becomes imperative to work as hard as possible to demonstrate your (virtuous) difference from everybody else.

That the Duke is being slightly disingenuous when he observes that a man of Angelo's quality needs to shrug off his stage fright and publicize his inner virtue is suggested by the Duke's own stated dislike of staging himself before the people's eyes. If he doesn't like to publicize *his* virtues, why should Angelo? Either the Duke is not being entirely candid about his disaffection for public show (does he like it more than he admits?), or he is not being sincere about his belief in Angelo's ability to govern virtuously. Either way there is something a bit fishy about his way of putting the matter. The speech betrays a contradiction in the Duke's motives, a contradiction he may be hiding from himself. He continues urging and admonishing Angelo:

> Spirits are not finely touched
> But to fine issues, nor Nature never lends
> The smallest scruple of her excellence
> But, like a thrifty goddess, she determines
> Herself the glory of a creditor,
> Both thanks and use. But I do bend my speech
> To one that can my part in him advertise.
> Hold, therefore, Angelo:
> In our remove be thou at full ourself.
> Mortality and mercy in Vienna
> Live in thy tongue and heart. (1.1.36–46)

The Duke continues his original vein of thought. Angelo needs to manifest his value. This imperative haunts us all. What am I worth? How can I know my value *before* it has been proved in society, which is to say, in the bustle of the marketplace? The Duke's language leans on a tension between morality (which is internal, spiritual, and universal) and ethics (which is external, social, and context-bound). Morally we are all equal, but when it comes to the ethical world of actual human relations, all kinds of invidious hierarchies emerge. For example, investors will not invest in just anybody. They will put their money into people who are blessed with creativity, talent, and a proven work ethic, in the hope that the risk of losing their capital will be minimized and they will see a good return on their investment. Hidden talent, "the smallest scruple of excellence," is Nature's seed capital, which "like a thrifty goddess" she "lends" to the debtor (Angelo), who is obliged to return "to the glory of the creditor" both thanks and interest on the loan. Harry Berger observes that this image puts the Duke in the position of creditor, to whom Angelo (the debtor) will owe both "thanks and use."[2] Optimists (and advocates of the free market) will be inclined to read the image positively. The Duke has the best interests of his client in mind. He has invested a great deal in Angelo, and it is now time to let the price system do its work. Will the investment pay off? Will others also see Angelo's value and agree with the Duke's choice? Only time will tell. Pessimists (and Marxists) will be less sanguine about the Duke's metaphor. All this talk of debt and credit suggests that the promotion of Angelo, far from being a selfless act on the part of the Duke, is a deliberate power move. By promoting Angelo, the Duke hopes to enrich himself. Berger (who is no Marxist) very much takes this latter view. The Duke will make Angelo pay for usurping the center. If this seems unfair and hypocritical of the Duke (and it does), then perhaps we should focus our attention on him instead of reserving our especial ire for his deputy.

The first scene closes with the Duke scurrying off while Angelo and Escalus scratch their heads and try to figure out what exactly they are supposed to do. The Duke has rather grandly said that Angelo will simply take over the Duke's identity—"be thou at full ourself." "Mortality and mercy," he adds, "Live in thy tongue and heart." But these are just words, not actual court cases requiring difficult ethical and legal arguments before delivering a judgment. The newly promoted deputy and his "secondary" (Escalus) stand rather haplessly holding their commissions. Escalus speaks first, and, unsurprisingly, he wants to know the scope of his power and authority: "A power I have, but of what strength and nature / I am not yet instructed" (1.1.80–81). Angelo is no less uncertain—"'Tis so with me" (1.1.82)—and he advises that they withdraw and discuss the matter further, presumably after they have both closely read their commissions, which I'm guessing are lengthy and extremely detailed.

The next scene takes us from the center to the periphery. We move from the office of high authority to the streets below, from the "categorical imperative" of the universal moral law to the messy world of actual ethical relations. Lucio and two gentlemen are discussing a rumor that the Duke may be involved in a plot with other dukes to overthrow the king of Hungary.[3] Why else would he have secretly left Vienna? The rumor turns out to be false, but this is less important than the fact that the Duke's subjects believe it to be true. Why do they believe it? Presumably, because there really is some kind of conflict drawing young men from the city to the battlefield. A few moments later, Overdone says that the war is one of the reasons that she is "custom-shrunk" (1.2.83). Later still, in the next scene, the Duke confirms that he has deliberately spread a rumor in the "common ear" that he has "traveled to Poland" (1.3.14–15). Hungary is not Poland, but we can safely assume that between Vienna and Warsaw the land is littered with all kinds of petty dukedoms and principalities, all of which will no doubt be engaging in various levels of belligerence with one another. In any case, the fact of war is less important than the rumor of it. Why? Because it spreads fear among the populace. If war is brewing on the horizon, how long will it be before it enters the city? In times of crisis, people naturally look to a strong and decisive leader, someone who will not be afraid to make tough but necessary decisions. The fact that it is the Duke who incites a false rumor about his whereabouts, which is interpreted by Lucio and his friends as an indication of an impending conflict, is slightly worrisome. Why would the Duke want to foment fear and anxiety among his subjects?

The sense of foreboding and uneasiness is amplified by Overdone's news that Claudio is to be beheaded "for getting Madam Julietta with child" (1.2.70–71). It is no surprise that the libertine Lucio takes a special interest in Claudio's case, as he is guilty (probably many times over) of the same crime as Claudio. Technically, Claudio is certainly guilty. He has made an unmarried woman pregnant. But the punishment (beheading) is disproportionate, and morally we are bound to find the law repugnant, particularly in Claudio's case, because he and Julietta are in love and betrothed. The only thing they lack is a marriage certificate, a fact that puts Claudio on the wrong side of the law punishing male fornicators with death. To our ears the law sounds ridiculous, but for a society without cheap and reliable contraception, not to mention a well-funded social welfare system, it is a spectacularly violent and therefore reasonably effective way to encourage men not to seduce young women whose children they have no intention of supporting. Needless to say, the law does not distinguish between the good intentions of Claudio and the bad intentions of someone like Lucio.

Claudio does not deny his guilt. He admits to Lucio that he is condemned because of "too much liberty" (1.2.125). He has given free rein to his desire and now he must suffer the consequences:

> Our natures do pursue,
> Like rats that ravin down their proper bane,
> A thirsty evil, and when we drink we die. (1.2.128–30)

This image of nature thirstily and eagerly pursuing evil is quite different from the one the Duke had applied earlier to Angelo. The Duke had suggested that Angelo has been hiding his virtue under a bushel and that it was high time he shared it with others so it could be properly admired and appreciated. We might call this the "optimistic" view of human nature. (Whether the Duke actually believes in this view of nature is another question.) Claudio's picture of human nature is much grimmer, much more Freudian. Rather than having a problem of hidden virtue, humans have a problem of hidden nastiness. If our desires are not tightly constrained, they will overwhelm civilization altogether. Lucio sees the wisdom of Claudio's remark: "If I could speak so wisely under an arrest, I would send for certain of my creditors. And yet, to say the truth, I had as lief have the foppery of freedom as the morality of imprisonment" (1.2.131–34).

When Lucio says that Claudio speaks "wisely," he means, presumably, not just that Claudio is showing remarkable equanimity for a man condemned to die but that his picture of human nature strikes him as accurate. We like to tell ourselves that we are in perfect control of our desires, but this is probably mostly wishful thinking. It's not that we aren't aware of the conflict between body and spirit. (On the contrary, we are all too aware of *that*.) Rather, it's that we frequently tell ourselves stories that justify or excuse our desires *once they have been satisfied*. Instead of the word leading the action, the action leads the (retrospective) word. We do something and then explain to ourselves why it was the rational or good or virtuous thing to do. This does not mean that *all* our actions are rationalizations after the fact.

It only means that once humans are able to represent their intentions to themselves and others, they frequently discover intentions or purposes they were unaware of at the time of the original action.[4] Of course, this means not only that we may tell ourselves self-exculpatory stories but self-accusing ones too. Jesus's admonition that we are only too eager to see the mote in our brother's eye but invariably fail to spot the beam in our own points up the difference between the self-exculpatory and the self-accusatory stories. By blaming someone else we may seek to get ourselves off the hook. Jesus's suggestion is that since most of us have enough sins to occupy a narrative that would outlast, to borrow Angelo's phrase, "a winter night in Russia," then the decent thing to do is to devote our attention to our own sins rather than the sins of others. In terms of the universal moral law, the self-accusatory story is preferable to the self-exculpatory one. Of course, believing that you can apply Jesus's gnomic formulations of the inner moral law ("Judge not, lest ye be judged") to all ethical situations is a fantasy. If it is a sin to accuse others, then secular law is by definition sinful, and the only option is to hand out mercy like birthday cake, which is what the Duke does at the end of the play. The Gospel message of universal clemency is most heartwarming, but it may not represent a realistic solution to the actual problems of human governance. It is the burden of Shakespeare's play to explore this conflict between universal morality and particular ethics. When is forgiveness a good idea and when is it just plain silly?

In the play's third scene we return to the Duke, who now occupies the same position as his subjects. He has vacated the bright legislative center and moves among his subjects in the dark corners of the human periphery. His position, however, is ambiguous, and this scene shows us why. He has not yet taken on his disguise, and his interlocutor (Friar Thomas) addresses him with the customary "Your Grace." When the scene opens, we are thrown midway into an ongoing conversation. The Duke is vigorously protesting something the friar has just suggested:

> No, holy Father, throw away that thought;
> Believe not that the dribbling dart of love
> Can pierce a complete bosom. Why I desire thee
> To give me secret harbor hath a purpose
> More grave and wrinkled than the aims and ends
> Of burning youth. (1.3.1–6)

The Duke is keen to dismiss the thought that his abdication has been prompted by illicit, or at least slightly disreputable, desires. Why the friar would assume that a secret romance is behind the Duke's hasty retreat from the spotlight is a thought worth dwelling on for a moment. Does the Duke have a history of this kind of thing? Lucio certainly believes he did. But Lucio is hardly a credible witness, and one is inclined to dismiss his attacks on the Duke's character as opportunistic and slanderous. Certainly, that is how the Duke sees them. But adopting the Duke's perspective on the matter may be as mistaken as adopting Lucio's. At any rate, we should probably defer the question of the Duke's unseemly peephole activities until we have a better understanding of why he abdicates. Friar Thomas is a more credible witness than Lucio, but there is no evidence (e.g., an illegitimate child) to back up the suggestion that the Duke is a dark horse when it comes to sexual philandering.

Whether or not the Duke is given to some behind-the-scenes hanky-panky, the point is that our private thoughts and desires are frequently in conflict with what is publicly and morally acceptable. The friar assumes, perfectly reasonably, that the Duke's abdication is prompted by a need for more privacy. Being in the public eye is tiring. We all need a place to unwind or decompress. This applies especially to public figures, whose authority depends, at least in part, upon their morally intact reputations. Being in the center is stressful and wearing. It's tough to play the role of the unspotted leader all the time. The Duke has already expressed his distaste for public adulation, and he will reiterate this aversion to the friar—"I have ever loved the life removed / And held in idle price to haunt assemblies / Where youth and cost witless bravery keeps" (1.3.8–10). Well, yes, but most of us, not just Lucio, would opt for the "foppery of freedom" over the "morality of imprisonment," unless of course the benefits of the center (prestige, status, money) are felt to outweigh its costs (resentment, envy, slander).

Now we can perhaps see the reason for Shakespeare's inserting the scene involving Lucio, Overdone, Pompey, and Claudio *before* he takes us to the Duke's private interview with Friar Thomas. The dribbling dart of love is something that affects us all, even those of us, such as the Duke, who profess to have a "complete bosom." For what love means here is not just sex but reciprocal human companionship. This sort of reciprocity is hard to create and maintain. We spend a great deal of time avoiding it because attending to the other, with all his or her impertinent demands on our time and attention, can be as tiring as waving to the admiring public from the palace balcony. At least in the latter case we don't have to have an actual conversation. Sometimes the masks we wear in public can be more satisfying and more reassuring precisely because they are oversimplified versions of our more complex private selves. The street scene has shown us multiple versions of what the Duke dismisses as "the dribbling dart of love" and the "youth and cost" of "witless bravery." First, we see the "witless bravery" of Lucio's talk of war with his companions; second, there are the purveyors of love's "dribbling dart," Overdone and Pompey, who worry that they may be forced out of business by the sudden crackdown on their operations; and third, there is the "cost" of "burning youth" in the form of Claudio's arrest for fornication, the evidence for which is furnished by the visibly pregnant but unwed Julietta. The street is filled with instances of the very thing the Duke says his complete bosom is armed to defend against. When I hear "complete bosom," I also hear an echo of Hamlet's description of the ghost armed in "complete steel." Needless to say, the association adds a slightly sinister note to the Duke's protestations. Hamlet could not withstand the ghost's temptation ("My fate cries out!"). Why should we believe the Duke is any less human? Doth the gentleman protest too much? Why does he insist on his bookish pursuits and his antipathy to burning youth? What makes him so sure Angelo will fail? Does the Duke speak from experience? Are Lucio's scandalous tales of the Duke not so fantastical after all?

After protesting that his darker purposes are not those of "burning youth" but more "grave and wrinkled," the Duke explains that he never intended to travel to Poland. Instead, he deliberately spread a rumor in the "common ear" to provide cover for his real (covert) aims, which appear to be twofold. First, he wants Angelo to clean up the mess resulting from his own failure to enforce the laws. Second, he wants to observe secretly "both prince and people" (1.3.45), presumably, to see how effective Angelo's cleanup will be. Our questions about the Duke's actions in the first scene appear now to be answered. We are given a reason for the abdication (the Duke has made a mess of things) and an explanation for his odd choice of deputy (Angelo is precise and can be depended upon to enforce the letter of the law).

One can see why the Duke did not volunteer this information directly to Angelo and Escalus. Not only would it have defeated his desire to go undercover, it also would have destroyed his ducal credibility. When you make a mess, the decent thing to do is clean it up, not pass it on to somebody else. Why then does he admit his failure to Friar Thomas? The latter's status as a friar is significant. The Duke engages the services of a professional confessor—or, as we might put it, a psychotherapist. If you need to get something off your chest, the friar can help. The friar himself speaks very little (six out of fifty-four lines), so we can hardly call the interaction a conversation. But that is as it should be. The therapist or confessor is there to listen, not to instruct, admonish, or otherwise speak for his subject. The Duke appears to be a regular client—"[N]one better knows than you / How I have ever loved the life removed" (1.3.7–8)—and shows a marked deference toward his confessor, addressing him repeatedly as "holy Father," (1.3.1) "[m]y holy sir," (1.3.7) and "pious sir" (1.3.16). Would it be too much to say the Duke *envies* the friar? Why else does he want to imitate the friar so closely, to the point that he will dress and talk like him? Does he envy the friar's free and ready access to other people's inner lives, their moral consciences? Does he fancy himself a good listener, a solver of people's moral and spiritual problems, a wise and compassionate shepherd among his wayward flock? It strikes me that the Duke feels he has missed his calling, which is spiritual, not earthly. Why else would he confess his abject failure when it comes to his earthly role as governor of the people? He is interested in the spirit, not messy human-made laws, which he regards with a kind of otherworldly disdain:

> We have strict statutes and most biting laws,
> The needful bits and curbs to headstrong steeds,
> Which for this fourteen years we have let slip,
> Even like an o'ergrown lion in a cave
> That goes not out to prey. Now, as fond fathers,
> Having bound up the threat'ning twigs of birch
> Only to stick it in their children's sight
> For terror, not to use, in time the rod
> Becomes more mocked than feared, so our decrees,
> Dead to infliction, to themselves are dead;
> And liberty plucks justice by the nose,
> The baby beats the nurse, and quite athwart
> Goes all decorum. (1.3.19–31)

The Duke reminds me of a parent who, confusing permissiveness with love, never disciplines his children and then throws up his hands in dismay when they throw food in a restaurant. The friar, upon hearing the Duke's remarkable confession, momentarily drops his mask as a professional listener to utter lines that betray his surprise. I quote the friar's slightly reproving lines and the Duke's even more remarkable (and remarkably defensive) response:

FRIAR THOMAS
                It rested in Your Grace
To unloose this tied-up justice when you pleased;
And it in you more dreadful would have seemed
Than in Lord Angelo.

DUKE
                I do fear, too dreadful.
Sith 'twas my fault to give the people scope,
'Twould be my tyranny to strike and gall them
For what I bid them do; for we bid this be done
When evil deeds have their permissive pass
And not the punishment. Therefore indeed, my father,
I have on Angelo imposed the office,
Who may in th'ambush of my name strike home,
And yet my nature never in the fight
To do in slander. (1.3.31–43)

As A. D. Nuttall points out, Machiavelli could hardly have asked for a more diligent student than the Duke, who appears be following the philosopher's advice to the letter.[5] If you have a violent job to do, give it to your most ruthless deputy. Once he has cleaned things up (and he will), you can let him take the inevitable hit for all the displeasure he will have aroused among your subjects. (Machiavelli, citing the example of Cesare Borgia, suggested that you execute your deputy once he's cleaned up your mess.) Thus, you achieve your practical goal, which is to restore order as quickly as possible, but without blemishing your own spotless reputation.

Remembering that the Duke's interview with the friar has the structure of a confession (in which the sinner does all the talking), we should note the self-exculpatory language used by the Duke. He admits his fault (he failed to enforce the laws), but only to excuse himself from fixing his own mess. It would (he implies) appear too dreadful and too tyrannical for him to change *his* behavior. To rephrase more bluntly the same point: "My tender conscience takes precedence over the maintenance of law and order in Vienna." The Duke doesn't have the guts to do his job. This argument, Nuttall says, "is slightly more poisonous" than the straightforward Machiavellian one. And it is more poisonous because it follows Machiavelli's sage advice to the prince ("Get the ruthless deputy to do your dirty work") while simultaneously trying to preserve one's tender and merciful conscience. "Such a process," Nuttall writes, "is hard on the more sentimental sort of conscience, and the Duke is struggling to keep his untroubled by wrapping it in a tissue of evasions."[6]

Nuttall is one among a growing number of late twentieth-century critics skeptical of the view that the Duke is a benevolent tester, teacher, and dispenser of mercy.[7] Graham Bradshaw agrees with Nuttall and argues that what we see in 1.3 is Shakespeare's "mordant exposure of the play's self-appointed *deus ex machina* and surrogate dramatist."[8] For both Nuttall and Bradshaw, the play systematically criticizes the Duke's view that the ethical problem of social disorder can be reduced to the absolute moral imperatives of one's inner conscience ("Judge not, lest ye be judged"). Hence the Duke's evasiveness in his confession to the friar. The Duke will only admit to being at fault by pleading that his moral conscience prevents him from upholding the law. "Men of tender conscience," Nuttall writes, "may preserve their charity intact, but only so long as others are willing to tarnish theirs a little."[9] Both Nuttall and Bradshaw anticipate Berger's yet more damning view that the Duke is not merely evasive but complicit in the creation of iniquity in Vienna. The Duke puts Angelo on the throne because he wants to enjoy the satisfaction of seeing him fall, at which point he can generously swoop in to make a great show of forgiving him.

Berger sees in the Duke's confession in 1.3 a hidden motive for the Duke's choice of deputy. At the very end of the scene, the Duke says something that clashes with his previous statements; he shifts the focus from the ethical problem of maintaining civic order to the moral problem of Angelo's inner virtue:

> Lord Angelo is precise,
> Stands at a guard with envy, scarce confesses
> That his blood flows or that his appetite
> Is more to bread than stone. Hence shall we see,
> If power change purpose, what our seemers be. (1.3.50–54)

Berger relates these lines back to the Duke's protestation that he has a "complete bosom" immune to the "dribbling dart of love." Angelo, it appears, feels the same way about himself. Lucio, in the next scene, will describe Angelo as "a man whose blood / Is very snow broth; one who never feels / The wanton stings and motions of the sense" (1.4.57–59). Berger regards this second, very different intention of the Duke's (to test Angelo's virtue) as a distraction from the first problem, which was to restore order in Vienna. Why does the Duke shift his focus from Vienna to Angelo in his confession to the friar? What ultimately motivates his decision to abdicate and install Angelo as his substitute? Is it the need to restore order in Vienna, or is it the need to test Angelo's virtue? The Duke cannot hope to do both because the two projects are mutually exclusive, as Angelo himself realizes. The judge may be more sinful than the person he passes judgment upon, but that does not make the law invalid. On the contrary, it means that if the judge gets judged for the same crime, he, too, will be convicted. That is what the impartiality of the law means, and it is something that Angelo, to his credit, vigorously upholds (and why he doesn't beg for mercy when his crime of fornication is discovered).

Berger regards the Duke's confession in 1.3 as crucial evidence that the Duke is not merely a detached observer of other people's faults but the "enabler" of those same faults.[10] But why would the Duke want to enable or conspire in the production of evil? Because it makes for a nicely melodramatic narrative of self-exculpation and atonement. If you can't beat 'em, join 'em. If you can't raise the moral standards of the city, sink with the rest. The one snag is those who still insist on their superior virtue. What do you do with the likes of Angelo and Isabella? Well, you have no choice but to drag them down too. You have to prove that their virtue is as stained as that of the hoi polloi. They are no better than Lucio, Barnardine, Pompey, Overdone, et al. This is a tricky thing to do, but the Duke is an ambitious and inventive man and not at all deterred by conventional standards of decorum. He will happily poke into other people's private lives. He will snoop and prowl and cajole until he has put all the pieces in place for the final act, his big reveal. Like one of Agatha Christie's brilliant detectives, he will wait until the last moment before he assembles all parties to regale them with the tale of his awesome omniscience, which will render everyone in his stunned audience (except the irrepressible Lucio) literally speechless. Nuttall hints that this diabolical Iago-like desire may be the motive behind the Duke's rather cryptic reference to Angelo ("Hence shall we see, / If power change purpose, what our seemers be"). "Is it," Nuttall asks, "too curious to detect in this speech a certain relish of anticipation?"[11] Not at all! The Duke is rubbing his hands together in eager anticipation. Nuttall also detects in the Duke's words a "Lucio-like sneer at the chastity of Angelo."[12] This picture accords well with Berger's view that the Duke deliberately puts Angelo in the hot seat, not because he thinks he will succeed in cleaning up Vienna, but because he predicts he will be tempted to abuse his power and stain his virtue. In other words, the Duke's strategy is designed to gain greater control over his subjects. By accessing his subjects' private lives, he will be able to put them in his debt and control them all the more effectively. Mercy is being weaponized as a strategy of theatrical self-centralization. As Berger puts it, "He will abdicate as duke only to return as confessor and savior of the city's souls."[13] It turns out that the Duke abdicates only so he can set the stage for his miraculous and evil-vanquishing return. One can only imagine that the thrill of acceding to the center has worn rather thin. Why else would he feel the need to replay it?[14]

The next scene takes us to the convent of the votarists of Saint Clare, where Isabella is preparing to take her vows. There is an irony to the timing of this scene. Isabella's brother has just been condemned for the most carnal of acts (impregnating a woman), while his sister is on the threshold of surrendering herself to lifelong celibacy and spiritual devotion. Just before she can take her vows, however, Lucio arrives to tell her about her brother's misfortunes. Francisca, who has been informing Isabella of the various rules of the order, excuses herself because, as she explains, sworn votarists may not speak with men unless they are chaperoned by the Mother Superior and their faces are covered. The point of such modest behavior is to reduce the likelihood of any sexual frisson occurring between female votarist and male visitor. If Lucio had arrived a day later, or perhaps even an hour later, Angelo would not have been tempted, because under no circumstances would he have been able to interview Isabella alone. One suspects that the presence of a disapproving Mother Superior would have dampened any enthusiasm he might have felt for the veiled Isabella, even if she had been allowed to speak with the fervor and freedom of her former (unsworn) self. I doubt she would have been able to, given that it is Lucio who encourages her to speak more passionately to Angelo, and, presumably, his presence in the interview would have been strictly forbidden by the Mother Superior. In short, the order of Saint Clare has its own means for imposing the "needful bits and curbs to headstrong steeds" (1.3.20). This symmetry between Isabella and Angelo, both of whom welcome a tight restraint on human desire, is further highlighted by the presence of Lucio, who (as his name suggests) is much looser when it comes to his sense of how the reins of desire should be handled. Lucio personifies precisely what the Duke fears: the untrammeled liberation of desire.

Isabella thinks that Lucio is mocking her when he refers to her as "a thing enskied and sainted" (1.4.34), but what his language suggests is, rather, the universal conflict between body and spirit that the Duke uses as an excuse to explain his failure to maintain social order. Lucio explains the situation to Isabella:

> Your brother and his lover have embraced.
> As those that feed grow full, as blossoming time
> That from the seedness the bare fallow brings
> To teeming foison, even so her plenteous womb
> Expresseth his full tilth and husbandry. (1.4.40–44)

Lucio speaks for the view, particularly resonant among the lower characters in the play, that sexual desire is natural and good. As Nuttall observes, this view is, paradoxically, consonant with the Duke's (high Christian) view, echoed by Isabella, that since all men are imperfect sinners, judges must forgive rather than punish.[15] Both low and high views have the same ethical consequence—namely, to excuse, tolerate, and (ultimately) enable a healthy dose of vice in the community. No doubt this is one reason for Shakespeare's pairing of the Duke with Lucio, who sticks to his illustrious mentor like a "burr" (4.3.177). Despite the Duke's repeated attempts to put as much distance as possible between himself and Lucio, the libertine's shadow haunts, to the very end, "the old fantastical Duke of dark corners" (4.3.156–57).

Lucio's description of Angelo echoes the Duke's description of him from the previous scene:

> Upon [the Duke's] place,
> And with full line of his authority,
> Governs Lord Angelo, a man whose blood
> Is very snow broth; one who never feels
> The wanton stings and motions of the sense,
> But doth rebate and blunt his natural edge

> With profits of the mind, study, and fast.
> He—to give fear to use and liberty,
> Which have for long run by the hideous law
> As mice by lions—hath picked out an act,
> Under whose heavy sense your brother's life
> Falls into forfeit. He arrests him on it
> And follows close the rigor of the statute
> To make him an example. All hope is gone,
> Unless you have the grace by your fair prayer
> To soften Angelo. (1.4.55–70)

This picture of Angelo is familiar to us because it reproduces, very closely, the Duke's earlier portrait of him as a man who "scarce confesses / That his blood flows or that his appetite / Is more to bread than stone" (1.3.51–53). We also see reproduced the image of the law as an "o'ergrown lion in a cave / That goes not out to prey" (1.3.22–23). The natural order of things has been reversed when mice mock lions. Only one thing is added to the picture here, and it is significant. Angelo is as studious and bookish as the Duke. The detail is significant because it undermines the Duke's attempt to differentiate himself from Angelo. If Angelo is a seemer, perhaps the Duke is as well. This possibility is repeatedly suggested by the close connection between the Duke and his alter ego, Lucio.

Why is it that Lucio seems to be so well informed about the Duke's clandestine movements? Lucio is the one who announces, in 1.2, the Duke's sudden departure to conspire with the other dukes against the king of Hungary. Then, in 1.4, he explains to Isabella that the Duke has deliberately deceived eager young men like himself hoping for military action:

> The Duke is very strangely gone from hence;
> Bore many gentlemen, myself being one,
> In hand and hope of action; but we do learn,
> By those that know the very nerves of state,
> His givings-out were of an infinite distance
> From his true-meant design. (1.4.50–55)

Lucio is the victim of the Duke's disinformation strategy, but so are we. When the Duke deputizes Angelo, he does not explain where he is going or why the abdication is necessary. We are as surprised as Lucio when the

Duke discloses to Friar Thomas that his abdication is motivated by the hope that Angelo will rigorously enforce the laws and, in doing so, succumb to the same temptations he seeks to extinguish in others. In short, Lucio echoes our own double take: the Duke's public "givings-out" turn out to be "an infinite distance / From his true-meant design."

But who are Lucio's sources? Who are these mysterious insiders who "know the very nerves of state"? The question may seem impertinent. Shakespeare is not writing a spy novel, and we should not expect him to be giving us realistic metonymic details about the espionage of secret agents. But it also misses the point, which is that Lucio is the Duke's coconspirator. Both men attack Angelo's moral purity, which they see as inhuman and therefore implausible. The Duke attacks from on high ("Judge not, lest ye be judged"), whereas Lucio attacks from below (Angelo cannot be immune to the all-too-human desire to seed the "bare fallow" and bring the "plenteous womb" to "teeming foison"). It turns out that Lucio is absolutely indispensable to the Duke's (vaguely and evasively formulated) desire, first, to entrap Angelo and second, to find himself and his deputy sexual partners. Without Lucio, Isabella would not have been fetched from the convent, Angelo would not have been tempted, the bed trick could not have been used, and the Duke would not have had someone to propose to at the end. All of which suggests Lucio speaks for—one might even say personifies—something within the Duke himself. The quality of mercy droppeth as the gentle rain from heaven, but it helps if the supplicant is also an extremely attractive young woman. When Lucio calls Isabella an "enskied and sainted" "immortal spirit," he is not mocking her. On the contrary, he is all too aware of her transcendent beauty, which makes her the perfect emissary to plead for Claudio's life. Isabella doesn't seem to realize that she possesses this power to seduce our most virtuous-seeming judge:

LUCIO
         All hope is gone,
  Unless you have the grace by your fair prayer
  To soften Angelo. And that's my pith and business
  Twixt you and your poor brother.

ISABELLA
                  Doth he so
  Seek his life?

> LUCIO
> > He's censured him already,
> And, as I hear, the Provost hath a warrant
> For 's execution.
>
> ISABELLA
> > Alas, what poor
> Ability's in me to do him good?
>
> LUCIO
> Assay the power you have.
>
> ISABELLA
> My power? Alas, I doubt.
>
> LUCIO
> > Our doubts are traitors,
> And makes us lose the good we oft might win,
> By fearing to attempt. Go to Lord Angelo,
> And let him learn to know, when maidens sue,
> Men give like gods, but when they weep and kneel,
> All their petitions are as freely theirs
> As they themselves would owe them. (1.4.68–83)

Lucio is no novice when it comes to recognizing female beauty and the temptations of the flesh. He understands the power Isabella possesses, and he urges her to use it to the fullest. Angelo will not be able to resist when she kneels and weeps before him.

Lucio's prediction turns out to be true, but what most readers don't see is that it turns out to be true twice over. When Isabella weeps and kneels a second time, this time before the Duke himself, he too goes weak at the knees. The difference is that he has the decency to propose marriage, something Angelo is reluctant to do until the Duke forces him to marry Isabella's substitute, Mariana. Three of the final four marriages leave a distinctly sour taste in one's mouth. Only Claudio and Juliet appear to love one another. None of the other couples appear well matched. I interpret this as another of the play's many ironic comments on the Duke's diabolical strategy. He can force people to get married, just as he can hand out mercy like birthday cake, but that does not mean that the marriages will be happy or that the ethical challenges in Vienna have been solved. Quite the contrary.

Liberty Plucks Justice by the Nose

In 2.1 we return to the sacred halls of high justice. Angelo lectures Escalus on precisely the same point made by the Duke to the friar in 1.3:

> We must not make a scarecrow of the law,
> Setting it up to fear the birds of prey,
> And let it keep one shape till custom make it
> Their perch and not their terror. (2.1.1–4)

The metaphor is different, but the message is the same. Angelo refers to a scarecrow, whereas the Duke refers to overgrown lions and unused birch whips, but both intend the same meaning. If you don't punish according to the letter of the law, then the criminals will be emboldened. Pretty soon the city will become a breeding ground of sexual licentiousness and other unsavory criminal activities. Liberty plucks justice by the nose, and quite athwart goes all decorum. If the Duke could hear Angelo speak, he would swoon with pleasure to hear his disciple reproducing almost verbatim the very same sentiments he had expressed earlier. The difference, of course, is that Angelo announces these sentiments loudly and without embarrassment so that they ring through the hallways of justice, echoing into the streets below, where at this very moment the industrious Elbow is fighting the good fight against wickedness and debauchery. The Duke, on the other hand, cannot in good conscience make the same ringing endorsement of the law. Instead, he has to deliver his defense of it sotto voce behind the scenes to a man of the cloth, who (one assumes) is unlikely to begrudge the Duke this (rather cavalier) desire to place the needs of his tender conscience above the needs of his subjects and his city. Escalus nicely expresses the view that the pangs of one's merciful and compassionate conscience must be factored into the judge's application of justice:

> Ay, but yet
> Let us be keen and rather cut a little
> Than fall and bruise to death. Alas, this gentleman

> Whom I would save had a most noble father!
> Let but Your Honor know,
> Whom I believe to be most strait in virtue,
> That, in the working of your own affections,
> Had time cohered with place, or place with wishing,
> Or that the resolute acting of your blood
> Could have attained th'effect of your own purpose,
> Whether you had not sometime in your life
> Erred in this point which now you censure him,
> And pulled the law upon you. (2.1.4–16)

Escalus makes three different points. First, we should administer justice with a light touch. We must imitate the skilled surgeon with his life-preserving scalpel, not the executioner with his head-removing axe. Presumably, he means that Claudio's case does not deserve the full penalty (death), and they should lighten the sentence. Second, he appeals to straightforward nepotism: "[T]his gentleman / Whom I would save had a most noble father!" Assuming this line is not uttered as an aside, I can only imagine the look of contempt on Angelo's face. This line of thought isn't going to get Escalus anywhere, so he quickly shifts tactics. The third point is the one Escalus spends the most time on. It is the argument from compassion or empathy. Can Angelo imagine himself committing the same crime? If he can, shouldn't this make him reluctant to punish Claudio?

One can only surmise that Escalus's compassionate disposition is the reason why the Duke did not appoint Escalus, despite his seniority over the much younger Angelo, to the job of top judge. The Duke wanted a man with some backbone, an impartial enforcer of the law, not a man too much like himself, whose tender conscience had proved, by his own admission, a cowardly and dishonest impediment to the ethical imperative to maintain law and order in Vienna. The state of Angelo's inner conscience is a private matter rather than a legal or ethical one, so it has no bearing on Claudio's case. The Duke may believe it to be his prerogative, as God's appointed deputy, to peer into the inner consciences of his subjects, but from a practical and ethical standpoint this desire, which strikes me as rather creepy, is a distraction from the main task of the magistrate, which is to see that the city's laws are impartially enforced and upheld.

There is, however, the possibility that the Duke did not really care about the depravity of Vienna's brothels and slums. The Duke's lament to Friar Thomas about the general moral turpitude of Vienna, where liberty plucks justice by the nose, may have been a smokescreen designed to conceal the Duke's real intention, which was quite specifically to test Angelo's murderous intent. In that case, as Nuttall observes, the Duke becomes not just a ruthless Machiavel but a diabolical "white Machiavel," an angel with horns.[16] Rather than acting in the best interests of the city by getting Angelo to reduce the skyrocketing crime rates, the Duke is conducting a secret and private moral experiment. Just as Hamlet tests Claudius by staging his Mousetrap play, so too the Duke tests Angelo by making his deputy the arbiter of life and death in Vienna. The latter, however, is a much more diabolical experiment than Hamlet's. Hamlet suspects Claudius is a fraud and a murderer. But he isn't sure, so he invents a test in the hope of getting further evidence. The Duke, on the other hand, suspects that Angelo is a fraud, has evidence that he is dishonorable (the broken engagement to Mariana), and predicts that he will abuse his position, but he gives him the job anyway. This shows a greater degree of premeditation and, commensurately, a greater degree of resentment. At the very least, it suggests a remarkable level of contempt for his people, whose criminality the Duke has explicitly directed his precise and rigorous deputy to sniff out and punish to the full extent of the law. But if the real reason for the strict deputy's promotion is not the general wickedness of Vienna (a big problem) but the wickedness of Angelo (a small problem), why risk other people's lives to make this point? Why jeopardize the lives of countless ordinary citizens like Claudio, who are, technically and legally, "fornicators" but otherwise morally unremarkable, by putting a man in charge who refuses to acknowledge the difference between consensual sex and rape? How could the Duke not have known this fact about Angelo beforehand? Isn't there some kind of vetting process that is designed to weed out sociopaths like Angelo? Either the Duke is incompetent or he, too, is a sociopath. I find the latter hypothesis the most plausible. The Duke knows that "Angelo is precise" (1.3.50), which means that he knows that Angelo will enforce the laws blindly and ruthlessly, which means that he knows that the prisons will fill up and heads will roll.

Remember that Hamlet's decision to stage a play is spontaneous. He gets the idea only after hearing a speech about the avenging Pyrrhus, which he had explicitly asked the lead player to perform. Hamlet compares himself negatively to the player, who appears to be able to adopt whatever outward manner he wants despite the fact that he has no motivation other than the desire to appear "in character." How can the actor look so convincing with so little motivation? Why Hamlet imagines Claudius to be less capable of disguising his true feelings than the player is something Hamlet does not bother to consider. He simply says, "The play's the thing / Wherein I'll catch the conscience of the King" (2.2.605–6). Were Hamlet in the Duke's shoes, he might have said, "In holy friar's robes I go, / To catch the conscience of Lord Angelo." But I tend to think he would never have promoted Angelo in the first place. He would have taken one look at the precise Angelo and promptly decided he was morally unfit for office. The key difference between Hamlet and the Duke is that Hamlet lacks the Duke's considerable gift for self-deception and self-exculpation. Hamlet suspects Claudius because he suspects himself. He knows his own mind is as foul as Vulcan's stithy. That's why he doesn't trust the ghost, which he suspects may be a product of his own resentful and filthy imagination.[17] The Duke, on the other hand, hasn't the faintest clue that his imagination is as foul as Angelo's. On the contrary, he devotes a great deal of his considerable energy to hiding this fact from himself.

Bearing the above thoughts in mind, let's return to Escalus's arguments against Claudio's death sentence. The first is that it is too harsh. Most readers today would agree and, presumably, most playgoers in Shakespeare's day would have felt the same way, despite the obvious liberalization in attitudes toward sex, crime, and punishment that have occurred in the West in the last four hundred years. We are the beneficiaries of a long-term ethical, economic, scientific, and technological revolution that was only just beginning in Shakespeare's day. To be a bit more precise, the ethical revolution had been going on for a while, but the economic, scientific, and technological revolutions, which followed the ethical one, were yet to be launched. We have, thanks to effective contraception and a robust welfare safety net, relaxed the religious and ethical taboos on sex outside marriage. The preindustrial state, on the other hand, had to rely much more heavily on negative ethical injunctions (religion) backed up by state coercion (law enforcement). Thou shalt not commit adultery or premarital sex! And, if you do, woe betide you if the king or his deputies find out. In other words, the stakes were a good deal higher, and you could forfeit your life for doing something that today we believe to be a universal human right.

Nonetheless, Claudio's punishment is unduly harsh even by the standards of Shakespeare's day.[18] Claudio and Juliet are betrothed, and the gentleman appears to have no intention of leaving her stranded with a child she can't support. The risk of Claudio's actions throwing society into a tailspin of disorder appears to be minimal. I note in passing, however, that the reason the marriage was delayed, according to Claudio, is that they were waiting for her family's approval, without which there would be no dowry. This factor is not insignificant and points up the ethical and economic considerations that accompany Claudio's actions. Juliet is stuck with her child, but will Claudio stick with her? Angelo broke off his engagement with Mariana when it became evident that her dowry was not forthcoming. Mariana was not pregnant (Angelo had not bedded her), which is a crucial and all-important difference between the two engagements. Nonetheless, the rejection appears mean-spirited given that it occurred in her hour of need. Raising a family, however, requires more than just love and compassion. It also requires commitment, hard work, and some decent start-up funds.

If Escalus, in his desire to lighten Claudio's harsh sentence, speaks for common sense, why does Angelo ignore his argument? Angelo, as the Duke had said to the friar, is very "precise" (1.3.50). Like Shylock, he believes in following the letter of the law. "What's open made to justice," Angelo says, "That justice seizes" (2.1.21–22). Unlike Shylock, however, Angelo is not driven by a desire for revenge. He has nothing personal against Claudio. On the contrary, he prides himself on his detachment from any personal involvement in the individuals of particular cases. If he should be brought before the law, he would expect the same absolute impartiality:

When I that censure him do so offend,
Let mine own judgment pattern out my death
And nothing come in partial. (2.1.29–31)

This is as it should be. The law applies universally to everyone. There is not one law for the lower sort and another for the higher-ups. Angelo is a severe logician, a devout believer in the rule of modus ponens. *If p, then q.* If you commit fornication, then you must die. Since Claudio fornicated, he must die. Put whomever you want into the formula (Claudio, Lucio, Angelo, the Duke himself); the result must always be the same.

One might feel that Angelo's application of the law is too rigid, too idealized, and, ultimately, impractical and unethical. It is impossible to factor out *all* human feeling for the simple reason that the law is an instrument of imperfect human beings. Angelo ends up fetishizing the law, forgetting that the law cannot be separated from the ethical contexts in which it is made and applied. When pressed by Isabella to be merciful, Angelo refuses to allow that he can intervene: "It is the law, not I, condemn your brother" (2.2.85). But this is an ethical sleight of hand. The law does not condemn and punish. Humans do. Offloading one's guilt onto the law is convenient but dishonest. The fact that Angelo does not have to cut off Claudio's head himself is, I think, a contributing factor in Angelo's rationalization of justice as a product of the rule of modus ponens.

What about Escalus's other arguments? The second one (nepotism) isn't serious, and he quickly switches tactics by pressing his third and final argument: Can't you see yourself doing what Claudio did? Do you really want to put this man to death for doing something that any one of us could easily be guilty of? This is a version of the first argument, but instead of focusing on the disproportionate severity of the punishment, it focuses on the humanity of the accused. We are all weak and imperfect. Any one of us could have slipped up like Claudio. There but for the grace of God go I. So goes the argument from compassion and empathy.

Angelo's response to this argument is, again, to depersonalize it. He refuses to accept that pity for the accused has any part to play in the application of justice:

> 'Tis one thing to be tempted, Escalus,
> Another thing to fall. I not deny
> The jury, passing on the prisoner's life,
> May in the sworn twelve have a thief or two
> Guiltier than him they try. What's open made to justice,
> That justice seizes. What knows the laws
> That thieves do pass on thieves? 'Tis very pregnant,
> The jewel that we find, we stoop and take't
> Because we see it; but what we do not see
> We tread upon and never think of it. (2.1.17–26)

On one level this rebuttal makes perfect sense. If I get pulled over for speeding, it is no argument for me to say, "But officer, have you never exceeded the speed limit before?" It's unlikely the officer would respond to my question, but I can imagine him saying something along the following lines: "Sir, I speeded all the way to this location. As I set up my speed trap, I counted a dozen speeding cars. You're the lucky driver I actually managed to clock on my speed gun. Congratulations!" What's open made to justice, that justice seizes.

Of course, both the crime and the punishment are very different in Claudio's case, but from a strictly *logical* point of view the difference is unimportant. You are either following the rules or breaking them. If you are breaking them, then you have to suffer the consequences. *If p, then q*. Speed limits are necessary because the likelihood of injury increases dramatically with speed. But we have to admit that speed limits get broken all the time, and not just by thrill-seeking young men in fast cars. The husband whose pregnant wife suddenly experiences urgent labor contractions may decide that at two o'clock in the morning, on a deserted highway, it is in the best interests of all parties if he nudges the car over the posted speed limit so he can get to the hospital before his wife delivers the baby. Emergency responders break speed limits and traffic laws all the time, and their vehicles are purposely equipped with lights and sirens to indicate that they are in a "state of exception" and the normal rules of the road do not apply. In other words, extenuating circumstances are a necessary part of human judgment. When Angelo defers to the impersonal logic of the law, he is, paradoxically, abdicating his role as judge. He makes no attempt to distinguish between, for example, Claudio's case and more flagrant abusers of the law, such as Lucio or Pompey or Overdone. As far as he is concerned, all fornicators are law breakers, and if he found out about Lucio, he would no doubt condemn him to death too.

It is not hard to grasp the ethical incoherence of Angelo's position. What is more difficult to explain is the fact that the Duke seems to have promoted Angelo *because of* his deputy's reputation for interpreting the law so inflexibly. Apparently, he wanted Angelo to be a hard-ass, to apply logically and impartially the law of modus ponens. If justice is to stop liberty from plucking justice by the nose, it is time for justice to get tough. What justice sees, that justice must prosecute. The Duke deliberately overlooked Escalus, the more humane and lenient judge, because he is too much like the Duke himself. The upshot of this peculiar decision is the hilarious scene in which Angelo's inhuman and rigid interpretation of the law is juxtaposed with

Escalus's failure to apply the law at all. After failing to persuade Angelo to be more lenient in Claudio's sentencing, Escalus utters a quiet prayer for Claudio:

> Well, heaven forgive him, and forgive us all!
> Some rise by sin, and some by virtue fall;
> Some run from breaks of ice and answer none,
> And some condemnèd for a fault alone. (2.1.37–40)

Clearly, Escalus's conscience is deeply troubled. He feels complicit in Claudio's sin—"God forgive us all!" Whether this is because as a senior administrator in Vienna's Department of Justice he feels complicit in Claudio's death, or whether he simply feels morally incapable of condemning Claudio because he too is a sinner, is unclear. It may be that Escalus is himself unsure of the distinction between his inner moral conscience and his ethical obligation to uphold the law. Certainly, his argument that Angelo would do well to *imagine* himself committing the same crime as Claudio is a moral and aesthetic argument rather than an ethical one. The moral and aesthetic argument asks you to examine your internal scene of representation, your innermost conscience, and imagine yourself being tempted by the same crime. Your conscience says, "I am a sinner like him! Let us therefore forgive him!" The ethical argument, on the other hand, dispenses with the internal judge and asks for the facts: "Did this man break the law? If he did, are there any mitigating circumstances I should know about that may lighten the penalty or even allow me to dismiss it altogether?" It is an extraordinary fact that neither Escalus nor Isabella ever mentions the extenuating circumstances of Claudio's case. Never do they mention (a) the betrothal, (b) the witnesses to the pledge, or (c) the pending dowry.[19] Instead they hammer home the dramatically vivid but rather impractical point that we are all sinners and mercy is the only option. One can only imagine that they are as blind as Angelo to the actual facts of the case. Paradoxically, both sides collude in obscuring the ethical reality upon which judgment should be based. The logician is blinded by the law of modus ponens. The advocates of mercy are blinded by God's universal moral law ("Judge not, lest ye be judged"). The result is this extraordinary tragicomedy, in which each side conspires in the evasion of justice.

To see this, we have only to examine what happens next in Vienna's high court. Like most justice systems, Vienna's is not dominated by high-profile cases like Claudio's. Most crimes are committed by those who have, for whatever reason, been forced to grow up on the street where they are subject to the predatory influence of the underworld. Soliciting, drunkenness, theft, drug trafficking—these are the sorts of run-of-the-mill crimes that get prosecuted daily in the courts. Elbow enters with "two notorious benefactors" (2.1.50), Pompey and Froth, both of whom he wants prosecuted for illegal activities. Pompey is a tapster in Mistress Overdone's brothel. His position as bartender is a cover for his role as a professional bawd in the illegal business of prostitution. Master Froth is "of fourscore pounds a year" (2.1.195) and one of Overdone's regular customers. Elbow, a determined and loyal constable, is hampered by his imperfect linguistic skills. What is so funny (and so deeply ironic) is that while everyone knows that Froth and Pompey are guilty, it becomes impossible to spell it out in plain English because of (a) Elbow's frequent malapropisms, (b) Pompey's penchant for punning and circumlocution, and (c) Froth's reluctance to speak at all (as his name suggests, Froth is too drunk or too stupid or too spineless to say anything). Angelo obviously finds this tomfoolery beneath his dignity and barely says anything at all. Halfway through the interview and still no nearer to learning the facts, he throws his hands up in exasperation, dumps the case into Escalus's lap, and leaves. His only contribution to the entire interview has been to correct Pompey's first malapropism ("malefactors" for "benefactors"). His frustration is evident when, storming out in disgust, he says he hopes Escalus will "find good cause to whip them all" (2.1.138).

It is easy to sneer at Angelo, whose refusal to show any patience or compassion is evident. But Escalus hardly fares any better. Indeed, one could say he fares worse. Escalus knows full well what Pompey is up to, but he makes absolutely no effort to enforce the law against fornication or bawdy houses. After having lamented that Claudio had the bad luck of being caught ("[S]ome condemnèd for a fault alone") where others have gotten away scot-free ("Some run from breaks of ice and answer none"), Escalus conspires in creating the very conditions he laments by *failing* to prosecute Elbow's case:

ELBOW

What is't Your Worship's pleasure I shall do with this wicked caitiff?

ESCALUS

Truly, officer, because he hath some offenses in him that thou wouldst discover if thou couldst, let him continue in his courses till thou know'st what they are.

ELBOW

Marry, I thank Your Worship for it.—Thou see'st, thou wicked varlet, now, what's come upon thee: thou art to continue now, thou varlet, thou art to continue. (2.1.183–92)

Instead of attempting to apply the law, Escalus ignores it altogether. Elbow's unintentional abuse of language, his failure to shift smoothly from his intentions to shared meaning (language), mirrors Escalus's peculiar view of justice. Good intentions are more important than ethical consequences. Just as Elbow abuses language, so too Escalus abuses justice. Pompey and Froth are to *continue* their illegal activities. Liberty is to continue plucking justice by the nose. Rather than enforce the law, Escalus seeks to reform Froth and Pompey by giving them a stern lecture about the immorality of bawdy houses. He tells Froth that if he continues to associate with the likes of Pompey, he will come to no good: "They will draw you, Master Froth, and you will hang them" (2.1.205–6). Froth does not pick up on either the threat or the pun. Instead, he answers with a pun of his own, which suggests that he will go straight back to his old habits: "For mine own part, I never come into any room in a taphouse but I am drawn in" (2.1.208–10). We can safely assume that Escalus's warning falls on deaf ears.

Escalus's threats to Pompey are equally ineffectual. He threatens him with whipping, hanging, and beheading, but the cheeky Pompey remains merrily undaunted:

I thank Your Worship for your good counsel. [*Aside*] But I shall follow it as the flesh and fortune shall better determine.
Whip me? No, no, let carman whip his jade.
The valiant heart's not whipped out of his trade. (2.1. 250–54)

The final verse couplet underscores how Liberty (Pompey) gets the better of Justice (Escalus). Of course, we approve of Escalus's lenience because

Pompey is good fun. But it's clear that Escalus's work on behalf of Justice assiduously and systematically undermines Angelo's attempt to restrain Liberty. Escalus's last words are addressed partly to himself and partly to the Justice who stands beside him:

> Mercy is not itself, that oft looks so;
> Pardon is still the nurse of second woe.
> But yet—poor Claudio! There is no remedy. (2.1.281–83)

Given that Escalus has quite deliberately chosen *not* to apply Vienna's "strict statutes and most biting laws" (1.3.19), these words come as a surprise. Why does he appear to agree with Angelo's point of view? Why does he say that a too-liberal inclination to dish out pardons leads to increased rather than reduced criminality? Should we read these words not as a tough-minded affirmation of Angelo's point of view but, rather, as an attempt at self-exculpation? One can imagine Escalus here laconically searching for reasons to *excuse* or *justify* Claudio's bad luck: "Somebody must be punished, otherwise liberty will run amok. Chaos cannot be tolerated. It's too bad it's Claudio, but I tried my best to reason with Angelo. Nothing more can be done. There is no remedy." Are Escalus's final words an attempt to offload the guilt he feels at his failure to defend Claudio? If we interpret the speech in this way, we may want to reassess Escalus's liberal and kind-hearted treatment of Pompey and Froth. In this context, mercy becomes an evasive and self-deceiving strategy of atonement and self-exculpation. Escalus has no real interest in the facts of Elbow's case. Instead, he uses it as an opportunity to salve his own conscience. Obviously, this represents a serious breach of his responsibilities as a judge. Horrified at his complicity in Claudio's death, Escalus responds by turning a blind eye to other infractions, as though he were trying to compensate for Angelo's strictness. It is almost as if Escalus revels in the linguistic opacity of the case before him. Shielded from the dismal facts (poverty, prostitution, drunkenness) by the barrage of Elbow's malapropisms and Pompey's puns, Escalus conspires in the evasion of the facts by participating in the delightfully mischievous wordplay:

ESCALUS
>   Come you hither to me, Master Tapster. What's your name, Master Tapster?

POMPEY
Pompey.

ESCALUS
What else?

POMPEY
Bum, sir.

ESCALUS
Troth, and your bum is the greatest thing about you, so that in the beastliest sense you are Pompey the Great. Pompey, you are partly a bawd, Pompey, howsoever you color it in being a tapster, are you not? (2.1.212–21)

Escalus cannot resist punning on Pompey's name. Later he will say, "Pompey, I shall beat you to your tent and prove a shrewd Caesar to you" (2.1.246–48). Of course, this is funny and in the spirit of Pompey himself, who revels in the ambiguity and slipperiness of language. But it is also an evasion of the facts. Having attached a proper name to the man who stands before him, Escalus is struck by a hilarious pun. He connects Pompey's backside, which is evidently oversized, to the famous Roman general. One might characterize the pun as an Elizabethan version of Cockney rhyming slang (Pompey Bum = Pompey's big ass = Pompey the Great). The pun works by the doubly referential nature of words, which refer both to other words and to objects in the real world. In this case, Pompey's surname *Bum* is also a common noun, *buttocks*. On hearing the surname, Escalus notices Pompey's buttocks, which are larger than most. Another word for large is *great*, which can be substituted for Pompey's surname. Hence "Pompey the Great." What makes all this punning slightly disturbing is the fact that it enables Escalus to avoid his responsibilities as a judge. By participating in the general evasion of worldly reference, Escalus can salve his wounded conscience. But the practical consequence of the wordplay is that nothing gets done to fix the real social problems in Vienna.

If Escalus illustrates the shameless conspiracy between Justice and Iniquity, Angelo represents the attempt by Justice to reassert its former dignity and power. Faced with this new threat to its liberty, Iniquity will seek to breach the walls of Justice by launching a sneak attack. The sneak attack is extremely cunning because it comes in two waves. The first wave is the more predictable one. It is headed by Lucio, who imagines (rightly) that he has identified the Achilles' heel in Angelo's plan to defeat Iniquity. He will tempt him with a woman who is not only young and beautiful but more virtuous than Angelo himself. What makes the sneak attack especially cunning is that this first move is followed by a second, even sneakier maneuver that masterfully anticipates and outflanks Angelo's seemingly invincible countermove as head of justice. The Duke will deliver the coup de grâce when he reveals that Justice and Iniquity coexist in *the same person*. In a dramatic exposé designed to grip his shocked and speechless audience, the Duke will force Angelo's smutty interior into the public spotlight, where it will be judged and found grievously wanting. Angelo will be caught with his pants down, and, as Machiavelli sagely advised, that is the time for the prince to deliver his glorious death blow. "Judge not, that ye be not judged: for with what judgment ye judge, ye shall be judged; and with what measure ye mete, it shall be measured to you again" (Matthew 7:1–2). The severe and upright judge, having done his job and clamped down on Vienna's excessive liberality and licentiousness, will be hoisted by his own petard. It promises to be very satisfying theater, if not a wholly satisfying conclusion to the perennial human conflict between justice and liberty, morality and ethics, equality and hierarchy, center and periphery.

The Great Seduction

It is no exaggeration to say that the scene in which Isabella pleads Angelo to spare her brother's life is the greatest seduction scene in all of Shakespeare. The fact that the seducer is a chaste novice nun and the seducee a stern and passionless judge is what makes the scene so unexpected and therefore all the more extraordinary.[20] Nobody sees the seduction coming except Lucio. He hardly says a word, but his presence is necessary to indicate that Angelo is being tempted by Isabella's beauty and passion, not by her words. If he found her words persuasive, he would have pardoned Claudio on the spot.

Lucio realizes that the way to beat Angelo is not by logical argument, which is the judge's strong suit, but by a sneak attack on his carnal desires. That is why he urges Isabella to argue her case more passionately and feelingly. He knows that her ardent belief in God's boundless love and mercy is the key to drawing out her irresistible beauty, passion, and femininity.

Initially, Isabella's performance is a complete failure. She is hesitant and wooden, and Angelo remains unmoved. She is so intimidated by the august judge that she ends up practically making Angelo's argument for him. She says she abhors her brother's "vice," which she modestly refuses to name (she can't bring herself to use the word *fornication*), and, furthermore, that the vice deserves the full "blow of justice" (2.2.32–33). Then she asks, in a bizarre non sequitur, that Angelo condemn "his fault, / And not my brother" (2.2.38–39). Angelo points out the illogicality of her request:

> Condemn the fault, and not the actor of it?
> Why, every fault's condemned ere it be done.
> Mine were the very cipher of a function,
> To fine the faults, whose fine stands in record,
> And let go by the actor. (2.2.40–44)

Legally speaking, the "fault" (fornication) is by definition already condemned by law. The point of the justice system is not to redefine or debate the laws. That is the task of legislators, human or divine, who are responsible for crafting or, in the case of God, decreeing the laws in the first place. The point of the justice system is to identify the perpetrators of the crimes already defined in the law books. The law is not a game in which imaginary faults are discovered and condemned while the perpetrators in the real world get away scot-free. Isabella, rather like Escalus in the previous scene, seeks to divert attention away from the specific facts of individual cases to the abstract representation of criminality within the individual's internal scene of representation. Let us condemn the *abstract idea* of fornication, which may be represented internally within the mind or externally on the stage as a personified (but not individualized) abstraction (Mr. Fornication); but let us not condemn poor Claudio, who is the innocent victim of the *evil idea* of fornication. Isabella's (Platonic) argument is another version of Escalus's moral and aesthetic argument. Because we can imagine ourselves committing the same crime as Claudio, who thus becomes an Everyman victimized by Fornication, it is unfair to condemn any *particular* individual. We are all victims of the Evil Idea, which lurks within each individual's unconscious, waiting to pounce on the unsuspecting superego.

Isabella obviously finds Angelo's logic impeccable because she congratulates him on his explanation: "Oh, just but severe law! / I had a brother, then. Heaven keep your honor!" (2.2.45–46). She thinks the interview is over and obediently makes to leave, but Lucio stops her at the door. He admonishes her and tells her what she has to do if she is to win Angelo over:

> Give't not o'er so. To him again, entreat him!
> Kneel down before him; hang upon his gown.
> You are too cold. If you should need a pin,
> You could not with more tame a tongue desire it.
> To him, I say! (2.2.47–51)

As far as Lucio is concerned, it is time for the cunning enemy to bait the hook. He will use a saint to catch a saint. Some rise by sin and some by virtue fall. Lucio rises by sin, Angelo and Isabella by virtue fall. Shakespeare delights playgoers and readers with the paradox that our good angels also wear the devil's horns.

Readers of this scene (but not playgoers watching a convincing performance) are too easily distracted by Isabella's eloquent defense of mercy. Her words are indeed moving, and there is no better spokesperson for mercy in all of Shakespeare. She exceeds even Portia in that regard. But if we pay too much attention to her words, we miss the irony that what moves Angelo is not her beautiful words but her beautiful body and, equally important, her highly seductive control of it. In this respect, the key lines are uttered not by Isabella but by Lucio; they indicate Angelo's rising sexual desire. Lucio, a serial fornicator, personifies what is taking place within Angelo.

When Lucio directs Isabella to kneel down before Angelo and hang upon his gown, he has in mind a highly suggestive erotic image that Isabella and Angelo would be the last people on earth to admit harboring in their pure and virtuous breasts. The mere suggestion of such a shameless and indecent thought sends the better sort, which includes Angelo and Isabella but also many morally upright readers and playgoers, into blustering fits of indignant denial. The disgusting shame of the image is simply too horrible to contemplate. What makes this scene so extraordinary and so compelling on the stage is that the abstract morality-play contest between Justice and Mercy is also a highly plausible, naturalistic seduction scene, in which Isabella plays the role of the tempter and Angelo the role of seducee:

> What's this, what's this? Is this her fault or mine?
> The tempter or the tempted, who sins most, ha? (2.2.170–71)

Of course, it would be outrageous to suggest that Isabella *intended* to seduce Angelo. Nothing could have been further from the young novitiate's chaste mind. But can we ever be 100 percent sure of this fact? The line between intended and unintended acts is not as crystal clear as we would like to believe. Humans are constantly circling back to their actions and putting them into new (imagined) contexts and under new perspectives. When precisely in this symbolic and hermeneutic process do actions become vividly and clearly intentional? How do we distinguish between the fault and the actor of it? Isabella herself admits to this difficulty when she confesses, in the play's final scene, that she believes Angelo was seduced by her great beauty: "I partly think / A due sincerity governed his deeds, / Till he did look on me" (5.1.453–55). Why does she reveal this fact about herself only at this very late stage? When does she decide that she is the temptress who has the upper hand in the seduction of the mighty Lord Angelo? Could it have something to do with the fact that this man who was once so powerful is now condemned to a pitiful death?

Shakespeare is, by now, something of an expert when it comes to depicting the tragic protagonist's transgression of prohibited desire. The most famous temptation scene in Shakespeare is conducted by that master seducer, Iago, who knows that the key to a successful seduction is not to express oneself directly and clearly, in neatly packaged true-or-false propositions. The resentful desires of our dark imaginations are much too covert and wily to be caught out by the cold light of logically verifiable statements. Only by indirection do we find direction out. Desire specializes in the oblique *sneak attack*. It does not express itself in lucid and plain-spoken propositional statements, but with mocking questions, insinuations, and doubts:

> Utter my thoughts? Why, say they are vile and false,
> As where's that palace whereinto foul things
> Sometimes intrude not? Who has that breast so pure
> But some uncleanly apprehensions
> Keep leets and law days, and in sessions sit
> With meditations lawful? (*Othello* 3.3.149–54)

Iago's point is well taken. No matter how pure the breast, no matter how impregnable the armor guarding the "complete bosom," unclean thoughts will pollute the inner sanctity. Iago's metaphor of "leets and law days" has particular resonance in the context of *Measure for Measure*. Unclean thoughts hold their sessions side by side with lawful ones. Inside the inner sanctum of Justice, Iniquity holds its court too.

Iago encourages Othello to paint for himself, in fantastic sordid detail, an image of Desdemona as the "cunning whore of Venice" (4.2.93). The picture is false, but the truth of the picture is not what is most important. What is centrally important is the fact that the picture can be painted at all. That is the point Iago makes in the above lines. Independently of the facts of the case, independently of whether Desdemona is a fornicatress or not, foul desires have an uncanny knack of finding their way from the darkest depths to the unhappy surface, where they drift unbidden into our thoughts like so much unwanted flotsam and jetsam. Lucio represents one half of Iago's function; the Duke represents the other. Lucio's function is to steer Isabella into Angelo's arms, just as Iago steered Desdemona into Cassio's. In fact, Iago didn't really have to do anything. Cassio was such a lady's man, so attentive to Desdemona on the quayside in Cyprus, that watching the two harmlessly flirting together gave Iago the idea that the dashing and handsome lieutenant must already be sleeping with the general's beautiful young wife. All he has to do is casually suggest this preposterously plausible idea to Othello, who promptly decides that there can be no other explanation for his wife's obvious enjoyment of the younger man's company.

Lucio's task is more challenging. He has to eroticize Isabella in Angelo's mind. Since her thoughts are decidedly spiritual and uncarnal, this is no easy task. He calls her "enskied and sainted" (1.4.34) because he recognizes her essentially ethereal and otherworldly character. But this turns out to be an advantage. Angelo is repelled by the crude showiness of the prostitute's "double vigor" (2.2.191), the attempt to add to her natural beauty by wearing heavy makeup, high heels, tightly fitting clothes, and fake eyelashes. Angelo's taste in women is evidently a bit more refined than what one can expect to find in Mistress Overdone's House of Iniquity. Whereas Pompey and Overdone pander to the desires of the cruder sort, Lucio will pander to Angelo's more refined tastes. He will pluck Isabella from the embrace of God and place her in the halls of high justice where she will go head-to-head with the secular judge. Who will win? The advocate of God's mercy and the inner moral conscience, or the conservative spokesman of law and order? Whose laws should we follow, God's absolute moral law ("Judge not, lest ye be judged!"), or the hidebound rules of the ancient city ("What's open made to justice, / That justice seizes!")?

The scene certainly has the appearance of a courtroom drama (not unlike the trial scene in *The Merchant of Venice*). But if we focus too narrowly on the arguments made by Isabella and Angelo, we miss the fact that this is also a temptation scene. The contest occurs on two levels simultaneously. It is a contest between Justice (Angelo) and Mercy (Isabella), but it is also a contest *within* Angelo, whose ensuing inner conflict is the result of a sneak attack by the irrepressible libertine Lucio. Lucio's job is to ignite a desire that has long lain dormant in the otherwise cold and passionless Angelo.

After he prevents Isabella from leaving and urges her to return to Angelo with more passion ("Kneel down before him; hang upon his gown. / You are too cold."), Lucio delivers eight more asides. These interjections indicate Angelo's rising passion. In the first of these, after she has meekly suggested Angelo could pardon Claudio if his "heart were touched with that remorse / As mine is to him" (2.2.58–59), Lucio repeats his earlier admonishment, "You are too cold" (2.2.61). Isabella tries again, this time invoking, Portia-like, the notion that nothing becomes power so well as mercy: "Not the king's crown, nor the deputed sword, / The marshal's truncheon, nor the judge's robe" (2.2.65–66). She then plays the judge-not-lest-ye-be-judged card: "If he had been as you, and you as he, / You would have slipped like him; but he, like you, / Would not have been so stern" (2.2.69–71). Angelo has heard this before, of course, and he responds, with a touch of impatience, "Pray you, begone" (2.2.171). The dismissal suggests his characteristic irritation at ineffectual and superficial moralizing, but it may also indicate a subconscious intuition that he might not be able to resist *her* and so wants her out of his presence. The imperative ("begone") has no effect because Isabella remains rooted to the spot. She is warming to her theme:

ISABELLA
    I would to heaven I had your potency,
    And you were Isabel. Should it then be thus?
    No, I would tell what 'twere to be a judge
    And what a prisoner.

LUCIO [*aside to Isabella*]
                      Ay, touch him; there's the vein.

ANGELO
>Your brother is a forfeit of the law,
>And you but waste your words. (2.2.72–77)

Isabella may be wasting her words, but, given that the words are a pretext to keep her in Angelo's presence, what is important is not so much what she says but how she says it. This is not to argue that Angelo is impervious to the meaning of her utterances. On the contrary, the cold and lifeless words that Angelo has been so adept at dissecting logically begin to take on new and unexpected life as he feels an unbidden passion rising within him. In referring to Angelo's "potency" and then asking him to imagine switching places with her so that she has his potency and he is her "prisoner" (or a supplicant for a prisoner under her power), a number of images race through Angelo's mind, not all of them decent. Yes, he has potency. What if he were to abuse that potency? But she has potency too. Is she exerting her (sexual) power over him? Does he want to submit? Lucio obviously approves of this train of thought. "Ay, touch him," he says, "there's the vein." Touch him both literally and metaphorically. Hang on his gown, kneel before him, make him your prisoner. Lucio sees a breach or "vein"—a crack—opening in Angelo's defensive wall. We are also invited to think of blood pulsating through Angelo's veins, swelling, tumescent. Blood thou art blood. Lust courses through the judge's veins.

There is now unquestionably some erotic tension, most (but not all) of it unconscious, as the interlocutors begin to spar with one another. Isabella delivers her most impassioned lines yet:

>Alas, alas!
>Why, all the souls that were, were forfeit once,
>And He that might the vantage best have took
>Found out the remedy. How would you be,
>If He, which is the top of judgment, should
>But judge you as you are? Oh, think on that,
>And mercy then will breathe within your lips,
>Like man new-made. (2.2.77–84)

Logically, this is a restatement of Escalus's argument that since we are imperfect beings it is hypocritical for us to condemn others for crimes we could easily be convicted of ourselves. Isabella, however, strips the argument of its skeptical humanist mooring and draws the optimistic soteriological conclusion. Only the heavenly and merciful Redeemer can judge us. Whereas Escalus resigned himself to the skeptic's view that there was "no remedy" (2.1.279, 283) and that the best option was to admonish and cajole but not punish (to bark, not bite), Isabella defers all justice, whether restorative or punitive, to God. Our job is not to admonish, let alone punish. It is, rather, to glory in God's endless patience and beneficence. The image of God's bottomless love is contagious. Isabella can feel the divine spirit moving within her. Now she exhorts Angelo to share her rapture. Can he feel it too? Does he feel like a "man new-made"?

I am quite certain he does feel the spirit moving within him, though it is a good deal more earthy and indecent. Her quickening pulse and breathlessness are symptoms which Angelo (and Lucio) cannot fail to pick up on. We know that she has touched him in all the right places because he does not dismiss her. On the contrary, he is enjoying her presence. He wants to feast upon her. She must not leave and nor must he. He is not persuaded by her evangelical argument, but he wants to keep the discussion going just so he can admire her beauty. He takes each of her statements seriously and each time offers a patient rebuttal. It is the opposite of his impatient treatment of Elbow, Pompey, and Froth. She is a woman worth his time and attention. She repeats herself, but he does not mind:

ISABELLA
    Good, good my lord, bethink you:
    Who is it that hath died for this offense?
    There's many have committed it.

LUCIO [*aside to Isabella*]
                                  Ay, well said.

ANGELO
    The law hath not been dead, though it hath slept.
    Those many had not dared to do that evil
    If the first that did th'edict infringe
    Had answered for his deed. Now 'tis awake,
    Takes note of what is done, and like a prophet
    Looks in a glass that shows what future evils,
    Either now, or by remissness new-conceived

> And so in progress to be hatched and born,
> Are now to have no successive degrees,
> But ere they live, to end. (2.2.92–104)

Logically, her argument is not, in Lucio's words, "well said." It is no argument to say that because other guilty parties have evaded justice, Claudio should too. But Lucio is not referring to her logic but to her capacity to command Angelo's attention, to take him prisoner, to seduce him with this unexpected mix of virtue, innocence, piety, passion, eloquence, and beauty.

Angelo finds himself compelled by her words not because of what they mean in the abstract (their logic), but because it is she who utters them. He is transfixed by her pious fervor. Her language seems to take on the power of a divine imperative. He is almost ready to believe the injunction "Judge not, lest ye be judged!" "Yet show some pity" (2.2.104), she implores. Angelo feels compelled to take her imperative utterance seriously. Before, when Escalus had made the very same argument, he had dismissed it. Pity, Angelo had replied, was no part of the law. What's open made to justice, that justice seizes. Now he gives the idea serious consideration. She must not think that he is incapable of compassion. He no longer relies on his earlier argument that the law's impartiality trumps human compassion. Now he argues that his punishment of offenders demonstrates his capacity to show pity for the victims:

> I show it most of all when I show justice;
> For then I pity those I do not know,
> Which a dismissed offense would after gall,
> And do him right that, answering one foul wrong,
> Lives not to act another. Be satisfied;
> Your brother dies tomorrow. Be content. (2.2.105–10)

This is a better argument than Angelo had made previously. It is not the judge's place to be merciful on behalf of victims. Only the victims can forgive the offender, not some neutral third party who has not suffered the offender's violence. If the judge makes leniency and mercy a habit, he risks reproducing or even exacerbating the offense for precisely the reasons Angelo gives. The desire for justice is motivated not by the offender but by the offender's victims. Isabella will soon discover this truth. Here, however, her defense of mercy, eloquent though it is, remains ungrounded in the experience of injustice. In another of the play's many ironies, Isabella will experience injustice (and, consequently, a sincere desire for justice) only after she has argued for the abrogation of earthly justice on the assumption that God alone is qualified to judge and condemn. The fervency of her belief in the superiority of divine justice over the sinfulness of human justice motivates her characterization of Angelo as a petty officer aping Jove's thunder:

> ISABELLA
> Could great men thunder
> As Jove himself does, Jove would never be quiet,
> For every pelting, petty officer
> Would use his heaven for thunder,
> Nothing but thunder. Merciful heaven,
> Thou rather with thy sharp and sulfurous bolt
> Splits the unwedgeable and gnarlèd oak
> Than the soft myrtle; but man, proud man,
> Dressed in a little brief authority,
> Most ignorant of what he's most assured,
> His glassy essence, like an angry ape
> Plays such fantastic tricks before high heaven
> As makes the angels weep; who, with our spleens,
> Would all themselves laugh mortal.
>
> LUCIO [*aside to Isabella*]
> Oh, to him, to him, wench! He will relent.
> He's coming, I perceive't.
>
> PROVOST [*aside*]
>   Pray heaven she win him! (2.2.115–30)

Let's begin with the asides by Lucio and the Provost. Why does Shakespeare include them? They seem awkward and unnecessary. Modern directors and actors, uncertain what to make of them, often omit them altogether. But they are necessary for Shakespeare's dramatic picture of Angelo's fall. We are witnessing a temptation scene in which Lucio's presence indicates the overthrow of Angelo by sexual desire. Why does Lucio call Isabella a "wench"? A. R. Braunmuller and Robert Watson, editors of the most recent Arden edition, observe in an explanatory note that the term is not "necessarily disparaging, but certainly not respectful."[21] Given that Lucio had earlier declared Isabella to be "enskied and sainted," the term comes as something of a shock, even from Lucio's mouth. The point, however, is not the effect Isabella has on Lucio, but on Angelo. When Lucio calls her "wench," he is voicing Angelo's desire. Angelo is the one who would like to take her in his arms, call her his "wench," and do heaven knows what else with her. To put the point in dramatic and allegorical terms, Angelo feels the libertine within himself struggling to break free. He wants to be Lucio. But, of course, he cannot admit this to himself or anyone else, which is why Lucio is necessary to complete the picture of Angelo's inner turmoil. Later, Angelo will admit to himself that he would prefer to be a libertine than a grave judge:

> Yea, my gravity
> Wherein—let no man hear me—I take pride,
> Could I with boot change for an idle plume,
> Which the air beats for vain. (2.4.9–12)

But during his first interview with Isabella, he is unprepared to recognize that a piece of Lucio lurks within him, which is precisely why Shakespeare includes Lucio in the temptation scene. He personifies the feelings Angelo hides both from himself and others. Angelo is not trying to hide his light under a bushel (as the Duke claimed), he is hiding his foul desires under a bushel (as the Duke suspected). When Lucio says, "He's coming," the Arden editors note that he means Angelo is "yielding," but they add that the "bawdy senses" of "sexually forward" or "climaxing sexually" are "not far away."[22] I agree that these bawdy connotations, which Lucio never fails to exploit in his language elsewhere, are also intended here. Why else would Shakespeare have gone to the trouble of putting the most randy man in Vienna side by side with Angelo and Isabella? Justice is about to be unseated, not by Piety, but by Iniquity.

The Provost's aside ("Pray heaven she win him!") is more straightforward. We can take it to express the sincere wishes of the Provost, who has from the start objected to Claudio's death sentence. I do not think the line is addressed to Lucio. It is, rather, a form of self-addressed speech, an almost involuntary ejaculation that reflects the audience's sympathetic desire to see Isabella triumph for her brother's sake. What is ironic is that this seemingly harmless desire to see a cruel punishment averted leads to further ethical problems. Isabella wins Angelo over, but not in the sense either she or the audience had hoped for. That is why I don't believe that the Provost's aside is addressed to Lucio, who would not be at all surprised by Angelo's indecent proposal. He, too, wants Isabella to win, but he knows that it will take more than an eloquent speech about God's mercy to do so. More underhanded tactics will also have to be employed.

A final point about the Provost: his presence here is unusual. Normally he would be overseeing the custody and punishment of inmates in the prison. His visit to Angelo was prompted by the hope that he could change Angelo's mind about Claudio, but his counsel was indignantly rejected by the stern judge. Why then is he still present? He has remained at Angelo's special request. For some reason, Angelo wants the Provost to attend this interview. My guess is that he wants another official in the room with him. Perhaps he also wants to prove to the Provost how firm he is. He will not budge even when the condemned man's sister pleads for her brother's life.

What about Isabella's speech? What are we to make of it? What makes it so powerful that not just Angelo, but Lucio and the Provost are moved? It is certainly true that humans are easily seduced by the desire for power and authority. Shakespeare's histories and tragedies assume the basic truth of this idea. What is less often remarked, however, is the concomitant of desire, which is the experience of *thwarted desire* or *resentment*. The center has by definition a very strict limit on the number of occupants it can tolerate. Ideally, occupancy should be restricted to one individual (one territory, one ruler), though of course there is a ladder in descending order of rank as you move from the center toward the periphery (king, duke, marquis, earl, viscount, baron, knight, etc.). Having more than one person in the center merely creates ambiguity about who occupies the center, which necessitates a contest to reduce the number of occupants until only one king (or, more rarely, one queen) is left. That is why you can have only one king but multiple dukes. The dukes are kings-in-waiting (though, obviously, for most the waiting will be in vain).[23] For anyone with a realistic shot at getting to the top, or near the top, the rules of the game are taken very seriously. As *Julius Caesar*'s Brutus understands, resentment is kept more or less in check by the desire to get to the next (upward) rung on the ladder.[24] But what happens when you reach the top? Brutus worried that once ambition had nowhere left to go, it would turn into contempt and scorn, which is to say, into unchecked (and therefore maximally destructive) resentment. The winner would turn his back on his fellows and scorn the base degrees by which he did ascend. In fact, Brutus need not have worried. While it is certainly possible that resentment may occur, it may occur at any point on the ladder, even at the very the bottom. As long as there is someone beneath you, even if only the humble dog, contempt is always an option. You may not be able to kick your boss, but you can certainly kick your dog.

But there is another option that Brutus, who obviously didn't believe in the Judeo-Christian God, did not consider. This is the option Isabella offers. She rules out contempt at every point on the ladder, even at the very top. The gradations on the ladder are insignificant compared to the absolute difference between God and man. It doesn't matter if you're the Duke of Vienna or the king of Hungary; your proud authority is brief and petty. This picture cuts resentment off at its source. There is no point in desiring the center's social and political prestige because, morally speaking, it doesn't get you anywhere. Your achievement will always look insignificant next to God's absolute moral superiority. The best option, therefore, is to focus on tending your inner conscience from the comfort and security of the periphery. As we have already discussed, this is hard work, and there are no guarantees you will be saved. All the more reason, therefore, to buckle down and prove your inner moral virtue. Max Weber thought this was the secret to the Protestant work ethic. Isabella's solution is to enter a convent, which appears to offer her the ideal *private* space to cultivate her inner virtue. It turns out that both Angelo and the Duke disagree with her. Angelo rides roughshod over her personal career goals. The Duke appears to be more gentlemanly about the matter, but the fact that she does not reply to his unexpected marriage proposal suggests that she may be experiencing more than a little resentment. It is hard not to sympathize with Isabella, whose career goals have been thwarted three times by three different men who appear to think their desires are more important than hers. First Angelo, then Claudio, and finally the Duke himself all make indecent proposals to her. Angelo gets the ball rolling by demanding to have sex with her. Claudio conspires, unhappily and reluctantly, with Angelo's desire by asking her to sacrifice her chastity. (Admittedly, his circumstances are rather unusual, so we tend to downplay his complicity.) Finally, the Duke appears to want her sex too. The fact that he proposes marriage makes his offer appear more honorable than Angelo's. The point, however, is not whether marriage is an honorable pathway to sex (it is), but whether Isabella's desires are being taken seriously. On what grounds can we assume that the convent is the wrong place for Isabella? Surely the only person who can answer this question is Isabella.

She doesn't, so neither can we. One assumes the irony is not lost on her. The Duke has been thundering like Jove himself for almost the entirety of the play's final act. She must be thinking, "Oh boy, here we go again."

How much of Isabella's great speech Angelo actually absorbs is difficult to tell. We know he is distracted by her great beauty and finds it increasingly difficult to focus on her arguments. Suffice it to say that if she does persuade him that his authority is brief and not to be taken too seriously, he may take her at her word and decide that all the hard work he's put in to get the spot of top judge is rather pointless next to his overwhelming desire for her. Of course, he doesn't voice this belief directly to her. Only later, in his second soliloquy, does he confess it: "The state, whereon I studied, / Is like a good thing, being often read, / Grown sere and tedious" (2.4.7–9). After Isabella's impassioned speech, Angelo is, unusually, at a loss for words. The only line he can utter is, "Why do you put these sayings upon me?" (2.2.138). Isabella is on the brink of total victory, and she clinches the matter by repeating the argument from empathy, which Escalus had made earlier that day:

ISABELLA
                    Go to your bosom;
    Knock there, and ask your heart what it doth know
    That's like my brother's fault. If it confess
    A natural guiltiness such as is his,
    Let it not sound a thought upon your tongue
    Against my brother's life.

ANGELO [*aside*]
    She speaks, and 'tis such sense
    That my sense breeds with it. (2.2.141–48)

Why does she now succeed where moments before she—and, still earlier, Escalus—had failed? She succeeds now because before Angelo had not been seduced. He had (most emphatically!) not been seduced by Escalus. Nor had he been seduced by Isabella's initial tentative and lukewarm attempts. His blood remained untouched by sexual desire. The law against fornication therefore remained an abstract rule, and he had applied it with coldly impartial logical precision. Now, however, he grasps the warm human context of this particular law because he feels a burning desire to trespass against it. When Escalus had suggested that romantic circumstances similar to Claudio's could have heated Angelo's normally snow-broth blood, Angelo had scoffed at the idea, which seemed all the more ridiculous coming from the mouth of Escalus, a man whose age and appearance suggested the barrenness of winter, not the "teaming foison" of the "plenteous womb" in spring (1.4.43). Escalus has the distinct disadvantage of being old, wrinkly, and white-haired, and he therefore could not convincingly demonstrate the "resolute acting" of the "blood" (2.1.12) either in himself or Angelo. Isabella is not similarly hampered by her age or sex. As she warms to her theme and enacts her extraordinary passion for the merciful and loving Heavenly Father, she literally heats Angelo's blood into a teeming foison. He feels a sudden overwhelming desire to possess her. His bosom loudly confesses a natural guiltiness, as indicated in the prominence Shakespeare gives to the panderer Lucio, who has coaxed the image of Isabella's passionate surrender to God into Angelo's darkest and foulest thoughts. The seduction scene is over. Iniquity's sneak attack on Justice has triumphed.

Alone, Angelo marvels at how his once crystal-clear vision of the law has been muddied by hideous and foul impulses he never knew he possessed:

> What's this, what's this? Is this her fault or mine?
> The tempter or the tempted, who sins most, ha?
> Not she, nor doth she tempt; but it is I
> That, lying by the violet in the sun,
> Do, as the carrion does, not as the flower,
> Corrupt with virtuous season. Can it be
> That modesty may more betray our sense
> Than woman's lightness? Having waste ground enough,
> Shall we desire to raze the sanctuary
> And pitch our evils there? Oh, fie, fie, fie!
> What dost thou, or what art thou, Angelo?
> Dost thou desire her foully for those things
> That make her good? Oh, let her brother live!
> Thieves for their robbery have authority
> When judges steal themselves. What, do I love her,
> That I desire to hear her speak again
> And feast upon her eyes? What is't I dream on?
> Oh, cunning enemy that, to catch a saint,
> With saints dost bait thy hook! (2.2.170–88)

In the context of Shakespeare's other temptation scenes, the most remarkable thing about this soliloquy is how fully aware Angelo is of the fact he has been tempted. No other protagonist expresses with such lucidity the moral contradictions of his position. Not even Hamlet comes close to Angelo's self-consciousness of the paradox that the center exists only because of the desiring attentions of those on the periphery. How can he, in good conscience, condemn Claudio for the same crime he commits in the privacy of his moral and aesthetic imagination? Indeed, his crime (should he commit it) is much worse because he wants to ravage a pure and virtuous novice nun. She is sexually forbidden, which only makes his desire more evil—and more urgent. Why then does he commit it? Angelo is like the doctor who, after carefully listing all of the harmful effects of smoking to his patients, steps out of his office and lights a cigarette. He knows the risks, but he smokes anyway. There is a peculiar disjunction between the lucidity of Angelo's moral reasoning, on the one hand, and his sexual desire, on the other. One almost feels that Angelo is saying, "Well, I'm telling you folks in the audience that I'm about to do a *very bad thing*. I know it's bad, I've told everyone else it's bad, and I've punished everyone I've caught doing it, but I'm going to do it anyway. Behold Angelo the Hypocrite!" The notion that he is a false seemer, a morally righteous judge in appearance only, is particularly evident in his second soliloquy:

> O place, O form,
> How often dost thou with thy case, thy habit,
> Wrench awe from fools and tie the wiser souls
> To thy false seeming! Blood, thou art blood.
> Let's write "good angel" on the devil's horn,
> 'Tis not the devil's crest. (2.4.12–17)

It is, in fact, rather hard to believe that Angelo is caught off guard by the sudden flow of blood in his loins. His description of the change within himself is too clinical and too self-aware. It does not suggest the impetuousness of youthful and inexperienced desire. Angelo is no lovesick Romeo or Claudio bowled head-over-heels by a Juliet or Julietta. Like Angelo, these lovers fall, but they never compare their fallen selves with their unfallen selves in the lucid and objective moral terms Angelo does:

> Never could the strumpet,
> With all her double vigor—art and nature—

Once stir my temper; but this virtuous maid
Subdues me quite. Ever till now,
When men were fond, I smiled and wondered how. (2.2.190–94)

Rather than romantic love, Angelo is driven by the much seedier idea of *lust*, as though he were aware that he was performing a role in the Duke's rather clichéd and exaggerated morality tale. He is the serious (moralizing) version of Lucio. Being a good sport, he agrees to wear the devil's horns, though naturally it is not a role he relishes: "Let's write 'good angel' on the devil's horn, / 'Tis not the devil's crest." He can't seem to shake the feeling that he is about to become the butt of a massive practical joke.

The False Friar

Meanwhile the Duke, from whom we have not heard since 1.3, is now disguised as a humble friar. He has made his way to the city's increasingly congested prison where, as he explains to the Provost, he wishes "to visit the afflicted spirits" (2.3.4). It goes without saying that prison is an excellent place to minister to those in need of spiritual guidance. Where else will he find so many fallen souls in one convenient location? If Angelo's job is to identify and punish the criminals, the Duke's job is to attend to their ailing souls. If the Duke was hoping that Angelo would furnish him with a robust list of needy clients, he now sees that hope fulfilled. The prison is overflowing with fallen souls. Thankfully, his first case appears to be an easy one (though they quickly get much harder, especially when he encounters the intractable Barnardine):

DUKE
  Repent you, fair one, of the sin you carry?

JULIET
  I do, and bear the shame most patiently. (2.3.19–20)

Juliet proves to be most eager to confess her sin and repent. But the Duke is a thorough man. He wants to make sure Juliet is not simply saying what she thinks her confessor wants to hear. He must ascertain if the repentance is sincere. Just as Angelo may not "condemn the fault" and excuse "the actor of it" (2.2.40), so too the Duke must zero in on the actor's conscience to make sure it is still firmly attached to the fault committed. Condemning a fault unattached to a guilty conscience would be to condemn the fault and not the actor of it:

> I'll teach you how you shall arraign your conscience,
> And try your penitence, if it be sound
> Or hollowly put on. (2.3.21–23)

Sins, if they are to be sins and not simply mistakes or accidents, must be committed wholeheartedly and sincerely with the full awareness that one is being tempted into a sin. It is hardly a sin if you don't know that what you did, or are about to do, is morally *verboten*.

Whether the law against fornication should also be interpreted in this way is another matter. Is Angelo guilty of fornication because he *intended* to commit it and, after the deed, sincerely believed he had committed it? Legally, the crime did not take place, but morally it did. The bed trick is the Duke's ultimate diabolical practical joke. (Who is the angel with horns now?) By this device, he is able to test Angelo's conscience without himself conspiring in a crime (e.g., whore-mongering, soliciting, conspiracy to commit fornication). Instead, the Duke conspires with Angelo's conscience, but the conspiracy goes no further than that. He will abet the temptation by providing a warm body in the dark (Mariana's), but he will manage to stay on the right side of the law, unlike Mistress Overdone, Pompey, and Lucio, all of whom he scolds for moral sinfulness *leading to* criminal behavior. In short, the Duke walks a fine line between moral faults (sins) and illegal infractions against the state (crimes). He is like the physician who inoculates the patient against a disease by administering a small but nonlethal dose of the disease. Guilt is the powerful inoculant the Duke injects into his sinful patients.

This distinction between the moral definition of a sin and the legal definition of a crime may seem beside the point, but it informs much of the play, including this little scene between the Duke and Juliet. Why else would the Duke belabor the point that Juliet's repentance must be sincere? If it is not sincere, there is a risk that the offender will re-offend. He repeats his statement that, first, she has committed not only a crime against the state but, more damagingly, a moral crime against God (a sin) and, second, that hers was of a "heavier kind" (2.3.29) than Claudio's. It is unclear why hers is of a heavier kind, unless *heavier* means that she literally has to bear the earthly burden of the sin by carrying a child in her womb, delivering it, and then raising it by herself. In any case, Juliet repeats her willingness to confess and repent:

JULIET
    I do confess it and repent, Father.

DUKE
    'Tis meet so, daughter. But lest you do repent
    As that the sin hath brought you to this shame,
    Which sorrow is always toward ourselves, not heaven,
    Showing we would not spare heaven as we love it,
    But as we stand in fear—

JULIET
    I do repent me as it is an evil,
    And take the shame with joy. (2.3.30–37)

One gets the impression that the Duke is showing a few beginner's jitters in his role as "ghostly father" (5.1.131), confessor of souls. He keeps badgering Juliet about her sincerity, as though this confession business is a bit new to him and he hasn't quite got the knack of reading his subject's mind. Juliet seems a trifle impatient, because she interrupts him, restating her sincere desire to repent by adding, emphatically, that her sin was "evil" and that she takes "her shame with joy," as if to say, "How much more emphatic would you like me to be, Friar?" Juliet finds herself in the same predicament as Hamlet responding to his mother's innocent inquiry about his peculiar black dress-up ("I know not seems, Madam"). Hamlet, like Juliet, finds himself straining to prove his sincerity, to separate his inner being, which is alone authentic, from the external "trappings" of collective representation. The latter includes not just the clothes you wear but the language you use. The fact that language is by definition collective or shared paradoxically undermines the claim to inner authenticity. You can only claim your inner authenticity in language that is by definition *not* your own. The desire to transcend this predicament by reaching deep into one's inner soul leads not to individual authenticity but to the kind of absurd malapropisms evident in Elbow's abuse of conventional meaning.

As the reference to Hamlet suggests, the aim is to point up the difference between mere show and inner moral conviction. We have just heard Angelo's remarkably self-conscious soliloquy bemoaning his lack of authenticity. Outwardly he is the stern voice of law, order, and restraint, but inwardly he would like nothing better than to unleash his wicked desire for Isabella. The soliloquy is interrupted by the brief scene in which the Duke probes Juliet's inner conscience. We are then taken directly back to Angelo, who continues to ponder the disparity between his inner being and his outward appearance:

> When I would pray and think, I think and pray
> To several subjects. Heaven hath my empty words,
> Whilst my invention, hearing not my tongue,
> Anchors on Isabel; Heaven in my mouth,
> As if I did but only chew His name,
> And in my heart the strong and swelling evil
> Of my conception. (2.4.1–7)

Like Hamlet and Julietta, Angelo has that within which passes show, but it is a morally depraved inwardness that most of us are too ashamed to display in public. The Duke is a sensitive leader and evidently disagrees with the hard line his deputy is taking. Rather than shame criminals publicly by ostentatiously displaying their crimes and punishments for all to see, he prefers to minister to each fallen soul separately and individually. He will allow himself a rather shocking exception to this general rule in the final act's scene of public humiliation in which Isabella, Angelo, and Lucio receive a generous dose of good old-fashioned retribution. But as a rule, the Duke's preferred approach to justice is merciful and preventative rather than vengeful and punitive. His wager is that by ministering to his people's inner spiritual and moral needs he can also manage the ethical problem of social injustice. Whether the Duke is right about the effectiveness of this "soft" approach to law and order is debatable, and we must be cautious before deciding that his aesthetic centrality, evident in the multiple roles he plays (duke, friar, and amateur playwright), gives him a special moral license and, in that sense, a free pass from the reader or playgoer.[25]

Liberty Plucks Justice by the Nose Again

The next scene between Isabella and Angelo is a sequel to the great seduction scene the day before in which Iniquity (Lucio) triumphed over Justice (Angelo). Lucio is no longer necessary to Shakespeare's dramatic and allegorical picture because Justice has become indistinguishable from Iniquity. Morally, Angelo is no different from Lucio. Both men have given free rein to their (sexual) desires. Lucio pays for illegal sex in brothels, and Angelo wishes to bribe Isabella to have illegal sex with him. Lucio's task was to breach the walls of Justice by launching a sneak attack on Angelo's sexual desire. With the sensuous blood coursing urgently through his veins, Angelo attempts to seduce Isabella. Unlike the fashionable man-about-town and serial fornicator, however, the judge is inexperienced in the role of worldly seducer. Isabella is also inexperienced and does not know how to respond to the judge's unexpected proposal. The result is an excruciatingly uncomfortable exchange in which each seems willfully bent on misunderstanding the other.

Angelo thinks he can seduce Isabella by rational argument. If he can get her to understand the impeccable logic underlying the bargain (sex in exchange for her brother's life), she will concede his point and therefore her body. For him, the seduction is ultimately reducible to a matter of strict logic, seduction by modus ponens: "If you have sex with me, your brother lives. If you do not, he dies. Which is it to be?" The problem is that Isabella does not think of sex in this rather stripped-down, highly unromantic fashion. Indeed, Isabella tries not to think of sex at all. For her, sex is something other people do. The whole point of her entering a convent was to avoid the business altogether. The upshot is that while Angelo repeatedly attempts to infer via hints and oblique insinuations the indecent terms of his proposal, Isabella repeatedly misunderstands him. The deliberate use of ambiguous and evasive language results in an absurd evasion of meaning by both parties. Just as Escalus, Elbow, Pompey, and Froth conspired in the evasion of justice, so too Angelo and Isabella conspire in the evasion of Angelo's dark desire. In the end, Angelo has no choice but to spell it out in plain English, at which point Isabella reacts with predictable horror.

At first, Angelo hints that Claudio's life may be prolonged. Yes, he says, he is condemned by law to die, "Yet may he live awhile; and, it may be, / As long as you or I" (2.4.35–36). Isabella interprets this to mean Angelo is willing to grant a temporary "reprieve" so she may fit his soul for death (2.4.39). Irritated by her obsession with the soul, he reminds her of the filthy vices of the body, over which he has the full coercive power of the law:

> Fie, these filthy vices! It were as good
> To pardon him that hath from nature stolen
> A man already made, as to remit
> Their saucy sweetness that do coin heaven's image
> In stamps that are forbid. (2.4.42–46)

Fornication is just as bad as murder and will be punished accordingly. Isabella's reply, "'Tis set down so in heaven, but not in earth" (2.4.50), opens the door to Angelo's wish to focus on what Isabella, not God, can do to save Claudio:

> Say you so? Then I shall pose you quickly:
> Which had you rather, that the most just law
> Now took your brother's life, or, to redeem him,
> Give up your body to such sweet uncleanness
> As she that he hath stained? (2.4.51–55)

Angelo tries to seduce Isabella by evasively alluding to a hypothetical if-then scenario: "If you really want to save your brother, you need to give me something in exchange for my judicial pardon." But Isabella evades his meaning by insisting on interpreting the exchange in terms of her relationship to God: "I had rather give my body than my soul" (2.4.56). No price can be put on the soul. It is therefore pointless to try to compare it to anything merely earthly, including her brother's life. Angelo doggedly tries to push her from this stubborn focus on the soul: "I talk not of your soul. Our compelled sins / Stand more for number than for account" (2.4.57–58). In other words, "Quit worrying about your soul, sins committed under duress are not sins." Isabella refuses to take his meaning. She will not countenance the filthy bargain he is trying to press on her.

Angelo tries a slightly different tactic by borrowing her moral terms: "Might there not be a charity in sin / To save this brother's life?" (2.4.63–64). If one sins for charitable reasons, doesn't the charity outweigh the sin? Angelo wants her to think of charity and sin as commodities that can be exchanged (your sex for my pardon), but Isabella refuses to weigh sin and charity together. A charitable act is by definition without sin: "I'll take it as a peril to my soul, / It is no sin at all, but charity" (2.4.65–66). Angelo takes her to mean that she is willing to put her soul in peril by sinning to save her brother: "Pleased you to do't at peril of your soul / Were equal poise of sin and charity" (2.4.67–68). If you're content to put your soul in danger for your brother's sake, you are weighing sex, in one hand, against your brother's life, in the other. This is surely a bargain, given that God weighs murder and fornication as sins of equal weight. Angelo implies he is underselling God by a hefty margin. But Isabella disputes the premise of his argument and sticks to her original view that there is no bargain to make. The matter is very straightforward: she is pleading for her brother's life. If Angelo wants to pardon Claudio, neither her plea nor his pardon can be sins.

Exasperated at her refusal to grasp his intention, Angelo spells it out more plainly. "Admit no other way to save his life . . . but that either / You must lay down the treasures of your body / To this supposed, or else to let him suffer. / What would you do?" (2.4.88–98). No longer able to evade the disturbing meaning of his argument, Isabella clings to the fact that it is offered as a counterfactual. Given this hypothetical situation, what would you do? He must, surely, be testing her. The alternative is too horrible to bear thinking about. Her answer is vehement, passionate, and sincere:

ISABELLA
> As much for my poor brother as myself:
> That is, were I under the terms of death,
> Th'impression of keen whips I'd wear as rubies,
> And strip myself to death as to a bed
> That longing have been sick for, ere I'd yield
> My body up to shame.

ANGELO
> Then must your brother die.

ISABELLA
> And 'twere the cheaper way.
> Better it were a brother died at once
> Than that a sister, by redeeming him,
> Should die forever. (2.4.99–109)

Her meaning is crystal clear. Not in a million years would she enter into such a filthy bargain. Her language, however, is bound to suggest otherwise, at least to Angelo's lascivious mind. If she wants to strip herself and go to bed with God, why not with me? Doesn't she recognize that by rejecting the offer, she is condemning her brother? Doesn't that make her "as cruel as the sentence" she slanders (2.4.110)?

Isabella goes back to her essential point, eloquently made in the seduction scene. Mercy cannot be ransomed:

> Ignomy in ransom and free pardon
> Are of two houses. Lawful mercy
> Is nothing kin to foul redemption. (2.4.112–14)

Angelo wants to say that mercy is a form of currency. It puts the forgiven into the debt of the forgiver. It has a price, and Isabella must pay it. Isabella argues that this is to misunderstand mercy, which has no price (it droppeth as the gentle rain from heaven). Angelo counters that her understanding of mercy makes a mockery of the law, which cannot be expected to reproduce the lofty standards of the all-merciful Heavenly Redeemer. Pardoning a criminal only encourages the vice in others:

> ANGELO
>> You seemed of late to make the law a tyrant,
>> And rather proved the sliding of your brother
>> A merriment than a vice.
>
> ISABELLA
>> Oh, pardon me, my lord. It oft falls out,
>> To have what we would have, we speak not what we mean.
>> I something do excuse the thing I hate
>> For his advantage that I dearly love.
>
> ANGELO
>> We are all frail. (2.4.115–22)

Isabella concedes that she may inadvertently have understated the gravity of her brother's crime, but this was only a manner of speaking and not her intention. Angelo seizes on this admission, which he wants to see as a weakness of character ("We are all frail"). If she concedes that she does not always mean what she says, maybe when she says no, she really means yes. The two are now at extreme cross-purposes. Isabella hears his "We are all frail" and imagines he has conceded her point that it is unjust to condemn her brother for a common human weakness. Angelo recoils from her interpretation. He does not mean that men are weak, though he knows, all too well, that he is weak. He wants to say women are weak—"women are frail too" (2.4.125). This reduces Isabella to his own (fallen) level. She agrees that women are weak, but she thinks that by agreeing she may persuade him that Claudio's transgression is not exceptional and deserves forgiveness. At this point, Angelo thinks he has her cornered. She's admitted her weakness. All he has to do is point out that her weakness is natural. She should give in to her desires, as he has given in to his:

ANGELO
> I do arrest your words. Be that you are,
> That is, a woman; if you be more, you're none.
> If you be one, as you are well expressed
> By all external warrants, show it now
> By putting on the destined livery.

ISABELLA
> I have no tongue but one. Gentle my lord,
> Let me entreat you speak the former language.

ANGELO
> Plainly conceive, I love you.

ISABELLA
> My brother did love Juliet,
> And you tell me that he shall die for't.

ANGELO
> He shall not, Isabel, if you give me love.

ISABELLA
> I know your virtue hath a license in't,
> Which seems a little fouler than it is
> To pluck on others.

ANGELO
>   Believe me, on mine honor,
> My words express my purpose. (2.4.135–49)

Angelo believes in seduction by modus ponens. If all women are weak, then Isabella, who is a woman, is weak. Behind this impeccable logic, however, lies a much more suspect syllogism, which runs something like this: "I, who was once impervious to sexual desire, have succumbed to it. If I can succumb to it, then everyone can succumb to it, including you." Strictly speaking, this is a fallacy. One cannot argue from the particular case to the general ("I am guilty, therefore everyone is guilty"). Nonetheless, that is precisely what Isabella had encouraged Angelo to do when she asked him to look into his heart and "confess / A natural guiltiness" that was like her "brother's fault" (2.2.143–44). His experience, she argued, was generalizable. This is not a logical deduction but an inference from personal experience to the experiences of others. We may call it the argument from empathy.

It is a sad fact that most of us fail to live up to our noblest and loftiest ideals. The spirit may be willing, but the flesh is disappointingly weak. This statement is true insofar as it goes, but it misses the fact that the division between spirit and flesh is an invention of the spirit, which dubiously anthropomorphizes the flesh as its weak-willed and ill-behaved twin. Freud's concept of the unconscious, which is not only weak-willed but *intentionally* deviant, commits the same metaphysical sleight of hand.[26] At what point does the body become capable of intentional thought (whether or not thought is deviant)? Or to put the same point differently, at what point do humans become capable of representing themselves? When do they begin talking to one another?

The commonsense empirical answer to this question, ridiculed independently by Durkheim, Saussure, and Wittgenstein, is that some bright individual realized it would be convenient to attach external and publicly shared signs to the brilliant ideas he had in his head. How else could he share his brilliant ideas with others? But this is to assume the very thing we wish to explain, which is the origin of publicly shared signs or words. Ideas do not miraculously appear in the head waiting to get transported into other heads. This is to mistake ideas for perceptions. The latter are indeed unique and unshareable except by way of words. Words are not simply the external reflection of our unique and inmost perceptions. They are, rather, the means whereby our inner perceptions can be collectively organized by publicly controlled and socially mediated ideas. Ideas are the result of an arduous and lengthy training of the mind by the community's habits, in particular, by its words, where words are themselves the product of repeatedly directing individual perception, which is unruly and idiosyncratic, to collectively significant objects in the world. Durkheim understood the initiation of the individual into the collective representations of the community to be the function of ritual, and he elaborated a convincing theory to explain how this occurred.[27] Perception must become *collective attention* to specific (sacred) objects.[28] Language is the means whereby the chaos of inner perception and experience is transformed into the order of intentional thought. Without language, there can be no division between the spirit and the flesh, or between the conscious and unconscious mind.

What has this to do with Angelo and Isabella? Angelo began his tenure as deputy by strictly enforcing the law. He deliberately excluded his own feelings when he considered the cases before him. But now he has reached an impasse. He cannot separate his strong sexual desire for Isabella from his consideration of her brother's case. Her argument that he must knock at his heart and discover the same feelings that led her brother to run afoul of the law have had the desired effect. Angelo feels the same way toward her that Claudio had felt toward Juliet on that fateful evening when the two embraced one another. Isabella's argument from empathy has worked, though not quite in the manner she had hoped. Somehow, she has seduced Angelo, and now he is attempting to seduce her. How have things managed to go so awry?

Most human actions are not tied very securely to abstract philosophical principles. Rather, they are tethered to repeated scenes of human interaction around centrally significant or sacred objects. People do not worship because they have an inherent need to believe in some abstract principle (e.g., Goodness, Justice, Beauty, Morality, Power). They worship because other people worship. As Durkheim saw, these scenes of communal interaction are a form of collective representation, a means to synchronize or civilize the individual's otherwise completely wild, idiosyncratic, and unrestrained perceptions, feelings, associations, and behaviors. This process of synchronization is quite irrational, in the sense that there is no rulebook explaining how one gets from a generally shared principle or proposition to a specific feeling, passion, or emotion. Usually, it is the other way around. One gets to the abstract principle only after one has experienced the requisite group emotion. One only believes in Goodness as an abstract principle after one has the warm feeling of collective well-being. The Good is not something *up there* but something *in here*, where *in here* means not only in each individual but *in each individual within our group*. In other words, the Good is something that must be generated over and over again in scenes of ritual interaction with others. Of course, this is hard work and very demanding on one's time. If you try to rest on your laurels by putting on the august robes of your Very Important Position, someone is bound to notice, enviously or resentfully, that your desires and emotions conflict with theirs. This leads to the disturbing conclusion that someone has the wrong feelings. Isabella does her best to assume that Angelo harbors only pure thoughts and feelings, but once it becomes painfully evident that his thoughts and feelings are impure, she is forced to turn the accusing finger on him:

> Ha! Little honor to be much believed,
> And most pernicious purpose! Seeming, seeming!
> I will proclaim thee, Angelo, look for't!
> Sign me a present pardon for my brother,
> Or with an outstretched throat I'll tell the world aloud
> What man thou art. (2.4.150–55)

Angelo does not deny that his thoughts are impure. How could he? What he does deny is that this wide gap between her desire and his desire can be resolved in her favor. She wants a judicial pardon for her brother. He wants her sex. Why don't they make a discreet exchange that satisfies both parties? Isabella, however, is unprepared to sacrifice the high moral ground. She will not allow him to raze her sanctuary. He is the polluted one, and she has no intention of allowing him to pollute her. But how will she prove his inner filthiness to others? His feelings are his alone, and they can always be denied:

> Who will believe thee, Isabel?
> My unsoiled name, th'austereness of my life,
> My vouch against you, and my place i'th' state
> Will so your accusation overweigh
> That you shall stifle in your own report
> And smell of calumny. (2.4.155–60)

Ambushed by Lucio's sneak attack, Angelo makes his countermove in the form of a highly indecent proposal. His position at the center appears to make him invulnerable, but he has not anticipated the Duke's master stroke, which will be to launch a second sneak attack, this time on the inner sanctum itself. Angelo's conscience will be turned inside out. The angel will have to wear his horns in front of everyone.

The Cunning Enemy

The Duke's task of ministering to the increasing number of fallen souls in Vienna's prison is becoming harder. Juliet was a relatively easy case, but her lover is proving more intractable. Unsurprisingly, the prospect of his imminent execution dampens his enthusiasm for any last-minute moral instruction. What is the point of a lecture on his moral shortcomings if he is going to die? The Duke must sense that Claudio is not the most devout of souls, because this time he pursues a completely different tactic. He never mentions God, heaven, or the immortal soul. Instead, in a long and tortuous speech, he attempts to drive home the point that death is the end of everything, so Claudio might as well get used to the idea. It is hardly an uplifting speech and certainly not something one would expect from one of God's holy emissaries. The Duke, of course, is not a real friar, but this only seems to make his grim lecture even worse. Why would he inveigle his way into Claudio's confidence only to dash all hope? A. P. Rossiter points out that critics who interpret the Duke as a benevolent and merciful stand-in for God conveniently ignore this speech, which is utterly devoid of any kind of redemptive or hopeful message.[29] Why does the Duke not only deny Claudio the hope of an afterlife but also the hope that his life might yet be spared? What is the point of this terribly bleak message?

It is difficult to explain the shifty Duke's motivations, but one thing that emerges clearly in this scene is the huge gap between Claudio's point of view and the Duke's. Claudio is, understandably, getting increasingly nervous as his appointment with the executioner draws near. His last hope is Isabella. Will she persuade Angelo to grant him a pardon? The Duke's advice is to assume that she will not: "Be absolute for death. Either death or life / Shall thereby be the sweeter" (3.1.5–6). In other words: "Prepare yourself for the worst, because then you will not be disappointed whatever the outcome. In the unlikely event that the news is good, you will be all the happier." The Duke goes on to describe life as a thing only "fools would keep" (3.1.8), because it is subject to so many unpleasant and inconstant influences. We spend our lives desiring happiness, but we're never satisfied. The best thing about life is sleep, which is what death brings. Why fear death when life is so miserable and unrewarding? Really, we should welcome death.

This sort of advice represents the worst type of arrogance and condescension. It smugly assumes that the person who is about to lose his head should listen to someone whose head is in no danger at all explain how fear of the executioner's axe is irrational because life is actually not as pleasant as people generally think. The arrogance is quite stupefying. Not only does it make the wholly unjustified assumption that life is equally unpleasant or depressing for everyone, it also assumes that this sort of intellectual game can have the slightest effect on someone whose head is about to be chopped off. The Duke thinks he can prepare Claudio for death by arguing that life is reducible to a peculiar way of speaking, a matter of mere metaphor or world picture. If you use the right metaphors, your picture of life as something you want to hold on to will change into something you want to let go. After the Duke goes on for forty-seven excruciating lines of this sort of tone-deaf wordplay, Claudio says, "I humbly thank you. / To sue to live, I find I seek to die, / And, seeking death, find life" (3.1.41–43). I can only imagine he says this to get the Duke out of his cell as quickly as possible. It is clear from what Claudio says to his sister moments later that he has lost none of his zest for life and would dearly love to hang on to it for as long as possible.

When Isabella arrives to give Claudio the bad news that he must die, it's clear she's nervous. She fears he won't share her devout belief in her chastity. She begins by asserting that he must prepare his soul for its heavenward ascent. When Claudio asks, "Is there no remedy?" (3.1.59), she refuses to answer directly. Instead, she questions his honor, which she fears will weaken if she divulges the terms of Angelo's bargain:

> Oh, I do fear thee, Claudio, and I quake
> Lest thou a feverous life shouldst entertain,
> And six or seven winters more respect
> Than a perpetual honor. Dar'st thou die?
> The sense of death is most in apprehension,
> And the poor beetle that we tread upon
> In corporal sufferance finds a pang as great
> As when a giant dies. (3.1.73–80)

Isabella adopts the same strategy as the Duke when she argues that, in terms of physical suffering, there is no difference between a beetle's pain and the pain experienced by a giant. Presumably, she means that Claudio should imagine his death as swift and painless. He will suffer no more than the beetle squashed underfoot by an inattentive walker. Claudio's reaction shows that he was merely being polite when he said to the Duke that his poetic speech had persuaded him to welcome death. "Why give you me this shame?" he says, "Think you I can a resolution fetch / From flow'ry tenderness" (3.1.81–83). Claudio is annoyed that Isabella should imply that his ability to face death courageously and honorably is a matter of mere metaphor and flowery speech. To ward off this tactic, Claudio uses a metaphor of his own. He asserts that if he must die, he "will encounter darkness as a bride" whom he will "hug" in his "arms" (3.1.84–85). Isabella seizes on this image, which echoes her own highly sentimental image of death as an erotic union between herself and God:

> There spake my brother! There my father's grave
> Did utter forth a voice. Yes, thou must die.
> Thou are too noble to conserve a life
> In base appliances. (3.1.86–89)

Isabella, somewhat desperately, reminds Claudio of his filial duty to uphold his father's honor. She does not want him to throw his patrimony away because of an ignoble fear of death. As Harold Goddard points out, Isabella puts herself in the unflattering and highly ambivalent position of the ghost in *Hamlet*.[30] Tempted by a voice from beyond his father's grave, Hamlet is torn between revenge (represented by the ghost) and love (represented by Ophelia). He chooses the ghost, and the consequence is death—not just for Claudius but for Polonius, Ophelia, Rosencrantz, Guildenstern, Laertes, Gertrude, and Hamlet too. Isabella comes dangerously close to the same (male) violence that overwhelms Shakespeare's tragic protagonists. In her desperation to steer Claudio away from Angelo's shameful bargain, she forgets that her brother is unlikely to be at his most sympathetic when it comes to *her* plight. Death is for him not some distant abstract notion that he can safely intellectualize. It is a "fearful thing" (3.1.117) that completely dominates his attention. Anything that can delay his appointment with the executioner is a life raft thrown to a drowning man. He will not let go of any hope, even the hope that Isabella may be persuaded to accept Angelo's filthy bargain. As she had secretly feared, when she does reveal Angelo's despicable terms, Claudio clings to this last glimmer of hope:

ISABELLA
> Dost thou think, Claudio:
> If I would yield him my virginity,
> Thou mightst be freed!

CLAUDIO

                    Oh, heavens, it cannot be.

ISABELLA

Yes, he would give't thee, from this rank offense,
So to offend him still. This night's the time
That I should do what I abhor to name,
Or else thou diest tomorrow.

CLAUDIO

Thou shalt not do't.

ISABELLA

Oh, were it but my life,
I'd throw it down for your deliverance
As frankly as a pin.

CLAUDIO

                    Thanks, dear Isabel.

ISABELLA

Be ready, Claudio, for your death tomorrow.

CLAUDIO

Yes. Has he affections in him,
That thus can make him bite the law by th' nose
When he would force it? Sure it is no sin,
Or of the deadly seven it is the least.

ISABELLA

Which is the least?

CLAUDIO

If it were damnable, he being so wise,
Why would he for the momentary trick
Be perdurably fined? Oh, Isabel!

ISABELLA

What says my brother?

CLAUDIO

                    Death is a fearful thing.

ISABELLA
And shamèd life a hateful. (3.1.97–118)

Isabella fears Claudio's constancy of soul. The will to live outweighs the rather more abstract focus on one's spirit. No doubt there is an inverse relationship between the will to live and the capacity to focus on one's soul. In the face of life-threatening violence, all bets about one's soul tend to fade into the background. The focus is not on one's soul, which is much too abstract and distant, but on one's *survival*. This general rule is not disproved by the proverb that "there are no atheists in the foxholes." When threatened with imminent death, most of us—even lifelong atheists—are willing to compromise on our most deeply held principles. Belief in principled moral abstractions follows, rather than leads, the will to live. If God can help me live, then I will pray to him all the more fervently, even if such prayers were something I formerly held in contempt.

Claudio is no different from most people faced with imminent violent death. Abstractly, he is aware that he should protect his sister's chastity. But the threat of life-ending violence to *his* person weakens his capacity to believe in the sanctity of *her* chastity. He wonders, naturally, whether a sin undertaken to save someone's life really can be considered a sin and, if it can, whether lechery is not in fact the least of the seven deadly sins. Surely Angelo would not willingly endanger *his* soul? Of course, Claudio is rationalizing lechery, just as Isabella is rationalizing Claudio's death. When she asserts that she would instantly have accepted Angelo's terms if he had asked for her life rather than her virginity, one cannot help but feel skeptical. The notion of her martyrdom remains an abstraction. How might her point of view change were she, not her brother, faced with imminent violent death? Would she feel the same devotion to death that she asserted earlier to Angelo ("[W]ere I under the terms of death, / Th'impression of keen whips I'd wear as rubies, / And strip myself to death as to a bed / That longing have been sick for" [2.4.100–103])? The idea of his imminent death fills Claudio with anxiety and fear:

Ay, but to die, and go we know not where,
To lie in cold obstruction and to rot,
This sensible warm motion to become
A kneaded clod, and the delighted spirit

> To bathe in fiery floods, or to reside
> In thrilling region of thick-ribbèd ice;
> To be imprisoned in the viewless winds
> And blown with restless violence round about
> The pendent world; or to be worse than worst
> Of those that lawless and incertain thought
> Imagine howling—'tis too horrible!
> The weariest and most loathèd worldly life
> That age, ache, penury, and imprisonment
> Can lay on nature is a paradise
> To what we fear of death. (3.1.119–33)

As these words make painfully clear, Claudio is anything but ready to die. All Isabella can say in response is, "Alas, alas!" (3.1.134). She is genuinely moved by her brother's fear. When he implores her to accept Angelo's terms and save his life, however, her sympathy turns to revulsion and furious condemnation:

> CLAUDIO
>   Sweet sister, let me live.
>   What sin you do to save a brother's life,
>   Nature dispenses with the deed so far
>   That it becomes a virtue.
>
> ISABELLA
>   Oh, you beast!
>   Oh, faithless coward! Oh, dishonest wretch!
>   Wilt thou be made a man out of my vice?
>   Is't not a kind of incest, to take life
>   From thine own sister's shame? What should I think?
>   Heaven shield my mother played my father fair!
>   For such a warpèd slip of wilderness
>   Ne'er issued from his blood. Take my defiance,
>   Die, perish! Might but my bending down
>   Reprieve thee from thy fate, it should proceed.
>   I'll pray a thousand prayers for thy death,
>   No word to save thee. (3.1.135–49)

How did we get to this unhappy clash of viewpoints? What happened to the merciful and empathetic Isabella? How can she change so quickly from eloquent champion of mercy and empathy into someone who says *this*?

Obviously, Isabella is exaggerating, but why? Her beliefs are being questioned and the exaggerated manner of her response suggests that her convictions are not as secure as she imagines. How else are we to explain the hyperbole? Only someone deeply insecure about her beliefs would react in this hyperdefensive and exaggerated fashion. It seems she may be guilty of the same moral backsliding as Angelo. There appears to be a considerable discrepancy between her inward and outward selves. Outwardly, she behaves like the pious and virtuous novice nun she appears to be, but her inner virtue has been tested and, unfortunately, she has come up short of the high benchmark she set for herself when she had suggested that proud man, dressed in a little brief authority, was wont to ignore his glassy essence and behave like an angry ape. Like Angelo, she too has been hoisted by her own petard. Happily, the Duke is waiting in the wings to rescue her fallen soul.

After Isabella delivers her condemnatory and accusing speech to Claudio, there is a dramatic change in tone, indicated by the shift from verse to prose. The Duke, who has been observing unseen the unhappy exchange between brother and sister, realizes that his pastoral therapy isn't working. He will have to be more aggressive in his tactics if he is to have any effect on the harder cases, which include Angelo, Isabella, and Claudio, not to mention Barnardine, whose conscience the Duke utterly fails to reach. Angelo appears to be a hypocrite and abuser of power. Isabella's virtue also appears to be somewhat tarnished, and, at any rate, she now appears to condone Angelo's death sentence, which automatically makes her suspect in the Duke's eyes. As for Claudio, well, he just doesn't want to die, and all the Duke's pretty speeches about death appear to have had zero effect on him. The Duke does some quick thinking and settles on a plan. First, he tells Claudio that Angelo was merely testing Isabella's virtue and was never going to pardon Claudio. How does he know this fact? Because he is "confessor to Angelo" (3.1.169). Let us leave aside the troubling fact that our friar seems remarkably cavalier with the sacred confidences of the souls he confesses. Of course, we do not believe that he has actually confessed Angelo. He is not a real friar but a duke trying to shepherd his unruly subjects into some moral order. Remember that cruel physical coercion would damage *his* conscience, not to mention his reputation as a kind, benevolent, and much-loved prince. It is necessary, therefore, to tell the occasional white lie. This lie, however, is rather painful, at least to Claudio, who now thinks that he will die tomorrow. The Duke does nothing to dissuade him of this extremely painful and anxiety-inducing belief. He says flatly, "Tomorrow you must die. Go to your knees and make ready" (3.1.171–72). With his last hope gone, Claudio resigns himself to his fate. He now feels bad that he asked Isabella to do something that would merely have led her to fail a purely hypothetical test of her virtue. It seems his head is destined to be separated from his body after all. "Let me ask my sister pardon," he says, "I am so out of love with life that I will sue to be rid of it" (3.1.173–74). But Claudio never speaks to his sister again, not even in the final scene when they are reunited. Henceforth he will be a silent prop in the Duke's cunning trial of Lord Angelo's virtue. Like Hamlet (but far more successfully), the Duke will catch the conscience of a king. He will make Hamlet's "mousetrap" look amateurish and feeble by comparison. He plans to produce something much more effective, and Isabella will be his star witness.

Consider the Duke's problem. He has just overheard Isabella tell her brother that Angelo is prepared to grant a pardon if she sleeps with him. It seems he has caught the virtuous deputy with his pants down. As he predicted, there appears to be a wide discrepancy between Angelo's foul (inward) desires and his virtuous (outward) appearance. But how will he prove this discrepancy? How will he take Angelo's inner foulness and expose it to the clear light of day? When Isabella indicates that she would like nothing better than to denounce Angelo publicly so she can get justice, he points to the essential difficulty:

ISABELLA
    But, oh, how much is the good Duke deceived in Angelo! If ever he return and I can speak to him, I will open my lips in vain, or discover his government.

DUKE
    That shall not be much amiss. Yet, as the matter now stands, he will avoid your accusation; he made trial of you only. (3.1.193–99)

Note the shift in the Duke's narrative voice in his final sentence. He moves from the statement made from *his* point of view to a statement made from

Angelo's point of view. "As the matter now stands," the Duke says, "Angelo will evade or deny your accusation—he was only testing you." Of course, the Duke does not really believe Angelo was testing Isabella. What he means is that Angelo will deny Isabella's accusation by claiming that he was only testing her. This is an example of free indirect speech, the kind of thing we'd expect to find in a Jane Austen novel, in which we shift seamlessly between the narrator's point of view and that of the internal characters. The Duke shifts from his external perspective to adopt the internal viewpoint of one of his characters. He is thinking Angelo's thoughts, anticipating Angelo's words. If challenged, Angelo will say, "I made trial of her only. You can't seriously believe I wanted to sleep with her. Are you quite mad?"

Why is this significant? It is significant because the Duke is trying to become the controlling figure of the dramatic narrative by putting the other characters inside *his* narrative. He wants to turn the showing into a telling, the drama of tragic conflict into a sentimental education of the audience member, whom we may take the liberty here of calling a *reader* or *interpreter* of the Duke's narrative. And he aims to do this by means of his narrative point of view. The Duke's utterance is an example of free indirect speech because we seem to overhear Angelo *through* the voice of the narrator, as indicated by the use of the third-person pronoun ("he"). We are, as it were, simultaneously inside Angelo's head and outside it. Angelo does not refer to himself in the third person when thinking about himself. This shift from first person to third person mirrors the shift from Angelo's thinking to the Duke's thinking about Angelo's thinking. We are shifting from the Duke's perspective to Angelo's and back again. The Duke, in short, is trying to become an external narrator, a commentator on his characters' inner thoughts.

How successful is he? Let's just say he faces a steep uphill battle. In particular, he faces two related challenges. The first is the obvious epistemological problem: How does he get inside another person's head? The second is the more interesting one; it is the generic or formal problem: How does he transcend this stage or scene, in which he is merely one among many other characters all existing on the same plane of reality, to become the narrator of these other characters who are now *internal* to his narrative? Let's address the second problem first. Since we are dealing with a dramatic representation rather than a philosophical treatise, addressing the formal or generic issue will help us think about the epistemological problem.

What challenges does the Duke face in his effort to become the external narrator of a dramatic scene in which he also an internal actor? The British philosopher Peter Goldie points out that a narrative assumes a difference between at least two points of view: that of the external narrator and that of the internal character.[31] To take the most basic form of narrative, autobiographical thinking or thinking about oneself, this distinction between internal and external characters maps onto a distinction between the narrating self and the narrated self. The narrating self thinks of itself as an internal character in a narrative, whether in the past or future, and reflects on this difference between internal and external viewpoints. The external viewpoint is the privileged position, in the sense that it reflects on the more limited perspective of the internal character. For example, reflecting back on my conversation with a friend yesterday, I feel slightly ashamed that I spent most of the time talking and very little time listening. At the time, I thought I was being a scintillating conversationalist, making all kinds of smart jokes and clever observations, but now I realize that most of my remarks were rather platitudinous and that my friend's silence was an expression of polite boredom rather than an appreciation of my brilliant wit. Next time we have coffee, I resolve to spend less time talking and more time listening.

As this example suggests, narrative thinking is a form of dramatic irony in which the internal character knows less than the external character. In the case of autobiographical narrative, this distinction between internal and external perspectives is located in a single mind. The self reflects on itself by situating itself at the center of an internal scene of representation where it is free to imagine past or future versions of itself. In Shakespeare, the conventional method for representing this form of narrative thinking is the soliloquy, which is a form of self-addressed speech.[32] The self addresses a past or future version of itself. Shakespeare often uses soliloquies to indicate that a character is undergoing an internal moral or spiritual crisis. Angelo provides a pertinent example:

> What's this, what's this? Is this her fault or mine?
> The tempter or the tempted, who sins most, ha?
> Not she, nor doth she tempt; but it is I
> That, lying by the violet in the sun,
> Do, as the carrion does, not as the flower,

> Corrupt with virtuous season. Can it be
> That modesty may more betray our sense
> Than woman's lightness? Having waste ground enough,
> Shall we desire to raze the sanctuary
> And pitch our evils there? Oh, fie, fie, fie!
> What dost thou, or what art thou, Angelo?
> Dost thou desire her foully for those things
> That make her good? Oh, let her brother live!
> Thieves for their robbery have authority
> When judges steal themselves. (2.2.169–84)

The normally cold and stony Angelo feels an unexpectedly warm desire for Isabella. The feeling takes him totally by surprise, and he is thrown into a deep moral conflict between his past and present selves. His former self had looked coldly on Claudio's predicament. Incapable himself of any sexual passion, Angelo felt no empathy toward Claudio, whom he had looked down on contemptuously as a weak and inferior being undeserving of pity or mercy. His current self, however, is remarkably changed. After experiencing a similar sexual passion, he feels empathy for Claudio and now sees the injustice of his former hardline position. The fact that most of Angelo's sentences are not descriptive statements but questions ("What are thou?") or imperatives ("Oh, let her brother live!") indicates that the normally hyperrational and hyperlogical Angelo has been unseated by a passion he does not fully understand. His inner turmoil, the conflict between his past and present selves, is reflected in his incapacity to think clearly about what he should do. On the one hand, he wants to "raze the sanctuary" (violate Isabella); on the other, he wants to confess his sins, repent, and make amends by pardoning Claudio. Angelo is split between two morally incompatible versions of himself. He knows what he should do. He should confess his sins, repent his fault, and pardon Claudio. But in the end, he ignores his better self and gives in to his base desires. He is a man to "double business bound," whose worser self triumphs over the better.

Angelo's soliloquy is a classic case of autobiographical narrative thinking. But what happens when a character treats not merely himself but others as internal characters in his narrative? When this happens, a character becomes the author or narrator of other people's stories, not just of his own. Angelo becomes not merely a character reflecting on himself but a character reflecting on himself in somebody else's narrative. In other words, we get not just Angelo's perspective on his former self but the narrator's perspective on Angelo's perspective on his former self. Obviously, this shift from internal character to external narrator creates a further discrepancy between internal and external perspectives. Now it is not just the self representing other versions of itself but the self being observed unseen by another self who also has the power to see into the other's mind.

The Duke seems at times to approach the extraordinary position of being the narrator of the play unfolding before our eyes.[33] After he observes from his place of hiding the appalling scene in which Isabella condemns her brother, he steps out from the shadows and tries to take control of the narrative, to push it in the direction *he* wants it to go. He sees the narrative is on a grim and tragic course. The conflict between Claudio's, Angelo's, and Isabella's perspectives is too great to lead to anything but at least one death (Claudio's), and doubtless many more, following the logic of the old talion law ("an eye for an eye"). The Duke, however, believes he can save the principal characters both from themselves and each other with a surgical and precisely timed intervention. For the plan to work, however, a fair amount of deception will be necessary. In particular, in order to get Isabella and Angelo to see the light and avert the looming crisis, the Duke aims to keep them in the dark and on a tragic path for as long as possible. He orchestrates matters so that both Angelo and Isabella end up committing the same sins they condemn so forthrightly in others. Only once they have been made to see their own fallibility and imperfection will he play his final trump card.

When we read a novel, we must distinguish between the narrator and the author. Likewise, we cannot assume that the controlling character in the play (the Duke) is the author or playwright (Shakespeare). To borrow a term we usually apply to novels, the Duke is at best an *unreliable narrator* of the scenes he stages. More precisely, he is a fallible and imperfect ruler, whose undercover operation does little to dispel our suspicions about his all-too-human fallibility. He is most emphatically *not* the stage equivalent of an omniscient, benevolent, and merciful God. In the first place, he is not omniscient. He repeatedly fails to anticipate the actions of those whose consciences he attempts to penetrate and expose. For example, he is surprised by Angelo's order that Claudio's head be chopped off despite the fact that Isabella has, as far as Angelo is aware, held to her part of the bargain. Second, he is hardly benevolent. He does nothing to dissuade Claudio he is about to be executed; he allows Isabella to believe that her brother has been executed; and he seems to take a bit too much pleasure in humiliating Isabella, Angelo, and Lucio in the final scene over which he works so assiduously to assume absolute control. Finally, the mercy he shows seems more strained than unstrained. If mercy droppeth as the gentle rain from heaven, the Duke's version of it thunders like an angry ape. His grandstanding show trial at the end is enough to make the gods weep. The Duke's actions appear to be designed to put himself in the best possible light. Why else would he choose this moment to propose to Isabella? He seems to believe that he deserves her hand because he has preserved her brother's life, a fact he reveals at the last minute with great satisfaction when he distributes pardons like confetti. No doubt his offer is a step up from Angelo's filthy bargain, but Isabella might be forgiven for thinking that, despite the improved terms, it is still an exchange of one thing for another (her sex for the Duke's prestige) and in this sense falls short of divine love and mercy.

Peephole Therapy

The early suspicion we had that the Duke was holding something back when he handed power to Angelo is now emphatically confirmed. The Duke has a plan, but he needs Isabella to play her role as bait in this second wave of the sneak attack on Angelo. She must return to Angelo and accept his bargain. The Duke is following through on Lucio's ambush of Justice by Iniquity. He will encourage Iniquity to trespass on the inner sanctum. However, the trespass must be legal. Angelo must believe he is guilty of fornication, but the Duke will not allow the sin to be an illegal act. He must have sex and believe it to be immoral, but it must be technically legal so that the Duke himself cannot be accused of running a high-class bawdy house for discerning gentlemen like Angelo.

The deep moral and ethical problems of this plan do not appear to worry the Duke, whose mealy-mouthed descriptions of what he is doing suggest a fair amount of evasion and self-deception. For instance, his first soliloquy shows none of the pained self-questioning we witnessed in Angelo's soliloquies. Instead, we hear some trite and platitudinous moralizing:

> He who the sword of heaven will bear
> Should be as holy as severe;

> Pattern in himself to know,
> Grace to stand, and virtue go;
> More nor less to others paying
> Than by self-offenses weighing.
> Shame to him whose cruel striking
> Kills for faults of his own liking!
> Twice treble shame on Angelo,
> To weed my vice and let his grow!
> Oh, what may man within him hide,
> Though angel on the outward side! (3.2.254–65)

One might characterize this soliloquy as a public service announcement. The Duke steps forward to address the audience by pointing out the moral of the story. Beware hypocrisy! The Duke is not reflecting on himself, as Angelo and Isabella had done in their soliloquies. Rather, he is reflecting on the drama in general and, in particular, on the sins of others. In case we didn't grasp the message clearly enough, he helpfully reminds us of the salient point: Angelo is a hypocrite! But don't worry, the Duke knows his dirty secret and will craftily use it against him:

> Craft against vice I must apply.
> With Angelo tonight shall lie
> His old betrothèd but despisèd;
> So disguise shall, by the disguisèd,
> Pay with falsehood false exacting
> And perform an old contracting. (3.2.270–75)

Angelo thinks he is being clever by using his power to have sex with Isabella, but the Duke is even more clever because he will trick Angelo into honoring a contract with a woman who loves him (even if Angelo doesn't love her). One disguise (Iniquity disguised as Virtue, the angel with horns) will be met with another (Mariana disguised as Isabella), and thus one falsehood will repay another. The Duke's trick will undermine Angelo's. The tit-for-tat logic of these lines echoes the play's title. Measure will be answered with measure. Angelo's crafty deception will be answered by the Duke's.

Many critics explain the peculiar rhythm and tone of these lines as a symptom of the play shifting gears, rather clunkily, from tragedy to comedy. The Duke steps forward to offer a sort of prologue to the impending comic resolution. The singsong rhyming tetrameter couplets indicate that we have entered a new genre, one in which the clash of competing desires will be resolved comically (everyone lives) rather than tragically (everyone dies). This shift in tone is confirmed when the next scene begins with a song, which is not something we typically expect in a tragedy.[34]

There is no question that there is a shift from tragedy to comedy. Many critics, however, are unhappy with the result. Most of the discussion revolves around the Duke, as he is the one who orchestrates the shift. For example, Harriet Hawkins is disappointed by the "ducal solutions," which she finds "hopelessly inadequate in the face of the psychological, sexual, and moral conflicts they are supposed to have resolved."[35] It is not simply a case of an improbable comic ending—many of Shakespeare's comedies have improbable endings. Rather, the problem is that the Duke's solutions run roughshod over what was so interesting in the first half of the play. Richard Wheeler explains the problem as follows: "The completion of the comic design centered in the wise and benevolent Duke is made possible by theatrical maneuvers that limit its scope and blunt its force. They create a comic whole smaller than the sum of its parts. The idealization of the Duke is necessary in order to complete this design, but can only be accomplished by suppressing potential links between Vincentio and deep psychological conflict."[36] Wheeler goes on to compare the Duke to Othello. Both are older men who marry (or propose to marry) a much younger woman. The difference is that the corruption of sexual desire into jealousy and resentment is "deflected away from Vincentio, who is kept always at least once removed from this corruption." This allows Shakespeare to push the conflict toward a comic resolution: "The distance imposed between the Duke and those who participate directly in the force of conflict in *Measure for Measure* allows Shakespeare to develop a comic design presided over by judicious authority, by Vincentio presented as a wise, strong, merciful leader."[37] For Wheeler, however, the Duke's apparent immunity to the conflict affecting the other characters creates an imbalance between the tragic and comic halves of the play. "With the completion of the comic design," Wheeler writes, "Vincentio's 'part' in Angelo is no longer part of himself, no longer corresponds to anything in Shakespeare's characterization of the Duke." The Duke is spared the violence that threatens the other characters. "Shakespeare," Wheeler says, "uses Angelo as a scapegoat who suffers in his person the consequences of a conflict Vincentio is thereby spared."[38]

Berger takes Wheeler's argument a step further. We should not be tempted to see the Duke as an idealized figure. That is the way the Duke prefers to see himself, but we should not be taken in by his self-flattery. "It makes a considerable difference," Berger writes, "whether we think of Vincentio as merely the observer of corruption or its enabler."[39] But why would the Duke want to encourage corruption? Because (Berger says) he is addicted to an idea of himself as "confessor and savior of the city's souls."[40]

Berger's picture of the Duke is indeed quite damning. The crucial piece of evidence Berger cites in favor of this picture is when the Duke reveals to Friar Thomas that he has deliberately let slip the strict statutes and most biting laws of the city. Why have things gotten so bad in Vienna? Because the Duke is addicted to handing out pardons! The trouble is that after fourteen years of pardoning, the effect is, unsurprisingly, wearing off. His subjects now take it for granted that they can get away with murder (quite literally, in the case of Barnardine). So what does the Duke do? He hands enforcement over to his strict and severe deputy. Angelo will remind the Duke's subjects of the real value of (the Duke's self-aggrandizing acts of) mercy. Once Angelo has restocked Vienna's prisons and strictly enforced the death penalty, the Duke will have a whole new slate of victims eager to confess, repent, and be pardoned. We can fully expect that after having had a taste of Angelo's severity, the Duke's chastened subjects will be ready to throw themselves before their prince and beg for mercy. The very thought of it produces paroxysms of delight in the Duke.

The advantage of Berger's perspective is that one is less inclined to see the play as a generic failure or problem. Neither fish nor fowl, the play starts out as a tragedy, then turns into a comedy. The result is a hopeless mishmash of conflicting genres. The difficulty with this view is that it attributes the ethical problem of the Duke's actions to external factors. Shakespeare was experimenting with genres and failed—or at least he didn't quite manage to pull it off. Berger insists that the notion that there is a conflict among competing genres misinterprets the problem, which is not external or generic but created by the Duke himself. To see this, however, we must first be clear that the Duke is not Shakespeare, or a proxy for Shakespeare. Once we admit this fact, we must read the Duke's speeches as we would read any other character's speeches. What motivates him to say what he does? What picture of himself is he trying to present to his interlocutors and to himself? What is he concealing from himself or the other characters? In short, we must understand him just as we would any of the other characters—that is, as an imperfect and fallible narrator of versions of himself and those around him.

Consider, for instance, the soliloquy we have just looked at. Rather than seeing it as a generic marker (the Duke steps forward to comment, chorus-like, on the play, thereby signaling the shift from tragedy to comedy), we should consider it at face value. Why does the Duke speak this way? Whom is he trying to convince? The most obvious answer is that he is trying to convince himself. More precisely, he is trying to convince himself that he is better than Angelo. Given how far Angelo has fallen, one might think that this is no great challenge. Clearly, on the evidence so far, no one is worse, morally speaking, than the hypocritical deputy. But precisely because Angelo has been caught red-handed, the Duke's speech comes off as pompous and self-aggrandizing, as though he were crowing about his moral superiority. If, as Berger argues, the Duke is addicted to pardoning, then his plan to replenish his client base and reform his subjects so they are, once again, ripe for pardoning is working better than he anticipated. Not only has Angelo restocked the prisons with freshly fallen souls, he has also implicated himself in the general moral corruption and therefore requires, like the many other fallen souls, the Duke's spiritual counsel and reform:

Twice treble shame on Angelo,
To weed my vice and let his grow! (3.2.262–63)

David Bevington, who is keen to see this speech as the Duke speaking "chorically on behalf of everyone," glosses "my vice" as "vice in everyone except Angelo."[41] But if we accept Berger's argument, we should read this speech not as the Duke speaking on behalf of others ("everyone") but as the Duke speaking on behalf of himself. In other words, when he says "my vice" he means, precisely, *his* vice, not the personified vice of an abstract Everyman.

Imagine if Angelo had successfully weeded out the Duke's vice (negligence, cowardice, vanity, pride) *without* letting his own vices grow. Imagine if he had succeeded in cleaning up the city, whose strict statutes and most biting laws the Duke had, for wholly self-indulgent reasons, let slip. Lurking in the back of the Duke's mind there must have been a certain amount of doubt and anxiety, perhaps even fear. Would his devious plan work? Would it deliver him the client base he was so eagerly hoping for? What if Angelo succeeded in reforming the citizens of Vienna *without* the Duke's interference? What if Angelo's severe enforcement of the law had the effect of cleaning up the moral and spiritual problems left in the wake of the Duke's lackluster performance as the city's judicial and penal authority? That would have been the Duke's worst nightmare. Not only would he be left with no lost souls to confess and forgive, but he would have been outshone by his own deputy. Imagine Vienna without moral corruption! What would there be left for him to do? Happily for the Duke, this embarrassing and humiliating situation does not come to pass. Instead, Angelo unwittingly offers up to him the perfect punchline to the highly moving and sentimental story of the return of our beloved prince. The Duke will show everyone why he is Vienna's best-loved and most-exalted leader. Vincentio the Merciful will vanquish his shameless and much-hated deputy. He couldn't have asked for a more perfect storyline.

Berger, whose view of the Duke I have been summarizing, is one among a growing number of recent critics who oppose the idea that the Duke is an admirable, benevolent leader who graciously models the uncompromising moral reciprocity of the Gospel message ("Judge not, lest ye be judged"). Bradshaw, another of the Duke's detractors, notes the peculiar fact that the Christian reading of the play, which reaches its zenith in Wilson Knight's 1930 essay *"Measure for Measure* and the Gospels" but can be traced back to A. W. Schlegel's 1808 *Lectures on Dramatic Art and Literature,* was somehow missed by "our two greatest Christian critics," Samuel Johnson and Samuel Taylor Coleridge, both of whom felt that the Duke was wrong to forgive Angelo.[42] Bradshaw argues that the oddly anti-Christian perspective of Johnson and Coleridge and the more conventional Christian perspective of Knight and others *both* miss the point, which is that "the final scene, the Duke's verdicts, and the Duke himself are all problematic *by design.*"[43]

Bradshaw's main point is that the play sets up and explores a series of dialectical relationships that cannot be reduced to one side of the dialectic. The Christian interpretation, epitomized in Knight's reading of the play, seeks to resolve the problem of social disorder by reducing it to a problem of the inner moral conscience. As long as one's conscience is sound, then the problem of social disorder disappears. Once Angelo understands the need for mercy, he is rehabilitated, and that is why the Duke lets him live. The same goes for Isabella. Once she falls to her knees and pleads for Angelo's life, she too discovers genuine mercy, and that is why she "wins" the Duke's hand in marriage, which may be understood symbolically as, in Knight's words, "the marriage of understanding with purity; of tolerance with moral fervor."[44] For Bradshaw, this optimistic reading ignores all those elements in the play that undermine the idea that justice can be reduced to the condition of one's inner moral conscience. Foremost among these is the problem of social disorder in Vienna, which the Duke explicitly highlights in his confession to Friar Thomas and which he says Angelo has been tasked with fixing precisely because he can be relied upon to enforce the city's "strict statutes and most biting laws" (1.3.19). As Bradshaw trenchantly puts it, these "problems of secular government and justice" that Angelo is obliged to address "are not to be routed, like a vampire, by a brandished cross."[45]

While both Berger and Bradshaw are highly critical of the Duke's moral authority, Berger is less interested in the dialectic between morality and ethics, or mercy and justice, and more interested in the Duke's self-representations. Berger, who calls the Duke "an intriguer, a practicer, a pious fraud," finds his character interesting precisely because he is so bad.[46] Like Iago, he deserves our special attention. And just as we read the soliloquies of Shakespeare's most notorious villain with a grain of salt, so too we must not be hoodwinked by the Duke's self-representations and self-justifications. Berger thus flips the picture of the noble and all-merciful Duke on its head. The Duke would like to be seen as noble and merciful, and that is certainly the way he represents himself both to others and to himself. But if we accept this picture, we have sorely missed the deeper irony that a close reading of his speeches and their immediate contexts cannot fail to demonstrate. "He works," Berger writes, "behind the back and from behind the arras—voyeuristically, duplicitously, furtively, even maliciously. . . . [H]is stage 'presence,' his style of self-representation, delivers a hilariously devious, irritable, energetic, histrionic, and bumptious protagonist who manages somehow to be simultaneously the life of the party and its killjoy."[47] It turns out the Duke is even more devious than Iago. And the proof is that almost nobody suspects him!

The question this raises is the same one that exercises critics faced with the task of explaining Iago's motivation. What motivates these two diabolical practical jokers?[48] In Iago's case, the joker's *resentment*, which is made transparently clear to us in soliloquy after soliloquy, seems totally disproportionate to the facts of the case. Pointing to the failed promotion, or the suspected adulteries of Iago's wife, merely begs the question. These are not facts. They are, rather, stories Iago tells himself, stories whose main function appears to be to justify or excuse or exacerbate resentment, both his own and that of his interlocutors (e.g., Roderigo's, Othello's). In other words, resentment preexists anything Iago says about why he is resentful. As the temptation scene makes vividly clear, Iago's function is to nurse resentment from its hiding place until it blossoms on the stage in the full violent ferocity of the play's final act.

Can we say something similar about the Duke? Can we read his speeches as narratives of attempted self-exculpation, stories he tells himself to feel better about himself? Berger believes that this is a plausible hypothesis, and he pursues it with all of his characteristic sharpness and ingenuity. The Duke is shy and terribly bad at his job. After fourteen (or perhaps as much as nineteen) years of incompetence, Vienna is in a bad state, and it's clear that something drastic must be done.[49] So the Duke fires himself and hands the job over to his protégé. The tough new deputy can be relied upon to enforce the laws. Of course, the Duke cannot say to Angelo that he is replacing an incompetent predecessor. (That would be slanderous!) But it's clear from what the Duke says to Friar Thomas that the predecessor was indeed incompetent and that Angelo, rather than the more senior Escalus, was selected precisely because he could be relied upon to do what the Duke failed to do, namely, uphold the law and punish offenders. This much is indisputable. But Berger adds a kicker. The Duke is *dishonest* as well as incompetent. This takes Bradshaw's argument a step further, and it is worth pausing to spell out the exact nature of the difference between their otherwise closely allied interpretations.

Bradshaw argues that the Duke's incompetence, evident in his confession in 1.3, is not a flaw in the play's design but one of its strengths. When in the final act the Duke attempts to resolve the fundamental anthropological tension between (universal) morality and (particular) ethics via a state-sponsored program of universal reconciliation and mercy, we are meant to understand this as an instance of exemplary Shakespearean irony. Shakespeare is criticizing, perhaps even mocking, the Duke's naiveté, not applauding it. If God's moral law (judge not, turn the other cheek, note the beam in your own eye first, etc.) takes absolute precedence over secular law, then justice can never be served. When the Duke triumphantly hands out pardons, he makes a mockery of the city's laws and the notion of secular justice. Bradshaw insists on the play's careful and systematic exploration of the dialectical tension between Christian morality and secular ethics, a tension he finds present in the play's multiple ironies:

> On the one hand, there is the highly coloured and implausibly contrived movement towards a "happy" closure, involving Italianate plot contrivances and moated grange lyricism; on the other hand, the "low-life" scenes become more seamily "realistic" in the scenes involving Lucio, Barnardine, Pompey and Abhorson, while the ironic parallels between *three* cases involving promises to marry expose the unprincipled, capricious and self-regarding nature of the Duke's legal and moral thinking. The ensuing ironies expose the arrogant naviety concealed within the commonplace Renaissance comparisons (such as we find in Sidney or Ben Jonson) which see the Poet as Prince or even a god, who creates a universe or commonwealth and dispenses ideal justice; put crudely, it is as if Shakespeare is reminding us that life is not like stories, and that only a moral idiot, or somebody who sees life through the spectacle of books, would expect a work of art to resolve the problems which are—as this work of art so disturbingly shows— wholly intractable.[50]

For Bradshaw, the point of the play is very much its irony, the lack of resolution, the intractability of reconciling mercy and justice. If we don't grasp this irony, then we have missed the play's major theme, which is to point up the tension between morality and ethics, mercy and justice, God's law and secular law, the (universal and monolithic) sacred center and the (multiple and competing desires of the) human periphery.

Berger very much agrees with Bradshaw's insistence on the play's ironies. One of those ironies is that the Duke is not the paragon of benevolent leadership he represents himself to be. But whereas Bradshaw claims that the Duke's incompetence in the practical task of secular governance is part of the play's overall design, one side of the dialectic between (naive, self-regarding) mercy and (coldhearted, cynical) justice, Berger argues, more insidiously and damningly, that the Duke is deliberately and maliciously—in a word, *dishonestly*—incompetent. Far from being naive or a "moral idiot," he is more dishonest and calculating than the archvillain Iago. The Duke maliciously colludes in the spread of iniquity. Why?

Because he takes great pleasure in wringing his hands over it. Here is how Berger puts it:

> But there is possibly a more troubling element in the bad faith of the project, which I mentioned above when I suggested that this voyeuristic temptation of Angelo may supply a kind of model, an intensified version, a continuation, of the passive-aggressive policy he had pursued the previous fourteen or nineteen years: countenancing—in effect licensing—the licentiousness he complains about; that is, countenancing it so that he can complain about it. The liberty he permits and his subjects abuse, the authority he bestows and Angelo abuses, give him an advantage similar to the one Portia gains and describes when she bestows the ring on Bassanio in *The Merchant of Venice*:
>
> > I give . . . this ring,
> > Which when you part from, lose, or give away,
> > Let it presage the ruin of your love,
> > And be my vantage to exclaim on you. (3.2.171–74)
>
> As an ethical strategy, the Duke's policy is also illuminated by the chilling words Brutus uses to depict the proper way for an assassin-to-be to approach his task: "[L]et our hearts, as subtle masters do, / Stir up their servants to an act of rage, / And after seem to chide 'em."[51]

The Duke is like Iago but worse. At least Iago is honest about his resentment in his soliloquies. The Duke, on the other hand, deliberately conceals his resentment behind a veil of hypocritical piety and smug moralizing.[52] He tempts his victims into the center so he may bring them down by the sheer force of his superior moral conscience, his virtuousness. For Berger, the Duke's humble friar act is brazenly and stunningly fraudulent. Angelo is the clearest victim of the Duke's diabolical strategy. The promotion seems like an honor, but in reality it provides the occasion for the Duke's revenge on both his deputy and his unruly and licentious subjects. He watches the deputy fall, exposes him publicly, sentences him to death, and pardons him. A similar narrative of humiliation and shame applies to Isabella. He watches her fall, dangles the bed trick as a way out, lies about her brother's death, gets her to humiliate herself publicly as a fornicatress, condemns her to prison, produces her unbeheaded brother, then proposes to her.

Escalus describes the Duke as "[o]ne that, above all other strifes, contended especially to know himself" (3.2.227–28). If we accept Berger's argument, we must finish Escalus's thought by adding, "but he failed miserably." The Duke's self-representations are shot through with evasion, self-pity, self-exculpation, and self-deception.[53] Angelo's soliloquies, in comparison, are refreshingly (and painfully) honest. Whether this is because the Duke is too narrowly focused on the mote in Angelo's eye to notice the beam in his own is a question worth asking. Berger picks up on Wheeler's argument that the forced comic resolution pushes the Duke implausibly above the fray, leaving Angelo to bear full responsibility for the crisis. "Shakespeare," Wheeler says, "uses Angelo as a scapegoat who suffers in his person the consequences of a conflict Vincentio is thereby spared."[54] Berger assents to the spirit of this claim but insists that a further substitution is necessary to avoid displacing the Duke from the play (where he belongs) to some blissfully conflict-free zone outside it (e.g., Shakespeare, God, Jesus, personified Mercy, Kant's categorical imperative, Rawls's original position, etc.). As far as Berger is concerned, Angelo suffers not because Shakespeare uses him as a scapegoat but because the Duke does.

I agree with Berger that an ethical evaluation of the Duke is best served by sticking to what he says (and does) and what other characters say about him (and do in response to him). We must avoid displacing the ethical problem of what motivates the Duke by redescribing it in terms of a nonethical but more easily graspable problem, such as the play's relation to its source-texts,[55] or its use of generic archetypes,[56] or a performance problem,[57] or a Darwinian sociobiological imperative.[58] Berger's approach can be summarized by a series of questions. How does the Duke represent himself with respect to the central dramatic conflict? Does he see himself as doing harm or good? This way of putting it may make it seem that the dramatic world can be easily divided between good and bad characters (Angelo = bad; the Duke = good). But though the internal characters certainly conspire in presenting themselves as either good or bad, the ethical facts are usually more complex, especially in Shakespeare. As Berger's close readings of Shakespeare's plays demonstrate, even seemingly good or admirable characters frequently trade on self-exculpating narratives of victimhood in which they project their violence onto others. Berger takes Lear's line "I am more sinned against than sinning" as paradigmatic of the self-exculpating narrative. By projecting his faults onto others (not just Cordelia but Goneril and Regan too), Lear labors strenuously (if not always successfully) to avoid unpleasant emotions such as shame and guilt.[59]

This shift in perspective has the advantage of humanizing the Duke (warts and all). It also nicely fits with Goldie's distinction between internal and external narrative perspectives. There is no such thing as a perspectiveless or characterless narrative. If the Duke has a story to tell, it is by definition from *his* perspective, not Shakespeare's or God's. If something strikes us as contradictory or obfuscating in his narrative, the most useful hypothesis to pursue is not that Shakespeare lost his concentration or mishandled his genres (one can always pull that rabbit out of the hat) but that the Duke has a reason, whether he is fully aware of it or not, for being contradictory or obfuscating or dishonest. As we have already had occasion to see in our analysis of Isabella's seduction of Angelo, human actions rarely follow clean, smooth, well-lit, logical paths. Instead, they tend to veer off suddenly and unpredictably. It is only afterward that we round off the sharp edges (so to speak) by explaining or excusing or otherwise rationalizing why we did what we did. Why did Claudio have sex with Juliet? Why does Elbow have sex with Mrs. Elbow? Why does Froth drink in a brothel where sex is available all the time? Why did Angelo not have sex with Mariana but then want to have sex with Isabella? Why does Lucio want to have sex whenever he can? Why does the Duke vociferously deny that he has any sexual appetite but then propose marriage to a beautiful young woman who doesn't want to have sex with anyone? This last question is particularly suggestive given that the Duke shadows his protégé extremely closely. His penchant for voyeurism and spying is, frankly, creepy. It becomes positively obscene when we factor in his lively interest in other people's sex lives. He is the peephole Duke—or, as Lucio puts it, "the old fantastical Duke of dark corners" (4.3.156–57). The claim that the Duke is given to eccentric and thoroughly un-duke-like behavior is not in itself original. Most of the critics cited above offer their own explanations for the Duke's underhanded tactics, not all of them convincing.[60] I propose a different explanation. If we don't accept the optimistic (Christian) view that the Duke has figured out how to create heaven on earth, how to get his subjects to turn their cheeks and pluck out the beams in their eyes, there must be other reasons for his peephole tactics. No doubt these reasons will be less edifying than the kind of gnomic formulations of the moral law found in the Gospels. Yet they will also be more interesting precisely because they are not represented as imperative moral commands ("Judge not," "Note the beam in your own eye," "Turn the other cheek," "Love thy neighbor," etc.) but as *dramatic scenes* in which we identify with, and are simultaneously alienated from, the internal character's resentful and shameful desires.

Razing the Sanctuary

It is a curious fact that there is only one unattached young woman in the play (Isabella). Stage productions usually add a few prostitutes, which makes sense given that the play makes liberal reference to bawdy houses and whores, such as the unmarried Kate Keepdown whose child Lucio has fathered. But other than prostitutes like Kate, the only unambiguously single and available woman is Isabella. The two other unmarried young women are both betrothed—Juliet to Claudio, and Mariana to Angelo. Angelo, of course, has called off his engagement to Mariana, but she appears to consider the betrothal still very much a live fact, as does the Duke when he assures her that the bed trick is 100 percent kosher. Meanwhile, Francisca the nun is attached to God, Overdone is married to her ninth husband, and Mrs. Elbow is pregnant and has a craving for stewed prunes. This means that the only truly eligible woman in the play is Isabella, but of course she is determined to make herself ineligible by following Francisca's example and becoming a full-time nun and a bride of God.

Now consider another curious set of facts. Isabella is hauled, in the nick of time, from her planned initiation into a life of celibacy and made the object of an illegal sexual conspiracy by no less than four different men. On each occasion, Isabella is unchaperoned, and her chastity is put under severe strain. First, Lucio recalls her from the nunnery to plead for Claudio; his intervention is necessary to coax Isabella's sex appeal out into the open. The sensual language he uses to describe Juliet's pregnant condition—"[A]s blossoming time . . . the bare fallow brings / To teaming foison, even so the plenteous womb / Expresseth his full tilth and husbandry" (1.4.41–44)—seems purposely designed to embarrass or provoke Isabella into doubting her wish to become a nun. The next assault on her virginity is Angelo's indecent and brazen proposal. There follows the unhappy exchange with her brother in which Claudio suggests she accept Angelo's filthy bargain. Technically, she is not alone with her brother, as the Duke is spying on them, but as far as brother and sister are concerned, they are alone. By this stage, it is clear that Isabella is fighting a losing battle to protect her virginity. Events seem to be conspiring to overthrow her aspiration to become a nun and devote herself exclusively to spiritual matters. The man at the center of this assault on her chastity is the much-hated Angelo, but it is in fact the fourth man in this series who attacks her chastity the most persistently and devastatingly. I am referring, of course, to the Duke. After overhearing how Angelo has proposed to trade his power to pardon Claudio for her sex, the Duke swoops in to place himself between Angelo's desire and Isabella. But instead of protecting her chastity, he conspires to destroy it. His dodgy bed trick involves a substitution of Mariana's body for Isabella's, which leaves Isabella sexually available for the Duke. He will prevent Angelo from razing Isabella's sanctuary, but only by razing it himself. One might object that this is too horribly sordid and filthy for a man who professes to be a regular do-gooder. But if Angelo can dream up this kind of filthy bargain, why can't the Duke? Why should we trust the purity of the Duke's thoughts any more than we trust the purity of Angelo's? After all, we have just seen the most passionless man in Vienna succumb to heated sexual passion. Isn't it possible that "the dribbling dart of love" (1.3.2) might unseat the Duke too?

Angelo remarks that what tempts him is precisely Isabella's unsullied purity. He looks down on the common whores of Vienna's red-light district, but the beautiful and chaste novitiate has an unusual power over him. His fishing metaphor—"Oh, cunning enemy that, to catch a saint, / With saints dost bait thy hook!" (2.2.187–88)—suggests that he feels threatened by Isabella's saintliness. She is too much like himself, and he therefore treats her as a rival whom he must either coerce or destroy. By razing her saintliness, he ensures his own reputation for spotless virtue remains unrivaled.[61]

René Girard sees in Angelo's words the ugly specter of mimetic rivalry, which certainly makes a great deal of sense.[62] Like doth quit like, and measure still for measure. The self feels threatened by the other when the other is too much like the self. But given that our desires are, as Girard says, learned by imitating others (rather than spontaneously welling up from within, which merely confuses human desire with biological appetite), it follows that the self inevitably comes into conflict with others whose desires the self imitates. It is significant, I think, that both Isabella and Angelo are understudies in their respective vocations or disciplines. Angelo is a student of the law; Isabella, a novice nun. Both are also extremely ambitious and competitive. Angelo has spent most of his young life buried in law books. He wants to be the top judge in the realm, and it appears he has fulfilled his ambition when the Duke makes him, rather than Escalus, his substitute. But now he is unnerved by this other young student, who seems even more devoted to *her* cause. Her interpretation of the law is unschooled and idiosyncratic, but he can't deny that her perspective makes a certain amount of sense. This must be enormously upsetting. How can he, a learned student of the law, be so easily defeated by a novice nun who knows nothing about legal matters? No wonder he wants to do dirt on her, raze her to the ground, destroy her scolding sanctity. Angelo's sexual passion is motivated by a healthy dose of highly unerotic resentment.

Angelo is confused about his feelings. He thinks he may be in love, but plainly that is not the case. He wonders if it is lust, but, though certainly closer to the mark, it still doesn't capture Angelo's true feelings. If he were experiencing overwhelming lust, he would want to have sex with her in his office and be done with it. But instead, he delays and plans meticulously. The most plausible explanation is that Angelo is motivated by resentment. He resents her saintliness. More precisely, he wants to raze the sanctuary because she is a threat to his identity. It is not just her beauty that threatens him; it is, even more, her zealous attachment to her beliefs. She is too much like him. Indeed, she is much better than him because she seems to be more sincere, more authentic, more passionate, more devoted to her cause. She is clearly more virtuous, and she may even understand the law better because she refuses to be distracted by legal niceties.[63] While Angelo parses the if-then clauses of the legal fine print, she goes straight to the human heart of the matter: "What gives you the moral right to chop off my brother's head?" It is a question Angelo tries to sidestep, but in the end, he can't. Hence the anguished soliloquies and his enormous guilt.

At least he experiences guilt. The same cannot be said for the Duke, whose attempt to seduce Isabella is even creepier than the resentful actions of his deputy. It is almost as if Shakespeare gives us, in descending order of moral suitability, a lineup of disreputable romantic partners for the play's only eligible woman. Lucio is a scoundrel and a womanizer, but at least women know what they are getting. Even Isabella, who is mightily inexperienced in erotic banter and foreplay, is not fooled by Lucio's winning phrases and sexual flattery. Angelo is more dangerous because he is more resentful. He uses his power to coerce Isabella into sexual degradation. He fails, of course, but not because of the Duke's timely intervention. Isabella does not need the Duke to rebuff Angelo's clumsy and ham-fisted advances. Readers, playgoers, and critics have been fooled into believing that the Duke's intervention in the third act makes him a suitable romantic partner. But if the Duke truly had Isabella's best interests in mind, he would never have coerced her into, first, conspiring in the bed trick and, second, humiliating her by getting her to claim, in public, that she fornicated with Angelo.

These considerations help to explain why Shakespeare highlights Isabella's vulnerability once she leaves the sanctuary of the convent. Most readers see the irony of Isabella desiring a "more strict restraint" (1.4.4) in a city that, thanks to the Duke's deliberate promotion of "too much liberty" (1.2.125), is more famous for its brothels and nightlife than its convents. But I think equally significant are the details of how votaries may interact with men:

> LUCIO (*within*)
>   Ho! Peace be in this place!
>
> ISABELLA
>   Who's that which calls?
>
> FRANCISCA
>   It is a man's voice. Gentle Isabella,
>   Turn you the key, and know his business of him.
>   You may, I may not; you are yet unsworn.
>   When you have vowed, you must not speak with men
>   But in the presence of the prioress;
>   Then if you speak you must not show your face,
>   Or if you show your face you must not speak.
>   He calls again. I pray you, answer him. (1.4.6–14)

Most editors indicate that Francisca exits after she has explained to Isabella that her vows prevent her from answering the door. J. W. Lever, however, argues that "Francisca the nun surely does not leave the novice Isabella alone with Lucio."[64] He suggests that she stands discreetly to one side instead.

There is no clear evidence to suggest whether she exits the stage or merely stands silently to one side. The rules of her order state that she may not speak to men unless she is chaperoned by the Mother Superior; but there is no rule saying she cannot be in the presence of men. (That would be an awkward rule—even nuns occasionally need to step outside to do the shopping.) In any case, the point is not really whether or not Francisca is present but that Isabella is on the threshold of being declared off-limits to men. Personally, I am in favor of Lever's suggestion that Francisca remains to keep a watchful eye on Lucio, whom we know to be a notorious womanizer. Once Isabella steps outside the convent, she becomes vulnerable to male attention, and this is indicated by the fact that in her first interview with Angelo it is Lucio who keeps a watchful eye on her, not a member of the order of Saint Clare, let alone the Mother Superior. But we must also remember that Angelo has explicitly invited the Provost to stay for the interview, and I think this is partly motivated by Angelo's sense of proper decorum. Angelo does not want to be alone with this young woman, whom he immediately sees is also highly attractive, and he doesn't trust Lucio, whose appearance smacks too much of the dissolute libertine.

In their second meeting, Isabella *is* unchaperoned. If we accept Lever's argument, it is also the first occasion in which she is alone on stage with a man. In the first meeting, Angelo has been merely irritated by her intrusion. The second time, he greets her with pleasure: "How now, fair maid?" (2.4.30). Calling her "fair" is a big step for Angelo. Lucio has already called her "[g]entle and fair" (1.4.24) as well as "enskied and sainted" (1.4.34). And soon the Duke will be repeating the word in his mealy-mouthed riffing on the dangers of being fair: "The goodness that is cheap in beauty makes beauty brief in goodness; but grace, being the soul of your complexion, shall keep the body of it ever fair" (3.1.183–85). He's trying to pay her a compliment. Evasion is a specialty of the Duke's, however, so one is not quite sure. Angelo, after some evasion of his own, manages to get directly to the point:

> I have begun,
> And now I give my sensual appetite the rein.
> Fit thy consent to my sharp appetite;
> Lay by all nicety and prolixious blushes
> That banish what they sue for. Redeem thy brother
> By yielding up thy body to my will,
> Or else he must not only die the death,
> But thy unkindness shall his death draw out
> To ling'ring sufferance. (2.4.160–68)

Angelo thinks he has been undone by Satan, the cunning enemy, but we know better. He has been undone by the Duke, whose plan has always been to do dirt on the spotless Angelo: "Hence shall we see, / If power change purpose, what our seemers be" (1.3.53–54). He has promoted Angelo because he wants to see him fall. What Angelo wants to do to Isabella—raze the sanctuary—the Duke does to Angelo *and* Isabella. In Vienna, it seems there is more than enough resentment to go around, and the Duke leads the way. Having created waste ground enough, he resents those few remaining spots of virtue. They are an affront to his moral and political authority and must be dragged through the dirt until their light is extinguished too.

I stated earlier that Lucio, Angelo, and the Duke form, in descending order of moral fitness, a line of highly suspect romantic partners for Isabella. The Duke is the least fit of all because he hides his illicit desires behind a façade of do-good self-righteousness. After discovering, to his great titillation and satisfaction, that his virtuous deputy wants to do dirt on Isabella, he pulls her aside and encourages her to conspire in her own sexual entrapment because of the great "love [he has] in doing good" (3.1.200). So much for grace keeping the body ever fair. Instead of protecting Isabella by sending her straight back to the convent, he uses her as bait. The cunning enemy is not Satan, it is the Duke. And the most cunning part about the Duke is that he deceives almost everybody, himself included. The only man who is not deceived is Lucio, who turns out to be the most honorable member of this disreputable threesome competing for the young lady's attentions. At least Lucio, for all his airy sexual puffery, is motivated by a sincere desire to save his friend Claudio.

Why does the Duke intervene when he does? The obvious answer is that he has just discovered an intolerable miscarriage of justice and therefore has no option but to intervene immediately. But if that is the case, why does he insist on remaining disguised as a friar? Here the answer is less obvious. If we say that he is interested in mending people's souls and the only way for him to do that is to remain disguised as a friar, then we minimize the seriousness of the crisis.[65] Angelo's resentment, if allowed to continue unchecked, will deliver not justice but death. It should by now be pretty obvious that Angelo is unfit for office. The Duke had already darkly hinted to Friar Thomas the likelihood of this outcome. Why then did the Duke promote Angelo?[66] It is not merely a case of the police officer handing out speeding tickets while he, concealed behind his badge and uniform, speeds with impunity. Angelo is not some petty police officer. He has the power to sentence people to death. Nor is it simply a case of Angelo being a fornicator. Claudio's crime was to have consensual sex with his fiancée. Angelo wants to *coerce* Isabella into having sex with him. Anyone who uses the word *fornication* to describe both cases is, like poor Elbow, simply abusing the English language. But a man who uses the word not only in this very imprecise and loose sense but also as a legal pretext to indiscriminately condemn all fornicators to death is either certifiably insane or a sociopath. Either way the conclusion is inescapable: Angelo must be removed from office immediately. So, yes, there is a serious moral problem with the deputy (he's a sociopath), but it might be advisable to remove him from office before worrying about the condition of his inner soul.

The Duke's response to the looming crisis is, to put it mildly, measured. He answers measure for measure a bit too precisely, as though he were fascinated by Angelo's aberrant behavior and wanted to observe it more closely, understand it more fully, perhaps even emulate it himself. In short, his response is to mirror or imitate Angelo's sexual fantasy. Rather than remove Angelo from office, he encourages the sadly misguided deputy to follow through on his plan to have coercive sex with Isabella. The peephole Duke is titillated by Angelo's sexual deviance and wants see his subject act out his resentful fantasy. Angelo must believe he is having sex with a young and beautiful novice nun. He must believe he has spoiled and polluted God's virginal bride. Talk about razing the sanctuary! The good friar aims his resentment squarely at God himself. If Angelo allows Iniquity to breach the walls of Justice, the Duke invites the cunning enemy into God's inner sanctum. There is, to quote *Julius Caesar*'s Brutus again, no "cavern dark enough" to hide the "monstrous visage" of "conspiracy."[67] It has penetrated not only the bright halls of justice but the inner sanctum of the individual conscience. Where's that palace whereinto foul things sometimes intrude not? There is no breast so pure but some uncleanly apprehensions keep leets and law days and sit with meditations lawful.

Why does the Duke dismiss the Provost when he interviews Isabella? In itself, the good friar's desire to speak privately with one of his erring clients is unremarkable. He is, after all, a professional confessor of souls (except that he isn't).[68] What *is* remarkable is the fact that the private interview reproduces the same asymmetries of power so evident in Isabella's second interview with Angelo. Unchaperoned by Lucio or the Provost, Isabella was, in that interview, vulnerable to Angelo's assault on her chastity. He had taken full advantage of his power by leaving her with a painful ultimatum:

"If you don't have sex with me, your brother dies a long and painful death." It is all she can do to confess the truth to her brother, who (unsurprisingly) fails to give her the comfort and reassurance she longs for because he is too preoccupied with the image of his head being separated violently from his body. At this point, the Duke intervenes, but instead of providing relief for the brother and comfort to the sister, which he could easily do as Vienna's imperial authority, he interviews each of them separately.

Detectives always divide suspected perpetrators before interviewing them. If the suspects can't keep their stories straight, then something fishy is going on. The Duke does the opposite. He divides brother and sister so he can deliberately mislead them with different versions of the "facts." He tells Claudio that Angelo was only testing Isabella's virtue; there will be no stay of his execution, and he must prepare himself for death (again!). When Angelo described his feelings as a "desire to raze the sanctuary" (2.2.178), he used the image of a razed church to picture his resentment of Isabella. The Duke doesn't need to use a metaphor. He literally pollutes the sanctuary.[69] By impersonating a friar, he inveigles his way into his subjects' private lives so he can throw dirt on them. The resentment of this extraordinary act is cleverly disguised by the Duke as a "love . . . in doing good," but as recent commentators have noticed, when you look reasonably closely at what the Duke actually does, the goodness seems to be nothing more than cheap moralizing. To adapt the Duke's own riddling words to Isabella, "The goodness that is cheap in piety makes piety brief in goodness." Scratch the surface and the Duke's pious façade crumbles to dust. The friar is a lecherous Peeping Tom. When Isabella, frantic to protect her virginity, disowns her brother and screams, "Mercy to thee would prove itself a bawd" (3.1.152), she exaggerates. But it is no exaggeration to say that the Duke proves himself a bawd by dangling Isabella in front of Angelo only to swap her with Mariana at the last minute. And he does it in the name of pious mercy and doing good! One wonders what the Mother Superior would have thought if she were present at Isabella's interview with the Duke.

We are now getting a clearer picture of the Duke as Angelo's sinister doppelgänger, a devious imitator of Angelo's desire, a rival for Isabella's sex, and a fellow competitor for the center. The older and more experienced man has pushed his protégé into the center with the aim of watching him flounder. The plan is working perfectly, and it is time to reel in the prize. Unfortunately for the Duke, one man seems to be on to him.

Why is the Duke's private interview with Isabella immediately followed by the shenanigans involving Elbow, Pompey, and Lucio? Because it shows that there is little difference between Pompey's pimping and the Duke's conspiracy to entrap Angelo. Though evasive about his own involvement in the sex trade, Pompey is refreshingly candid about the relationship between pimping and the law. Earlier, Escalus had asked Pompey if he thought pimping to be a "lawful trade" (2.1.225). Pompey had replied, "If the law would allow it, sir" (2.1.226). He went on to compare the outlawing of the sex trade to state-enforced celibacy, which he characterized as a genocidal assault on the city's youth and their unborn children: "Does Your Worship mean to geld and splay all the youth of the city?" (2.1.229–30). Unlike Pompey, the Duke cannot afford to be so candid about his interest in the sex lives of his subjects. Why else would he furiously attempt to ward off Pompey's presence—"Fie, sirrah, a bawd, a wicked bawd!" (3.2.20)—if he did not feel that he was himself guilty of being a "wicked bawd"? When the Duke asks Elbow to explain Pompey's "offense" (3.2.14), Elbow describes Pompey as a thief, not a bawd. So why does the Duke chastise Pompey for being a bawd? Either he already knows Pompey is a bawd, or he guesses Pompey is a bawd, or he is so focused on not being accused of being a bawd that he accuses someone else instead. I think the last hypothesis is the most plausible. Perhaps faint pangs of guilt also encourage him to imagine that Pompey is a bawd. Elbow says they have found a "picklock" (3.2.18) on Pompey, and this image may suggest to the Duke not thievery but the sexual symbolism of a key (penis) inserted into a keyhole (vagina). Later, Isabella will show the Duke the keys she has to unlock the two doors that enclose the dark and secret place in which Angelo is to steal her virginity. The fact that Isabella holds the keys is significant. She has, on the Duke's advice, taken over Pompey's function and become a procurer of sex for other people. This danger was signaled in her first stage appearance when Francisca described the reasons she couldn't open the door to Lucio. "Turn you the key" (1.4.8), she had said to Isabella, as if to say, "I can't put myself in danger, but you can." But by turning the key and letting Lucio in, she was also letting herself out. Removed from her sanctuary, Isabella becomes vulnerable to, in her own phrase, "abhorred pollution" (2.4.184). The Duke does nothing to protect her chastity. On the contrary, he conspires in polluting it, first symbolically when he enlists her in the conspiracy against Angelo that requires her to admit publicly to fornication, then not so symbolically when he proposes to her.

Meanwhile, Lucio's presence in this scene reinforces the point that the Duke is Angelo's doppelgänger. We saw how Lucio's function in the seduction scene was akin to Iago's function vis-à-vis Othello. His presence was necessary to show that Angelo is being seduced by "filthy vices" (2.4.42) he never knew he possessed. The desire is "filthy" because it remains hidden and unconscious, repressed. The only way Angelo knows how to deal with it is in private and behind closed doors. He must conceal it from others, which is why he is so resentful of Isabella's virtue. "How can she be so pure when I am so polluted?"

At least Angelo knows enough about himself that he can ask this question. The Duke knows less about himself than Angelo, who is a much brighter student of desire. Hence Lucio's nagging presence beside the Duke throughout the second half of the play. The Duke would like to think of himself as the good conscience of his subjects, and most especially the good conscience of Angelo. But Angelo's conscience is not where the chief problem lies. His conscience is fully functional. We witness it pumping frequent doses of guilt into the anxious deputy's mind. The problem is that Angelo ignores it. Nothing the Duke does changes Angelo's conscience. Once his crime is discovered, Angelo wants to be executed. Death will be a release from all the guilt he experiences. Like Macbeth, Angelo feels guilty from the beginning, even before he commits the foul act. He knows it is wrong, yet he does it anyway.

The Duke, on the other hand, does not appear to know he has a problem. He razes the sanctuary while telling himself that he loves doing good. He is the classic case of the exculpating self-deceiver, which is why Lucio stubbornly sticks to him like a "burr" (4.3.177). The Duke would have Pompey out of his sight, and Elbow duly marches him off to his cell. But Lucio cannot be removed so easily. Lucio accuses the Duke of being a womanizer who "had some feeling of the sport" (3.2.116), as well as being a "drunk" (3.2.124), "shy" (3.2.127), "superficial, ignorant, unweighing fellow" (3.2.136). Most readers take the Duke's side and sympathize with his indignant feeling that he is the unfair target of Lucio's "envy" (3.1.137), "malice" (3.1.144), and "slanderous tongue" (3.1.182). I am not so sure. Certainly, if we assume that Lucio's main function in the play is to do dirt on the Duke, then we will be inclined to say that his words are slanderous. But Shakespeare is much more subtle in the way he uses his minor characters to reflect faults *within* the major characters. We have already seen how Lucio reflects the emergence of an unknown passion within Angelo. Once Angelo becomes aware of this passion, Lucio disappears from Angelo's office and never pesters him again. He is no longer necessary to represent what Angelo doesn't know about himself for the simple reason that Angelo acknowledges—to himself, if not to others—that he is a hypocritical fraud.

In the second half of the play, Lucio switches his attention exclusively to the Duke. Just as he did with Angelo, his presence indicates foul desire *within*. The difference is that the Duke never admits that he has foul desires. Instead, he repeatedly insists on his honorable "bringings-forth" as a true "scholar, statesman, and soldier" (3.2.141–42). When Lucio says he "was an inward of his" (3.2.127), I think we are meant to interpret this literally. Lucio represents a part of the Duke himself. That is why Lucio says his "secret" is "locked within the teeth and lips" (3.2.131–32). He knows the Duke's inwardness not because he is an intimate friend of the Duke's (he isn't), but because he personifies a secret and hidden part of the Duke. "I know what I know" (3.2.148), Lucio says, unmoved by the Duke's fervent denials. He knows what he knows because he embodies an aspect of the Duke that the Duke stubbornly and repeatedly denies.

The Duke desperately tries to expel Lucio. He tries every exculpatory trick in the book. He accuses Lucio of slander, envy, and calumny and, in the final scene, sentences him to whipping and hanging. But the exculpation doesn't work. Lucio simply pops back up again like an indestructible cartoon character. As long as the Duke accuses Lucio of slander and envy, he will never rid himself of Lucio, who will continue to stick to him obstinately like a burr. The first step to ridding himself of Lucio is to acknowledge that he possesses all those qualities he finds so abhorrent in Lucio, including desire (for prestige, recognition, women) and resentment (when that desire is thwarted). Lucio's slander of the Duke is a reflection of the Duke's unhealthy delight in snooping into the private lives of his subjects. He spies on his subjects so he can do dirt on them. He encourages their iniquity so he can wring his merciful hands and, in Brutus's icily cynical words, "after seem to chide 'em" so as to appear "not envious" (*Julius Caesar*, 2.1.178–79). The Duke is, in short, the chief conspirator when it comes to spreading resentment in Vienna.

Why does Lucio lie about Friar Lodowick in the play's final scene? Why does he insist, after slandering the Duke in front of the friar, that it was not him but the friar who slandered the Duke? The scene is certainly very funny. Lucio appears to be digging himself into a deep hole because he doesn't know that the friar he accuses of slander *is* the Duke. It is no longer his word against the friar's but his word against the Duke's, and he is highly unlikely to win that contest. But there is more going on here than an amusing gag. Significantly, it is Lucio who unhoods the friar:

LUCIO
> Come, sir, come, sir, come, sir; foh, sir! Why, you bald-pated, lying rascal, you must be hooded, must you? Show your knave's visage, with a pox to you! Show your sheep-biting face, and be hanged an hour! Will't not off?
>
> *[He pulls off the friar's hood, and discovers the Duke. Angelo and Escalus rise.]*

DUKE
> Thou art the first knave that e'er mad'st a duke. (5.1.359–64)

Lucio accuses the friar of using his hood as a screen behind which he can spread malicious lies. Just as the Duke aims to expose Angelo, so Lucio aims to expose the friar. It turns out that the friar *is* a fraud. The friar is not really a friar, but rather the Duke masquerading as a friar. Oddly, in the final moments of the scene when everybody is on stage (except for Lucio, who has been carted off to prison), nobody appears to be unduly concerned about the fact that they have been deceived. The Duke has not only fraudulently confessed Isabella, Mariana, and Julietta; he has also fraudulently prepared Claudio and Barnardine for death. Furthermore, he has lied, quite deliberately, to everyone, none more painfully than Isabella. How do we explain this peculiar fact? Are we to understand the deafening silences of Isabella, Angelo, Claudio, and Juliet as signs of stifled protest? Or are we rather to understand that the Duke is, in Angelo's phrase, a "power divine" (5.1.377) who overawes his subjects like God? The last possibility seems the least plausible. Certainly Lucio is not overawed. On the contrary, he remains conspicuously vociferous to the end. Nor does it seem satisfactory to appeal to Shakespeare's carefree or clumsy use of the conventions of romantic comedy. If the conclusion strikes us as forced or unsatisfying, then the least plausible hypothesis is that Shakespeare, rather than an inattentive reader, is to be blamed for incompetence.

When the Duke removes himself from the center to lurk in the dark corners of the anonymous periphery, he gives himself the freedom to participate in the periphery's resentment of the center, in what Brutus calls "monstrous conspiracy." It is important to recall that the change in Vienna's leadership is not precipitated by a genuine crisis in political authority. The Duke refers vaguely to the laxity of his rulership, but Vienna has not been invaded by hostile forces, nor has there been a coup or insurrection from within. On the contrary, the Duke abdicates for purely self-interested reasons. His fragile ego makes him extremely sensitive to criticism and, after years of benign neglect of the city's strict laws out of a misplaced desire to be well liked, the Duke realizes that his policy of permissiveness has been an abject failure. Keen to avoid becoming the target of public slander and resentment, the Duke imposes his office on Angelo. When Lucio, in the play's final act, accuses Friar Lodowick of slander, he acknowledges the fact that the periphery is the locus of personal freedom, including the freedom to slander the center. Because the center appears to thwart human desire, it also appears to deserve the resentment leveled at it. But the power to defer the multiple conflicting desires of the periphery is a product not of the sacred center but of the aesthetic imaginations of the peripheral human actors, who cannot all simultaneously possess the center. The center is represented internally within the scenic imaginations of the individuals situated on the desiring periphery.[70] The center would not exist without the collective attentions of the periphery, the "[m]illions of false eyes" (4.1.59) that are "stuck upon" (4.1.60) the central figure making him "the father of their idle dream" (4.1.63). The Duke's forlorn lament on "back-wounding calumny" (3.2.180) and "the slanderous tongue" (3.2.182) captures not only his (former) discomfort as an occupant of the center but also his (current) satisfaction at being able to participate freely in the resentment aimed at his substitute. When Lucio slanders the old Duke in front of Friar Lodowick, he unwittingly reminds the Duke of his complicity in exacerbating rather than deferring resentment.

In short, the Duke wants to have his cake and eat it too. He wants to enjoy the center's prestige and "divine power," but without suffering any of its human costs. Hence his cunning scheme of appointing Angelo to absorb the resentment that has built up during the past fourteen years or more of his deliberate misrule. The plan appears to work. All are so focused on the fraudulent judge that they forget the fraudulent friar—all except Lucio, that is. When Lucio reminds the Duke that it was he who had exposed him— "Your Highness said even now I made you a duke" (5.1.526–27)—the Duke agrees to remit two of Lucio's three punishments. He will not be whipped and hanged, but he must marry Kate Keepdown. When Lucio, unable to resist a joke says, "Marrying a punk, my lord, is pressing to death, whipping, and hanging" (5.1.533–34), the Duke replies, "Slandering a prince deserves it" (5.1.535). The message is clear. What irritates the Duke most is the fact that he has been slandered. Lucio explains he "spoke but according to the trick" (5.1.515–16). *Trick* is usually glossed as *fashion* or *custom*. Lucio spoke merely as was his custom, habit, or wont; the Duke should not take undue offense. But one can't help also hearing the word's primary meaning, "a crafty or fraudulent device of a mean or base kind" (*Oxford English Dictionary*). Lucio is not the only person to engage in crafty tricks. On the contrary, the Duke is the self-professed master when it comes to the application of "[c]raft against vice" (3.2.270). All of his crafty tricks have been leading up to this climactic scene. He will first chastise his naughty subjects, then magnanimously forgive them. The more despairing and desperate the situation, the more spectacular does his act of mercy become. The crafty peephole Duke of dark corners connives in creating as much conflict as he possibly can, saving his final self-centralizing, self-aggrandizing coup de grâce until the very last moment.

Mad Fantastical Tricks

The ace up the Duke's sleeve is that Claudio is not dead. Only he and the Provost know this fact, and it is imperative that they guard the secret closely if the Duke is to get the maximum effect out of his show trial of Angelo and Isabella, the two unwitting protagonists of what he intends to be a gripping matinée performance. The Duke has meticulously arranged everything down to the tiniest detail. First, he throws up a smokescreen to unbalance Angelo and Escalus, sending deliberately confusing letters that are clear on one essential point: they are to meet him at the city gates where any disaffected subjects craving "redress of injustice ... should exhibit their petitions in the street" (4.4.9–10). Then he gives instructions to Friar Peter to coach Isabella and Mariana about where they are to stand and what they are to say when the Duke enters the city. Earlier, he had directly informed Isabella that, if she follows Friar Peter's advice to the letter, she will have "revenges to [her] heart" (4.3.135).

The big day arrives and the good folk of Vienna line the streets to witness the return of their lost prince. Isabella does as she is told. She throws herself on her knees and begs the returned Duke for "justice, justice, justice, justice!" (5.1.26). She accuses Angelo of being "forsworn," "a murderer," "an adulterous thief," a "hypocrite," and "a virgin-violator" (5.1.40–43). She confesses to giving her "chaste body / To his concupiscible intemperate lust" (5.1.102–3) only to be double-crossed by Angelo, who forswore his oath and executed her brother the next day. The Duke scoffs at her story, declaring it unbelievable, and demands to know who "hath set [her] on" (5.1.117). When she admits that Friar Lodowick had urged her to accuse Angelo, he arrests her for slander and orders that Lodowick be summoned for questioning. This is Friar Peter's cue, first, to defend Lodowick's good name and, second, to explain that Angelo has been wrongfully accused by Isabella and that he has a witness to prove it. Mariana steps forward to explain that Angelo had slept with her, though he thought he was with Isabella. Angelo, emboldened by the Duke's apparent faith in him, confesses that he knows Mariana and that he was once betrothed to her, but he denies having slept with her or indeed anyone. It is his word against theirs, which is of course what he had pointed out to Isabella when she had threatened to accuse him. Believing he has the Duke's full support, Angelo now requests permission to try these "poor informal women" himself (5.1.244), declaring his strong suspicion that they are the "instruments of some more mightier member / That sets them on" (5.1.245–46). Angelo is right, but the "mightier member" is someone well above Angelo's pay grade, which spells disaster for him. Delighted that Angelo has taken the proffered bait, the Duke accepts the offer, expressing his sincere hope that Angelo will "punish" the malefactors "to [his] height of pleasure" (5.1.248). He hastily exits to change costumes. The next bit is the part he is especially looking forward to.

When he returns (disguised once more as the humble friar), he points an accusing finger at the fraud seated pompously on the dais. How can this imposter speak for the Duke? He is a villain compared to the royal prince of Vienna. The poor women have no hope of receiving justice from this *interloper*:

> But oh, poor souls,
> Come you to seek the lamb here of the fox?
> Good night to your redress! Is the Duke gone?
> Then is your cause gone too. The Duke's unjust,

> Thus to retort your manifest appeal,
> And put your trial in the villain's mouth
> Which here you come to accuse. (5.1.305–11)

One is tempted to respond to this delectable speech by saying, "It takes one to know one." The Duke describes Isabella and Mariana as lambs who have unwittingly walked into the trap set by the wily Angelo. But Angelo has been outfoxed by the cleverest fox of them all, the crafty Duke of dark corners. Compared to the Duke, everyone is a lamb. No one outfoxes this Duke. And the cleverest part of it is that the Duke presents himself not as the wily and predatory fox but as the merciful shepherd. He does not kill his lambs. He only threatens to kill them, and when they shake with fear, he takes great delight in pardoning them.

Escalus does his best to defend Angelo. After all, his authority is also being impugned since he, too, represents the Duke. If this lowly friar can get away with such outrageous slander, who knows what will become of representative authority in Vienna. Escalus orders the friar to be taken to the rack, where he'll be painfully stretched "[j]oint by joint" (5.1.320). The friar, however, will not allow it. Instead, he absurdly claims to speak for the Duke himself: "Be not so hot. The Duke / Dare no more stretch this finger of mine than he / Dare rack his own" (5.1.321–23). It's an inside joke that nobody (except the offstage audience) gets. But the Duke is used to enjoying his jokes privately. He is now warming to his theme, and the next bit gives him particular pleasure:

> My business in this state
> Made me a looker-on here in Vienna,
> Where I have seen corruption boil and bubble
> Till it o'errun the stew; laws for all faults,
> But faults so countenanced that the strong statutes
> Stand like the forfeits in a barber's shop,
> As much in mock as mark. (5.1.324–30)

It is more or less the same complaint he made to Friar Thomas, but with one notable difference. This time he can point his finger squarely at Angelo. The heavy burden he carried into his confession with Friar Thomas is finally lifted from his shoulders and placed on the hapless deputy. Corruption has been boiling and bubbling in Vienna for many years, but now the

Duke, under cover of his monkish disguise, can vent publicly and forthrightly what he earlier could only express secretly to his confessor. What is to be done about this sad state of moral affairs in Vienna? The Duke has an answer for that too. The deputy must pay for it. After all, he stuck his neck out—or, rather, he had it stuck out for him by the Duke. Now it is time to cut it off. The Duke is getting ready for his punchline, but first he must revert to his former princely self. It is time to lay aside the humble-friar act.

Enraged by the impious friar's scandalous accusations, Escalus orders that he be arrested: "Slander to th' state! / Away with him to prison" (5.1.330–31). Angelo, keen to line up further witnesses for the state's prosecution of Lodowick, asks Lucio for his testimony: "What can you vouch against him, Signor Lucio?" (5.1.332). Lucio testifies that the friar called the Duke "a fleshmonger, a fool, and a coward" (5.1.341-42). Lodowick coolly denies that he ever called the Duke any such thing: "I protest I love the Duke as I love myself" (5.1.349). It is another inside joke, but the joke is about to made public. When Lucio lays his hands upon the "bald-pated, lying rascal" (5.1.360) and removes his hood, the joke turns deadly serious. The accusers—Angelo, Escalus, and Lucio—find themselves suddenly in the position of the accused. They have dared to assault a true prince. They are imposters, mere representatives of justice. He is Justice itself.

Escalus is immediately pardoned. His fault was merely to be ignorant of the truth. Angelo, however, cannot be forgiven. He knew the truth of his crime, yet he chose to hide it. As for Lucio, he also knew the truth, not of the friar's true identity, but of the fact that he had slandered a prince. The Duke promises to deal with Lucio later. Angelo is the big fish, who has been well and truly hooked. Oh, cunning enemy that to catch a saint, with a saint has baited the hook! Ever since the Duke darkly hinted to Friar Thomas that Angelo was an unsuitable substitute, we have been anticipating a reckoning. Now, after much intrigue by the dark prince, the moment of reckoning has arrived. The Duke seats himself at the head of the dais and begins the accounting of his protagonists' souls. This is done quite openly, before the city gates, with the entire populace eagerly looking on.

Angelo immediately drops to his knees. He is not a stupid man. He sees that there is no legal loophole for him to slip through. The time for hiding behind the law has long passed. It is now a battle for his soul, and here, strangely, the idea of his death comes as a comfort to him. Death will, once and for all, put an end to the constant piercing guilt he feels:

> O my dread lord,
> I should be guiltier than my guiltiness
> To think I can be undiscernible,
> When I perceive Your Grace, like power divine,
> Hath looked upon my passes. Then, good prince,
> No longer session hold upon my shame,
> But let my trial be mine own confession.
> Immediate sentence then and sequent death
> Is all the grace I beg. (5.1.374–82)

Has Angelo suddenly got religion? Is he now a true believer in the notion that the prince is God's anointed deputy on earth? Has he finally come around to Isabella's argument that the only power worth worrying about is God's heavenly power over the immortal soul? Angelo's words are striking precisely because they make no reference to secular law. Angelo's concern is exclusively with the condition of his soul. The words he uses—"guiltiness," "power divine," "shame," "confession," "grace"—refer to his spiritually fallen condition, not to a legal definition of a crime. Angelo feels bad because he has sinned, not because he has committed an illegal act as defined in the law books. Legally, it is debatable whether he has, in fact, committed a crime. As Isabella points out later, he has not committed the crime of fornication. He reneged on his deal with Isabella, but that in itself is not a crime. Legally speaking, the only crime Angelo has committed is the crime of bribery or corruption, and it's not clear what the penalty for that is in Vienna. At any rate, Angelo does not confess to these specific crimes. Instead, he confesses tout court. "I am full of sin. Please put me to death and end my misery."

But the Duke has no intention of ending Angelo's misery. He has been waiting a long time for this moment and has no wish to shorten the experience. He orders Friar Peter to marry Angelo and Mariana at the nearest church. While the shotgun wedding is performed offstage, he apologizes to Isabella for failing to save her brother, blaming the speed of Angelo's order, which came so soon on the heels of the deflowering in the dark and secret garden. This is a nice touch because it prepares Isabella for what comes next, the punchline we have all been waiting for. As soon as Angelo returns a married man, the Duke condemns him to death, citing the Old Testament talion law:

"An Angelo for Claudio, death for death!"
Haste still pays haste, and leisure answers leisure;
Like doth quit like, and measure still for measure. (5.1.417–19)

Advocates of the Christian reading regard this as the climax of the play. The Duke is testing Isabella. She believes her brother to be dead and has screamed for "justice, justice, justice, justice!" (5.1.26). Now the Duke offers her justice. Will she take this opportunity afforded by the old law of the talion (an eye for an eye) to avenge herself on Angelo? Or will she go to her bosom, knock there, and ask herself what's in her heart that is like Angelo's fault? Mariana, having finally landed her husband, is understandably loath to give him up, and she now implores Isabella to kneel with her and beg the Duke to forgive Angelo. The Duke insists that Angelo's death is recompense for Claudio's; if Isabella were to beg for mercy, she would be dishonoring her dead brother, whose "ghost his pavèd bed would break, / And take her hence in horror" (5.1.443–44). All eyes are on Isabella, whose first authentic step in the world outside the nunnery is about to be taken. She kneels beside Mariana and, therefore, passes the Duke's test. She becomes an advocate of mercy and God's divine law (judge not, turn the other cheek, observe the beam in your own eye, and so on). The absolute and universal moral law wins over particular and context-bound ethics. Mercy wins over justice, love over vengeance, Jesus's ethic over the lex talionis. Mercy breathes within Isabella's lips, and she is born again, "[l]ike man new-made" (2.2.84).

The difficulty with this reading, quite apart from the problems we have already considered, is that Isabella does not actually ask the Duke to forgive Angelo. Instead, she makes the legal argument that Angelo is not guilty of the same crime as Claudio and therefore cannot be punished for fornication. Whereas her brother "did the thing for which he died," Angelo's "act did not o'ertake his bad intent" (5.1.457–59). Legally, there are no grounds for executing Angelo. The Duke cannot condemn a man for having foul thoughts: "Thoughts are no subjects, / Intents but merely thoughts" (5.1.461–62).

It must be mildly discomfiting for the Duke to hear himself being corrected on a legal matter. If he had hoped that Isabella would produce another marvelous speech on the absolute supremacy of mercy over the talion law, he is sorely disappointed. Presumably, that is why he waves Isabella's legal argument aside—"Your suit's unprofitable" (5.1.463)—and abruptly switches tactics.[71] He orders the kneeling women to stand and turns his attention to the Provost, whom he has co-opted into his final coup de théâtre, which he now hastens to deliver. He asks the Provost why Claudio was executed at such an odd hour. This question provides the Provost with a pretext to fetch the prisoner Barnardine, whose "testimony" (5.1.474) will prove that the Provost is guiltless in Claudio's clandestine execution. The Provost returns not just with Barnardine, however, but with Juliet and the muffled Claudio too. The Duke, who is keen to get on with the show and play his last trump card, now needs to deal with a convicted murderer (Barnardine) without destroying the warm and generous atmosphere he is so desperately trying to create. Without batting an eyelid, he pardons Barnardine. What the family of Barnardine's victims think of this travesty of justice, the Duke does not bother to consider. He has more important matters to address, including his pièce de résistance, a proposal of marriage to Isabella. No doubt believing that there is no surer way to a woman's heart than to demonstrate his power over both life *and* death, he reveals, with a great flourish, that the brother she thought was dead is in fact very much alive. Grasping Claudio with one hand, he takes Isabella in his other. He has a suggestion to make. Since he has brought Claudio back to life, he can't put Angelo to death. Nonetheless, this act of delightfully unexpected male birthing deserves recompense. Just as he has miraculously produced a life, so too she must produce one for him. They must have sex, but of course it will be strictly legal and by the book:

> If he be like your brother, for his sake
> Is he pardoned, and for your lovely sake,
> Give me your hand and say you will be mine;
> He is my brother too. (5.1.501–4)

The fact that the sentence is presented as a conditional strengthens the sense of an exchange of like for like. If I give you this, you should give me that. One might paraphrase the Duke's sentence as follows: "If this man, whom you thought was dead, is indeed your brother, then I will pardon him, but only if you make him my brother too, namely, by marrying me." This is more or less a version of the deal Angelo offered Isabella, only the Duke is unafraid to do it publicly: "I have the power to pardon and I am willing to do it right now in front of everyone, but I expect something in return." Is it any wonder Isabella doesn't reply?[72]

Isabella's silence is awkward, to say the least. This is not the way the Duke imagined the scene would play out. Shouldn't she be throwing herself into his arms? It is hard to know exactly what the Duke is thinking, but it's not hard to guess Isabella's thoughts. She must be truly gobsmacked. She is being proposed to by a man who fraudulently posed to her as a friar, inveigled his way into her confidence, lured her into accepting the illicit sexual shenanigans with Angelo, lied to her about her brother's death, humiliated her in front of the entire city as a fornicatress, arrested her, pardoned her, then produced her unbeheaded brother. And now he wants to marry her. He must be a madman. At the very least, he is a complete ass. I think it is safe to say that the Duke's proposal comes as a nasty surprise to her. Unless we decide that her feelings are unimportant or that her character is suddenly discontinuous with the picture of her we have been building in our minds up to this point, there is no way to make the Duke's proposal of marriage look like a happy (comic) ending.

This much seems clear, and certainly critics have not been slow to point out that Isabella's silence cannot be taken to indicate her joyful acceptance of the Duke's proposal. But what about the Duke? What is he thinking? When did he decide that Isabella was an ideal bride for him? When did he discover that he *desired* her? I think the play is quite unambiguous about the answer to this last question. The Duke discovers his desire for Isabella when he learns of Angelo's desire for her. The fact that both men strenuously deny that they are susceptible to sexual passion is what brings them together. Isabella, whose name means *consecrated* or *pledged to God*, is the sacred object both men wish to do dirt on. Angelo wants to raze the sanctuary not because he is in love with Isabella but because she appears more virtuous than him. He resents her virtue and piety. The Duke, in turn, wants to do dirt on Angelo because Angelo appears more virtuous and pious than him. So, what does the Duke do when he sees the virtuous and pious Isabella? He wants to do dirt on her too. That is why he prevents her from returning to the convent and instead insists that she hold to Angelo's indecent bargain. Only once he has humiliated her as a fornicatress does he "forgive" her and offer her marriage.

Because he is so good at self-evasion, self-deception, and self-exculpation, it is hard to know exactly what the Duke is thinking. Nonetheless, I think that his awkwardness in the final scene tells us a great deal about him. His big reveal was supposed to be a triumph, but it falls horribly flat. This is particularly evident in his proposal to Isabella, which must be the most one-sided and unsuccessful marriage proposal in all of Shakespeare. The rule of thumb for a successful romantic relationship is that you must be honest with your partner. But the Duke, as we have seen, lies to himself habitually. If he is so dishonest with himself, how can we expect him to be honest with others? The motivation for the Duke's dishonesty is not hard to see. He is afraid of what he might find if he looks too closely at himself. He is desperate to ward off these threats to his fragile sense of self-respect. Hence his loud condemnation of those who appear to have succumbed to sexual depravity, including Angelo and all the lower characters. But the Duke's actions betray his hypocrisy. He is a sexual voyeur, the peephole Duke of dark corners. His lust for Isabella is mediated by Angelo's lust for her, and in both cases this lust can be traced to resentment, a depraved desire to do dirt on the success of others. The Duke's picture of female sexuality reminds one a bit of Hamlet's picture of female sexuality. It combines extreme sentimentality with extreme chauvinism, to which can be added more than a hint of dark lechery. In Hamlet's first soliloquy, he pictures Gertrude clinging to his manly father: "Why, she would hang on him / As if increase of appetite had grown / By what it fed on" (1.2.143–45). Recall that this implausible picture of the supine woman clinging sensuously and greedily to her male superior was also Lucio's image of how Isabella would seduce Angelo. She was to drop to her knees and submissively, but also sensuously and passionately, hang upon his gown. In co-opting Isabella and Mariana into the sexual conspiracy, the Duke had encouraged Angelo to enact his illicit desires, and one suspects that he did so partly because he was aroused by the same image. Why else would he have colluded in the sexual pollution of both women?

After the Duke plays his final trump card and brings Claudio back to life, the only person to speak other than the Duke is Lucio. Everyone else is speechless, including Isabella. Only Lucio has not lost his tongue. There is a good reason for this: he understands the Duke better than the Duke understands himself. That is why he can't be silenced. The Duke declares that he is in the forgiving mood, but there is one person he cannot forgive:

DUKE
    I find an apt remission in myself;
    And yet here's one in place I cannot pardon.

> [*To Lucio*] You, sirrah, that knew me for a fool, a coward
> One of all luxury, an ass, a madman—
> Wherein have I so deserved of you
> That you extol me thus?
>
> LUCIO
> Faith, my lord, I spoke but according to the trick. (5.1.509–16)

The Duke cannot pardon Lucio because pardoning Lucio would mean, to adapt Isabella's words, that he had gone to his bosom, knocked there, and asked his heart what it doth know that is like Lucio's slanders. Since the Duke cannot admit to being "a fool, a coward, / One of all luxury, an ass, a madman," he cannot forgive Lucio. Lucio speaks according to "the trick," not only because he is in the habit of talking this way, but also because the Duke is himself a trickster, a cheat, a fraud, a con man. The Duke cannot tolerate Lucio in his presence because Lucio reminds him too much of himself.

Lucio is carted off to prison because he slanders a prince. More to the point, he is removed from the scene because he risks exposing the Duke a second time.[73] If we consider each of the terms the Duke lists as instances of slander, we find that they are not slanderous at all but true. Neglecting his duties as governor, the Duke acted like a fool. Moreover, he did this because he wanted to be liked, which shows he is a coward who does not have the courage to enforce the law himself, instead giving the task to his inexperienced and unsuitable deputy. His peephole activities showed him to be given to a level of luxury (i.e., lechery) even more depraved than Angelo's because it remains unaccompanied by shame or guilt. Pardoning Barnardine was the act of a plain madman.[74] Finally, his humble-friar charade was the act of an ass that culminated in an absurd marriage proposal to Isabella, whose dignity he has trampled upon in the mad belief that she would be grateful to him when he produced her brother after cruelly lying that he was dead. The Duke makes sure he gets the last word, but it is Lucio who gets the last laugh. To borrow from Isabella's great speech, the pelting, petty Duke, dressed in a little brief authority, thunders like Jove himself, playing such fantastic tricks before high heaven as to make the angels, who would die of laughter if they were not immortal, weep instead.

To put the point in slightly more theoretical terms, the Duke's attempt to cheer everyone up with the good news that marriage and mercy will solve the perennial anthropological problem of resentment is met with awkward silence from his speechless and stunned interlocutors, who have become, precisely, not reciprocal dialogical linguistic partners but inferior subjects.[75] Their stunned silence suggests that the Duke's solution to Vienna's ethical problems comes not from a prolonged and infinitely deferrable negotiation among the equal members of the human periphery but from the authoritarian and unnegotiable center.[76] Only the Duke deserves to occupy the center because only the Duke can see godlike into the sinful souls of his humiliated clients who are now, more precisely, his chastened *subjects*. The appropriate offstage response to the Duke's final blustering show of mad self-centralization is an ironic shake of the head. Can this man really be serious? Either he's an ass (like Bottom) or a madman (like Lear). Take your pick. Then laugh at the ass, or weep at the madman.

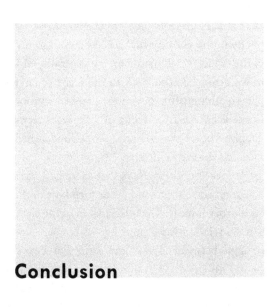

Conclusion

Lear's abdication, intended to secure his legacy forever in his last and greatest potlatch, leads not to triumph but disaster. All his children die before him, and the play ends ambivalently with the suggestion that political power will be divided among the handful of remaining English nobility, a small and forlorn group including Albany, Edgar, and Kent (though Kent refuses Albany's offer of power and appears to be readying himself for death). Lear's renunciation of the kingship, which begins with the ceremonial exchange of his kingdom for his daughters' love, ends in a war in which his daughters no longer exchange vows of love but violent blows. Instead of seeing his children prosper, he watches them die. His last potlatch succeeds only in driving him first to madness, then to the violent spectacle of the deaths of his three daughters, the youngest of whom dies in his arms in a scene so punishing it kills him.

Bradley saw in Lear's final moments a purifying release of the inner soul. Lear finally learns the moral lesson that what counts is not the power and prestige of the sacred monarchal center but the equality of souls on the human periphery. He has learned to love Cordelia unconditionally, and that is what purifies his soul at the end. But this is a curious illustration of the lesson of moral equality. It is equally possible, as Berger points out, that Lear's final moments suggest his stubborn refusal to acknowledge his complicity in the violence that has destroyed so many lives. The very structure of the scene, which insists on the centrality of Lear with the dead Cordelia in his arms, takes us back to the scene of envious rivalry with which the play so ominously begins. Lear's fantastic vision of himself kneeling before Cordelia in a private scene of reciprocal recognition between father and daughter never materializes. He is condemned to remain in the center, a sacrificial figure to the end.

The lesson of tragedy is that as long as the public center cannot be refused, reconciliation among the members of the human periphery remains an illusory fantasy. The relationship to the sacred center of the ritual scene is not a relationship among equals but, as Hegel pointed out, a permanent struggle between master and slave. For Lear's vision to come true, both he and his subjects have to renounce the sacral monarchy upon which the (agrarian) social order depends. Only in his madness on the heath, with the Fool and poor Tom for interlocutors, does he come close to such a release. Yet events quickly conspire to return him to the seat of monarchal power, beginning with Gloucester's ill-conceived plan to remove him to Dover. Lear's reconciliation with Cordelia depends fatally upon Lear regaining both his sanity and his former definition as a king. Lear's mad parody of kingship, as he strolls along the cliffs of Dover with flowers in his hair, is an attempt to escape the violence of the tragic center. But the parody turns into tragedy when he and Cordelia are reconciled. In the final scenes, he becomes once again the target of his envious rivals, a group that includes the reluctant Albany, who perversely declares that though his moral sympathies lie with Lear and Cordelia, he nonetheless feels obliged to fight against them because of the foreign army she commands. The presence of French troops on English soil reflects the underlying problem, which can be traced back to Lear's last failed potlatch. As far as Edmund, Regan, and Goneril are concerned, Lear and Cordelia are usurpers, envious competitors for the center, no better—or worse—than themselves. This contest for centrality is the very definition of tragedy, and no participant in the tragic scene, least of all the protagonists, can escape it.

Where Lear fails, Duke Vincentio appears to succeed. Though he too abdicates, his return to the center in the play's final scene is represented as a heroic triumph rather than a dismal (tragic) failure. Yet this optimistic assessment, much favored by interpreters like Wilson Knight, mistakes the Duke's self-satisfied and smug representation of himself for Shakespeare's. As many recent critics have pointed out, there is simply too much irony in the play to accept the Duke's resolution of the central tragic conflict as an unqualified success. What this darker, more ironic perspective suggests is that the final scene, in which the Duke distributes love and mercy like pigs and blankets at a tribal potlatch, has been deliberately choreographed by the Duke to elevate himself above his subjects. The Duke would implement the divine moral law in Vienna, but what his actions suggest is not the creation of heaven on earth but the reverse. His attempt to coerce his subjects is more invidious and cynical than anything Lear attempts to do. The Duke's mad plan makes Lear's "darker purpose" look childish and naive by comparison. If Lear's madness is partly due to old age and senility, the Duke's madness is a consequence of his sociopathic tendencies. Only a sociopath would grant the legally "precise" Angelo the power to punish fornication with death.

Where Lear seeks to exchange absolute power for his daughters' love and care, the Duke conspires in the fraudulent presentation of himself as a pious friar, a tactic designed to grant him greater access to his subjects' inner lives so he may control them all the more effectively. By this sleight of hand, he would seek not merely political but moral control. Not satisfied with political power, he usurps God's power to judge the inner consciences of his subjects. He tells Isabella that he has a love of doing good, but his Peeping-Tom tactics suggest a deliberate and systematic strategy of self-centralization and self-exculpation. By throwing dirt on others, he distracts negative attention from himself and tightens his grip on the political center. The Duke's final mad act is intended as an extravagant show of princely virtue, a spiritual potlatch in which royal pardons rather than consumables are distributed to his erring subjects. But as with all big-man extravagance, the Duke's potlatch has a singular political purpose. He aims to humiliate his rivals by shaming them publicly and hammering their guilty consciences. Only the Duke deserves to occupy the sacred center because only the Duke can see godlike into the sinful souls of his shameful and humiliated subjects.

W. H. Auden describes Iago as a malevolent practical joker because like all practical jokers he wants to control others without them knowing they are being controlled.[1] The punchline for the practical joker occurs when he reveals that his victims, who thought they were acting under their own volition, have in fact been secretly controlled by the joker. Auden's analysis of the psychology of the practical joker applies equally well to the Duke. Even more than Iago, the Duke wants to control his subjects, whom he treats as curious objects to be observed and manipulated, as in a laboratory experiment. He does not merely want to coerce them; he wants to inhabit their inner consciences, their souls. His abdication is undertaken as a mad attempt to admonish and coerce his subjects in a way only God can. He shadows Angelo so closely not merely because he wants to see him fail but because he expects him to fail. Giving Angelo governorship of the city is like giving an addict the drugs he craves or a child a bag of sweets. In each case the response is predictable. The Duke knows Angelo will not fail to resurrect Vienna's outdated law punishing fornication with death. The hapless deputy's sociopathic personality reflects the greater sociopathy of the Duke, who puts Angelo in charge as a means to tighten his grip on his subjects by tightening his grip on their consciences. But as the final scene demonstrates, the Duke's understanding of the inner lives of his subjects is an illusion, a mad fantastical trick, a fraud. He fails because the illusion of coercive power is based on the same fundamental asymmetry between center and periphery that unseats Lear. The Duke can only enjoy his central authority as a "power divine" if his subjects conspire in the same mad fantasy that he is God's anointed deputy who has a love of doing good. The most revealing moment in the final scene is not the Duke's tone-deaf marriage proposal to Isabella but his release of the murderer Barnardine. Earlier he had needed Barnardine's head and had labored hard to prepare the latter for the executioner's block. When another prisoner dies of natural causes and provides him with the required stage prop (a severed head), he abruptly forgets about executing Barnardine. Subsequently, when he stands once more as a prince before his subjects and needs to make a good impression, he releases Barnardine. Swept up in a feverish show of potlatch clemency, the Duke is keen to shine his godlike benevolence on everyone, including an unrepentant murderer. But what his impulsive release of Barnardine really shows is a reckless and contemptuous disregard for Barnardine's victim, the victim's family, and Barnardine's future victims (or are we to assume that Barnardine is miraculously healed by the Duke's benevolence?). The Duke's acts of mercy are, in short, pure stage acts, exercises in narcissistic self-glorification. Acts of justice they most emphatically are not.

Where Lear sought to trade his kingdom for his children's love, the Duke seeks to conjure love out of thin air. Lucio's description of his abdication as a "mad fantastical trick" is the truest thing anybody says about him. There is not a single scene in which the Duke can be said to approach the reciprocity between equals upon which the moral law depends. Even when he talks sotto voce to Friar Thomas, his only interest is to keep his conscience clean by setting up his deputy to take the heat for enforcing cruel laws he has deliberately let slip. The exchange is not so much a confession as an exercise in self-exculpation. When he subsequently disguises himself as a friar, he is by definition incapable of acknowledging the moral presence of the other because, as Auden's metaphor of the practical joker suggests, by concealing himself he shows contempt for his interlocutors, whom he treats as inferiors to be manipulated and controlled rather than equals to be acknowledged and loved. When he finally sheds his disguise, it becomes clear that the abdication and the humble-friar act were merely elaborate stage tricks designed to secure his grip on the center more firmly. In an extravagant show of potlatch clemency, the main function of which is to humiliate not only Angelo, but Escalus, Isabella, and Lucio, he seeks to elevate himself above all these lesser mortals. Yet for all his careful preparation, the show comes off as a series of cheap fantastical tricks. The attempt to control the periphery from the center ends up being a farce.

Shakespeare's early work is dominated by the romantic comedies in which he developed a fairly systematic picture of romantic love. Doubtless, he was influenced by the allegorical method of the medieval poets. Love, however, is challenged by resentment, and in the tragedies of Shakespeare's middle period, resentment triumphs. John Vyvyan argues that Shakespeare's final period, which is dominated by the tragicomedies and romances, is a dialectical synthesis of the comedies and tragedies.[2] In the tragedies, Shakespeare explores the problem of resentment, which he then "solves" in the tragicomic experiments of the romances. I am sympathetic to Vyvyan's view of the matter, but I also think that his analysis of what he calls "the Shakespearean ethic" could be sharpened by an application of some originary thinking.

In the tragedies, we see the sacrifice of the big man whose usurpation of the center must be punished. In the romantic comedies, the public scene of tragedy is abandoned for the more intimate sphere of reciprocal love.

In the light of Shakespeare's subsequent experiments in tragicomedy and romance, *King Lear* may be understood as a failed romance. Condemned to remain in the center, Lear is also condemned to lovelessness. Hence the poignancy of the final scene, in which Lear dies of a broken heart, cradling the lifeless body of his beloved Cordelia. Conversely, *Measure for Measure* may be considered a failed tragedy. After setting up Angelo to play the tragic role of central scapegoat, the Duke denies us the satisfaction of witnessing the scapegoat's comeuppance. It turns out that Angelo's occupation of the center is merely a diversionary tactic to distract us from the real usurper of sacred power. By presenting himself as a "power divine," the Duke seeks to persuade us that he holds all the cards, including the power to punish or forgive his erring subjects. But this power proves to be illusory. The Duke's mad antics resemble Lear's madness in the storm, with Lucio in the role of the Fool, who speaks the truth of the Duke's lunacy. If we superimpose *Measure for Measure* on *King Lear*, we find that the common factor is madness—and, more precisely, the madness of the exiled or eccentric big man. This raises the interesting question of whether exile represents a possible solution to tragic conflict. Can the big man exist as a permanent exile of the center without also going mad?

In his final masterpiece, Shakespeare addresses this question directly. Prospero is a big man without a political center. Like the Duke in *Measure for Measure*, he says he loves the life removed. But for someone who loves the life removed, he also appears unhealthily preoccupied with his displacement from the seat of ducal authority in Milan. Prospero's story appears similar to Lear's, but with one notable difference: he does not go mad. Nor does he engage in mad peephole activities like Duke Vincentio. Prospero does not spy on his subjects. How could he? He lives on an island in the middle of the Mediterranean Sea many leagues from his dukedom. If Lear's exile is brief and Vincentio's merely a pretext, Prospero's appears permanent.

Yet all is not so simple. Prospero solves the problem of his exile not by returning to Milan for revenge but, rather, by recreating the Milanese and Neapolitan courts on his fantasy island. This allows him to control the story of his romantic return to the center with an authority unparalleled in Shakespeare. Armed with his magic cloak and staff, Prospero becomes more powerful than King Lear and more omniscient than Duke Vincentio. If both Lear and the Duke are hampered by the fact that their subjects have minds of their own, Prospero appears to have solved this problem by turning his subjects into fictional characters whose minds he has untrammeled access to because he created them. Does this mean that Prospero's power is as madly illusory as Lear's or Duke Vincentio's? In terms of his political power, we must answer this question in the affirmative. As an exile, Prospero has zero political authority. But as an author or playwright, Prospero exerts absolute authority over his narrative, which he, like Lear and Duke Vincentio, but much more artfully and self-consciously, transforms into an epic personal battle between the forces of good and evil.

Does this represent an ethical solution to the problem of resentment depicted in Shakespearean tragedy? The full answer to that question must be deferred to another volume.[3] All I can say here is that Prospero's exile is quite different from either Lear's or the Duke's. The closest thing to it is Timon's exile in *Timon of Athens*, which is, curiously enough, Shakespeare's most thorough exploration of the ethical problem of the big man. It seems that in returning to this basic anthropological problem Shakespeare hit upon a possible solution.

Afterword

When I set out to write this book, I had originally thought to include a chapter on Prospero, who struck me as a fitting endpoint—the last big man, so to speak—to a discussion of Shakespeare's collection of oddball authority figures. But by the time I had finished discussing King Lear and the Duke of *Measure for Measure*, I realized that my reading of Shakespeare's final (single-authored) masterpiece would have to wait for another occasion, because Prospero, while in some ways similar to both Lear and the Duke, is clearly *not* a mad man. He is an exile, and his greater distance from the center—which is to say, his greater eccentricity or marginality—(partially) explains his immunity to the madness affecting the more central, and therefore always potentially tragic, figures of Lear and the Duke, both of whom exaggerate, without the slightest sense of irony, their political power as occupants of the center. But if I had paired Lear with Duke Vincentio, with whom could I pair Prospero?

The answer became obvious when I reread *Timon of Athens*. Prospero's precursor is this extraordinary protoromantic exile from ancient Greece, who is also, coincidentally, Shakespeare's most sharply drawn picture of the big man, as a number of recent commentators have pointed out. Both Timon and Prospero are among the most resentful of Shakespeare's protagonists. But they are also among the most successful when it comes to venting their resentment *nonviolently*, which is to say, deferring mimetic conflict by representing it. Timon is Shakespeare's only tragic hero who doesn't actually kill anyone. He doesn't even kill himself—unlike, for example, Shakespeare's more conventionally tragic hero-suicides, including Romeo, Brutus, Othello, and Antony, all of whom rather showily dispatch themselves after violently dispatching others. We don't know exactly how Timon dies, but I'm guessing he dies of starvation or possibly of a miscalculation about what his digestive system can tolerate when it comes to eating unidentified or misidentified roots. This is a nice irony. When Timon attempts to live like a solitary animal in the forest, he fails utterly because he doesn't know what to eat. His death is so miserable and nonviolent it is not fit to be represented on the (tragic) stage, which makes for a peculiar ending to an already peculiar tragedy. In abandoning Athens and becoming a vegetarian in the forest, Timon adopts the pose of the romantic exile, who inveighs against the immorality and injustice of the center.

In this regard, Prospero is an even more thoroughgoing romantic than Timon, to the point that one cannot really call him a tragic hero, unless we believe his melodramatic story that he was tragically deposed from his position of former centrality, which seems doubtful. His story of being cast adrift with his daughter on a rotten and leaky boat, which is also a well-stocked floating library and which delivers him to a magical island that doubles as his private aesthetic stage, smells—like the island's curious indigenous inhabitant—a bit fishy. But in the end, who really cares? The important point is that he dominates our attention with his highly imaginative story. In other words, Prospero succeeds where both Lear and the mad Duke of *Measure for Measure* fail. At least since A. C. Bradley, critics have noticed the similarities between Lear and Prospero, but only Prospero transforms his resentment into a self-consciously crafted autobiographical narrative of vengeance, penance, and forgiveness. The mad Duke of Vienna attempts to do something similar but without Prospero's sense of timing and dramatic irony. This explains why recent commentators tend to respond to the mad Duke's final "pardon party," to use Paul Yachnin's delightful phrase, with dumbfounded astonishment, which (once the initial shock passes) turns into a deeper skepticism about the Duke's stated motives.

In short, *Shakespeare's Mad Men* is both a sequel and a prequel. It is a sequel to the story of the big men who populate the great tragedies of Shakespeare's middle period, and it is a prequel to the story of the exiles who populate his last plays. I tell the first story in *Shakespeare's Big Men*. The story of Shakespeare's exiles is currently in preparation and will (I hope) bring my discussion of Shakespeare's ethical discovery procedures to a reasonably satisfying end. Much has been made of Prospero's resemblance to the all-seeing dramatist who holds a mirror up to the other characters. Much less has been made of Prospero's resemblance to the first-person narrator who attempts, not always successfully, to hold a mirror up to himself. Not to give away too much, there are some illuminating parallels to be drawn between Prospero and the self-exculpatory narrators of Yann Martel's *Life of Pi* and Ian McEwan's *Atonement*, including that they all seek, sometimes rather desperately, to protect their centrality by a barrage of words. This ought to be a lesson to all writers to get to the point. Let me therefore end by acknowledging those who have helped to give this book its own modest measure of centrality.

Though written during the height of the coronavirus pandemic when I was on sabbatical and therefore (mercifully!) unaffected by the mass shift from in-person to online teaching, this book has its origins in my teaching of Shakespeare. I am grateful to my students, whose indispensable role as *in-person* interlocutors gently but firmly encourages me to express my thoughts as clearly as possible. I am also grateful to the following readers of the manuscript: Paul Kottman, for his faith in the larger project and *Shakespeare's Mad Men* in particular; Erica Wetter, for her skillful stewardship of the manuscript once it fell into her hands; and three anonymous reviewers, whose comments on the manuscript I found to be invaluable. I could not ask for more agreeable attention from Adriana Smith for copyediting and Susan Karani for overseeing the book's production. Finally, I wish to thank Sheila Jones for filling my life with many wonderful surprises (some human, some not), including the illustration on the cover of this book.

Notes

Introduction

1. Richard van Oort, *Shakespeare's Big Men: Tragedy and the Problem of Resentment* (Toronto: University of Toronto Press, 2016).

2. Maynard Mack, *Everybody's Shakespeare: Reflections Chiefly on the Tragedies* (Lincoln: University of Nebraska Press, 1993), 260.

3. Harold Bloom, in *Shakespeare: The Invention of the Human* (New York: Riverhead Books, 1998), regards the Duke as a mad sociopath who comes close to Iago in his desire to control and manipulate others. For Bloom, Barnardine is the only sane character in a mad play. Only Barnardine, Bloom writes, "has the wisdom to stay perpetually drunk because to be sober in this mad play is to be madder than the maddest" (359). Bloom calls the final long scene, in which the Duke attempts to exert absolute control over the actions and thoughts of his subjects, "a perfectly mad coda" (379).

4. Marshall Sahlins, "Poor Man, Rich Man, Big-Man, Chief: Political Types in Melanesia and Polynesia," *Comparative Studies in Society and History* 5, no. 3 (1963): 285–303.

5. See Eric Gans, *The End of Culture: Toward a Generative Anthropology* (Berkeley: University of California Press, 1985), esp. 150–62, and *Science and Faith: The Anthropology of Revelation* (Savage, MD: Rowman & Littlefield, 1990), esp. 32–47. Recently, Marshall Sahlins, in "The Original Political Society," *HAU: Journal of Ethnographic Theory* 7, no. 2 (2017): 91–128, seems to have come around to Gans's position. He is now calling for "a Copernican Revolution in the sciences of society and culture" (117), a shift from an anthropology that understands the sacred as a reifying projection of existing (secular) human relations to an anthropology that sees the "original political society" in the relationship between human periphery and sacred center. "Human political power," Sahlins writes, "is the usurpation of divine

power" (119). Sahlins's evidence for this claim is the presence within egalitarian hunter-gatherer societies of a highly developed hierarchy among the sacred beings who govern these societies. Sahlins calls these sacred beings "metapersons," and he argues that they should be understood to be the prototype of personhood as such. These sacred beings or metapersons have the power "to impose rules and render justice that would be the envy of kings" (93). It follows that the sacred precedes and structures the development of social hierarchies in agrarian societies. The original political society is therefore not the agrarian state but, more fundamentally, the human relation to the sacred. In other words, the political and the sacred are coeval, which is to say (with Gans), *originary*.

6. Harry Jaffa, in "The Limits of Politics: *King Lear*, Act 1, Scene 1," in Allan Bloom with Harry V. Jaffa, *Shakespeare's Politics* (1964; repr., Chicago: University of Chicago Press, 1981), 113–45, is one of the few critics to have noticed that far from being a mere fairy tale, Lear's love test is a pretext for a serious ethical problem—namely, the problem of political succession. "If Lear is, in fact, Shakespeare's greatest king," Jaffa writes, "and if it is true that to perpetuate such a rule is an even greater task than to establish it, then the opening of *King Lear* shows us the old king confronted with the supreme problem of his great career—that of providing for the succession to his throne" (114).

7. Ernest Gellner, *Plough, Sword and Book: The Structure of Human History* (Chicago: University of Chicago Press, 1989). The Islamic proverb is cited as an epigraph to the first chapter.

8. The reader may be surprised by the omission of Northrop Frye from this list of anthropological critics. Is he not an "originary" anthropological thinker? Frye's literary anthropology can be traced to the last great Victorian anthropologist, James George Frazer. Despite the sophistication of Frye's taxonomy of literary archetypes, when pushed to explain the origin of these archetypes, he falls back on a positivist (i.e., pre-Durkheimian) account of symbolic representation. Thus, he explains the origin of culture as an attempt to synchronize an archetypal symbolic pattern, whether in ritual, myth, or literature, with the individual's *non-cultural perception* of seasonal change. Consider, for example, this passage from his *Anatomy of Criticism: Four Essays* (Princeton, NJ: Princeton University Press, 1957): "A farmer must harvest his crop at a certain time of the year, but because he must do this anyway, harvesting itself is not precisely a ritual. It is the expression of a will to synchronize human and natural energies at that time which produces the harvest songs, harvest sacrifices, and harvest folk customs that we associate with ritual" (120). But where does this passion to synchronize "human and natural energies" come from? Frye assumes precisely what he needs to explain, namely, the capacity to represent the world symbolically. In this sense, Frye's originary scene is not all that different from Max Müller's account of the origin of myth in the individual's

perception of the awesome spectacle of the rising sun. As Durkheim pointed out, if the sun rises every day, why would a solitary and prelinguistic protohuman find this habitual sight awesome, which is to say, worth representing collectively? Significance comes not from nature but from humans collectively and symbolically representing themselves in the figure of the sacred (i.e., the god or "metaperson"). It follows that representation cannot be derived empirically by a psychology of iconic and indexical associations between naturally occurring phenomena such as the rising sun or the passage of the seasons. Frye is on firmer ground when he writes that Frazer's "*Golden Bough* is, from the point of view of literary criticism, an essay on the ritual content of naïve drama: that is, it reconstructs an archetypal ritual from which the structure and generic principles of drama may be logically, not chronologically, derived.... The *literary* relation of ritual to drama, like that of any other aspect of human action to drama, is a relation of content to form only, not one of source to derivation" (109). Frye touches on the essential problem here, which is the relation of form to content or, to put it in more overtly linguistic terms, the relation of the word to its object. This problem is not unique to literature; it concerns any use of symbolic reference, which is basically a means for designating central (scenic) significance or, to use Frye's term, "content." In the end, however, Frye's literary anthropology remains too wedded to the positivism of a pre-Durkheimian—and a fortiori a pre-Derridean or pre-Gansian—account of symbolic culture.

9. See, in particular, Gans, *End of Culture* and *Originary Thinking: Elements of Generative Anthropology* (Stanford, CA: Stanford University Press, 1993). The term *genetic* is used here in the most general sense of "relating to origin or development" (*Oxford English Dictionary*). Concepts such as desire and resentment are cultural categories and, in that sense, assume the existence of cultural institutions such as language, religion, and art. A hypothesis seeking to explain the latter must therefore also be historical, which is to say, the particular cultural elements we wish to explain must be *genetically* traceable to historical precursors going back, ultimately, to the first cultural moment or institution. The "originary hypothesis" assumes that the fundamental cultural institution is language, the origin of which it is the purpose of the hypothesis to explain. The hypothesis is not an empirical hypothesis but rather a heuristic by which to understand the general historical development of more complex cultural forms—such as, for example, Shakespearean drama.

10. Robert McCrum, "'Perfect Mind': On Shakespeare and the Brain," *Brain: A Journal of Neurology* 139, no. 12 (2016): 3011, https://doi.org/10.1093/brain/aww279.

11. Terrence Deacon, *The Symbolic Species: The Co-evolution of Language and the Brain* (New York: W. W. Norton, 1997), 34. Deacon specializes in the study of Darwinian evolutionary processes. If a neuroscientist can make the claim that the brain evolves in response to the origin of outside-the-brain social and symbolic processes, then humanists should not be shy about repeating it. The claim strikes

me as an urgent call to action for those in the humanities, who should put aside their misguided fascination for pseudoscience and scientism. On the topic of scientism in the humanities, see Raymond Tallis, *Aping Mankind: Neuromania, Darwinitis and the Misrepresentation of Humanity* (Durham, UK: Acumen, 2011).

12. How do I know that chimpanzees don't use language? Isn't it possible that I simply haven't figured out how to speak "chimpanzee"? The short answer to this question is that if wild chimpanzees used language, they would be able to represent their interests collectively both to themselves and to others (e.g., the United Nations, the governments of the countries in which they live, researchers like Jane Goodall, etc.) rather than have humans speak for them—by, for example, setting up chimpanzee sanctuaries such as the one in Gombe National Park in Tanzania. For the long answer, see Deacon's *Symbolic Species*. A useful introduction to this question is Robbins Burling's beautifully lucid discussion in *The Talking Ape: How Language Evolved* (Oxford: Oxford University Press, 2005).

13. Deacon, *Symbolic Species*, 52.

14. For an ontogenetic account of the joint attentional scene, see Michael Tomasello, *The Cultural Origins of Human Cognition* (Cambridge, MA: Harvard University Press, 1999).

15. See, for example, Deacon's analysis of the many language-training experiments of chimpanzees in part 1 of *Symbolic Species*. I have discussed the relevance of Deacon's work to literary studies in "Cognitive Science and the Problem of Representation," *Poetics Today* 24, no. 2 (2003): 237–95.

16. Jacques Derrida, *Of Grammatology*, trans. Gayatri Chakravorty Spivak (Baltimore: Johns Hopkins University Press, 1976).

17. I have deliberately kept my summary of the originary hypothesis brief because I think the best test of the hypothesis is to put it to work in a reading of *King Lear* and *Measure for Measure*. For a more detailed summary of the hypothesis as well as an account of some of the convergences between generative anthropology and recent Shakespeare criticism, see the first two chapters of *Shakespeare's Big Men*. If the interested reader would like to delve further into generative anthropology, I recommend beginning with Gans's *Originary Thinking*. This book provides a clear exposition of the hypothesis, which Gans then applies to the areas of language, religion, ethics, and aesthetics.

18. Paul A. Kottman, in *Love as Human Freedom* (Stanford, CA: Stanford University Press, 2017), makes much the same point when he observes that the spectacular advances in science and technology that have so transformed the world in which we live cannot themselves explain this world. "We may," Kottman writes, "find ourselves empowered by modern science to bring into being nuclear weapons, medical cures, mechanical demands on our time and attention—but none of these phenomena can be fully explained or evaluated *by* the natural-scientific discoveries

that gave rise to them." "The social authority of the scientific method as a social practice or institution," Kottman continues, "cannot itself be evaluated by means of the scientific method" (16). Kottman's specific aim is to carve a space within the humanities for a philosophical anthropology that addresses fundamental categories of human self-understanding, in particular, the notion that "love is a fundamental form of human self-education" toward freedom and rationality (3).

19. On the idea of Shakespeare as a precursor to modern anthropology, see my "Shakespeare and the Idea of the Modern," *New Literary History* 37, no. 2 (2006): 319–39.

20. Gans, *Originary Thinking*, 2 (Gans's italics).

21. There appears to be increasing dissatisfaction in Shakespeare studies with the historicist orthodoxy. See, for example, William Kerrigan, *Hamlet's Perfection* (Baltimore: Johns Hopkins University Press, 1994), esp. chap. 1; Edward Pechter, *Shakespeare Studies Today: Romanticism Lost* (New York: Palgrave Macmillan, 2011); Paul A. Kottman, "Why Think about Shakespearean Tragedy Today?," in *The Cambridge Companion to Shakespearean Tragedy*, 2nd ed., ed. Claire McEachern, (Cambridge: Cambridge University Press, 2013), 240–61; Michael Bristol, "Vernacular Criticism and the Scenes Shakespeare Never Wrote," in *Shakespeare Survey*, vol. 53, ed. Peter Holland (Cambridge: Cambridge University Press, 2000), 89–102, and "Macbeth the Philosopher: Rethinking Context," *New Literary History* 42, no. 4 (Autumn 2011), 641–62; Ewan Fernie, *The Demonic: Literature and Experience* (London: Routledge, 2013); and Amir Khan, *Shakespeare in Hindsight: Counterfactual Thinking and Shakespearean Tragedy* (Edinburgh: Edinburgh University Press, 2016).

Chapter One

1. See Gans, *Originary Thinking*, part 2, esp. chap. 9. Gans applies the term "neoclassical" to medieval and Renaissance art to indicate the changed ethical context into which the art of the ancient Greeks, including classical tragedy, was inserted in the Renaissance. According to Gans, what distinguishes classical from neoclassical art is not merely the changed content of the artwork but rather the different ethical context from which the artwork emerges. In the West, the ethical transformation is a consequence of the spread of Christianity in the medieval period. For a magisterial survey of early modern tragedy, as well as a skeptical appraisal of the dominance of the romantic idea of tragedy in recent critical thought, see Blair Hoxby, *What Was Tragedy? Theory and the Early Modern Canon* (Oxford: Oxford University Press, 2015). In reminding us that early modern tragedy cannot simply be reduced to the pre-romantic, Hoxby draws our attention to some neglected authors of early modern tragedy, a genre which was understood much more elastically by Shakespeare's contemporaries than by their romantic successors. The "philosophy of the tragic" developed by the German idealists in the late eighteen and early nineteenth centuries has

been, Hoxby asserts, "an obstacle to our interpretation of most of the tragedy that was produced in early modern Europe between 1515 and 1795" (293). In Hoxby's view, this development has led to the lionization of Shakespeare at the expense of other authors who don't fit the romantic philosophy of history so well.

2. See Harry Berger Jr., *Making Trifles of Terrors: Redistributing Complicities in Shakespeare* (Stanford, CA: Stanford University Press, 1997), which is devoted to exploring the hypothesis that Shakespeare's characters collude in the suffering represented on the stage. Berger's specific analyses of *King Lear* can be found in chapters 3 and 4. In his highly sympathetic review of Berger's book, Michael Bristol, in "Recent Studies in Tudor and Stuart Drama," *Studies in English Literature, 1500-1900* 38, no. 2 (Spring 1998): 363-409, notes that "Berger is doing what the best critics have always done. He is simply trying to understand and articulate his own relationship to Shakespeare, and the best way to do that is to test his response against what other people have thought and felt about their own relationship to the same material" (402). I agree that criticism is, in the end, deeply personal and that the best critics proceed, first, by getting to know the text as intimately as possible (by reading it closely multiple times) and, second, by testing their response by comparing it to what other intelligent readers have said about it throughout the ages. For sympathetic appraisals of Berger's work, see "Forum: Harry Berger, Jr.'s *Making Trifles of Terror: Redistributing Complicities in Shakespeare*," in *Shakespeare Studies* 27 (1999): 19-73, which includes short essays by Lena Cowen Orlin, Lynn Enterline, Angus Fletcher, Lois Potter, Marshall Grossman, and Stanley Cavell. See also the essays collected in Nina Levine and David Lee Miller, eds., *A Touch More Rare: Harry Berger, Jr., and the Arts of Interpretation* (New York: Fordham University Press, 2009). For a much more negative account of Berger, see Richard Strier, "The Judgment of the Critics That Makes Us Tremble: 'Distributing Complicities' in Recent Criticism of *King Lear*," in *Shakespeare and Judgment*, ed. Kevin Curran (Edinburgh: Edinburgh University Press, 2017), 215-34.

3. René Girard argues, in *A Theater of Envy: William Shakespeare* (New York: Oxford University Press, 1991), that the point of the abdication scene is to dramatize the "crisis of Degree." When Lear abdicates, he replaces the order of external mediation (sacred hierarchy) with the disorder of internal mediation. Sacred hierarchy is dissolved, leaving only the bare reality of mimetic rivalry, which is consequently free to flourish. The love test is a transparent example of mimetic desire reduced to its bare minimum in the competition between rivals: "The king invites his three daughters to exhibit their love for him, each one in turn; instead of preventing all mimetic competition among them, as his role demands, he foolishly incites it: he proposes himself as an object of competitive desire" (181). For Girard, Lear exhibits the same narcissism as a modern-day supermodel or celebrity. He incites rivalry among his admiring disciples and then is shocked when they turn on him.

4. Wilson Knight, "The Embassy of Death: An Essay on *Hamlet*" in *The Wheel of Fire: Interpretations of Shakespearean Tragedy* (1930; repr., London: Routledge Classics, 2001).

5. A. C. Bradley, *Shakespearean Tragedy: Lectures on "Hamlet," "Othello," "King Lear," "Macbeth"* (1904; repr., London: Penguin, 1991), 295–96.

6. Bradley, 292.

7. In a sharp comment, Marvin Rosenberg, in *The Masks of King Lear* (Berkeley: University of California Press, 1972), notes that "Cordelia is the first to reveal her private self, her inner conflicts, and to expose publicly, much more than she is allowed to be consciously aware of, the underside of her nature" (56–57). This is but one instance of what Rosenberg calls the "*Lear* dialectic," the clash of polarities and opposites generating ambivalence and paradox at every level, whether linguistic, poetic, dramatic, psychological, philosophical, or anthropological. Here, it is the clash of the private and public spheres, with Cordelia representing the former and Lear (and his court) the latter. Rosenberg is generally very sensitive to the play's dramatic, linguistic, and psychological details, but in his discussion of the play's first scene he misrepresents Bradley's picture of Cordelia when he accuses Bradley of falsely characterizing her as "the ultimate Christ figure . . . enskied and sainted" (57). Certainly, Bradley's overall impression of Cordelia is extremely positive (surely not incorrect?), but as usual Bradley does not allow an abstraction—in this case, Lucio's description of Isabella as "a thing enskied and sainted" (1.4.34), which Bradley does not hesitate to apply to Cordelia's relative status in the Shakespearean pantheon of heroines—to interfere with his *specific* analysis of the scene. Far from seeing Cordelia as "a thing enskyed and sainted" (Bradley 291) in the opening court scene, Bradley argues that her silence is deliberately antagonistic and that it barely conceals her pride and resentment. I find it curious that Rosenberg should misrepresent a critic whose insights are so convergent with his own. Is this an instance of the fashion among academic critics for de rigueur Bradley bashing?

8. Berger, *Making Trifles of Terrors*, 42.

9. Berger, 43.

10. Berger, 44.

11. Berger, 27.

12. Bradley, *Shakespearean Tragedy*, 292.

13. Bradley, 292.

14. John Vyvyan, in *Shakespeare and the Rose of Love: A Study of the Early Plays in Relation to the Medieval Philosophy of Love* (1960; repr., London: Shepheard-Walwyn, 2013) and *Shakespeare and Platonic Beauty* (1961; repr., London: Shepheard-Walwyn, 2013), examines Shakespeare's use of the metaphor in *Love's Labour's Lost*, *Romeo and Juliet*, and *All's Well That Ends Well*, but it occurs elsewhere as well.

15. Here is how Bradley puts it: "He loved Cordelia most and knew that she loved him best, and the supreme moment to which he looked forward was that in which she should outdo her sisters in expressions of affection, and should be rewarded by that 'third' of the kingdom which was the most 'opulent.' And then—so it naturally seemed to him—she put him to open shame" (231). Stanley Cavell picks up on Bradley's hint that shame lies at the core of Lear's reaction.

16. Stanley Cavell, "The Avoidance of Love: A Reading of *King Lear*," in *Must We Mean What We Say? A Book of Essays* (New York: Charles Scribner's Sons, 1969), 290.

17. I think this is why Shakespeare presents Laertes as a competitor to the throne in the fourth act when the people cry, "Laertes shall be king!" Politically Laertes is not a serious candidate and has never been represented as such. But ethically the point is clear. Laertes's candidacy is based on his willingness to accept the role of violent revenger. Like Hamlet and Fortinbras, he is the son of a murdered father.

18. Friedrich Nietzsche, *On the Genealogy of Morals*, trans. Walter Kaufmann and R. J. Hollingdale (New York: Vintage Books, 1989), especially book 1. See also Max Scheler, *Ressentiment*, trans. Lewis B. Coser and William W. Holdheim (Milwaukee, WI: Marquette University Press, 1994).

19. William Empson, in *The Structure of Complex Words* (London: Chatto & Windus, 1977), notes the conflict between Lear's stated religious motivations (he wants to set his soul in order before he dies) and the political ramifications of the abdication. Upon hearing Lear's opening speech, an Elizabethan audience, Empson says, "would feel a very practical disapproval for any plan to divide England and thereby risk civil war," but they would also "naturally interpret the speech in religious terms" and so understand the king's religious motivations (127).

20. Orwell makes this point in his 1947 essay "Lear, Tolstoy and the Fool." See George Orwell, *Collected Essays* (London: Mercury Books, 1961).

21. In an extraordinary reading of the play's first scene, Jaffa, in "Limits of Politics," 113–45, observes that "Cordelia can be the cause of that love which Lear's great soul needs only if Lear removes himself from, or removes from himself, every vestige of his monarchy in this world" (136). Jaffa argues that Lear reaches the limits of politics when he tries to solve the political problem of succession. The plan he devises is a good one: he means to give Cordelia the best part of his kingdom and, therefore, eventually the crown, while also maintaining good relations with Cornwall and Albany (via the rich dowries that accompany the love test). Cordelia, however, ignores the political problem and confronts her father with the truth, which is the truth of the exchange between lover and beloved. In granting Cordelia the more opulent third (and, therefore, the crown), Lear professes his love to her. He makes Cordelia the beloved, as everyone recognizes. But this action leads to a conflict between the hypocrisy of politics and the truth of love: "He does not know, however,

that, by becoming the lover, the only bounty he has to offer is his love and that Cordelia, as beloved, can only cause his love by refusing to surrender the sovereignty which he has himself now thrust on her. Ironically, Lear is attempting to command Cordelia at precisely the moment and in the very situation in which his relation to her has been reversed, and she has become the commanding one, for, when Lear turned to Cordelia to hear her profession, she had already ascended to the throne. It was not the throne of Britain, but rather the invisible throne prepared by nature for those of surpassing virtue" (135).

22. See G. W. F. Hegel, *The Phenomenology of Spirit*, trans. J. N. Findlay (Oxford: Oxford University Press, 1977), esp. the section "Lordship and Bondage." See also Alexandre Kojève, *Introduction to the Reading of Hegel*, ed. Allan Bloom, trans. James H. Nichols (Ithaca, NY: Cornell University Press, 1969).

23. The phrase is John Vyvyan's, who uses it in his analysis of Hamlet. See John Vyvyan, *The Shakespearean Ethic* (1959; repr., London: Shepheard-Walwyn, 2011), 44.

24. The disguised Kent says he is forty-eight, but Bradley, citing the frequent references to Kent's old age and gray hairs, believes he is probably in his sixties. See Bradley, *Shakespearean Tragedy*, 284.

25. Bradley, *Shakespearean Tragedy*, 283.

26. Bradley, 284.

27. Bradley, 283.

28. See, for example, H. A. Mason, in *Shakespeare's Tragedies of Love: An Examination of the Possibility of Common Readings of "Romeo and Juliet," "Othello," "King Lear," and "Antony and Cleopatra"* (London: Chatto & Windus, 1970). Mason observes that Lear, after his abdication, hardly conducts himself as a man who is meekly crawling toward death. On the contrary, his hunting and feasting are a burden on his host (Goneril). This sets up a debate. Is Lear abusing his host or is she abusing him? This debate is figured by Goneril, on the one hand, and Kent, on the other. For Mason, Kent "is very much a function and very little a character" (184). When Kent is placed in the stocks, we witness an allegory in miniature. Kent's behavior is certainly excessive and his punishment therefore deserved. Mason also thinks that Kent's behavior is implausible. Why does he indulge in such excess? The answer is that Kent represents the riotous behavior of Lear's knights and, therefore, of Lear himself: "For it may then cross our minds that Kent's uncharacteristic unmannerliness was, as it were, by replacing that of his knights, an extension of Lear. He for the moment *is* Lear's guilt, his unnatural folly" (191).

29. Tracking the use of the word *fool* in the play, Empson, in *Structure of Complex Words*, tackles the problem of Lear's final speech in which he delivers the line "And my poor fool is hanged!" (5.3.311). Lear is referring to Cordelia, but why does he call her his "fool"? Empson questions the idea, often cited by editors, that Lear uses the word *fool* strictly as a term of endearment. The association between fool-

ishness and madness is too strongly developed in the play to allow us to ignore the primary meaning of *fool*. Empson believes that Lear is returned to his state of madness in the storm: "Lear is now thrown back into something like the storm phase of his madness, the effect of immediate shock, and the Fool seems to him part of it. The only affectionate dependent he had recently has been hanged, and the only one he had then was the Fool: the point is not that they are alike—it is shocking because they are so unlike—but that he must be utterly crazy to call one by the name of the other" (152).

30. Mack, *Everybody's Shakespeare*, 245. Mack is actually talking about the Fool as a "reflection" of "Lear's inner experiences" (245), but his larger argument is that the minor characters are frequently used by Shakespeare as "dramatic shorthand" (245) for "goings-on in the King's brain that only occasionally bubble to the surface in the form of conscious apprehensions" (246). I am in full agreement with Mack on this point, which fits closely with Vyvyan's discussion of Shakespeare's use of the minor characters.

31. Berger describes "the conventional reading" as the view "which accedes to Lear's perspective in viewing him as the foolish victim of his two cruel daughters" (34). Against this view, Berger argues that Lear's desire for vengeance is a bad-faith tactic to hide the truth from himself. More precisely, his contempt (not just of his bad daughters but of Cordelia too) is a mask behind which he hides his hatred of himself for his failures as a king and, most especially, as a father. Berger thus divides Lear's cruelty into two contradictory impulses. There is his "darker purpose," which is his desire to stir up maximal conflict and rivalry among others by projecting onto them the bad feelings and hatred he secretly harbors toward himself, and there is his "darkest purpose," which is the recognition of his complicity in the violence that spreads like a miasma across the stage. In Berger's reading, Lear struggles mightily to protect himself from becoming aware of his darkest purpose. That way madness lies. Even Lear's madness, Berger says, is a desperate attempt to hide from himself his own guilt and complicity. In other words, Lear always reverts to the view that he is more sinned against than sinning.

32. If we are squeamish about committing the so-called intentional fallacy, we can say the "perspective of the text" instead of "the perspective of Shakespeare." The distinction, of course, is merely a manner of speaking. "Shakespeare" is a shorthand for saying "the perspective that transcends the perspective of the individual characters," in other words, the perspective of the text. It goes without saying that the evidence for Shakespeare's perspective is textual. This includes not just *King Lear* but Shakespeare's other aesthetic texts. Even if we found Shakespeare's secret diary, in which he recorded his sincere account of what he intended his plays to mean, this would change nothing. "Shakespeare" would still refer to the "perspective of his aesthetic texts." The alternative would be to say that there is no distinc-

tion between the aesthetic and non-aesthetic texts (e.g., Shakespeare's diary). My assumption, however, is that the distinction exists.

33. See Wilson Knight, "*King Lear* and the Comedy of the Grotesque," in *Wheel of Fire*.

34. Since human desire is by definition mimetic (i.e., shared), it is also conflictive. This is Girard's fundamental insight. We cannot both possess the same object. Hence the universality of resentment, which is the experience of dispossession from the desirable human center. In her landmark exploration of this experience of dispossession, Mary Shelley portrays Victor Frankenstein's monster as permanently denied entry into the human scene of domestic bliss that he observes so enviously from his position on the periphery. For an analysis of *Frankenstein* from this perspective, see my "A Race of Devils: *Frankenstein*, Romanticism, and the Tragedy of Human Origin," in *Spheres of Action: Speech and Performance in Romantic Culture*, eds. Alexander Dick and Angela Esterhammer (Toronto: University of Toronto Press, 2009), 124–46.

35. Michael Ignatieff, in *The Needs of Strangers* (London: Chatto & Windus, 1984), observes that the notion of universal human rights is based on a contradiction between the universal and the particular. Needs can only be conceived in terms of their historical particularity. When Lear speaks of his "need" for a "retinue of knights," this "counts as a need only within a given time and place, a given zone of safety guaranteed by a history of obligations and commitments. To call this need into question by the standards of some abstractly equal conception of what all humans might need is nonsensical" (31).

36. In *The Crisis of the Aristocracy, 1558–1642*, abr. ed. (Oxford: Oxford University Press, 1967), Lawrence Stone notes that by the sixteenth century the need for armed retainers among the peerage had become mostly symbolic, coercive power having given way to displays of prestige and conspicuous consumption. "As late as the 1570's," Stone writes, "the Earl of Oxford was accompanied not only by his gentlemen followers, but also by 100 tall yeomen in livery with the Blue Boar recognizance on the left shoulder" (102). "There can be little doubt," Stone says, "that the function of these bravoes in the late sixteenth century was as much one of display as military force," and by "the early seventeenth century" most of the great houses had dispensed with armed retainers altogether, "for the ingredients of prestige had now shifted to more showy but less warlike items" (103). Stone's larger argument is that the "crisis of the aristocracy" can be traced to a "social revolution of far-reaching consequences" in which the Tudors were successful "in weaning the landed classes from their ancient habits of violence and subjecting them to the discipline of the law" (121). Stone points to many factors in this process of gradual pacification of the warlike impulses of the aristocracy, but chief among them are what he calls "changes in occupational habits and in the mental and moral climate of opinion"

(116). "By 1640," Stone writes, "the bellicose instincts of the class had been sublimated in the pursuit of wealth and the cultivation of the arts" (116). As Lear's attachment to his knights suggests, brute force can only take you so far. Coercive power is backed up by symbolic power, which obviously offers more opportunities for those less adept at wielding a sword.

37. Berger, *Making Trifles of Terror*, 35.

38. Comparing Shakespeare's representation of the "crisis of degree" in *King Lear* and *A Midsummer Night's Dream*, Girard says that Lear "is not really interested in the truth, and his grandiloquent dialogue with the storm is little more than a senior citizen's equivalent of the midsummer night capers" (*Theater of Envy*, 183). For Girard, Lear's night on the heath performs much the same function as the lovers' night in the woods: both scenes reveal what happens to the social order when a mimetic crisis breaks out. Girard's exclusive focus on the latter tends to obscure any interest in the hero's inner conflict, which is arguably the main focus of the tragedies.

39. Mason, *Shakespeare's Tragedies of Love*, 198. Mason's comments come after he cites Lear's line, "Here I stand your slave, / A poor, infirm, weak, and despised old man" (3.2.19–20).

40. Berger, *Making Trifles of Terror*, 34.

41. Berger, *Making Trifles of Terror*, 36.

42. Here is the full speech, which I never tire of rereading:

> I was born free as Caesar; so were you;
> We both have fed as well, and we can both
> Endure the winter's cold as well as he.
> For once, upon a raw and gusty day,
> The troubled Tiber chafing with her shores,
> Caesar said to me, "Dar'st thou, Cassius, now
> Leap in with me into this angry flood,
> And swim to yonder point?" Upon the word,
> Accoutred as I was, I plungèd in
> And bade him follow; so indeed he did.
> The torrent roared, and we did buffet it
> With lusty sinews, throwing it aside
> And stemming it with hearts of controversy.
> But ere we could arrive the point proposed,
> Caesar cried "Help me, Cassius, or I sink!"
> Ay, as Aeneas, our great ancestor,
> Did from the flames of Troy upon his shoulder
> The old Anchises bear, so from the waves of Tiber

> Did I the tirèd Caesar. And this man
> Is now become a god, and Cassius is
> A wretched creature and must bend his body,
> If Caesar carelessly but nod on him.
> He had a fever when he was in Spain,
> And when the fit was on him I did mark
> How he did shake. 'Tis true, this god did shake.
> His coward lips did from their color fly,
> And that same eye whose bend doth awe the world
> Did lose his luster. I did hear him groan.
> Ay, and that tongue of his that bade the Romans
> Mark him and write his speeches in their books,
> Alas, it cried "Give me some drink, Titinius,"
> As a sick girl. Ye gods, it doth amaze me
> A man of such a feeble temper should
> So get the start of the majestic world
> And bear the palm alone. (1.2.97–131)

43. Cassius wants to kill Mark Antony as well as Caesar, but Brutus advises against it because doing so will make them appear envious murderers rather than self-sacrificing purgerers: "This shall make / Our purpose necessary, and not envious; / Which so appearing to the common eyes, / We shall be called purgerers, not murderers" (2.1.178–81).

44. In an earlier draft, I used the word *emotion* to describe the protagonist's inner state (e.g., "He was overcome with resentful *emotions*"). However, Thomas Dixon, in *From Passions to Emotions: The Creation of a Secular and Psychological Category* (Cambridge: Cambridge University Press, 2003), argues that the "category of emotions, conceived as a set of morally disengaged, bodily, non-cognitive and involuntary feelings, is a recent invention" (3) that does not predate the nineteenth century. The so-called harmful split between emotion and reason, decried by theorists like Robert Solomon, is, Dixon argues, itself a product of modern theories of the emotions. Early theorists, such as Augustine and Aquinas, not to mention Plato and Aristotle, took a much more holistic approach to the passionate and reasoning parts of the human soul. Obviously, Shakespeare's picture of the human "passions" similarly encompasses a general picture of the human soul. In short, resentment is not simply an involuntary emotion but a defining condition of human personhood, which cannot be understood independently of the (originary) scene of human interaction. Shakespeare does not think of resentment as a purely inner state but as a product of the *dramatic scene*. Hence the importance of temptation scenes in Shakespeare's picture of the individual soul.

45. See van Oort, *Shakespeare's Big Men*.

46. Quarto 1 has "doom" instead of "gift," which underscores the fact that the gift is really a curse.

47. Mason, *Shakespeare's Tragedies of Love*, 198.

48. Bradley, *Shakespearean Tragedy*, 262–63.

49. See, for example, the introduction to Girard's *Theater of Envy*.

50. Kent repeats the line, "Good my lord, enter," four times in the space of twenty-two lines.

51. Empson observes that Lear's encounter with Edgar "is much more pointed if you take the original abdication as an attempt to renounce the world, but one which had too much calculation in it, so that he is now trying desperately to find what a real renunciation would be" (*Structure of Complex Words*, 138).

52. Richard's sly campiness (winking at the audience, crooking his finger at us, etc.) is brilliantly emphasized by Ian McKellen in his performance of the role in Richard Loncraine's extremely entertaining and well-crafted 1995 film adaptation of *Richard III*.

53. Berger, *Making Trifles of Terror*, 55.

54. Noticing that the "horror of sex appears for the first time as soon as he is mad," Empson suggests that Lear's obsession with sexuality, far from being an "irrelevant introduction of Shakespeare's own neuroses," fits with the theme of madness. "The clown," Empson notes, "has all along made jokes about sex which imply that the daughters will do harm," and in those scenes in the hovel, in which Edgar, the Fool, and Lear exchange "bawdy jokes," we see Lear come closer to the (feigned) madness of Edgar and the (real) lunacy of the Fool (*Structure of Complex Words*, 137–38).

55. At the beginning of the scene, before Edmund and Goneril depart, each sister suggests a different way to punish Gloucester. Regan says, "Hang him instantly," and Goneril says, "Pluck out his eyes" (3.7.4-5). Perhaps Goneril's suggestion is lurking in the back of Cornwall's mind throughout the interview with Gloucester. The violent image of eyes being plucked out occurs earlier, when Lear says, in reply to Goneril's suggestion that he "disquantity" (1.4.246) his train of knights, that he would rather "pluck" out his own "fond eyes" (1.4.300-301) than let them weep. In 3.7, the idea becomes a reality.

56. S. L. Goldberg, in *An Essay on "King Lear"* (Cambridge: Cambridge University Press, 1974), observes that Gloucester is important because without him, the evil characters don't seem so evil and Lear's mad night on the heath doesn't seem very serious: "Without Gloucester in the play, the attitudes and behaviour not just of Edmund, Goneril, Regan and Cornwall, but of others too, would seem less serious, less meaningful. It might have seemed, for instance, that there was nothing for Lear to get so worked up about in Goneril and Regan's attitude over the knights,

or that his madness is merely a pathological condition" (89). I agree with Goldberg's observation, but he doesn't take the next step, which is to see that Gloucester's blindness is also a reflection of the audience's blindness. We are the ones who have demanded a scapegoat precisely in order to give these rather undignified and petty actions of the protagonist dignity and moral seriousness. When Gloucester is blinded, we feel that Lear's rage is fully justified. With one hand, Shakespeare anticipates and encourages our rage; with the other, he ironizes and criticizes it.

57. Mason, in *Shakespeare's Tragedies of Love*, calls it "cheap moralising" (222). Berger, in *Making Trifles of Terror*, says that Edgar, nervous about revealing his full complicity in his father's death, reverts to moral platitudes: "He has by now displaced the deep shock of complicity, has assumed the savior's mantle and feels capable of pronouncing judgment" (64).

58. In an illuminating and provocative commentary, Janet Adelman, in *Suffocating Mothers: Fantasies of Maternal Origin in Shakespeare's Plays, "Hamlet" to "The Tempest"* (London: Routledge, 1992), argues that Edgar's moralizing is but one instance among many of patriarchal scapegoating in which the (absent) figure of the mother is blamed for social disorder. "In simultaneously marking the mother's child as illegitimate and locating the place of female begetting as the father's scourge," Adelman writes, "the Gloucester plot plays out a bizarre fantasy in which social anxieties about illegitimacy and patriarchal inheritance are fused with psychological anxieties about sexuality and masculine identity" (106). Adelman reads Lear's madness as a response to the darkness within himself, which he consistently represents in sexist terms as female hysteria or the "suffocating mother." I agree that despite Lear's strenuous efforts "to separate himself from [Goneril's] corrupt femaleness, he finds himself pregnant with her. . . . [A]ttempting to smell out the faults of others, he finds the stench of the sulphurous pit on his own hands" (113). I am less convinced, however, by Adelman's claim that "Shakespeare is complicit in Lear's fantasy" (125) of big-man dominance. On the contrary, Lear's tragedy stems precisely from his refusal to renounce the sacred center, which in agrarian societies has always been the site of violent male contestation. Peter Kishore Saval, in *Shakespeare in Hate: Emotions, Passions, Selfhood* (New York: Routledge, 2016), argues that Edgar's reference to the "dark and vicious place" fits into a larger set of oppositions in the play (e.g., male/female, father/mother, light/dark, order/chaos, culture/nature). *King Lear* moves progressively from order to chaos, light to dark, male to female. Lear's problem is that he refuses to acknowledge his dependency on the darker aspects of his nature, which ultimately are traceable back to the child's dependency on its mother. In exposing himself to the elements, Lear gains self-knowledge. However, this self-knowledge is not discursive, in the manner of Montaigne's *Essays*, but rather an acknowledgment of his dependency on darker feelings—in particular, on the emotions of humiliation and shame.

59. Bradley, *Shakespearean Tragedy*, 271.

60. Cavell writes: "In a play in which, as has often been said, each of the characters is either very good or very bad, this revelation of Edgar's capacity for cruelty—and the *same* cruelty as that of the evil characters—shows how radically implicated good is in evil; in a play of disguises, how often they are disguised" ("Avoidance of Love," 283). Like Berger, Cavell is unconvinced that there is such a wide margin between the good and bad characters.

61. For a philosophical definition and discussion of the notion of an "epistemological crisis," see Alasdair MacIntyre, "Epistemological Crises, Dramatic Narrative, and the Philosophy of Science," *Monist* 60, no. 4 (1977): 453–72. MacIntyre argues that epistemological crises occur when our customary narratives of sense-making break down. These epistemological crises are a common theme of literature. MacIntyre cites *Hamlet* (though he could have cited *King Lear*, or indeed any of Shakespeare's major tragedies), and he chides philosophers for failing to take account of the fact that their claims are always bound by a narrative framework "in which good or bad character helps to produce unfortunate or happy outcomes" (456).

62. As recently as the night before Lear's division of the kingdom, father and son were on good terms. In 1.2, Edmund asks Edgar when he last saw his father. Edgar replies, "The night gone by" (1.2.156), adding that they spoke for two full hours. Edmund asks, "Found you no displeasure in him by word or countenance?" "None at all," Edgar replies (1.2.159–61). On the surface at least, father and son were on amiable terms.

63. For a very different reading of the Dover cliff scene, one that reads the encounter between Gloucester and Poor Tom along Levinasian lines, see James Kearney, "'This Is Above All Strangeness': *King Lear*, Ethics, and the Phenomenology of Recognition," *Criticism* 54, no. 3 (Summer 2012): 455–67.

64. Harold Goddard, *The Meaning of Shakespeare* (Chicago: University of Chicago Press, 1960), 2:151–52.

65. In his analysis of exorcism in *King Lear*, Stephen Greenblatt, in *Shakespearean Negotiations: The Circulation of Social Energy in Renaissance England* (Berkeley: University of California Press, 1988), accepts the traditional "optimistic" reading of this scene. "Edgar," Greenblatt writes, "tries to create in Gloucester an experience of awe and wonder so intense that it can shatter his suicidal despair and restore his faith in the benevolence of the gods" (118). Despite its sophisticated new-historicist focus on the texts of demonic possession and exorcism, Greenblatt's argument is ultimately very close to Goddard's, at least when it comes to his interpretation of the cliff scene.

66. Goddard, *Meaning of Shakespeare*, 2:151.

67. The fashionable idea that humanity, especially that most pernicious part

of it known as the West, is going down the toilet has been disputed on empirical grounds by Steven Pinker, in *The Better Angels of Our Nature: Why Violence Has Declined* (New York: Penguin Books, 2011). Needless to say, Pinker's book has been mostly ignored by the pessimists in the humanities.

68. Cavell, "Avoidance of Love," 284.

69. Cavell says that Edgar's *"revealing himself* would seem the surest and most immediate way" to "cure his father of the desire to commit suicide" ("Avoidance of Love," 282).

70. I will discuss the Duke's "mad fantastical trick" in the next chapter.

71. Berger, *Making Trifles of Terror*, 63. Referring to the cliff scene, Berger says: "It is nevertheless the case that this is an act of symbolic parricide: the old man (and old Adam in Gloucester) must be 'killed' so that the father and son may slough off the former life and be reborn together. The problem is that Edgar can never fully rid himself of the fiend, and in his second attempt to cure Gloucester the parricide is less symbolic" (63). In the next sentence, Berger calls Edgar's "brief tale" the "execution of Gloucester."

72. Citing this particular assertion by Berger as an instance of the many "astonishingly bizarre claims" (215) made by both Berger and Cavell, Strier, in "Judgment of the Critics," defends the traditional view of the play, in which the good characters are mostly good and the bad characters are mostly bad. Strier regards the readings of Cavell and Berger as perverse and unbalanced and concludes that "what is needed in literary criticism is something like ordinary awareness and common sense" (228). I find this conclusion disappointing and anticlimactic. If literary criticism is supposed to devote itself to ordinary awareness and common sense, why bother reading Shakespeare at all? He is hardly most people's idea of "ordinary awareness" or "common sense." The constructive way to refute a critic with whom you strongly disagree is to provide your own reading of the text. Strier appears to be more bothered by the fact that Cavell and Berger have been reasonably influential in the small (but adventurous) world of *Lear* criticism.

73. "In her mind," Cavell writes, "the man she is sending on his way to Dover is the man she *knows* is sent on his way to Dover: in her paroxysms of cruelty, she imagines that she has just participated in blinding her father" ("Avoidance of Love," 281).

74. Cavell, "Avoidance of Love," 281–82.

75. Berger stresses that Gloucester wants "to stay clear of Edgar's speaking presence." The distance is necessary, Berger adds, because it "is a way of making sure his suspicions will remain unchallenged by the son he fears to confront" (*Making Trifles of Terror*, 59).

76. I am relying on Eric Gans's analysis of morality and ethics in chapter 3 of *Originary Thinking*.

77. John Holloway, *The Story of the Night: Studies in Shakespeare's Major Tragedies* (London: Routledge & Kegan Paul, 1961), 97.

78. See John Milton, *Paradise Lost*, ed. Gordon Tesky (New York: W. W. Norton, 2005). In book 5, Eve describes her dream in which she (a) stumbles on "the Tree / Of interdicted Knowledge" (51–52), (b) watches an angel-like figure eat its fruit, (c) follows the angel's example, and (d) discovers her own exalted godlike superiority:

> Forthwith up to the clouds
> With him I flew and underneath beheld
> The earth outstretched immense, a prospect wide
> And various, wond'ring at my flight and change
> To this high exaltation. (86–90)

79. In a remarkable passage, Kottman, in *Love as Human Freedom*, connects Eve's self-consciousness of herself as a sexual being to God's prohibition of the fruit of the Tree of Knowledge: "By picking the fruit and offering it to Adam, Eve offers not just fruit, nor a species-level behavioral response to instinctual hunger, nor rational deliberation, but her own *self-conception*. She offers herself" (82). Kottman calls this "Eve's knowledge" and sees it as the originary condition of, ultimately, the modern idea of sexual love as mutual respect and human freedom. I am sympathetic to Kottman's literary-anthropological approach to understanding the emergence of "love as human freedom," but I think that the idea of mutual reciprocity that he finds in the (idealized) act of love is dependent upon a more fundamental form of reciprocal exchange, namely, that which takes place in the originary scene of language. Eve cannot know herself as a sexual being unless she represents herself as such, which is to say, unless she situates herself at the center of a counternarrative to existing (ritual) narratives. Eve's "forbidden knowledge" of herself as a sexual being begins, as Kottman points out, as a dissatisfaction with mythical or sacred narratives that explain her "fruitfulness" as an emanation of the divine center. In usurping the center, Eve participates in a historical process of desacralization. By making herself a new center, she recreates sacrality in the context of her reciprocal partnership with Adam. Kottman's wager is that this process of desacralization is overall a positive one. I tend to agree, but for some possible reservations, see Catherine Wilson's review of Kottman's "Love as Human Freedom" in *Notre Dame Philosophical Reviews*, November 28, 2017, https://ndpr.nd.edu/reviews/love-as-human-freedom.

80. This seems to be what Matthew Kendrick, in "Refusal in *Measure for Measure*: Shakespeare with Žižek," *Angelaki* 25, no. 6 (2020): 37–50, is driving at when he notes that power lies neither in the law nor in the central figurehead of the law (the king) but in the *signs* of the law, which is to say, in the originary deferral between the word and its sacred object. Kendrick traces this originary difference to Žižek's

(Lacanian) account of the subject's desire for "illicit enjoyment" (40). I'm sympathetic to Kendrick's idea of power involving the anthropological category of desire *as mediated by the sign*, but I think that Gans offers a clearer account of the origin of desire than either Lacan or Žižek.

81. Thus Goddard reads the scene as the last attempt by "the furies of war and murder" to "possess . . . the old man's soul." The assault, however, is unsuccessful. When Lear sinks to the ground crying, "Let me have surgeons; I am cut to the brain," the purification is complete. "It is," Goddard writes, "as if the lacerations had been made less in the attempt of those demons to tear their way into his soul than in tearing their way out from it forever. When we next see the King, with Cordelia restored, his 'insanity' is of the celestial, not the infernal, brand" (*Meaning of Shakespeare*, 2:155).

82. I think I have summarized Cavell's argument accurately, but in case I haven't, here is what he says:

> This is the scene in which Lear's madness is first broken through; in the next scene he is reassembling his sanity. Both the breaking through and the reassembling are manifested by his *recognizing* someone, and my first question is: Why is it Gloucester whom Lear is first able to recognize from his madness and in recognizing whom his sanity begins to return? . . . Given our notion that recognizing a person depends upon allowing oneself to be recognized by him, the question becomes: Why is it Gloucester whose recognition Lear is first able to bear? The obvious answer is: Because Gloucester is blind. Therefore one can be, can only be, *recognized by him without being seen*, without having to bear eyes upon oneself. ("Avoidance of Love," 278–79)

83. Cavell, "Avoidance of Love," 280.

84. Berger suggests that Lear's ambiguous line—"This' a good block" (4.6.183)—refers to the executioner's block. The usual glosses are that it refers to a hat (i.e., by metonymy, the block being the wooden mold for a felt hat), or to a mounting block to get on to a horse (Lear earlier refers to his boots, which may be hunting boots), or to the block or wooden manikin used as target practice for jousting knights on horseback.

85. Shakespeare has prepared us for this image of Lear running into the corn. This is how Cordelia described him two scenes earlier:

> Alack, 'tis he! Why, he was met even now
> As mad as the vexed sea, singing aloud,
> Crowned with rank fumiter and furrow weeds,
> With hardocks, hemlock, nettles, cuckooflowers,
> Darnel, and all the idle weeds that grow

> In our sustaining corn. A century send forth!
> Search every acre in the high-grown field
> And bring him to our eye. (4.4.1–8)

The fact that Lear runs into the "high-grown field" of "our sustaining corn" suggests that it is harvest season or autumn. But the fact that he wears "cuckooflowers" suggests that it is spring. The ambivalence reflects the twofold nature of Lear's sacrifice. He is both victim and hero, dying scapegoat-god and bringer of life.

86. In a shrewd and perceptive essay, Nicholas Luke, in "Avoidance as Love: Evading Cavell on Dover Cliff," *Modern Philology* 117, no. 4 (2020): 445–69, suggests that Cavell's notion of avoidance relies too heavily on an idealized notion of the face-to-face encounter. Luke argues that it would be better to understand representation, especially theatrical representation, as involving a dialectical or paradoxical play between avoidance and recognition. Edgar performs many roles and wears many masks because he is trying to recreate his relationship to his father from scratch. Critics like Cavell and Berger are too hard on Edgar when they accuse him of torture. Only by wearing these masks can "father and son begin to speak truth and speak love for the first time" (459). Luke's account of aesthetic play, especially toward the end of his essay when he speaks of the "creative play of avoidance and recognition" as a "sacred" "transfiguration" capable of transforming the "ordinary" into "something aesthetically beautiful and existentially meaningful" (468), reveals him to be in the (romantic) tradition of Bradley and Goddard. Like them, he sees in Lear's final moments a gesture toward "the alternate romance reality of the late plays, in which fathers and daughters will be reunited and the lifeless rise" (464). I am sympathetic to Luke's reading of the play, particularly to his sense that Shakespeare's art may be conceived as a "radical resacralization of the world" (468).

87. In his account of his experiences in the death camps of Nazi Germany, Viktor Frankl, in *Man's Search for Meaning* (1959; repr., Boston: Beacon Press, 2006), explains that after the initial experience of shock and horror, prisoners underwent a kind of "emotional death," which gradually inoculated them to the many brutalities of life in the death camps. For example, new arrivals would avert their eyes in shame and horror when they saw a guard beating a fellow prisoner, but eventually the prisoner would grow accustomed to these daily horrors and would no longer "avert his eyes.... By then his feelings were blunted, and he watched unmoved" (20–21).

88. Berger, *Making Trifles of Terror*, 45. Berger finds "a touch of smugness" (45) in Cordelia's allusion to Christ ("It is thy business that I go about"), and he sees this as of a piece with her general strategy of presenting herself as a merciful and forgiving savior. The biblical reference is to Luke 2:49, "And he said unto them, How is it that ye sought me? Wist ye not that I must be about my Father's business?"

89. With apologies to Munro Leaf, I have changed the happy ending to fit Shakespeare's own adaptation of the Lear story, the happy ending of which Shakespeare evidently saw as an inaccurate picture of the contest for centrality.

90. Berger, *Making Trifles of Terror*, 302.

91. After observing that "the late sixteenth and early seventeenth centuries are characterized by an exceptional speed of turnover of land" among the peerage, Stone, in *Crisis of the Aristocracy*, points out that a major reason for this turnover was "the failure to provide a male heir" (76–77). Stone estimates the attrition rate of noble families at around 40 percent and remarks that the selling of peerages by the Crown was necessary simply to "plug the gaps." Otherwise, "in 250 years or so there would be no one left to sport a title" (79). Stone's larger point, however, is not that the peerage was experiencing unprecedented attrition rates (it wasn't—40 percent strikes him as moderate) but rather that the very concept of the peerage, with its incessant demand for ever-increasing and frequently suicidal "conspicuous consumption" (86), was under attack. The overselling of peerages by the Crown was, in this sense, merely a symptom of a larger crisis wrought by "the puritan conscience," which had little respect for the extravagant excess of the court and its envious imitators among the aspiring members of the nobility. "By 1641," Stone declares, "rust was eating into the shackles of the Great Chain of Being" (21). In this context, Lear's last "potlatch" should be seen as the death throes of an outmoded ethical system. The fact that Lear has daughters instead of sons, and therefore feels he has to auction off their love with portions of his estate, emphasizes the underlying problem.

92. "When he murmurs, 'Yet Edmund was beloved,'" Bradley writes, "one is almost in danger of forgetting that he had done much more than reject the love of his father and half-brother" (*Shakespearean Tragedy*, 279).

93. "The dying Edmund," Goddard writes, "mortally wounded by Edgar in their duel, changes his mind too late. Edgar's account of their father's death of mingled grief and joy obviously touches him. It is as if the incipient prompting to goodness that may for just a moment be detected in Iago in the presence of Desdemona had survived into another life and come to bud in Edmund" (*Meaning of Shakespeare*, 2:160).

94. Amir Khan, in *Shakespeare in Hindsight*, argues that Edmund's last-minute conversion highlights the contingency of tragedy and forces us to reassess the necessity of Edmund's villainy. "We can," Khan writes, "read Edmund as the preeminent moral agent in the play not because he, like Cordelia, is eminently 'good,' but because he is the only character in the play who acknowledges the universe as contingent" (69). Khan's larger argument is that "counterfactual thinking" encourages us to read the plays as if for the first time. By asking questions like, "Why does Edmund convert and want to do good?" we see the radical contingency of Cordelia's death, and this opens up all kinds of ethical reassessments of the play's

characters. Perhaps Edmund is not so bad after all? Perhaps Cordelia is worse than we imagined? The title of Khan's chapter on *King Lear* is "Reversing Good and Evil: Counterfactual Thinking and *King Lear*." Though Khan does not cite Berger, he acknowledges Cavell's influence on his reading of the play.

95. Cavell, "Avoidance of Love," 282.

96. Kenneth Burke, *Kenneth Burke on Shakespeare*, ed. Scott Newstok (West Lafayette, IN: Parlor Press, 2007), 188.

97. Of Edmund's dying effort to do some good, Bradley writes, "There is something pathetic here which tempts one to dream that, if Edmund had been whole brother to Edgar, and had been at home during those 'nine years' when he was 'out,' he might have been a very different man" (*Shakespearean Tragedy*, 279).

98. Bradley, *Shakespearean Tragedy*, 269.

99. Bradley, 270.

100. Bradley, 298.

101. Goddard, *Meaning of Shakespeare*, 2:171.

102. Berger, *Making Trifles of Terror*, 64.

103. Berger notes that Edmund's first soliloquy, despite gleefully positioning him in the role of rebel and villain, nonetheless betrays his dependency on traditional structures of authority in, for example, primogeniture and knightly etiquette: "The soliloquy that begins with a counter-patriarchal appeal to Goddess Nature ultimately reveals itself as an act of *reauthorizing* the father" (*Making Trifles of Terror*, 316). In the same chapter, he remarks that in *The Merchant of Venice* the Christians use "the very practices" they "stigmatize in the Jew. Their mercy is revenge—not a gentle rain, but a ton of bricks" (318). I admire Berger's capacity to tease out so deftly the ethical contradictions in the language used by Shakespeare's characters. Berger is silent, however, on the historical and anthropological implications of his close readings of Shakespeare. There are occasional nods to Jacques Lacan and, in this particular chapter, to Norbert Elias's thesis of "the internalization of social control" (329). But he offers no hypothesis about why such control might be necessary, or indeed what distinguishes modern instances of social and cultural control from premodern ones. One might express the point by asking, "What makes your analysis of Shakespeare specifically ethical?" If by *ethical* Berger means that he is interested in the moral self-appraisals of the characters and how these self-appraisals are influenced by the discursive communities constructed by the language of the play, then what is to distinguish Berger's ethical criticism from the criticism of, say, A. C. Bradley, other than a more rigorous attention to the language of the text? But why do humans have language? On this fundamental anthropological question, Berger offers no answer.

104. Citing John Vyvyan's claim that Shakespeare's last plays were "less concerned with the art of theatre than with the science of life" (*Shakespearean Ethic*, 4),

Paul Kottman, in "Why Shakespeare Stopped Writing Tragedies," *Journal of Medieval and Early Modern Studies* 49, no. 1 (2019): 113–35, argues that "Shakespeare came to understand" that "the unmet demands of mutual intelligibility and reciprocity in human affairs . . . could not be adequately grasped in tragic drama" (114) and that Shakespeare's recognition of this fact is evident in Prospero's plea to the audience, in the epilogue to *The Tempest*, that he be released and set free from the spell of aesthetic centrality that both he and the audience conspire in creating. Kottman interprets Prospero's plea along Hegelian lines as "a farewell to art's highest vocation as a sensuous presentation of the Absolute" (131), but he also points to the decline of "religiously sanctioned rituals" and the emergence of "a modern, secular, market-driven world" (120) requiring "new modes of recognition between audience and performer" (121). Kottman does not spell out the exact nature of this new mode of recognition, but he seems to be alluding to the everyday ethical interactions between individuals in a market stripped of centralizing sacred ritual. This new economic sphere eschews the asymmetries of ritual and aesthetic modes of interaction with the center. Of course, we are always free to walk out of the theater, but the aesthetic space represented by the dramatic stage forces our attention onto central figures, such as Lear and Cordelia, over which we have no control.

Chapter Two

1. The notable exception is Timon, whose death is so miserably untragic and nonviolent that he has to die offstage.

2. Berger, *Making Trifles of Terrors*, 345.

3. Why the king of Hungary? In George Whetstone's *Promos and Cassandra*, a major source text for *Measure for Measure*, the king of Hungary is the prototype of the Duke of Vienna. In Whetstone's play, the king appoints Promos governor of the city of Julio. Promos condemns a young man (Andrugio) to die for breaking the law against fornication. The young man's sister, Cassandra, pleads for her brother's life, which Promos agrees to spare if she sleeps with him. She does, but he reneges and sends Cassandra her brother's head. She complains to the king of Hungary, who forces Promos to marry her and then condemns him to death, but she pleads for his life. It turns out her brother is still alive—a kindly jailor committed a subterfuge by sending Cassandra the head of an executed felon instead. The king forgives Promos and advises him to be a good husband. In the light of Shakespeare's source, Lucio's itching to participate in a military action against the king of Hungary seems like an inside joke. Lucio never misses an opportunity to slander the high and mighty, whom he suspects of being a good deal less pure and virtuous than they make themselves out to be. Since a king outranks a duke, he sides with the dukes against the king. When it turns out that this conspiracy against the king of Hungary was just a ruse fabricated by the Duke, Lucio turns his calumny on the Duke instead.

Well might the Duke bemoan "back-wounding calumny" as he moves in disguise among his people, all the while conducting little impromptu opinion polls of himself. In the age of social media, the Duke would be hungrily counting his ratings and followers.

4. Peter Goldie, in *The Mess Inside: Narrative, Emotion, and the Mind* (Oxford: Oxford University Press, 2012), explains that all narratives assume a distinction between internal and external characters. This applies not just to the fictional narratives of literature but to the everyday autobiographical narratives we tell ourselves. All narratives assume a gap between the narrator and the narrated, the external and internal narrative perspectives. This gap in narrative perspective is why we may discover new facts about ourselves that we did not notice until we consciously represented these facts in a narrative. In other words, by representing ourselves we also acquire the means to transform ourselves. I will return to Goldie's useful distinction when I discuss the Duke's attempt to control the narrative in the second half of the play.

5. A. D. Nuttall, "*Measure for Measure*: Quid Pro Quo?," *Shakespeare Studies* 4 (1968): 231–51.

6. Nuttall, "Quid Pro Quo?," 244.

7. The benevolent view of the Duke is well represented by Wilson Knight's essay "*Measure for Measure* and the Gospels," in *Wheel of Fire*. Knight claims that the "Duke, like Jesus, is the prophet of a new order of ethics" (88). For an ethical reading of the play sympathetic to Knight's argument, see also Vyvyan, *Shakespearean Ethic*, chaps. 6–8. For a more recent defense of the Christian argument, see G. M. Pinciss, "'Heavenly Comforts of Despair' and *Measure for Measure*," *Studies in English Literature, 1500–1900* 30, no. 2 (Spring 1990): 303–13. Pinciss argues that "the Duke's eccentricities" can be explained as Shakespeare's representation of "providential intervention" and that the Duke teaches "that through despair we can acquire the faith to believe that we will be saved not through our goodness but God's" (306–7). For a very different approach to this question, which nonetheless reaches the same optimistic conclusion that the Duke is a paragon of the merciful sacral ruler, see Debora Kuller Shuger, *Political Theologies in Shakespeare's England: The Sacred and the State in "Measure for Measure"* (New York: Palgrave, 2001). Unlike the above critics, Shuger is not really interested in reading *Measure for Measure*. Instead, she assumes that the Duke *is* a paragon of mercy and then looks to historical sources to back up this claim. Her main argument is that the Duke represents a penitential form of justice (associated with Anglicanism and James I) rather than a penal one (associated with Puritanism). Both of these "visionary theocracies" (131) deny the claims of the secular (liberal) state. As Stephen Guy-Bray drily notes in his review of Shuger, her argument only works if one ignores "the sadism of the Duke" (Review of *Political Theologies in Shakespeare's England: The Sacred and the State*

in *"Measure for Measure,"* by Debora Kuller Shuger, *Religious Studies and Theology* 22, no.2 (2003): 79).

8. Graham Bradshaw, *Shakespeare's Scepticism* (Brighton, UK: Harvester Press, 1987), 174.

9. Nuttall, "Quid Pro Quo?," 242.

10. Berger, *Trifles of Terror*, 358.

11. Nuttall, "Quid Pro Quo?," 239.

12. Nuttall, 239.

13. Berger, *Trifles of Terror*, 365.

14. One may be reminded of Prince Hal's words in *1 Henry IV* when he explains why he condescends to mix with the worser sort in the Boar's Head tavern:

> I know you all, and will awhile uphold
> The unyoked humor of your idleness.
> Yet herein will I imitate the sun,
> Who doth permit the base contagious clouds
> To smother up his beauty from the world,
> That when he please again to be himself,
> Being wanted he may be more wondered at
> By breaking through the foul and ugly mists
> Of vapors that did seem to strangle him. (1.3.189–97)

15. See Nuttall, "Quid Pro Quo?," 241.

16. Nuttall, 239. See also A. P. Rossiter, *Angel with Horns and Other Shakespearean Lectures*, ed. Graham Storey (London: Longmans, 1961). Like both Nuttall and Bradshaw, Rossiter is scornful of Wilson Knight's attempt to read *Measure for Measure* as a morality play in which the Duke plays the starring role of the merciful "Jesus-figure" (165).

17. Just before the Mousetrap play is performed, Hamlet says to Horatio:

> Observe my uncle. If his occulted guilt
> Do not itself unkennel in one speech,
> It is a damnéd ghost that we have seen,
> And my imaginations are as foul
> As Vulcan's stithy. (3.2.79–83)

18. For a close historical examination of the engagement process from betrothal to marriage, see Victoria Hayne, "Performing Social Practice: The Example of *Measure for Measure*," *Shakespeare Quarterly* 44, no. 1 (Spring 1993): 1–29. Hayne writes that "both church and society tended to wink at prenuptial sex as long as it had no permanent socioeconomic consequences in the form of a child," while "fornication in the absence of betrothal was regarded much more seriously" and "merited a full

public penance, usually before the assembled parish in church on Sunday or in the marketplace" (6). Hayne's larger argument is that attempts by religious extremists to make adultery or fornication a criminal offense punishable by imprisonment or even death were repeatedly rejected by more moderate parliamentarians, who represented the consensus "that there were widespread limits to how far the state, conceived as separate from the church, should intrude upon the personal and moral lives of subjects" (17).

19. Bradshaw argues that the law under which Claudio is condemned is not a general law against fornication but, more precisely, a law against fornication *leading to pregnancy*. Bradshaw supposes that this is why Isabella does not mention the contract between Claudio and Juliet, because "the argument would be legally irrelevant and inadmissible" (*Shakespeare's Scepticism*, 215). Obviously, a law prohibiting fornication is extremely challenging to enforce and only those who leave behind clear evidence (pregnancy, illegitimate children) are likely to get prosecuted. But even if we assume that Claudio is condemned not for fornication but because he got Julietta with child, this still doesn't change the fact that he and Julietta are betrothed, a fact that makes their case very different from, for example, Lucio's scandalous seduction of Kate Keepdown, who presumably turned to prostitution because Lucio refused to marry her after he fathered her child. Surely we should expect a judge to be interested in these factual distinctions. In any case, one can hardly expect Isabella, who is not a lawyer, to be particularly concerned about what is legally admissible when she pleads for her brother's life. In fact, most of her arguments are "legally irrelevant and inadmissible."

20. "It is one of Shakespeare's most effective outrages," Harold Bloom writes, in *Shakespeare: The Invention of the Human*, "that Isabella is his most sexually provocative female character, far more seductive even than Cleopatra, the professional seductress" (365).

21. A. R. Braunmuller and Robert Watson, eds., *Measure for Measure*, in *Measure for Measure* (London: Bloomsbury Publishing, 2020), 226, http://dx.doi.org/10.5040/9781474208086.00000042.

22. Braunmuller and Watson, *Measure for Measure*, 226.

23. The "most important single factor" in the decline of the power of the aristocracy in the sixteenth century, Stone writes, in *Crisis of the Aristocracy*, "was the shrinkage in numbers and in scale of the overmighty subjects of the Crown." This decline had many causes, from the biological failure to produce an heir to changes in moral attitudes toward the peerage itself, but chief among these causes Stone counts the deliberate policy of Tudor monarchs to reduce the power of the peerage by "refraining from building up new landed families to replace those which died out." "After 1572," Stone observes, "there was not a duke in the country until the revival of the title for Richmond and Buckingham by James I" (129).

24. See the previous chapter for a discussion of Brutus's metaphor of the ladder of ambition.

25. Greenblatt, in *Shakespearean Negotiations*, appears to give the Duke a free pass when he argues that the Duke is Shakespeare's representation of what happens when religious institutions are "transferred to the stage" (138). For Greenblatt, the Duke/friar becomes "an emblem of the playwright" in which religious "anxiety is emptied out in the service of theatrical pleasure" (138). Greenblatt notes that the religious version of what he labels "salutary anxiety" affects most especially the Protestant believer, who has no way of knowing whither his soul is bound. Will it be eternal perdition or eternal bliss? Greenblatt's argument assumes that the anxiety of the Catholic believer is much reduced, if not completely absent, because Catholics can hedge their bets through good works, confession, or outright bribery of those earthly officials tasked with shepherding one's soul into heavenly bliss. The demise of these "idolatrous" Catholic institutions opens the path to a newly energized secular and commercial theater. The latter steps into the vacuum left by the destruction of the older ritual methods for dealing with religious "anxiety," which is now, as per the hypothesis, ratcheted up to an extremely high pitch. Where are the people to vent their anxiety now? Greenblatt's answer: in the theater! Thus, Renaissance dramatists become the high priests in the "arousing and manipulating" of "anxiety" (133). In Shakespeare, this mastery is taken to an extreme. In representing the theatrical manipulations of the priesthood, Shakespeare undermines their religious purpose. Anxiety is not so much used to control the subject as it is *exposed* as a method of control. I'm inclined to agree with this last claim, but Greenblatt stops the analysis just as it begins to get interesting. After observing that there is a shift from ritual to theatrical modes of constraining mimetic desire, he doesn't venture an explanation for why this shift occurs. Instead, Greenblatt concludes with the following remark: "All that it [i.e., the Duke's reformist moral zeal] has done is to offer the spectators pleasure in the spectacle. But that pleasure is precisely Shakespeare's professional purpose, and his ironic reflections on salutary anxiety do not at all diminish his commitment to it as a powerful theatrical technique" (141–42). Why is Shakespeare committed to salutary anxiety as a powerful theatrical technique? What distinguishes the sacred and aesthetic uses of salutary anxiety, and why is this distinction useful or important? Greenblatt's new-historicist framework comes tantalizingly close to, but ultimately stops short of, an anthropological hypothesis capable of explaining this shift from the ritual constraint of desire to theater's deliberate arousal of it.

26. See Ernest Gellner's brilliant analysis of the philosophical and anthropological contexts of psychoanalysis in *The Psychoanalytic Movement: The Cunning of Unreason*, 3rd ed. (London: Blackwell Publishing, 2003).

27. See Émile Durkheim, *The Elementary Forms of Religious Life*, trans. Karen E.

Fields (New York: Free Press, 1995), first published in 1912 as *Les formes élémentaire de la vie religieuse*.

28. See Tomasello, *Cultural Origins of Human Cognition*.
29. Rossiter, *Angel with Horns*, 165.
30. Goddard, *Meaning of Shakespeare*, 2:55.
31. Goldie, *The Mess Inside*.
32. For a sophisticated attempt to systematize the study of Shakespeare's soliloquies using both computer-assisted quantitative methods and traditional literary analysis, see Marcus Nordlund, *The Shakespearean Inside: A Study of the Complete Soliloquies and Solo Asides* (Edinburgh: Edinburgh University Press, 2017).
33. Shakespeare's most fully developed experiment in a character who is also the author of the action performed on the stage is Prospero. Hence the irresistible urge among critics to associate Prospero with Shakespeare. I think this intuition is basically sound, not because I am sentimental about Prospero (on the contrary!), but because Prospero's aesthetic or "magical" power over his internal characters is self-consciously represented by Shakespeare as conditional upon the Duke's displacement from real political power. Prospero remains an exile for the duration of the play, which is to say, he never leaves the island.
34. Northrop Frye, in *Northrop Frye on Shakespeare* (Markham, Ontario: Fitzhenry & Whiteside, 1986), makes much of the shift from tragedy to comedy and pinpoints the transition in the moment the Duke steps forward to start talking in prose to Isabella.
35. Harriet Hawkins, *The Devil's Party: Critical Counter-interpretations of Shakespearian Drama* (Oxford: Oxford University Press, 1985), 72.
36. Richard P. Wheeler, *Shakespeare's Development and the Problem Comedies: Turn and Counter-turn* (Berkeley: University of California Press, 1981), 127.
37. Wheeler, 126.
38. Wheeler, 138.
39. Berger, *Making Trifles of Terrors*, 358.
40. Berger, 365.
41. William Shakespeare, *The Complete Works of Shakespeare*, 6th ed., ed. David Bevington (New York: Pearson Longman, 2009), 440.
42. Bradshaw, *Shakespeare's Scepticism*, 164. Bradshaw quotes Schlegel's observation that the play's "true significance . . . is the triumph of mercy over strict justice," which gives the impression that Schlegel's reading, like Knight's, is candidly in favor of the Duke. But Schlegel also notes that the Duke "is too fond of round-about ways; his vanity is flattered with acting invisibly like an earthly providence; he takes more pleasure in overhearing his subjects than governing them in the customary ways of princes." Schlegel suggests that Lucio's slanders of the Duke "are not wholly without foundation," and he groups the Duke with other unconsci-

entious "pious frauds," such as the meddling friars in *Romeo and Juliet* and *Much Ado about Nothing*, who "busy themselves in the affairs of others." In short, Schlegel is not unaware of the irony that undermines the Christian reading of the play. Schlegel's comments on *Measure for Measure* can be found in *A Course of Lectures on Dramatic Art and Literature*, trans. John Black (London: Henry G. Bohn, 1846), 387–88. These lectures were first delivered in 1808 in (coincidentally) Vienna.

43. Bradshaw, *Shakespeare's Scepticism*, 174.
44. Knight, *Wheel of Fire*, 107.
45. Bradshaw, *Shakespeare's Scepticism*, 176.
46. Berger, *Making Trifles of Terrors*, 336.
47. Berger, 336.
48. W. H. Auden, in "The Joker in the Pack," calls Iago a "practical joker" and notes that "there is something slightly sinister about every practical joker . . . who likes to play God behind the scenes" (255–56). Auden's remarks apply equally well, I think, to the Duke. See Auden, *The Dyer's Hand and Other Essays* (1948; repr., New York: Vintage Books, 1989).
49. The Duke states that he has let the laws slip for "fourteen years" (1.3.21), but Claudio says that "nineteen zodiacs" (1.2.165) of ducal laxity have passed. Noting the difference, Berger remarks, in an endnote, that the "inconsistency can be chalked up to compositorial or authorial nodding," but it also "makes sense for Claudio to exaggerate the time period and for the Duke to minimize it" (461n18).
50. Bradshaw, *Shakespeare's Scepticism*, 208–9.
51. Berger, *Trifles of Terror*, 365. Berger's reference to Brutus is apt. Later, Brutus will accuse Cassius of corruption and, in the same astonishing breath, demand money from Cassius to pay his legions because he "can raise no money by vile means" (4.3.72). Brutus is like the Duke in that he is happy for others to pay the price of getting their hands dirty as long as he can (a) keep his hands clean and (b) enjoy the rewards of their "dirty" money.
52. I have found only one critic who has not only noticed the Duke's resentment but placed it at the center of his interpretation of the play. Calling the Duke "a cynical old man of a slightly sadistic disposition" and "a badly disguised snooper who revels in the excrement of the human soul" (116), Piotr Nowak, in "Gods and Children: Shakespeare Reads *The Prince*," *Philosophy and Literature* 41, no. 1A (2017): 109–27, describes the play as "a story about the 'mercy' and 'magnanimity' of the old" under which lurks "a concealed agenda for revenge on the young, conceived in pure envy" (120). Many of Nowak's comments are insightful, but by associating resentment with old age, he undermines many of his best insights. Resentment is not the exclusive prerogative of the old. On the contrary, it affects all who feel dispossessed from the center, which is to say, everyone. Nowak's view of youth or childhood strikes me as far too idealized. For him the initiation into the scene of

resentment is a sign of old age—"In *Measure for Measure*, the failure of the young is certainly a lesson for them, and it brings something new into their lives: the founding capital for resentment" (126)—but even a five-year-old child can experience resentment, because the child knows what it feels like to be excluded from the center of admiration and resents it.

53. Noticing the Duke's convoluted and evasive way of speaking, Matthew Hunter, in "*Measure for Measure* and the Problem of Style," *ELH* 83, no. 2 (Summer 2016): 457–88, suggests that the Duke deliberately conceals his private life from the public sphere. Hence his resentment of Lucio, who speculates "over [the Duke's] private, sexual life" (472). I admire Hunter's close analysis of style, but his argument is very different from mine. He argues that the Duke's obscure way of talking reflects the attempt to protect one's privacy among strangers with whom one is increasingly forced to do business in growing commercial centers like London. *Measure for Measure* is an exploration of the dialectic between public and private that is a distinct preoccupation of city comedy, which deals with the bustle of the city marketplace rather than the faraway (heroic) worlds of romance or tragedy.

54. Wheeler, *Shakespeare's Development*, 138.

55. For a thoughtful discussion of the Duke's soliloquy, see N. W. Bawcutt, "'He Who the Sword of Heaven Will Bear': The Duke versus Angelo in *Measure for Measure*," *Shakespeare Survey*, vol. 37, ed. Stanley Wells, (Cambridge: Cambridge University Press, 1984). Though sensitive to the disparity between the (tragic) conflicts raised by the first half of the play and the (comic) solutions imposed by the Duke in the second half, Bawcutt ultimately explains the Duke's intervention in question-begging terms as the result of "Shakespeare's decision" (97) to go against his sources by keeping his heroine's virginity intact. This change necessitates the bed trick and, therefore, the Duke's intervention. But this explanation is just another way of distracting ourselves from an ethical examination of the Duke's motivations. Are we to believe that the Duke is motivated by Shakespeare's desire to adapt his sources?

56. See Frye, in *Northrop Frye on Shakespeare*. Frye's longstanding interest in the structural archetypes of literature means that he is willing to grant the Duke a fair bit of latitude. Since comedy's roots are to be found in ancient mythical archetypes such as the trickster figure, we may understand the Duke's prominence in the second half of the play by attending to these fundamental structural features. His machinations may seem implausible and psychologically suspect from the point of view of tragedy, but from the point of view of comedy they make sense. Thus the Duke is "a trickster figure who is trying to turn a tragic situation into a comic one" (150), while Mariana is "the spark plug of the second half of the play" (152), and her beautiful song shows that the tragedy is winding down and the comedy is ramping up. Frye's comments about the influence of structural archetypes are illuminating, but the fact remains that the Duke is not merely an archetype but an

all-too-human character. If we excuse or explain his behavior as a necessity of the archetype, we may ignore the most interesting thing about him, which is that he is dishonest about what he is doing, not just with others but also with himself. In the end, Frye's argument is a more sophisticated version of the notion that an apparent contradiction or implausibility in the plot or character can be explained by the fact that Shakespeare momentarily lost his concentration. In the case of the Duke, we excuse his deceitfulness by saying, well, this is just Shakespeare reproducing the trickster archetype.

57. Andrew Gurr, in *"Measure for Measure*'s Hoods and Masks: The Duke, Isabella, and Liberty," *English Literary Renaissance* 27, no. 1 (Winter 1997): 89–105, defends the traditional (optimistic) view that marriage represents a (comic) solution to "the different positions across the scale from absolute liberty to absolute law" (91). Thus, when Isabella removes her mask (traditionally worn by noblewomen when they venture out of the house) and Lucio removes Friar Lodowick's hood, we are meant to understand that the pair have abandoned their desire to retreat from the world—he to the monastery, she to the convent—and, accordingly, "are freed from their devotion to the rigorous law" (103). Gurr's argument about the use of hoods and masks is fascinating, but ultimately, he too attempts to answer the basic ethical question of what motivates the Duke by turning it into a different question about how the play might have been staged by Shakespeare.

58. Robert N. Watson, in "False Immortality in *Measure for Measure*: Comic Means, Tragic Ends," *Shakespeare Quarterly* 41, no. 4 (Winter 1990): 411–32, explains the critical habit of pointing to "the inadequacies of the comic resolution" (417), including the Duke's "immoral" bed trick and "implausible" head trick (429), as reflecting "an unwillingness to see the play's darker purpose ... which is to challenge the sentimental notion of our individual significance" (430) by noticing that the play is a "stubbornly socio-biological play," one that is "as subversive to more recent humanistic pieties as it is to medieval Christian ones" (427). For Watson, the play, in its relentless ironizing of everything sacred and meaningful, whether Isabella's chastity, Claudio's life, Angelo's devotion to the law, or God's everlasting mercy, affirms only the grim sociobiological imperative, which is the propagation of the species under the watchful eye of the state. The Duke, whom Watson calls the "Grim Breeder" (416), is an agent of the state, whose only interest is managing "the mechanism of biology" in "the procreative impulse" in order to preserve "social structures rather than individual consciousnesses" (424). Obviously, this view of the play is radically anti-ethical and antihuman. To the question, "What is culture?" Watson's response is ultimately no different from those of E. O. Wilson or Richard Dawkins. Culture is nature's way of propagating the species. *Measure for Measure* is just another evolutionary strategy, like the bee dance or chimpanzee tool use. But the very anthropomorphism of Watson's conception of the state—for

example, when he says that "the state is merely doing its best to harness, rationalize, even sentimentalize, the relentless march of nature" (424)—undermines his sociobiological premises and reintroduces the ethical via the backdoor. We can only talk about the state's desire to harness, rationalize, or sentimentalize by understanding the Duke's desire to harness, rationalize, or sentimentalize. In other words, we are back to the ethical problem of understanding the Duke's motivations, which cannot be so easily reduced to a sociobiological imperative. The leap from nature to culture is ever haunted by the ethical, which is to say, the anthropological.

59. Berger is much influenced by Stanley Cavell's view that Lear's madness is a form of shameful avoidance of the other. See Berger, acknowledgments to *Making Trifles of Terror*, ix-xxiv.

60. See also Carolyn E. Brown, "The Homoeroticism of Duke Vincentio: 'Some Feeling for the Sport,'" *Studies in Philology* 94, no. 2 (Spring 1997): 187–220. Brown pursues the hypothesis that the Duke is secretly in love with Angelo, who rebuffs the Duke's sexual advances. She sees the Duke as a veiled reference to King James, who was given to granting power to his male favorites. Despite the tendentiousness of much of the argument, Brown's observation that the Duke "conceals his desires" in order "to enhance his ducal image" (190) is insightful, and her sense that the multiple ironies and ambivalences in the play invite us "to puncture" the Duke's "saintly surface," which "he maintains" "so expertly" (190), is very much in line with the spirit of my argument. There are, in fact, many useful insights in this essay, but the overall argument suffers from two large—and, in my opinion, insurmountable—problems: (1) it seeks to prove its hypothesis by appealing, rather bizarrely, to extradramatic evidence (King James was fond of young men and made them his court favorites); and (2) it ignores a great deal of the counterevidence in the text itself.

61. In a fine analysis of "chastity as a natural form of power" and therefore as a way Isabella can resist "the political power of men," Barbara J. Baines, in "Assaying the Power of Chastity in *Measure for Measure*," *Studies in English Literature, 1500–1900* 30, no. 2 (Spring 1990): 283–301, argues that Angelo sees Isabella as a threat whom he wants to dominate "by robbing her of her chastity" (293). Baines perceptively notes that Isabella's language in her first interview with Angelo betrays a certain coquettishness that, however subconsciously, "presents her as pleading for a vice," which "invites Angelo to see her as a mirror image of himself as he succumbs to his desire for her" (294).

62. See Girard, *Theater of Envy*, 295–96.

63. Lucy Owen, in "Mode and Character in *Measure for Measure*," *Shakespeare Quarterly* 25, no. 1 (Winter 1974): 17–32, makes the point that Isabella understands the imperfect human context of the law much better than Angelo, whose view of the law is highly literal and legalistic. "Isabella," Owen writes, "sees farther than

Angelo into the implications of the comedy of human existence. She realizes that justice itself in human hands is liable to the same follies as other human activities" (25). Owen's larger argument is that the Duke is a "[p]rovidential figure" (32), "who speaks and acts throughout the play rather from his desire to help others and his knowledge of their natures than from any need of his own" (28). While I agree that the Duke certainly busies himself with the task of correcting the faults of others, I disagree that the Duke is himself faultless. Ultimately, Owens's argument suffers from the same difficulty affecting all perspectives which interpret the Duke as a providential figure. It becomes impossible to treat him as an imperfect human being.

64. J. W. Lever, ed., *Measure for Measure*, in *Measure for Measure*. The Arden Shakespeare Second Series (London: Bloomsbury Publishing Plc, 2015), 2–149, http://dx.doi.org/10.5040/9781408160237.00000030, xxvi.

65. Robert Pierce, in "Being a Moral Agent in Shakespeare's Vienna," *Philosophy and Literature* 33, no. 2 (2009): 267–79, argues that the Duke is an "idealist like Brutus" and adopts the friar disguise "to educate his subjects" (276). I think the comparison to Brutus is apt—he, too, wants to stir up the citizens to an act of rage and after seem to chide them—but I am far from agreeing that Brutus and the Duke are honorable idealists, though of course that is the way they like to see themselves.

66. Despite perceptively noting that the Duke's choice of Angelo is "an increasingly unsettling source of curiosity to us" (274), Cynthia Lewis, in "'Dark Deeds Darkly Answered': Duke Vincentio and Judgment in *Measure for Measure*," *Shakespeare Quarterly* 34, no. 3 (Autumn 1983): 271–89, subscribes to the view that the Duke represents the "ideal balance . . . between strict punishment and mercy" (288). Lewis makes many pertinent observations, including the notion that Lucio represents a part of the Duke and that "the Duke's excuse for giving his office to Angelo can appear self-serving and evasive" (275). But in the end she too idealizes the Duke and therefore understates the self-exculpatory function of the Duke's self-representations. She reads the final scene as revealing "the Duke's new-found openness towards his subjects" (286). I see no evidence of the Duke's openness at the end. On the contrary, the scene is stage-managed by the Duke to coerce his subjects into behaving in the way he wants them to.

67. For the "monstrous conspiracy" against love, see the previous chapter, esp. pp. 92–93.

68. Alexander Leggatt points out, in "Substitution in *Measure for Measure*," *Shakespeare Quarterly* 39, no. 3 (Autumn 1988): 342–59, that the Duke does not merely disguise himself as a friar but usurps the role with wholehearted and unabashed fraudulence. For instance, he confesses Juliet, Claudio, and Mariana. "For anyone who takes this sacrament seriously," Leggatt writes, "the implications of the Duke's conduct do not bear thinking about. There is no such thing as a substitute

priest, and the Duke's assumption of priestly power means, among other things, that he is giving false absolutions to people on the point of death" (357).

69. Marc Shell, in *The End of Kinship: "Measure for Measure," Incest, and the Ideal of Universal Siblinghood* (Stanford, CA: Stanford University Press, 1988), argues that the Duke is "the principal caitiff in *Measure for Measure*, the one whose conscious and unconscious intents Angelo acts out" (93). Angelo "acts out (gives birth to) Vincentio's desires and hence as substitute educates Vincentio by demonstration, without bringing the Duke into disrepute" (92). Shell concludes that the Duke, like his substitute, desires "to raze the sanctuary" and "wants to have sexual relations with" Isabella (91). Berger, in *Making Trifles of Terror*, finds the textual evidence for Shell's thesis too thin and objects that there is no evidence of ducal "hanky-panky" (465). I think Berger misses the point, which is that Angelo is a mediator of the Duke's illicit desires. There is no obvious sexual hanky-panky precisely because the hanky-panky is voyeuristically observed by the Duke of dark corners rather than enacted. I am sympathetic to Shell's reading of the Duke's forbidden desire for Isabella, but I trace the origin of this desire not to the incest taboo but to the originary scene of language upon which all symbolic interdiction depends, including the interdiction against incest. What brings Angelo and the Duke together is their shared resentment of the sacred center, a position they imagine Isabella—the "bride of God"—to have scandalously usurped.

70. See Gans, *Originary Thinking*, esp. chap. 7.

71. Anna Kamaralli, in "Writing about Motive: Isabella, the Duke and Moral Authority," in *Shakespeare Survey*, vol. 58, ed. Peter Holland (Cambridge: Cambridge University Press, 2005), argues that Isabella's plea for Angelo's life "takes [the Duke] completely by surprise and produces his rather clumsy rejection of her plea" (59). Kamaralli objects to the idea that the Duke is "testing" Isabella but accepts the widely held view that Isabella is pleading for mercy over (merely legal) justice. Kamaralli's heterodox defense of Isabella's intelligence, independence, and integrity is highly persuasive (and most welcome), but she stops short of including the Duke in the attacks on Isabella's virginity. I think the Duke can be included as the most deceitful of the male conspirators who assault Isabella's independence.

72. Gurr, in "Hoods and Masks," notes that the Duke's offer of marriage is a version of Angelo's offer of sex, the difference being that "Angelo's experience is a violent parody of the temptation that the Duke goes through more quietly, and with better restraint" (93).

73. In his analysis of the contested site of "sexual memory," Stephen Spiess, in "The Measure of Sexual Memory," in *Shakespeare Survey*, vol. 67, ed. Peter Holland (Cambridge: Cambridge University Press, 2014), observes that Lucio is the only character to contest the Duke's official narrative at the end. Spiess sees Lucio "as a figure of memory" whose "alternative framework through which audiences might

perceive the sexual politics of Shakespeare's Vienna" is also "that which state authority seeks to silence and suppress" (325). I agree with Spiess's claim that Lucio contests the Duke's attempt to impose *his* (official) narrative on his subjects, but I think that this claim is more easily understood when put in the ethical context of the Duke as a person rather than as a representative of the (imperial and sacred) center. It makes little sense to say "that the state itself possesses desire" (325). States do not desire, persons do. When the Duke dons the imperial mantle at the end, he "suppresses" the peephole narrative of desire he has vicariously experienced through his fallen—and now thoroughly humiliated—deputy. In other words, the Duke's official state narrative includes two steps: first, he humiliates Angelo by exposing the latter's fraudulent occupation of the imperial center; and, second, by this action he secures his greater legitimacy as the one true prince whose moral purity remains unrivaled. Hence his anger at Lucio, whose refusal to treat him as immune to the "dribbling dart of love" continues to position him as an equal—and therefore also a rival—rather than as an unrivaled prince.

74. In an illuminating and ingenious argument, Andrew Majeske, in "Equity's Absence: The Extremity of Claudio's Prosecution and Barnardine's Pardon in Shakespeare's *Measure for Measure*," *Law and Literature* 21, no. 2 (Summer 2009): 169–84, argues that the Duke's motivation has always been "to reestablish the rule of law in Vienna" by "refounding" the state (169). The problem is that this can only be achieved by extreme shock therapy administered along violent Machiavellian lines. The Duke adopts and adapts Machiavelli's strategy, first, by putting the severe Angelo in charge, who very precisely targets an upper-class citizen (Claudio) who has committed, everyone assumes, a harmless crime; and, second, by then distancing himself from Angelo (this is the ingenious part of the argument) by delivering a second shock, the "seemingly irrational pardon of Barnardine" that "precisely balances and counteracts Angelo's confoundingly strict application of the law in Claudio's case" (178). From the perspective of his subjects, the pardoning of Barnardine must appear "mad," but madness is what is necessary to refound the state: "The pardon is a breathtaking public display of the Duke's power over his subjects designed to surpass their comprehension" (178).

75. In an interesting argument, Paul Yachnin, in "The Laws of *Measure for Measure*," in *Shakespeare and Judgment*, ed. Kevin Curran (Edinburgh: Edinburgh University Press, 2017), 139–56, claims that the Duke's "pardon party" (142) is deliberately represented as a travesty of justice to encourage the offstage audience members to participate in the collective process of aesthetic, moral, and legal judgment. Yachnin reads the play as shifting focus from traditional notions of law-making associated with, first, the "law of sovereign will" (145) and, second, the "law of kind," which Yachnin defines as "our recognition of our shared rootedness in nature" (147), to a new type of law giving, which he calls the "law of judgment" (148). Yach-

nin associates the latter with the emergence of a public sphere in which private citizens are free to debate controversial political ideas. He argues that the early modern public theaters were key to cultivating a shared public space for open debate. The weird ending of *Measure for Measure* is a signal to the audience that its members, rather than simply accepting the edicts issued from the sacred monarchal center represented by the Duke, have to make up their own minds about how to judge both the Duke and the moral and legal problems the play raises.

76. In this sense, the Duke's mad potlatch of clemency resembles somewhat Timon's mad potlatch of charitable giving. E. S. Mallin, in "Charity and Whoredom in *Timon of Athens*," *Shakespeare Quarterly* 69, no. 2 (Summer 2018): 75–100, argues that *Timon of Athens* explores the ethical contradictions in the concept of charity. Timon's extravagant acts of gift-giving are designed to centralize the giver at the expense of the receiver. Like Lear on the heath, Timon ends up being ejected from the center. This experience is humiliating because it puts both men in the position of their formerly dependent clients. Hence their resentment, which is also a recognition of the injustice of *their own infractions* against the moral reciprocity of the human periphery. Unlike Lear or Timon, Vincentio never discovers the scandal of his usurpation of the center. (I should note that the terminology of center and periphery is mine, not Mallin's.)

Conclusion

1. Auden, "The Joker in the Pack," in *Dyer's Hand*.
2. Vyvyan, *Shakespearean Ethic*.
3. A book on the subject of Shakespeare's exiles is currently in preparation.

Bibliography

Adelman, Janet. *Suffocating Mothers: Fantasies of Maternal Origin in Shakespeare's Plays, "Hamlet" to "The Tempest."* London: Routledge, 1992.

Auden, W. H. *The Dyer's Hand and Other Essays.* 1948. Reprint, New York: Vintage Books, 1989.

Baines, Barbara J. "Assaying the Power of Chastity in *Measure for Measure*." *Studies in English Literature, 1500–1900* 30, no. 2 (Spring 1990): 283–301.

Bawcutt, N. W. "'He Who the Sword of Heaven Will Bear': The Duke versus Angelo in *Measure for Measure*." In *Shakespeare Survey*, vol. 37, edited by Stanley Wells, 89–97. Cambridge: Cambridge University Press, 1984.

Berger, Harry, Jr. *Making Trifles of Terrors: Redistributing Complicities in Shakespeare.* Stanford, CA: Stanford University Press, 1997.

Bloom, Harold. *Shakespeare: The Invention of the Human.* New York: Riverhead Books, 1998.

Bradley, A. C. *Shakespearean Tragedy: Lectures on "Hamlet," "Othello," "King Lear," "Macbeth."* 1904. Reprint, London: Penguin, 1991.

Bradshaw, Graham. *Shakespeare's Scepticism.* Brighton, UK: Harvester Press, 1987.

Braunmuller, A. R., and Robert Watson, eds. *Measure for Measure.* In *Measure for Measure*, 150–360. The Arden Shakespeare Third Series. London: Bloomsbury Publishing, 2020. http://dx.doi.org/10.5040/9781474208086.00000042.

Bristol, Michael. "Macbeth the Philosopher: Rethinking Context." *New Literary History* 42, no. 4 (Autumn 2011): 641–62.

———. "Recent Studies in Tudor and Stuart Drama." *Studies in English Literature, 1500–1900* 38, no. 2 (Spring 1998): 363–409.

———. "Vernacular Criticism and the Scenes Shakespeare Never Wrote." In *Shakespeare Survey*, vol. 53, edited by Peter Holland, 89–102. Cambridge: Cambridge University Press, 2000.

Brown, Carolyn E. "The Homoeroticism of Duke Vincentio: 'Some Feeling for the Sport.'" *Studies in Philology* 94, no. 2 (Spring 1997): 187–220.

Burke, Kenneth. *Kenneth Burke on Shakespeare*. Edited by Scott Newstok. West Lafayette, IN: Parlor Press, 2007.

Burling, Robbins. *The Talking Ape: How Language Evolved*. Oxford: Oxford University Press, 2005.

Cavell, Stanley. "The Avoidance of Love: A Reading of *King Lear*." In *Must We Mean What We Say? A Book of Essays*, 267–353. New York: Charles Scribner's Sons, 1969.

Deacon, Terrence. *The Symbolic Species: The Co-evolution of Language and the Brain*. New York: W. W. Norton, 1997.

Derrida, Jacques. *Of Grammatology*. Translated by Gayatri Chakravorty Spivak. Baltimore: Johns Hopkins University Press, 1976.

Dixon, Thomas. *From Passions to Emotions: The Creation of a Secular and Psychological Category*. Cambridge: Cambridge University Press, 2003.

Durkheim, Émile. *The Elementary Forms of Religious Life*. Translated by Karen E. Fields. New York: Free Press, 1995.

Empson, William. *The Structure of Complex Words*. London: Chatto & Windus, 1977.

Fernie, Ewan. *The Demonic: Literature and Experience*. London: Routledge, 2013.

"Forum: Harry Berger, Jr.'s *Making Trifles of Terror: Redistributing Complicities in Shakespeare*." *Shakespeare Studies* 27 (1999): 19–73.

Frankl, Viktor. *Man's Search for Meaning*. 1959. Reprint, Boston: Beacon Press, 2006.

Frye, Northrop. *Anatomy of Criticism: Four Essays*. Princeton, NJ: Princeton University Press, 1957.

———. *Northrop Frye on Shakespeare*. Markham, Ontario: Fitzhenry & Whiteside, 1986.

Gans, Eric. *The End of Culture: Toward a Generative Anthropology*. Berkeley: University of California Press, 1985.

———. *Originary Thinking: Elements of Generative Anthropology*. Stanford, CA: Stanford University Press, 1993.

———. *Science and Faith: The Anthropology of Revelation*. Savage, MD: Rowman & Littlefield, 1990.

Gellner, Ernest. *Plough, Sword and Book: The Structure of Human History*. Chicago: University of Chicago Press, 1989.

———. *The Psychoanalytic Movement: The Cunning of Unreason*. 3rd ed. London: Blackwell Publishing, 2003.

Girard, René. *A Theater of Envy: William Shakespeare*. New York: Oxford University Press, 1991.

Goddard, Harold. *The Meaning of Shakespeare*. 2 vols. Chicago: University of Chicago Press, 1960.

Goldberg, S. L. *An Essay on "King Lear."* Cambridge: Cambridge University Press, 1974.

Goldie, Peter. *The Mess Inside: Narrative, Emotion, and the Mind*. Oxford: Oxford University Press, 2012.

Greenblatt, Stephen. *Shakespearean Negotiations: The Circulation of Social Energy in Renaissance England*. Berkeley: University of California Press, 1988.
Gurr, Andrew. "*Measure for Measure*'s Hoods and Masks: The Duke, Isabella, and Liberty." *English Literary Renaissance* 27, no. 1 (Winter 1997): 89–105.
Guy-Bray, Stephen. Review of *Political Theologies in Shakespeare's England: The Sacred and the State in "Measure for Measure*," by Debora Kuller Shuger. *Religious Studies and Theology* 22, no. 2 (2003): 79–80.
Hawkins, Harriet. *The Devil's Party: Critical Counter-interpretations of Shakespearian Drama*. Oxford: Oxford University Press, 1985.
Hayne, Victoria. "Performing Social Practice: The Example of *Measure for Measure*." *Shakespeare Quarterly* 44, no. 1 (Spring 1993): 1–29.
Hegel, G. W. F. *The Phenomenology of Spirit*. Translated by J. N. Findlay. Oxford: Oxford University Press, 1977.
Holloway, John. *The Story of the Night: Studies in Shakespeare's Major Tragedies*. London: Routledge & Kegan Paul, 1961.
Hoxby, Blair. *What Was Tragedy? Theory and the Early Modern Canon*. Oxford: Oxford University Press, 2015.
Hunter, Matthew. "*Measure for Measure* and the Problem of Style." *ELH* 83, no. 2 (Summer 2016): 457–88.
Ignatieff, Michael. *The Needs of Strangers*. London: Chatto & Windus, 1984.
Jaffa, Harry V. "The Limits of Politics: *King Lear*, Act 1, Scene 1." In Allan Bloom with Harry V. Jaffa, *Shakespeare's Politics*, 113–45. 1964. Reprint, Chicago: University of Chicago Press, 1981.
Kamaralli, Anna. "Writing about Motive: Isabella, the Duke and Moral Authority." In *Shakespeare Survey*, vol. 58, edited by Peter Holland, 48–59. Cambridge: Cambridge University Press, 2005.
Kearney, James. "'This Is Above All Strangeness': *King Lear*, Ethics, and the Phenomenology of Recognition." *Criticism* 54, no. 3 (Summer 2012): 455–67.
Kendrick, Matthew. "Refusal in *Measure for Measure*: Shakespeare with Žižek." *Angelaki* 25, no. 6 (2020): 37–50.
Kerrigan, William. *Hamlet's Perfection*. Baltimore: Johns Hopkins University Press, 1994.
Khan, Amir. *Shakespeare in Hindsight: Counterfactual Thinking and Shakespearean Tragedy*. Edinburgh: Edinburgh University Press, 2016.
Knight, Wilson. *The Wheel of Fire: Interpretations of Shakespearian Tragedy*. 1930. Reprint, London: Routledge Classics, 2001.
Kojève, Alexandre. *Introduction to the Reading of Hegel*. Edited by Allan Bloom. Translated by James H. Nichols. Ithaca, NY: Cornell University Press, 1969.
Kottman, Paul A. *Love as Human Freedom*. Stanford, CA: Stanford University Press, 2017.
———. "Why Shakespeare Stopped Writing Tragedies," *Journal of Medieval and Early Modern Studies* 49, no. 1 (2019): 113–35.
———. "Why Think about Shakespearean Tragedy Today?" In *The Cambridge Com-*

panion to Shakespearean Tragedy, 2nd ed., edited by Claire McEachern, 240–61. Cambridge: Cambridge University Press, 2013.

Leggatt, Alexander. "Substitution in *Measure for Measure*." *Shakespeare Quarterly* 39, no. 3 (Autumn 1988): 342–59.

Lever, J. W., ed. *Measure for Measure*. In *Measure for Measure*, 2–149. The Arden Shakespeare Second Series. London: Bloomsbury Publishing, 2015. http://dx.doi.org/10.5040/9781408160237.00000030.

Levine, Nina, and David Lee Miller, eds. *A Touch More Rare: Harry Berger, Jr., and the Arts of Interpretation* (New York: Fordham University Press, 2009).

Lewis, Cynthia. "'Dark Deeds Darkly Answered': Duke Vincentio and Judgement in *Measure for Measure*." *Shakespeare Quarterly* 34, no. 3 (Autumn 1983): 271–89.

Luke, Nicholas. "Avoidance as Love: Evading Cavell on Dover Cliff." *Modern Philology* 117, no. 4 (2020): 445–69.

MacIntyre, Alasdair. "Epistemological Crises, Dramatic Narrative, and the Philosophy of Science." *Monist* 60, no. 4 (1977): 453–72.

Mack, Maynard. *Everybody's Shakespeare: Reflections Chiefly on the Tragedies*. Lincoln: University of Nebraska Press, 1993.

Majeske, Andrew. "Equity's Absence: The Extremity of Claudio's Prosecution and Barnardine's Pardon in Shakespeare's *Measure for Measure*." *Law and Literature* 21, no. 2 (Summer 2009): 169–84.

Mallin, E. S. "Charity and Whoredom in *Timon of Athens*." *Shakespeare Quarterly* 69, no. 2 (Summer 2018): 75–100.

Mason, H. A. *Shakespeare's Tragedies of Love: An Examination of the Possibility of Common Readings of "Romeo and Juliet," "Othello," "King Lear," and "Antony and Cleopatra."* London: Chatto & Windus, 1970.

McCrum, Robert. "'Perfect Mind': On Shakespeare and the Brain." *Brain: A Journal of Neurology* 139, no. 12 (2016): 3010–3. https://doi.org/10.1093/brain/aww279.

Milton, John. *Paradise Lost*. Edited by Gordon Tesky. New York: W. W. Norton, 2005.

Nietzsche, Friedrich. *On the Genealogy of Morals*. Translated by Walter Kaufmann and R. J. Hollingdale. New York: Vintage Books, 1989.

Nordlund, Marcus. *The Shakespearean Inside: A Study of the Complete Soliloquies and Solo Asides*. Edinburgh: Edinburgh University Press, 2017.

Nowak, Piotr. "Gods and Children: Shakespeare Reads *The Prince*." *Philosophy and Literature* 41, no. 1A (2017): 109–27.

Nuttall, A. D. "*Measure for Measure*: Quid Pro Quo?," *Shakespeare Studies* 4 (1968): 231–51.

Orwell, George. *Collected Essays*. London: Mercury Books, 1961.

Owen, Lucy. "Mode and Character in *Measure for Measure*." *Shakespeare Quarterly* 25, no. 1 (Winter 1974): 17–32.

Pechter, Edward. *Shakespeare Studies Today: Romanticism Lost*. New York: Palgrave Macmillan, 2011.

Pierce, Robert. "Being a Moral Agent in Shakespeare's Vienna." *Philosophy and Literature* 33, no. 2 (2009): 267–79.

Pinciss, G. M. "'Heavenly Comforts of Despair' and *Measure for Measure.*" *Studies in English Literature, 1500-1900* 30, no. 2 (Spring 1990): 303-13.
Pinker, Steven. *The Better Angels of Our Nature: Why Violence Has Declined.* New York: Penguin Books, 2011.
Rosenberg, Marvin. *The Masks of King Lear.* Berkeley: University of California Press, 1972.
Rossiter, A. P. *Angel with Horns and Other Shakespearean Lectures.* Edited by Graham Storey. London: Longmans, 1961.
Sahlins, Marshall. "The Original Political Society." *HAU: Journal of Ethnographic Theory* 7, no. 2 (2017): 91-128. http://doi.org/10.14318/hau7.2.014.
———. "Poor Man, Rich Man, Big-Man, Chief: Political Types in Melanesia and Polynesia." *Comparative Studies in Society and History* 5, no. 3 (1963): 285-303.
Saval, Peter Kishore. *Shakespeare in Hate: Emotions, Passions, Selfhood.* New York: Routledge, 2016.
Scheler, Max. *Ressentiment.* Translated by Lewis B. Coser and William W. Holdheim, with an Introduction by Manfred Fings. Milwaukee, WI: Marquette University Press, 1994.
Schlegel, August Wilhelm von. *A Course of Lectures on Dramatic Art and Literature.* Translated by John Black. London: Henry G. Bohn, 1846.
Shakespeare, William. *The Complete Works of Shakespeare*, 6th ed. Edited by David Bevington. New York: Pearson Longman, 2009.
Shell, Marc. *The End of Kinship: "Measure for Measure," Incest, and the Ideal of Universal Siblinghood.* Stanford, CA: Stanford University Press, 1988.
Shuger, Debora Kuller. *Political Theologies in Shakespeare's England: The Sacred and the State in "Measure for Measure."* New York: Palgrave, 2001.
Spiess, Stephen. "The Measure of Sexual Memory." In *Shakespeare Survey*, vol. 67, edited by Peter Holland, 310-26. Cambridge: Cambridge University Press, 2014.
Stone, Lawrence. *The Crisis of the Aristocracy, 1558-1641.* Abridged ed. Oxford: Oxford University Press, 1967.
Strier, Richard. "The Judgment of the Critics That Makes Us Tremble: 'Distributing Complicities' in Recent Criticism of *King Lear*." In *Shakespeare and Judgment*, edited by Kevin Curran, 215-34. Edinburgh: Edinburgh University Press, 2017.
Tallis, Raymond. *Aping Mankind: Neuromania, Darwinitis and the Misrepresentation of Humanity.* Durham, UK: Acumen, 2011.
Tomasello, Michael. *The Cultural Origins of Human Cognition.* Cambridge, MA: Harvard University Press, 1999.
van Oort, Richard. "Cognitive Science and the Problem of Representation," *Poetics Today* 24, no. 2 (2003): 237-95.
———. "A Race of Devils: *Frankenstein*, Romanticism, and the Tragedy of Human Origin." In *Spheres of Action: Speech and Performance in Romantic Culture*, edited by Alexander Dick and Angela Esterhammer, 124-46. Toronto: University of Toronto Press, 2009.

———. "Shakespeare and the Idea of the Modern," *New Literary History* 37, no. 2 (2006): 319–39.

———. *Shakespeare's Big Men: Tragedy and the Problem of Resentment*. Toronto: University of Toronto Press, 2016.

Vyvyan, John. *Shakespeare and Platonic Beauty*. 1961. Reprint, London: Shepheard-Walwyn, 2013.

———. *Shakespeare and the Rose of Love: A Study of the Early Plays in Relation to the Medieval Philosophy of Love*. 1960. Reprint, London: Shepheard-Walwyn, 2013.

———. *The Shakespearean Ethic*. 1959. Reprint, London: Shepheard-Walwyn, 2011.

Watson, Robert N. "False Immortality in *Measure for Measure*: Comic Means, Tragic Ends." *Shakespeare Quarterly* 41, no. 4 (Winter 1990): 411–32.

Wheeler, Richard P. *Shakespeare's Development and the Problem Comedies: Turn and Counter-turn*. Berkeley: University of California Press, 1981.

Wilson, Catherine. Review of "Love as Human Freedom," by Paul A. Kottman. *Notre Dame Philosophical Reviews*, November 28, 2017. https://ndpr.nd.edu/reviews/love-as-human-freedom.

Yachnin, Paul. "The Laws of *Measure for Measure*." In *Shakespeare and Judgment*, edited by Kevin Curran, 139–56. Edinburgh: Edinburgh University Press, 2017.

Index

abdication: King Lear's, 14, 22, 40, 42, 225, 242n3; Duke Vincentio's, 126, 131, 132, 213, 226
Abhorson, 197
Adam and Eve, 89, 47. *See* also Eve
aesthetic: as anthropological category, 8–11, 32, 213, 246n32; as experience, 5, 6; as mode of audience interaction, 259, 271n75; as play, 256n86; in Angelo's soliloquies, 164; in Escalus's argument, 144, 150; in new historicism (Greenblatt), 263n25; Prospero's use of, 264n33
aesthetics, 240n17
agrarian societies, 3, 49, 103–4, 117, 238n5, 251n58
agrarian states, 90
Adelman, Janet, 251n58
Albany, 5, 10, 30, 55, 82, 101, 107, 108–9, 113, 115, 225, 226, 244n21
allegorical figures: Cassius, 39; Edmund and Edgar, 67–68; Kent, 25–27; Lucio, 159, 169; Oswald, 97–98
allegory, 25, 245n28
Alonso, 2, 74
Amleth. *See* Saxo Grammaticus
Angelo, 2, 73, 117–224, 227–30

anthropology, viii, 6, 11, 237n5, 238n8, 241n18, 241n19. *See* also generative anthropology
Antonio, 2
Antony, Mark, 118
Aquinas. *See* Thomas Aquinas, Saint
Ariel, 2
Aristotle, 249n44
Auden, W. H., 227–28, 229, 265n48
Augustine of Hippo, Saint, 249n44
authority: abdication of, 2, 29, 126; Duke Vincentio's, 194–95, 206, 208, 228; Isabella's critique of, 160–62; Lear's, 18; 23, 24, 87, 90; political, viii, 3, 38, 47, 122, 213, 216, 231; sacred monarchal, 4, 9, 26, 117. *See also* power

Baines, Barbara J., 268n61
Barnardine, 131, 165, 183, 192, 197, 212, 220, 223, 228, 237n3, 271n74
Bawcutt, N. W., 266n55
Berger, Harry, Jr., vii, 2, 5, 13, 15–16, 19, 31, 35, 36–37, 38, 42, 57, 78, 96, 97, 102, 104–5, 107, 114, 115, 122, 130–32, 192–99, 226, 242n2, 246n31, 251n57, 253n71, 253n72, 253n75, 255n84, 256n86, 256n88, 258n103, 265n49, 265n51, 268n59, 270n69

Index

Bloom, Harold, 237n3, 262n20
big man/men, 1–2, 3–4, 5, 14, 20, 101, 227, 229, 230, 231, 233, 234, 251n58
Bradley, A. C., 14–15, 16, 18, 24–25, 27, 46–47, 69, 104, 107, 110, 111, 112, 225, 234, 243n7, 244n15, 245n24, 256n86, 257n92, 258n97, 258n103
Bradshaw, Graham, 130, 194–95, 196–97, 261n16, 262n19, 264n42
Braunmuller, A. R., 158
Bristol, Michael, 241n21, 242n2
Brown, Carolyn E., 268n60
Brutus, Marcus, 38–39, 40, 41–42, 92–93, 102, 118, 160, 161, 198, 207, 211, 213, 233, 249n43, 265n51, 269n65
Burgundy, 19, 107–8
Burke, Kenneth, 111
Burling, Robbins, 240n12

Caesar, Julius, 38–39, 41–42, 93, 148, 249n43
Cassius, Caius, 38–39, 41, 92, 93, 249n43, 265n51
Cavell, Stanley, 2, 5, 19, 69–71, 72–73, 78–79, 91–92, 93, 96, 100, 111, 242, 244n15, 252n60, 253n69, 253n72, 253n73, 256n86
Christianity, 9, 10, 241n1
Claudio (in *Measure for Measure*): and Angelo, 187; and Duke, 177–78, 183–84, 188, 202, 208, 212, 214, 219–20, 222, 265n49, 269n68, 271n74; and Escalus, 138, 139, 141–42, 144, 145, 147; and Isabella, 178–83, 201; and Juliet, 136, 200; and Lucio 206; as felon, 123–24, 126, 262n19; and seduction scene, 149, 150, 154, 157, 160, 161, 164, 170, 171, 175
Claudio (in *Much Ado about Nothing*), 73, 74
Claudius, King, 13, 20, 21, 37, 38, 39, 43, 45, 139, 140, 179

conscience: and inner moral law, 153, 161, 165–66, 188, 194–95, 207, 227, 228; Angelo's, 138, 140, 164, 166, 176, 182, 210; as sign of guilt, 2, 4; Barnardine's, 183; Duke Vincentio's, 119, 128, 130, 137, 182, 198, 210, 229; Escalus's, 144, 147–48; Juliet's, 168; Lancelot's, 74; Lear's avoidance of, 38–51; Portia as Brutus's, 92–93; puritan, 257n91
conspiracy: against Julius Caesar, 38; between Justice and Iniquity, 148; Duke's, 166, 201; for the center, 103, 104; Gloucester's, 63; monstrosity of, 86–102, 207, 213, 222, 259n3
Cordelia, 2, 200, 225–26, 230; and Gloucester, 61–62; and reunion with Lear, 47, 51 91, 94, 95, 100, 102; as contender for the center, 105–9, 115; as exile, 34; as Lear's scapegoat, 45; as love, 19, 22 37, 42–44; death of, 84, 103–4, 110, 111–13; in first scene, 13–19, 23–25, 27, 36
Coriolanus, vii
Coriolanus, 1, 2, 14, 24, 102, 118
Cornwall, Duke of, 27, 29, 30, 36, 52–55, 58–61, 63, 67, 69, 101, 103, 113, 244n21, 250n56

Deacon, Terrence, 6, 239n11
Derrida, Jacques, 7
Desdemona, 1, 15, 38, 40, 42, 153, 257n93
desire: as anthropological category, 8, 47, 89, 202; 213, 239n9, 255n80; Duke Vincentio's, 208–11, 221, 270n69, 271n73; for centrality, 4–5, 102, 105; Freud's definition of, 57; monstrosity of, 1, 107; prohibition of, 152; Shakespeare's representation of, 13, 42; sexual, 133; 135, 151, 158, 162, 164, 169, 172, 175, 191; spectator's, 62, 111; versus animal need, 32. *See also* mimetic desire

Dixon, Thomas, 249n44
drama, 11, 13, 27, 31, 154, 185, 190, 239n8, 239n9
dramatic irony, 56, 111, 186, 234
Duke, the. *See* Vincentio
Duncan, King, 38, 40
Durkheim, Émile, 7, 89, 174, 175, 238n8

ear: of envy, 50–51, 54–55, 66; of rumor, 123, 127
Edgar: and fantasies of parricide, 51–63, 97–102; and parable of cliff, 69–86, 96; and rivalry with Edmund, 105, 110, 114; and rumor, 65–68; and tragic center, 115; as reflection of Lear, 27, 31, 32, 36, 48–49, 50, 87, 91; in Nahum Tate's adaptation, 112
Edmund: and contest for centrality, 226; and fantasies of parricide, 51–63, 65–69, 76, 82, 101; and Goneril, 96, 250n55; as evil character, 250n56; as false love, 25, 27; in final scene, 103–15
Elbow, 137, 145–47, 156, 167, 169, 200, 207, 209, 210
Elias, Norbert, 258n103
empathy, 138, 142, 162, 174, 175, 183, 187
Empson, William, 244n19, 245n29, 250n51, 250n54
Enterline, Lynn, 242n2
envy: as avoidance of love, 70; and slander, 126; Cassius as personification of, 39; Duke Vincentio's, 211, 265n52; Lear's, 42, 50–51, 96; in Lear's love contest, 108; Oswald as personification of, 97–98; tragic hero's, 4. *See also* ear
equality, 38, 120, 149, 225, 226
Escalus: and argument from empathy, 138, 157, 162, 163; and Duke, 119, 122, 127, 199, 203, 214, 216, 217, 229; and evasion of justice, 145–49, 150, 151, 169, 196, 209;

ethics, viii, 122; 240n17, 260n7; as anthropological category, 5; conflict with morality, 125, 149, 195–97, 219
ethical discovery procedures: Shakespeare plays as, 9, 11, 102, 117, 234
Eve, 90, 254n78
exile: as a solution to tragic conflict, 230–31, 233–4; Cordelia's, 15; Edgar's, 85; Lear's, 34, 46, 61, 91; Gloucester's, 68; Prospero's, 230–31, 233, 264n33; Timon's, 233–34

Fernie, Ewan, 241n21
Fletcher, Angus, 242n2
Fool, the, 2, 27, 30, 32, 36, 46, 47, 49, 50, 55, 87, 226, 230, 245n29, 246n30, 250n54
forgiveness: as theme in *Measure for Measure*, 125; between Edgar and Edmund, 66; Claudius's desire for, 21; Gloucester's quest for, 68, 78, 79, 83, 85; in Shakespeare's plays, 74; Isabella's concept of, 173; Lear's desire for, 87, 103, 106; Prospero's narrative of, 234
Fortinbras, 20, 244n17
France, king of, 19, 46, 58, 61, 63, 66, 104, 107–9, 112
Francisca, 132, 201, 204–5, 209
Frankl, Viktor, 256
Frazer, James George, 238n8
Freud, Sigmund, 57, 174
Freudian, 124
Froth, 145–46, 147, 156, 169, 200
Frye, Northrop, 238n8, 264n34, 266n56

Gans, Eric, vii, viii, 3, 5, 7, 8, 10, 237n5, 239n9, 240n17, 241n1, 253n76, 254n80
Gellner, Ernest, 3, 263n26
generative anthropology, 10, 240n17
ghost, Hamlet's father's, 14, 20, 38, 39, 45, 63, 127, 140, 179, 261n17
Girard, René, vii, 14, 47, 202, 242n3, 247n34, 248n38

Index

Gloucester: and Lear, 86–87, 91–93, 95–96; and weeping, 63–69; and parable of cliff, 69–86; and parricide, 51–63, 97–101, 110–11; as go-between, 29; as victim of center, 103; in Nahum Tate's adaptation, 112; reconciliation with Edgar, 115; subplot, 23
Goddard, Harold, 71, 76, 96, 110, 113, 179, 255n81, 256n86, 257n93
Goldberg, S. L., 250n56
Goldie, Peter, 186, 200, 260n4
Goneril: and Albany's accusation of ingratitude, 5, 10, 113; and fantasy of parricide, 51–63, 67; and love contest, 18, 21, 23, 48; and Oswald, 25, 96; and objection to Lear's knights, 27–30, 32–33; as Lear's chastiser, 36, 42–46; and Lear's tears, 64; as caricature of evil, 69, 95, 97, 101, 200, 250n56, 251n58; as rival for center, 102, 226; as victim of center, 103, 104; in final battle, 109
Greenblatt, Stephen, 252n65, 263n25
Grossman, Marshall, 242n2
guilt: as anthropological category, 4, 5, 9, 45; Angelo's, 203, 210, 217; Claudio's, 124; Claudius's, 20; Duke Vincentio's use of, 166, 209, 223; Edgar's, 70; Gloucester's, 58, 68, 77, 78, 79; as sign of complicity, 16, 31, 95, 142, 147; Lancelot's, 79; Lear's, 2, 200, 245n28, 246n31; Macbeth's, 1
Gurr, Andrew, 267n57, 270n72
Guy-Bray, Stephen, 260n7

Hal, Prince, 104, 261n14
Hamlet, vii, 19–21
Hamlet: and drowning stage with tears, 63–65; and inner virtue, 120; as divided self, 73; as mad man, 1, 2, 45; as man of violence, 102, 118, 179, 244n17; compared to Angelo, 164; compared to Cordelia, 13–15;
compared to Duke, 139–40, 184, 222; compared to Juliet, 167–68; compared to Lear, 17–18, 19–21, 32, 37, 38, 47–48; in temptation scene, 39, 40, 42, 43, 127
Hawkins, Harriet, 191
Hayne, Victoria, 261n18
Hegel, G. W. F., 22, 226
Henry V. *See* Hal
hierarchical world picture, 3
hierarchies, ethical, 38, 72, 73, 82, 90, 122, 237n5
hierarchy, 23, 47, 75, 89, 149, 237n5, 242n3
Holloway, John, 86, 94
Horatio, 14, 39
Hoxby, Blair, 241n1
humanities, viii, 9, 71, 240n11, 241n18, 253n67, 259n104
Hunter, Matthew, 266n53
hunter-gatherers, 49, 50, 237n5

Iago: as master seducer, 152–53; as practical joker, 227, 265n48; compared to Duke, 131, 195–96, 197–98, 228, 237n3; compared to Edmund, 56, 66, 257n93; compared to Lear, 32; in temptation scene, 38, 40
Ignatieff, Michael, 247n35
Imogen, 15
injustice, 37, 52, 62, 63, 85, 114, 158, 168, 187, 214, 234, 272n76. *See also* justice
iniquity: disguised as virtue, 190; Duke as spreader of, 197, 207, 211; in Vienna, 130; versus justice, 148–49, 153, 159, 163, 169, 189
irony. *See* dramatic irony
Isabella: and big man, 4; and extenuating circumstances in Claudio's case, 144; as bride of God, 118; as Claudio's last hope, 177, 178, 179–83; as figure of mercy, 194; as object of Angelo's lust, 187, 200, 201; as victim

of Duke, 73, 74, 198, 202, 203–10, 212, 214–23, 227, 228, 229; as virtuous, 131; fetched by Lucio from convent, 132–36; in Duke's conspiracy, 183–85, 188–90; in second interview with Angelo, 169–76; in seduction scene, 149–68

Jaffa, Harry V., 238n6, 244n21
Jesus, 125, 199, 219, 260n7, 261n16
Juliet (*Measure for Measure*), 123, 127, 136, 141, 164, 165, 166, 167, 175, 177, 200, 201, 212, 220
Juliet (*Romeo and Juliet*), 164
Julius Caesar, vii, 21, 92
justice: and death, 206; and mercy, 151, 168, 195, 197, 219, 264n42, 270n71; arbitrariness of, 87–88, 121; as abstract principle, 175; as God's alone, 156; as implementation of law, 150, 157–58, 196; Duke as representative of, 217, 260n7; Edgar's tale as instance of, 114; Isabella's desire for, 184, 215; poetic, 31; versus liberty/iniquity, 137–49, 153–54, 159, 163, 169, 189, 207; travesty of, 220, 228, 271n75. *See also* injustice

Kamaralli, Anna, 270n71
Kearney, James, 252n63
Keepdown, Kate, 201, 214, 262n19
Kendrick, Matthew, 254n80
Kent: age of, 245n24; allegorical function of, 24–27, 245n28; as exile, 34, 51, 87; as representation of faith, 17, 18, 23; compared to Gloucester, 66; Cordelia's messages to, 61; outside hovel, 35, 46, 48, 250n50; prophetic words of, 42–43; ready for death, 225; spokesman of Lear's shame, 91, 95; violence of, 53; with Gloucester on heath, 52, 57–58; worthiness of, 115

Kerrigan, William, 241n21
Khan, Amir, 241n21, 257n94
King Lear, vii, 4, 11, 13–117, 230
Knight, Wilson, 14, 32, 194, 227, 260n7, 261n16, 264n42
Kojève, Alexandre, 245n22
Kottman, Paul, 240n18, 241n21, 254n79, 258n104

Lacan, Jacques, 254n80, 258n103
Lancelot, Gobbo, 74–75
Laertes, 17, 20, 48, 64–65, 73, 179, 244n17
language: and Adam and Eve 89; and coercion, 88; origin of, 7. *See also* symbolic representation
law: against fornication, 123–24, 162, 166, 262n19; and judgment, 271n75; and moral equality, 38, 123, 125, 196, 200, 227, 229; and shock therapy, 271n74v; and representation, 254n80; Angelo as student of, 202–3; Angelo's interpretation of, 127, 131, 137–39, 141–43, 150, 156–57, 163, 170, 172, 175, 193, 228, 268n63; as object of ridicule, 134, 137; Duke's failure to enforce, 118, 130, 213, 216, 223, 265n49; Duke's soft approach to, 168; Claudio as victim of, 169; Escalus's failure to apply, 144–46; Iago's image of, 152, 207; in preindustrial state, 140; Pompey's view of, 209; secular versus God's, 153, 197, 217–18, 219; talion, 188, 218
Leaf, Munro, 257n89
Lear, vii, 1–2, 3, 13–117, 200, 224, 225–31, 233–34; compared to Duke Vincentio, 118–19
Leggatt, Alexander, 269n68
Lever, J. W., 204
Levine, Nina, 242n2
Lewis, Cynthia, 269n66

liberty: Angelo's crackdown on, 118; Claudio guilty of, 124; Duke's encouragement of, 198, 204; Duke's representation of, 128, 139; Escalus's representation of, 147; Lucio's representation of, 134; versus justice, 143, 148, 149

love: as anthropological category, 5; avoidance of, 70, 93; Lear's rejection of, 14–22, 42–44, 48

Lucio: and Angelo, 131, 132, 165, 169; and Isabella, 132–36, 204–5, 207, 209; and rumor, 123; as abuser of law against fornication, 143; as father of Kate's child, 201, 262n19; as low-life, 197; as scoundrel, 203; compared to Lear's Fool, 2, 230; Duke's humiliation of, 168, 189, 229; relationship to Duke, 126, 166, 200, 206, 210–14, 217, 222–23, 259n3, 266n53, 267n57, 269n66, 270n73; role in seduction of Angelo, 149–63; and Claudio, 124

Luke, Nicholas, 256n86

Macbeth, vii
Macbeth, 1, 2, 21, 38, 40, 43, 102, 118, 210
Machiavelli, 129, 130, 149, 271n74
MacIntyre, Alasdair, 252n61
Mack, Maynard, 1, 27, 246n30
madman, 221, 223, 224
madness: as common factor in *Measure for Measure* and *King Lear*, 230; definition of, 1–2; Duke Vincentio's, 118, 223–24, 227; Lear's, 37, 58, 91, 92, 93, 225, 226, 227, 245n29, 246n31, 250n54, 250n56, 251n58, 255n82, 268n59, 271n74
Majeske, Andrew, 271n74
Mallin, E. S., 272n76
Margaret, Queen, 55–56, 62, 64, 110
Mariana, 74, 136, 139, 141, 166, 190, 200, 201, 202, 208, 212, 214, 215, 216, 218, 219, 222, 266n56, 269n68
Martel, Yann, 235
Mason, H. A., 35–36, 38, 46, 245n28, 248n39, 251n57
McEwan, Ian, 235
McCrum, Robert, 239n10
Measure for Measure, vii, viii, 2, 4, 11, 22, 73, 74, 117–224, 230, 233, 234
Menenius, 24
Merchant of Venice, The, 74, 154, 198, 258n103
mercy: Angelo's concept of, 187; allegorical figure of, 149, 199; Duke's, 125, 130, 132, 135, 136, 189, 192, 208, 214, 223, 227, 228, 260n7, 269n66; Escalus's, 144, 147; ethics of, 196–97, 265n52; God's, 160, 267n58; in *Merchant of Venice*, 258n103; Isabella's concept of, 74, 151, 153, 155, 157, 172, 183, 194, 219, 270n71; versus justice, 195, 264n42
Miller, David Lee, 242n2
Milton, John, 89, 90, 254n78
mimetic desire/rivalry, vii, 202, 242n3, 247n34, 263n25
morality, 5, 7, 122, 125, 149, 175, 195, 196, 197, 253n76
morality play/tale, 25, 39, 151, 165, 261n16
motive: as critical category, 16; for lying, 74; Cordelia's, 104, 109; Duke Vincentio's, 119, 121, 130, 131, 234, 270n71; Gloucester's, 59
Much Ado about Nothing, 73, 264n42
Müller, Max, 238n8

narrator: Duke Vincentio as, 185–86, 187–88, 193; and narrated, 260n4; Lear as, 31, 62; Prospero as, 235
narrative, internal and external perspectives of, 186, 200, 260n4
Nietzsche, Friedrich, 7, 10, 21

Nordlund, Marcus, 264n32
Nowak, Piotr, 265n52
Nuttall, A. D., 129, 130, 131, 132, 133, 139

Ophelia, 17, 19, 20, 42, 48, 64, 65, 104, 179
originary hypothesis, 239n9, 240n17
originary scene, 6, 8, 238n8, 249n44, 254n79, 270n69
Orlin, Lena Cowen, 242n2
Orwell, George, 118, 244n20
Oswald: and Edgar, 96–102; and Kent, 24–27; as object of Lear's violence, 43, 53
Othello, vii
Othello, 1, 2, 38, 40, 42, 43, 56, 66, 102, 118, 153, 191, 196, 210, 233
Overdone, Mistress, 123, 126, 127, 131, 143, 145, 153, 166, 201
Owen, Lucy, 268n63

parricide/patricide, 51, 57, 60, 62, 67, 76, 82, 97, 102, 253n71
Pechter, Edward, 241n21
Peter, Friar, 214, 218
Pierce, Robert, 269n65
Pinciss, G. M., 260n7
Pinker, Steven, 252n67
Plato, viii, 89, 249n44
Pompey, 126, 127, 131, 143, 145–48, 153, 156, 166, 169, 197, 209, 210
potlatch, 3, 118, 225, 226, 227, 228, 229, 257n91, 272n76
Potter, Lois, 242n2
power: and ambition's ladder, 41–43, 55, 160; Angelo as abuser of, 183, 206–7; arbitrariness of, 87; as abstract principle, 175; as manifestation of the sacred center, 88, 213, 218, 233, 237n5, 254n80; decline of among aristocracy, 262n23; Duke Vincentio's covert political strategy of, 119, 122, 132, 189, 202–3, 220, 227–28, 230, 271n74; Isabella's, 135–36, 155, 268n61; Lear's abdication of, 26–7, 47, 61, 91, 225–26; in agrarian societies, 49; king of France's desire for, 108; knights as representatives of, 34; Prospero's, 231, 264n33; symbolic nature of, 90, 247n36; versus moral reciprocity, 38. *See also* authority
primogeniture, 57, 258n103
Promos and Cassandra, 259n3
Provost, the, 136, 158, 159, 160, 165, 205, 207, 214, 220

reciprocity, 22, 23, 37, 38, 72, 73, 82, 126, 194, 229, 254n79, 259n104, 272n76
Regan: and fantasy of parricide, 51–63, 67–68, 76; and love contest, 18, 23, 48, 51; and Goneril, 25, 27, 32, 43, 46, 52; and Lear's shame, 45, 200; as Lear's chastiser, 36, 53–54, 79, 104; as Lear's kindred spirit, 42; as monstrous, 21, 55, 69, 95, 97, 101, 250n56; as rival for the center, 102, 226; as victim of the center, 103, 113; in final battle, 109; in bidding war with Lear, 30, 33
renunciation, 2, 4, 8, 17, 22, 43, 118, 225, 250n51
repentance, 20, 74, 79, 81, 83, 85, 86, 165, 166
representation. See *symbolic representation*
resentment: Angelo's, 203, 206; as anthropological category, vii, 4–5, 8, 38, 82, 102, 105, 117, 213, 224, 239n9, 247n34, 249n44; as impotent rage, 21; as thwarted desire, 160–61; audience's, 110; contest with love, 17, 48, 229; Cordelia's, 14–15, 107, 243n7; Cornwall's, 59; Duke Vincentio's, 118, 139, 198, 206, 207–8, 211, 222, 265n52, 270n69; ethical problem of, 10, 231; Gloucester's, 67–68, 78,

resentment (cont.)
  85–86; Lear's, 14, 272n76; Hamlet's, 20, 39; Prospero's, 234; Queen Margaret's, 56; Timon's, 233; tragic hero's, 1
Richard III, 55, 56, 250n52
Richard, Duke of Gloucester, 56, 104, 250n52
ritual, 3, 4, 226, 259n104; authority of, 117; Durkheim's theory of, 175–76; Greenblatt's reference to, 263n25; Northrop Frye's theory of, 238n8; sacrificial, 8, 94. *See also* sacred center
romance, 4, 229, 230, 256n86, 266n53
Romeo , 18, 102, 164, 233
Rosenberg, Marvin, 243n7
Rossiter, A. P., 177, 261n16
rumor, 61, 65, 123, 127. *See also* ear

sacred: and aesthetic play, 256n86; and hierarchy, 242n3; and Isabella, 221; and justice, 137; and law, 254n80; and market, 259n104; and monarchal authority/kingship, 9, 47, 50, 117, 225; and myth, 254n79; as anthropological category, 7, 9, 32, 175, 237n5, 239n8; as constraint, 26; big man as usurper of, 3–4; Duke Vincentio as representative of, 230, 271n73, 271n75; Greenblatt's concept of, 263n25
sacred center, vii, 8, 14, 47, 197, 213, 225, 226, 227, 251n58, 270n69
sacrifice, vii, 86, 111, 229, 256n85
Sahlins, Marshall, 3, 5, 237n4, 237n5
Saussure, Ferdinand de, 7, 174
Saval, Peter Kishore, 251n58
Saxo Grammaticus: *Amleth*, 21
scapegoat: Angelo as, 191, 199, 230; in *King Lear*, 16, 36, 44, 45, 67, 95, 112, 114, 251n56, 251n58, 256n85; in *Merchant of Venice*, 75; in *Richard III*, 55–56;
Scheler, Max, 244n18
Schlegel, August Wilhelm von, 194, 264n42
science 6: as method, 9, 11, 240n18
Sebastian, 2
sex: Angelo's desire for, 151, 162, 164, 169, 174, 175, 187, 190, 203; Angelo's pathological understanding of, 139; Duke's interest in, 118, 126, 135, 191, 200, 202, 206, 207, 208, 209, 220, 221, 222, 266n53, 268n60, 270n69, 270n72; Eve's, 254n79; Isabella's, 155, 163, 170, 171, 176, 189, 201, 262n20; Isabella's aversion to, 132, 161; Lear's horror of, 250n54, 251n58; Lucio as representative of, 133, 158, 159, 270n73; outside marriage, 261n18; playgoers attitude toward, 140; Vienna as hotbed of, 137
shame: Angelo's, 218; as anthropological category, 4, 5, 8, 69–70, 96; audience's, 111; Duke Vincentio's, 198, 223; in *Julius Caesar*, 92–93; Gloucester's, 68, 76-79, 100; Lear's, 2, 44–45, 91–92, 94–95, 200, 244n15, 251n58; among prisoners in Nazi death camps, 256n87
Shell, Marc, 270n69
Shuger, Debora Kuller, 260n7
Shylock, 74–76, 114, 141
Socrates, viii
soliloquy: in autobiographical narrative, 186–87; as part of temptation scene, 39, 41, 92, 164, 168; as public service announcement, 190; as self-justification, 195
Solomon, Robert, 249n44
Spiess, Stephen, 270n73
Stone, Lawrence, 247n36, 257n91, 262n23

Strier, Richard, 242n2, 253n72
symbolic representation, 5, 6, 8, 238n8.
   See also language

Tallis, Raymond, 239n11
Tate, Nahum, 112
Tempest, The, 22, 74, 258n104
temptation scene, 38–41, 152, 154, 158–59, 164, 196, 249n44
Thomas Aquinas, Saint, 249n44
Thomas, Friar, 125–26, 128–29, 135, 139, 192, 195, 196, 206, 216, 217, 229
Tomasello, Michael, 240n14
tragedy: anthropological problem of, 115; as contest for centrality, 17, 20, 104, 226, 251n58; as sacrifice of big man, 229; audience's complicity in, 111; lesson of, 82; paradox of, 23; classical versus neoclassical, 13, 241n1; ethics of, 4, 231, 257n94; *Measure for Measure* as, 190–93, 230, 264n34, 266n56; *Timon of Athens* as, 234; violent conflict of, 40;
tragicomedy, 4, 144, 230

unconscious desires, 57, 73, 150, 155, 174–75, 210, 270n69

Vincentio, Duke of Vienna, vii, 1–2, 22, 74, 117–224, 226–31, 233–34
violence: and scapegoating, 191, 199; and weeping, 59; audience's complicity in, 111; Cordelia's complicity in, 104, 107; humanity's, vii–ix, 10, 69, 114, 117, 181; Lear's, 28, 36, 40, 53, 226, 246n31; in Tudor aristocracy, 247n36; of the center, 24, 101; of Gloucester's blinding, 59–63, 68; of Shakespeare's tragic heroes, 102, 179
Vyvyan, John, 17, 229, 243n14, 245n23, 260n7

Watson, Robert N., 158, 267n58
Weber, Max, 161
Wheeler, Richard P., 191–92, 199, 264n36
Whetstone, George, 259n3
Wilson, Catherine, 254n79
Winter's Tale, The, 74
Wittgenstein, Ludwig, 7, 174

Yachnin, Paul, 234, 271n75

Žižek, Slavoj, 254n80

SQUARE ONE
First-Order Questions in the Humanities

Series Editor: **PAUL A. KOTTMAN**

DAVIDE TARIZZO
Political Grammars: The Unconscious Foundations of Modern Democracy

AMIR ESHEL
Poetic Thinking Today: An Essay

PETER MURPHY
The Long Public Life of a Short Private Poem: Reading and Remembering Thomas Wyatt

JON BASKIN
Ordinary Unhappiness: The Therapeutic Fiction of David Foster Wallace

PAULA BLANK
Shakesplish: How We Read Shakespeare's Language

PAUL A. KOTTMAN
Love as Human Freedom

ADRIANA CAVARERO
Inclinations: A Critique of Rectitude